BY THE SAME AUTHOR.

FOOTFALLS ON THE BOUNDARY OF ANOTHER WORLD.

BEYOND THE BREAKERS.

*** See Notices at the end of this Volume.

THE

DEBATABLE LAND

BETWEEN

THIS WORLD AND THE NEXT

WITH ILLUSTRATIVE NARRATIONS

BY

ROBERT DALE OWEN

AUTHOR OF

"FOOTFALLS ON THE BOUNDARY OF ANOTHER WORLD."

"Occurrences which, according to received opinions, ought not to happen, are the facts which serve as clues to new discoveries."—SIR JOHN HERSCHEL.

NEW YORK:

G. W. Carleton & Co., Publishers.

LONDON: TRUBNER & CO.

M.DCCC.LXXII.

Stereotyped at the
WOMEN'S PRINTING HOUSE,
Corner Avenue A and Eighth Street,
New York.

PREFACE.

"In Scripture we are perpetually reminded that the laws of the spiritual world are in the highest sense laws of Nature, whose obligation, operation, and effect are all in the constitution and course of things."—ARGYLL.

ONE of the best known and most brilliant among the triumphs of astronomical science was the prediction, in advance of actual discovery, of the existence and, approximately, of the place in the heavens, of a planet belonging to our solar system and revolving outside of Uranus.

Certain data had long been known to astronomers: as that planets, if subject to the sun's attraction only, would revolve in ellipses; but that, being subject also, in a feeble but appreciable degree, to the attraction of each other, this minor influence causes them to deviate from their true elliptic paths; and that these perturbations, as they are called, are calculable, so that each planet's exact place on any given day, past or future, can be ascertained.

Again, though Uranus was discovered as late as 1781, this planet had been seen, mistaken for a fixed star which afterward disappeared, and its place registered as such, as early as 1690; and it had been so noted, at intervals, by several observers throughout the eighteenth century.

It was also admitted that discrepancies existed between the observed places thus ascertained to have been occupied by Uranus, and the places which, it seemed, that planet ought to have occupied, all known perturbing influences being calculated; and when, after actual discovery, its tables were accurately kept for a series of years, it was further ascertained that this discrepancy between the tabular and the observed positions of the planet gradually increased up to the year 1822; then became stationary; then began to decrease. This indicated the permanent existence of an occult disturbing cause. That cause *might* be a planet exterior to Uranus.

With these data and assuming certain probable postulates as to the orbit and the mean distance from the sun of the supposed perturbing planet—after profound investigations exhausting the resources of analogy—a young Parisian observer* wrote to one of the principal astronomers of the Berlin Observatory, telling him where the required planet ought to be, and asking him to look for it. It was found that very night; and at less than two diameters of the moon's disk from the indicated spot.

If some LE VERRIER of Spiritual Science had taken note, twenty-five years ago, of certain perturbing agencies of which the effects were visible throughout the religious world, he might have made a prediction more important than that of the French astronomer.

For even then it could have been discerned—what, however, is much more evident to-day—that an old belief was about to disappear from civilized society; a change which brings momentous results in its train.

This change is from belief in the exceptional and the miraculous to a settled conviction that it does not enter into God's economy, as manifested in His works, to operate here except mediately, through the instrumentality of natural laws; or to suspend or change these laws on special occasions; or, as men do, to make temporary laws for a certain age of the world and discontinue these throughout succeeding generations. In other words, the civilized

* LE VERRIER. Mr. J. C. Adams, of the University of Cambridge, without knowing what the other was about, had engaged in a similar investigation and obtained a similar result, except that the spot indicated by him was nearly five lunar diameters distant from the true one. Dr. Galle, of Berlin, to whom Le Verrier wrote, received the letter on the 23d of November, 1846; and during the night of the 23d-24th November, he, aided by Encké, discovered Neptune.

world is gradually settling down to the assurance that natural law is universal, invariable, persistent.

The advent of this change conceded, a thoughtful observer, endowed with proleptic faculty, might have foreshadowed some of its consequents.

If natural law be invariable, then either the wonderful works ascribed by the evangelists to Christ and his disciples were not performed, or else they were not miracles.

If they were not performed, then Christ, assuming to perform them, lent himself, as Rénan and others have alleged, to deception. This theory disparages his person and discredits his teachings.

But if they were performed under natural law, and if natural laws endure from generation to generation, then, inasmuch as the same laws under which these signs and wonders occurred must exist still, we may expect somewhat similar phenomena at any time.

But an acute observer, looking over the whole ground, might have detected more than this.

He would have found two antagonistic schools of religious opinion; the one basing spiritual truth on the miraculous and the infallible, chiefly represented in a Church of vast power, fifteen hundred years old, which has held her own against bold and active adversaries, and even increased in the relative as well as the actual number of her adherents for the last three hundred years: the other, dating back three hundred and fifty years only, affiliating more or less with the spirit of the age, and so placing herself in the line of progress; yet with less imposing antecedents, with fewer adherents, and, alas! with adherents weakened in influence by a large admixture of Indifferents, and still more weakened by intestine dissensions on questions of vital moment; even on the religious shibboleth of the day—the question of uniform rule, or miracle; many of this latter Church still holding to the opinion that to abandon the doctrine of the Miraculous is to deny the works of Christ

Apparently a very unequal contest--the outlook quite discouraging! Our spiritual Le Verrier might at first so regard it, just as his namesake may have felt discouraged when he first confronted the difficulty of predicting where an unknown world could be found.

Yet if our observer had abiding faith in the ultimate prevalence alike of Christianity and of the doctrine of natural law, he might, in casting about for a way out of difficulty, have come upon a practical solution.

History would inform him that the works of Christ and his disciples, mistaken by the Jews for miracles, effectively arrested the attention of a semi-barbarous age, incapable of appreciating the intrinsic value and moral beauty of the doctrines taught. And analogy might suggest to him that if phenomena more or less resembling these could be witnessed at the present day, and if they were not weighted down by claims to be miraculous, they might produce on modern indifference a somewhat similar impression. Then, if he had faith that God, who has bestowed to overflowing the means to supply our physical wants, would, in His own good time, provide also for our spiritual needs—it might occur to him that the appearance, under our eyes, of powers and gifts more or less similar to those of apostolic times, was not unlikely to be the means employed. And, if he was a Christian, this surmise would be confirmed by reading that Jesus, himself exercising these powers and gifts, promised to his followers after his death similar faculties;* evidently not regarding them as exclusively his, or as restricted to the age he lived in.

Guided by such premises as these, our supposed observer of twenty-five years since—though living at a time when the terms "medium" and "manifestations" (in their modern sense) had not yet come up—*might have predicted the speedy appearance and recognition among us of* Spiritual Phenomena, resembling those which

* John xiv. 12.

attended Christ's ministry and the Apostles' labors. As Le Verrier, guided by positive data and credible postulates, wrote, in 1846, to Dr. Galle, telling him what *ought* to be found in the heavens; so might a far-sighted Christian observer have written to a friend, in the same year, declaring what *ought* soon to be witnessed on earth.

The occurrence among us of spiritual phenomena under law not only tends to reconcile Scripture and sound philosophy; not only helps to attest the doctrine of the universal reign of law; not only explains and confirms the general accuracy of the gospel narratives; but it does much more than this. It supplies to a struggling religious minority, greatly in want of aid, the means of bringing to light, even before unbelievers in Scripture, the great truth of immortality; and it furnishes to that same minority, contending against greatly superior numbers, other powerful argumentative weapons urgently needed in the strife.

Less cogent considerations than these would suffice in proof that the subject treated of in this volume is of unspeakable importance in the interests alike of science and of Christianity.

In the following pages I seek to show that Religion, such as Christ taught, though sure to prevail in the end, is yet, for the time, hard pressed; on one hand by the hosts enlisted under the banner of Infallibility, on the other by the vigorous pioneers of Science: and that in this strait experimental evidence of the existence of modern spiritual phenomena, if it can be had, would assist her beyond measure. I seek to show, also, that if we but observe as dispassionately as the Berlin astronomer did, we shall obtain, as to the reality and the true character of these phenomena, proof as conclusive as that which demonstrated the existence of our latest-found planet.

Twelve years ago I endeavored to aid in clearing the way. As Uranus had occasionally been seen, but not recognized as a planet for a century, so had spiritual phenomena been observed and noted from time to time in the past, yet not then taken for what they really were—occurrences under law. Regarding them in this light, I brought what seemed the best authenticated among them to public notice.*

In the present work, partly historical though chiefly filled with detached narratives in way of illustration, I could not well avoid touching incidentally on certain doctrines which seem to me less beneficial than popular. If I have not succeeded—as who fully succeeds?—in dealing candidly and dispassionately with contending creeds, it has not been for lack of earnest endeavor.

I was tempted into the field which I here occupy chiefly by a profound conviction *that it affords phenomenal proof of a life to come.* But phenomenal proof is far more convincing than historical evidence. Had the electric telegraph been invented and employed for a brief period two thousand years ago, and had telegraphy then become one of the lost arts, the old records of its temporary triumph, how well attested soever, if unsupported by modern example, would have created but feeble belief to-day.

Such reflections outweighed the reluctance one feels in bringing forward what has lain for a time under the world's taboo. Nor am I over-sanguine, nor especially desirous, of speedy result. New ideas, how true soever, are seldom respectable, in the worldly sense of the term. Like self-made men they win their way to distinction—as it is best they should—but slowly, by their own merits.

The reader will find some repetition in this volume. In discussing a subject with which the public mind has little familiarity it is difficult to avoid this; and, in such a discussion, a certain amount of iteration has its use.

* In a work published January, 1860 (*Footfalls on the Boundary of Another World*), I traced back the occasional appearance of spontaneous spiritual phenomena for two hundred years, supplying many examples.

TABLE OF CONTENTS.

BOOK I.

TOUCHING COMMUNICATION OF RELIGIOUS KNOWLEDGE TO MEN.

CHAPTER I.

BOOK IV.

IDENTITY OF SPIRITS.

BOOK V.

THE CROWNING PROOF OF IMMORTALITY.

BOOK VI.

SPIRITUAL GIFTS OF THE FIRST CENTURY APPEARING IN OUR OWN TIMES.

BOOK VII.

THE CONCLUSION OF THE WHOLE MATTER.

INDEX.

THIS VOLUME

ON A SUBJECT INTIMATELY CONNECTED WITH

THE PRESENT ATTITUDE OF THE RELIGIOUS WORLD

IS DEDICATED

TO THE PROTESTANT CLERGY:

TO WHOM, IN WAY OF PREFACE, THE FOLLOWING REMARKS ARE ADDRESSED.

"To every thing there is a season, and a time to every purpose under the heaven."—ECCLESIASTES.

For every man, according to his light and conviction, there exists a certain duty to society, be it humble or elevated, evinced in words or in daily acts. If, after jealous watch set on motive and strict diligence in probing the verity and weighing the worth of what one may have to say, the conviction still abides that it ought to be said, one may be unfaithful in remaining silent. With such care and under such impression I tender to you what follows.

My work has this one claim, at least, on your attention, that what is therein set forth, alloyed with misconception and circumscribed by short-sight though it be, has been written religiously under the dictate of candor and of conscience, as if every word were to be laid at the foot of the Almighty's throne.

You will admit the grave importance of my subject-matter,

since it refers, first to the present state of theology and the religious needs of the world; incidentally to the reality of plenary inspiration; again, to the character of what, in the gospels and epistles, are termed sometimes signs and wonders, sometimes spiritual gifts; and, finally and specially, to the question whether phenomena analogous to these have come to light in the present age.

A just view of these subjects, vital beyond measure as they are, is unspeakably essential to the advancement of man's spiritual part. It is to you we may properly turn for this. Your office, in itself considered and looking to the eminence of its duties, is the highest upon earth; for the spiritual part *is* the man —is and will be in other phase of life than this. You ought to be the leaders of mankind. But zeal, learning, and the sincerest piety even, suffice not for the maintenance of such a position. As the world grows older, the letter of the ancient law, ecclesiastical or secular, governs less, and the spirit of the age more. They only can lead the world's advance who act upon this truth.

A layman, inviting your attention as I do, has this apology: that, within the immunities of your churches, you are not favorably situated to hear outside truth. I think you hear less of it than any other body of men. It is a privilege fraught with temptation to speak once a week, year after year, secure against challenge or reply: for it tends to mislead speaker and hearers alike. Among those who approach you the greater number mistake submissive acquiescence for respect: but the best token of respect, in addressing any man, or any class of men, is outspoken frankness and plain dealing.

The common result of your position is to restrict, within sectarian limits, your habitual periscope. And thus others, transgressing routine bounds, may have come upon fields of research which you, within the pale, disparaging them as barren, never see. If, for example, any among you have given as much time and thought as I to the question whether, in our own day as in times gone by, denizens of another world occasionally influence, for good or evil, the concerns of this, it has not been my good fortune to know it. Yet, discreetly pursued, there is no inquiry more legitimate, none reaching farther in its ethical and religious results. Nor is it we, pursuing such studies, who should defend our course: it is they that neglect them who may properly be called upon to show warrant for their neglect.

It is a belief justified by the history of the world that God permits man to acquire fresh knowledge in measure commensurate with his wants, and at the times when he becomes able to bear it.* Every age has its special needs, industrial, political, social, spiritual. I think there are strong reasons for the opinion that, at the present time, we lack, to sustain wholesome, reformatory faiths and to correct old errors that have been mixed up with these, direct aid from spiritual sources. If the history written by the Evangelists be a record with any valid claim to authenticity, it enters into God's economy to grant unto men, at certain times, such aid. It is a question of fact to be decided by proper evidence, whether He is supplying it now. Certain it is that the historical records of two thousand years ago, standing alone, fail to bring home to the free-inquiring mind of to-day the same convictions which they wrought in our ancestors.† Modern belief in the Unseen urgently needs freshening and additional support.

This will appear the rather, if we scan dispassionately the actual position of the religious world; its attitude toward science and the dilemma in which it finds itself whether it accepts or rejects the accredited discoveries of the day. The more thoughtful among your number cannot have failed to

* John xvi. 12.

† "Doubts to the world's child-heart unknown
Question us now from star and stone;
Too little or too much we know,
And sight is swift and faith is slow:
The power is lost to self-deceive
With shallow forms of make-believe."

WHITTIER: *The Meeting.*

mark the signs of the times. They must feel that a stationary policy is no longer practicable. Scepticism is silently, but surely, undermining once-popular doctrines: the old ground is giving way under our feet.

Not that there is cause for alarm except to those who think the world can be saved by dint of drag-chains only. Religion is in no more danger of subversion than are the eternal hills of sinking away, for its foundations in the soul are firmer than theirs in the solid earth: but opinions that cannot stand before the world's growth must, sooner or later, be subverted, do what you will in their defence. It is in vain that we cling to antiquated perplexities of doctrine, if it shall prove that these have become as much out of place under the lights of the nineteenth century as would be the belief of five hundred years ago that the pillars of Hercules marked the western boundary of the earth.

Beyond doubt many of your number are earnest in their convictions that what they deem Orthodoxy needs no spiritual influx to sustain its progress or rectify its errors; that it has no unphilosophical spirit to be reformed, nor any pernicious fallacies to be retracted. But if they are right in this, some problems connected with the history of Protestantism are of very difficult solution.

I allude to certain incidents for which we must go back some three hundred and fifty years, and which connect themselves with the rise and progress of the great REFORMATION—with its wonderful successes and its remarkable reverses—especially during the first century and a quarter of its growth.

---

§ 2. SUCCESSES AND REVERSES OF EARLY PROTESTANTISM.

It was on the tenth of December, in the year 1520, that brave Martin Luther burnt the Papal bull of excommunication which Leo X. had reluctantly launched against him. Less than half a century passed—the German miner's son and his Medicean opponent both having died the while—and the spirit of the reformed religion had spread to the most distant and obscure corners of Europe. "What an immense empire had Protestantism conquered in the space of forty years!—an empire reaching from Iceland to the Pyrenees, from Finland to the summit of the Italian Alps." *

The whole of that vast empire had not, indeed, gone definitively over to the new faith. In England, Scotland, Denmark, Sweden, Iceland, Livonia, Prussia, Saxony, Hesse, Würtemburg, and the Palatinate; in the northern Netherlands and in several cantons of Switzerland; the Reformation had completely triumphed: while throughout France, Belgium, Bavaria, Bohemia, Westphalia, Austria, Poland, and Hungary, though the contest remained undecided, the tenets of Luther or of Calvin had taken strong hold of the public mind. In France, for example, the reformed doctrines, in their Calvinistic phase, had invaded every province of the kingdom; in Brittany and Normandy, in Gascony and in Languedoc, in Poitou, Touraine, Provence, and Dauphiné, a majority openly professed the Protestant faith. "Your Highness," wrote the Venetian ambassador at the Court of France, in 1561, to the Doge, "may rest assured that, with the exception of the lower classes who still zealously frequent the churches, all the rest have fallen away, especially the nobles, and almost without a single exception, the men under forty." He says further that not only priests, monks, and nuns had adopted this heresy, but even bishops and many of the most considerable prelates; adding

* RANKE: *Ecclesiastical and Political History of the Popes of Rome in the Sixteenth and Seventeenth Centuries.* Translated by Sarah Austin, 3 vols. 8vo, London, 1840. Vol. ii. p. 18.

Lest too frequent references interrupt this brief sketch, I omit these, hoping that the student will refer, for verification of my narrative, to the work itself, one of the most interesting contributions to history that has appeared during the present century; or if he prefers a compendium, he may consult an admirable one in Macaulay's well-known review of Ranke's work, to which, a few pages further on, I have alluded. The latest edition of Ranke's work in German (*Die Römischen Päpste*) is the fourth, Berlin, 1856.

that imprisonment, stripes, and the stake, having only served to aggravate matters, had been abandoned, and that the liberated prisoners went about congratulating each other that they had won the battle against adversaries whom they were learning to call the Papists.*

In Prussian Poland, the right of the chief towns to the exercise of religion, according to the Lutheran forms, was confirmed by express charters in 1557 and 1558; while, in Poland proper, Protestants even obtained possession of bishops' sees. In Hungary, in the year 1554, a Lutheran was elected palatine of the empire. In Bavaria a large majority of the nobles had embraced the new doctrines, and the duke himself occasionally attended Protestant worship. In Austria, the revolution of sentiment was still greater; the nobles studied at Wittenberg, under professors who had been Luther's disciples; the colleges of Austria proper were filled with Protestants, and it was asserted that about a thirtieth † of the inhabitants only remained faithful to the Pope. In the Netherlands, the deadliest persecutions failed to effect their object. The ferocity, scarcely human, of Alva, the putting to death, as it was calculated, of thirty thousand Protestants in the Low Countries alone, had been unavailing to arrest the progress of the new opinions. Spain and Italy—themselves not without taint of heretical doctrine—were the only European countries, of any

* MICHELI. These details will be found in his *Relazione delle cose di Francia l'anno* 1561. I have held strictly to his expressions: "gloriandosi," he says, "che aveano guadagnato la lite contra i Papisti, così chiamavano e chiamano li loro adversarii."

A foreign minister of the day may be supposed to have informed himself carefully on such matters, and one representing a Catholic country was more likely to underrate than to over-estimate the progress of the Protestant movement.

† Macaulay has it one *thirteenth*. In the latest edition of Ranke's work in the original German (vol. ii. p. 9), I find it *thirtieth*, as above: "Man wollte rechnen dass veilleicht nur noch der dreiszigste Theil der Einwohner Katholisch geblieben sei:" doubtfully expressed, it will be observed, as to the authority.

importance, that could be regarded, after a struggle of half a century, as still loyal to the Holy See.*

Now, if we imagine a man of fair parts and competent foresight, a spectator throughout the religious struggle of the sixteenth century, and one whose convictions coincided with those of Luther and his adherents; if we suppose this man, when two-thirds of the century had elapsed, looking narrowly at the changes wrought by the Reformation, and reflecting upon the probable religious future of Europe; what must have been his anticipations? Can we doubt his reasonable conviction that three or four decades more would witness the expiring throes of that venerable system of ecclesiastical polity, endowed with more than antediluvian vitality, which, from the Seven Hills, had stretched its spiritual sceptre over the world

* Some of the most reliable Catholic authors of that day may be cited in proof that Ranke has not exaggerated the situation. Paolo Tiepolo, spoken of by his contemporaries as a man of good head and excellent heart, resided nearly three years as Venetian ambassador at the court of Pius V. He was there in 1568, and has left, written in that year, a small work entitled: *Relazione di Roma al tempo di Pio IV. e Pio V.* Thence I take the following:

"Speaking of these European countries alone, which were wont not only to yield obedience to the Pope, but also to conform in all their rites to the customs of the Roman Church, celebrating their offices in the Latin tongue; it is ascertained that England, Scotland, Denmark, Norway, Sweden—in fine all the northern countries—are alienated from him. Germany is almost entirely lost; Bohemia and Poland are in great part infected; the Low Countries of Flanders are so thoroughly corrupted, that even under the remedies (!) which the Duke of Alva feels compelled to employ against them, they will hardly return to their former health. Finally France, by reason of these bad humors (questi mal humori) is full of confusion. Thus it appears that there remains to the Pontificate nothing healthy and secure (non pare che sia restato altro di sano e sicuro al pontefice) save only Spain and Italy and a few islands, together with certain districts in Dalmatia and Greece."

It is evident that in Rome itself, in 1568, Roman Catholicism was held, by its supporters, to be in imminent danger of dying out.

throughout a longer series of centuries than the successors of Romulus themselves had ruled from the Eternal City?

Yet how marvellously wide of the truth were such expectations, then cherished by millions! * Eighty years passed; the contest had been waged and had subsided; and in 1648 the rights and the boundaries of the rival Churches were determined by treaty. But how determined? Of the European countries which, in 1568, might have been regarded as the Debatable Land of theological controversy, every one without an exception,—France and Austria and Belgium; Bavaria, Bohemia, Poland, and Hungary; even Westphalia where the partitioning treaties were signed †—had fallen back into the Roman faith.‡ Not only had Protestantism lost them all, but, after the lapse of two hundred years more, she has never regained one. There is not a single European nation that is Protestant to-day, except those that had become Protestant more than three hundred years ago.

We, Christians outside of the Roman faith, have much to allege in reply. We claim that the national downfall of Spain from a proud preëminence was mainly due to the influence of

* By Luther himself, among them He said: "'The Pope is the last blaze in the lamp, which will go out, and ere long be extinguished, the last instrument of the devil."—LUTHER'S *Table Talk*, p. 196. And again: "The Pope stands like a tottering wall about to be overthrown." —*Same work*, p. 331.

† Yet Westphalia, like the rest of Northern Europe, had been overrun, during the preceding century, by Lutheran doctrines. The town-council of Paderborn had been Protestant; in Munster most of the priests had married; and the ruling Duke, William of Cleves, apparently anxious to conciliate both parties, had received the sacrament in his private chapel, sometimes according to the Catholic, sometimes according to the Protestant form.

‡ I would avoid the use of the terms Roman Church, Romanism, Roman Catholic—grating to the ears of many honest believers in Papal infallibility—if I could do so without virtually admitting the claim of the Church of Rome to be *the* universal Church. Catholicity is a necessary element of any Faith that is to become the religion of civilization.

her Catholic Church;* that civilization has been retarded in Italy and in Ireland by similar agency; and, in a general way, that the increase of wealth, enterprise, and intelligence has been greater north of the boundary established by the peace of Westphalia than south of it: nevertheless the geographical frontier between the two religions, as then agreed upon, has scarcely been changed at all from that day to this. So far as the comparative numbers of Protestants and Romanists have varied since that peace was made, the variation has been in favor of the Roman Catholic Church.† Even in countries the most thor-

* The extermination of the Albigenses, even the St. Bartholomew massacres, dwindle to petty proportion before the giant wrong perpetrated, at the instigation of the Spanish Church, in the expatriation of the Moriscoes, the unhappy remnant of the Moorish nation. "About one million of the most industrious inhabitants of Spain were hunted out like wild beasts, because the sincerity of their religious opinions was doubtful."—BUCKLE, *History of Civilization* (New York Ed. 1862), vol. ii. p. 49. Countless thousands were butchered on the road to Africa, and hundreds of thousands more perished, when cast loose on a savage coast, by the swords of the Bedouins and by famine in the desert. The scarcely credible particulars of this wholesale outrage and of the ruin to Spanish prosperity and power that followed it, will be found, with ample authentication, in the chapter from which I have quoted. Never was nation so terribly and so speedily punished as Spain for one of the greatest crimes against humanity ever perpetrated by a people claiming to be civilized.

See, for a few important words in this connection, Darwin's *Descent of Man*, vol. i. pp. 171, 172: (New York Ed.)

† According to the best modern statistical authorities there were in the year 1868—out of the total population of the world, numbering 1,375,000,000—

Total number of Catholics.................... 195,434,000
Total number of Protestants.................. 100,835,000

And, *in Europe*, the totals for the same year were:

Total number of Catholics.................... 142,117,500
Total number of Protestants.................. 68,028,000

More than *two Catholics*, it will be observed, *to every Protestant*, in Europe to-day.

And besides the Catholics proper (who alone are reckoned above),

oughly Protestant and in our own times, the inroads of Catholicism on the prevailing faith have been such as must arouse, in thoughtful minds, grave reflections. In a third of a century, to wit from 1833 to 1867, the number of Catholic churches in Great Britain had more than doubled, while the number of Catholic seminaries had increased upward of five-fold. Up to the year 1833—the year when the great Tractarian movement had birth in Oxford—there was not in the British Isles a single convent or one Catholic school: but within thirty-four years thereafter there were founded in Great Britain nearly three hundred of the former, and nearly four hundred and fifty of the latter. Surely a very noteworthy progress made in the present age and in the most Protestant country of the world, by the Church of Rome! *

But it is in our own country, above every other, that the recent gains of Romanism upon Protestantism are the most remarkable. At the close of the two centuries and a half that elapsed from the first settlement of Virginia to the year 1859, the number of Catholics in the United States had run up to two

there are the members of the Eastern phase of Catholicism, agreeing with the Western in a general way, even on the subject of the infallible authority of the Church, except that they restrict that infallible authority to the Œcumenical Councils. (Hagenbach's *History of Doctrines*, vol. ii. p. 234.) In 1868 they outnumbered the Protestants in Europe, there being, in that quarter of the world—

Total included in Greek and other Eastern Churches... 69,782,000.

At the present time, therefore, *less than one fourth of the Christians in Europe* are Protestant.

For these and other details see Schem's *Ecclesiastical Almanac* for 1869 (noticed in a subsequent note), pp. 81, 82, etc.

* In the Report for the year 1867–8 of the *Scottish Reformation Society* (founded in Scotland, in 1850, to "resist the aggressions of Catholicism"), tables are given, showing the exact numbers, which sum up as follows:

	Churches.	Convents.	Colleges and Seminaries.	Schools.
In 1833 there were......	497	none.	3	none.
" 1867 " "	1,143	294	16	442

millions and a half only: but at the end of the nine years that succeeded (namely in 1868), that number had doubled. Twelve years ago they were but a twelfth part of our population; to-day they constitute, probably, more than a seventh.

If we suppose the two great divisions of the Christian Church, respectively, to go on increasing among us at the same ratio for four terms of nine years each from 1868, the Catholics of the United States would, at the end of that time, exceed the Protestants in number by several millions.*

How wonderful, if one admits that Reason and Scripture were on the side of the Reformers, is all this! From the usual Protestant standpoint, how beset with difficulties in explanation!

---

§ 3. Inadequate Causes suggesting themselves.

Some minor causes bearing on this ebb and flow of opinion, yet accessory only, one readily perceives. The startling progress of the Lutheran movement, even during the first decade or two, convinced the astute Court of Rome, that thorough

* Schem's "Ecclesiastical Year-book" for 1860, and his Ecclesiastical Almanac for 1869, both published in this country by a most painstaking German statistician, professor of Hebrew in Dickinson College, have the well-earned reputation of being the most trustworthy documents extant among us on the subject of modern religious statistics.

In the first of these (at page 14) I find

Number of Protestants in the United States in 1859... 21,000,000
Number of Catholics in the United States in 1859....... 2,500,000

And in the second (at page 81)

Number of Protestants in the United States in 1868... 27,000,000
Number of Catholics in the United States in 1868....... 5,000,000

Showing that the Catholics had increased, in the nine years from 1859 to 1868, *one hundred* per cent., while the Protestants had increased, in the same time, *less than twenty-nine* per cent.

Those who will verify the calculation of future increase, supposing it to continue at the same relative ratio for four terms of nine years each, commencing with the year 1868, will find that in 1904, that is *in thirty-*

reformation within could alone enable it to resist the giant Reformation without. This conviction showed itself in the changed character of the Pontiffs chosen. Before the standard of heresy was raised on the banks of the Elbe, it had been a Sixtus IV., with his inhumanity and his unblushing nepotism; an Alexander VI., with his sensuality, and those children of his, the infamous Borgias; at best, the elegant luxury and lavish prodigality of a Leo X. But when the storm from Wittenberg swept over the land, and the time of need came, then there succeeded to these the corrective influence of such men as Paul III., earnest,* intelligent, and sagacious, and Paul IV., austere, impulsive, inflexible, and ruled by a single devotion, that of restoring to its primitive purity the ancient faith. And more home-reaching than the power of any Pope was the influence of a man† as remarkable in his way as the great Reformer himself; unlike him as one man could well be to another, yet as fiercely in earnest, as indissolubly wedded, body and soul, to one idea. As Luther was the animating spirit of the reformatory movement, so was Loyola of the reactionary one. And, for a time, the sway exercised over the religious mind of Europe and its dependencies, by the Spaniard, with his intensity and his asceticism, was little less than that which the stubborn and warm-hearted German exerted.

three years from to-day, there would be eighty millions of Catholics to *less than seventy-five millions* of Protestants, in the American Union.

It is very far from being my belief that any such result is compatible with the spirit of God's economy and the ceaseless march of human progress. But to avert it, some religious influences that have been at work for three hundred years must undergo radical change.

* This Pontiff, expressing to the Emperor Charles V., in 1537, his determination to carry out internal reform in the Church, writes: "Sarà con effetto, e non con parole." It was to be in deeds, not words.

† Ignatius Loyola's public career commenced twenty years later than Martin Luther's. The bull establishing the new Order was granted, at Loyola's earnest instance, by Pope Paul III., in 1540. The Order of Jesus was suppressed in 1773, but restored in 1814: in each case by Papal authority.

These things are to be taken into account; but do we find in them a solution of the difficulty? If the vices of the Papacy were weeded out, its errors of opinion remained. If Popes like the third and fourth Paul and Pius V., and Gregory XIII.,* sustained the honor and the cause of the Catholic Church: if Loyola and his coadjutors gave to it their fortunes and their lives,† were there not, opposed to these, Luther and Calvin and Melancthon and Zwingli, and a host of other apostles of the Reformation, as able and as devoted workers as any of which Catholicism could boast?

The sword, indeed, was used against the innovators: but persecution, unless its severity tend toward extermination, is in-

* The last two, however, Pius and Gregory, with the drawback of an inhuman spirit of persecution. Pius V. complained that the leader of the French Catholics, Count Santafiore, failed to obey the command he had given him to take no Huguenot prisoner, but "instantly to kill every heretic that fell into his hands." Here are his biographer's own words: "Pio si dolsi del Conte che non avesse il comandamento di lui osservato d' ammazzar subito qualunque heretico gli fosse venuto alle mani."—*Vita di Pio V.*, by CATENA.

When the news of the massacre of St. Bartholomew (1573) reached Gregory XIII., he celebrated that great event by a solemn procession to San Luigi. I can find no foundation for the apology, sometimes offered by Catholics for this; namely, that Gregory was ignorant at the time, that it *was* a general massacre. It is incredible that a religious movement involving the death, it is said, of fifty thousand heretics (RANKE, *Histor. Polit. Zeitschrift*, II. iii.), should not have been known in its true character, and at the earliest day, to so well-served and well-informed a court as that of Rome; to say nothing of the fact that the Romish Church has always held it a right and a duty to suppress heresy, if need be, by the death-penalty.

† It is to be borne in mind also, that the stern discipline and incisive austerity of the order of Jesus faded, ere long, into a spirit of compromise with the vices and even the crimes of the age. Speaking of the Jesuits in the middle of the seventeenth century, Ranke says: "The spirit which once animated them had fallen before the temptations and influences of the world, and their sole endeavor now was to make themselves necessary to mankind, let the means be what they might. . . . The secret operations of that awful tribunal which is established

sufficient, if unaided by mental and moral agencies, to arrest a reformatory movement so powerful and widespread as was that of Lutheranism in 1570. It proved insufficient in the early ages to check a weaker sect, the primitive Christians; although, under Decius in the middle of the third century, and yet more especially fifty years later under Dioclesian and Galerius, it showed itself in forms of death and of torture marked by a ferocity unparalleled in the history of the world. The martyrs in those days, greedy of death as the surest entrance to heaven, denounced themselves, by hundreds, to the authorities; * and their religious teachers found it necessary to exert their utmost authority in order to check this species of self-immolation. The spirit of the new religion passed unquenched through the fiery trial.

The counter-revolution which set in toward the close of the sixteenth century was evidently a recoil of opinion far more than a repression by force. Outside of Spain and Italy, no authority to the Inquisition was conceded, after the date of the Reformation, by temporal sovereigns; Spain was the chief scene of its horrors.† Nor can we ascribe to victories in the

in the inmost depths of the heart of man were thus changed into mere outward acts. A slight turn of the thoughts was held to exonerate from all guilt."—*History of the Popes*, III. pp. 139, 143.

* If Tertullian may be trusted, the entire population of a small town in Asia presented themselves before the proconsul, proclaiming their faith in Christianity and entreating him to carry into effect the Imperial decree and put them all to death. When, partially acceding to their supplication, he had executed a few and dismissed the rest, these departed bitterly grieving that they had been deemed unworthy of the glorious martyr-crown.

† The number of victims who suffered under the Spanish Inquisition will never be accurately known, yet it was undoubtedly greater than that of all the martyrs under the Pagan persecutions of the first three centuries. It is to be conceded that the Protestant faith was actually crushed out of existence in Spain, by the death of obdurate heretics and the extremity of terror in the survivors. At one time, about 1558, "there were converts in almost all the towns and in many of the villages of the ancient kingdom of Leon."—(McCrie, *Reformation in*

field the losses, in converts and in territory, of the Reformers. When the war waged by the Smalcalde League of Protestants against Charles V. was terminated by Alva's victory at Mühlberg,* that seemingly disastrous defeat scarcely at all arrested the progress of the new faith. Even to the terrible night of St. Bartholomew and the horrors that succeeded it, though for the time they undoubtedly crushed hope and spirit among the Huguenots, we cannot trace the state of feeling which prevailed throughout France, twenty years after the massacre, when Henry IV., Protestant and fearless soldier as he was, finding himself about to be deserted even by the most gallant of those Huguenot nobles whose swords had won for him the battle of Ivry, was fain to abjure his religion in order to secure a throne.†

No. Neither fortune of arms nor suffering by persecution; neither the serpent-wisdom of an Order of which the members were all things to all men, nor the cleansing of those shameless corruptions which had so scandalized the Augustinian monk, Martin Luther, when in 1510 he visited degenerate Rome—not any one of these incidents, nor all of them combined, can be accepted as even plausible explanation why Protestantism, after virtually conquering three-fourths of Europe in one half century, lost, in the next eighty years, full one-half of all she had gained.

Lost, and never recovered it; not after ten generations had passed; not down to the present day.

Spain, London, 1829, p. 231.) A Catholic historian (PARAMO, *Hist. Inquisitiones*), says: "Had not the Inquisition taken care in time, the Protestant religion would have run through Spain like wildfire." But that wary institution took the alarm in 1558; the first auto-da-fè was celebrated May 21, 1559, at Valladolid, in presence of Don Carlos and the Queen Dowager; and ere five years had passed, Protestantism was literally exterminated, from the Pyrenees to the Atlantic.

* In 1547.

† "Even the Protestant clergy had the wisdom to exhort the king, (Henry IV.) to return into the bosom of the Catholic Church. Calvinism, by the burdensome austerities of its moral censures, finished by losing its attraction for the nobles."—GERVINUS: *Introduction to History of Nineteenth Century*, pp. 47, 48.

If still there lingers in your minds a doubt whether one is justified in concluding that the reactionary movement dating from 1570 cannot be explained, as the result of incidental and extraneous agencies; or if you fall back, perhaps, on the position that the Reformation was premature in so rude a century as the sixteenth; then I pray you to interpret another episode in the history of the Lutheran movement, occurring two hundred years after Luther's time.

An episode connected with the days of the French encyclopedists, when Voltaire derided; when D'Alembert and Diderot wrote; when Paine discoursed of an age of reason, and Volney of the ruin of empires. In those days men witnessed, some with amazement and terror, some with exultation, what seemed a concerted attack upon all that was most ancient in opinion, and all that is usually held most sacred in religion. Let Macaulay, who has graphically described this uprising of scepticism, often allied with talent and learning, sometimes with philanthropy, briefly sum up to us the result:

"During the eighteenth century the influence of the Church of Rome was constantly on the decline. Unbelief made extensive conquests in all the Catholic countries of Europe, and in some countries obtained a complete ascendency. The Papacy was at length brought so low as to be an object of derision to infidels, and of pity rather than of hatred to Protestants.* During the nineteenth century this fallen Church has been gradually rising from her depressed state and reconquering her old dominion. No person who calmly reflects on what, within the last few years,† has passed in Spain, in Italy, in South America, in Ireland, in the Netherlands, in Prussia, and even in France, can doubt that her power over the hearts and minds of men is now greater than it was when the 'Encyclopedia'

* Ranke's history fully bears out Macaulay's view of the situation. After giving the particulars of the death, in France, of the aged and deposed Pius VI., in August, 1799, he adds: "In fact it seemed as if the papal power was now forever at an end."—vol. iii. p. 226.

† This was written in 1840.

and the 'Philosophical Dictionary' appeared. It is surely remarkable that neither the moral revolution of the eighteenth century, nor the moral counter-revolution of the nineteenth, should, in any perceptible degree, have added to the domain of Protestantism. During the former period whatever was lost to Catholicism was lost also to Christianity; during the latter, whatever was regained by Christianity was regained also by Catholicism. We should naturally have expected that many minds, on the way from superstition to infidelity, or from infidelity back to superstition, would have stopped at an intermediate point. . . . We think it a most remarkable fact that no Christian nation which did not adopt the principles of the Reformation before the end of the sixteenth century, should ever have adopted them. Catholic communities have, since that time, become infidel and become Catholic again, but none have become Protestant."*

Macaulay is right. All this *is* most remarkable. He to whom it supplies not theme for earnest meditation must be very careless, or very contracted in circle of thought.

---

§ 4. How explain the foregoing Episodes?

All that has been said and believed of human progress—how mighty Truth is, how sure to prevail over Error—is it pure

* Macaulay's *Essays*, New York Ed. of 1856, vol. iii. pp. 339, 340. The extract is from his celebrated review of Ranke's *History of the Popes*, an admirable essay, rather, on the Reformation and its ebbings and flowings, and its results. I am compelled to differ from Macaulay's inferences, while I admire, and in part have followed, his masterly array of facts.

It ought to be borne in mind, in connection with the reactionary movement in favor of Catholicism above spoken of as occurring during the early portion of the present century, that the terrors of the Inquisition had nothing to do in bringing it about.

fable? Or are we to believe that it is *not* against Error that Protestantism is losing the battle?

We have had recent official reminders what some of the claims of Roman Catholicism are. That Christ himself has invested the Pope with full authority to rule and govern the Universal Church; that the Pope may properly issue decrees, by his assured knowledge, by his own impulse and by the fulness of his apostolic power; that such decrees shall remain in force in all time to come, and shall never, on any plea, be revoked, or limited, or questioned, even though an Œcumenical Council, including the college of Cardinals, unanimously consents to their revocation.*

Other claims, asserted and maintained by the Church of Rome, may be culled from equally authentic sources.† The

* See, in confirmation, the "Constitution" issued by the present Pope, under date of December 4, 1869, to provide for the contingency of his death during the recent Œcumenical Council. It affirms that "to the Roman Pontiffs . . . our Lord Jesus Christ gave the full power to feed, rule, and govern the Universal Church." The Pope then goes on to declare: "Of our certain knowledge, our motion, and in the plenitude of our Apostolic power, we decree and ordain," etc., (giving details, excluding the council from all share in the election of a Pope, and declaring null and void whatever they may do, until a successor to the Papal chair shall be so chosen). Then he proceeds: "This decision must not be questioned, attacked, refuted, invalidated, retracted, legally revoked, or submitted to discussion. . . . We declare null and void whatever shall be done to the contrary, during the vacancy of the Apostolic See, by any authority whatever, whether by the authority of the Council of the Vatican, or of any other Œcumenical Council; even with the unanimous consent of the Cardinals that now are, or at any future time may be." And the document winds up by proclaiming that whoever shall "call in question this our declaration, decree, and will," or shall "dare to infringe them," or shall "make such an attempt," "let him know that he incurs the indignation of Almighty God and of the blessed Apostles Peter and Paul."—Translation made for the (London) *Vatican*, and officially published in the (New York) *Catholic Register* of January 22, 1870.

† As from the Canons and Decrees of the Council of Trent, which commenced its sessions in December, 1545, twenty-five years after the

unwritten traditions of the "Holy Catholic Church," as having been handed down to it from Christ, are to be received with the same veneration as the Holy Scriptures; of which last the Vulgate is the only authorized translation.* Tradition is to be received because the Holy Ghost dwells perpetually in the Church; the Vulgate, because the Church of Rome, which adopts it, has been kept free from all errors by the special grace of God. The seven sacraments† are divinely ordained; they are referred to Christ, since the institutes of the Church of Christ are communicated to that Church not by Scripture alone, but by tradition. Justification is not to be obtained by faith alone. The sinner is justified (so the Council of Trent voted), "through the merit of the most sacred passion and by the power of the Holy Ghost. . . . While man observes the commands of God and the Church, by the help of faith *and through good works*, he grows in righteousness and is justified more and more."‡ Justification, however, cannot dispense with the sacraments, by which it either begins, or when begun is continued, or when lost is regained.‖ All religious instruction, all interpretation of Scripture, must be given by ecclesiastical authority alone.¶ The visible Church is also the true

outbreak of the Reformation. These documents (*Canones et Decretæ Concilii Tridentini*, Roma, 1564) were passed chiefly during Sessions iv. to vii., xiii., xiv., and xxi. to xxv. They will be found in the *Historia del Concilio Tridentino*, by SARPI, 1629. The *Professio Fidei Tridentinæ*, drawn up (A.D. 1564) by order of Pope Pius IV., embodies them. It was subscribed by all candidates, may be regarded as the Confession of Faith of the Roman Church, and as having settled, for Roman Catholicism as against the Protestant heresy, all the chief points of doctrine. In Sarpi's work (at page 241 and elsewhere) will be found discussions on these matters.

* *Concil. Trident*, Sessio IV.

† Namely: 1. Baptism; 2. Confirmation; 3. The Eucharist; 4. Penance; 5. Orders; 6. Marriage; 7. Extreme Unction. Luther and Melancthon were inclined to add to the two usual Protestant sacraments (to wit, Baptism and the Lord's Supper) a third, that of Penance.

‡ SARPI: Sessio VI., c. VII., § 10. ‖ Sessio VII. ¶ Sessio IV.

Church, and no religious existence can be recognized out of her pale.*

With these doctrines was included the seclusion of the Bible even in its Latin version, much more in the vernacular, from perusal by any one not an ecclesiastic.†

Then, in later documents, we find the ideas of the Roman Church, touching the relations between science and religion, and the definition of the Papal claim to infallibility in religious teachings. Scientific research must not, on pain of anathema, be prosecuted in a spirit of freedom, if, in its progress, science should assert what contravenes the doctrines of the Church.‡ And forasmuch as "this See of St. Peter ever remains free from all error," when its sovereign head, the Pope, speaking "in virtue of his supreme apostolic authority," defines any "doctrine of faith or morals, to be held by the universal Church," he is infallible; and therefore "such definitions of the

* In addition, of course, are to be noted the well-known Romanist doctrines of the Real Presence, Intercession of Saints, Absolution by the Priesthood, and Purgatory including the efficacy of prayers for the dead.

† Anterior to any translations of the Bible into modern languages, the Vulgate had been declared, to all persons not in sacred orders, a sealed volume. The Œcumenical Council held at Toulouse, in 1229, passed a canon, prohibiting the laity from having the books of the Old and New Testament.—Concil. Tolos. Canon 14: *Sabbei Collect.*, vol. xi. p. 427.

‡ "If any one shall say that human sciences ought to be pursued in such a spirit of freedom that one may be allowed to hold as true their assertions, even when opposed to revealed doctrine; and that such assertions may not be condemned by the Church; let him be anathema."

"If any one shall say that it may, at any time, come to pass in the progress of science, that the doctrines set forth by the Church must be taken in another sense than that in which the Church has ever received, and yet receives them; let him be anathema."

The above, translated for the (New York) *Catholic World*, by some of the bishops attending the Council, are sections 2 and 3 of Canon IV. of the Œcumenical Council of the Vatican, promulgated April 24, 1870. —See *Catholic World* for June, 1870.

Roman Pontiff are irreformable (irreformabiles) of themselves, and not by force of the consent of the Church thereto." This dogma, also, not to be contradicted on pain of anathema.*

The peculiar religious ideas, then, against which Protestantism, during three centuries, has failed to make head, are substantially these: A Spiritual Sovereign of Christendom (elected, from time to time, by a College of Cardinals), divinely ordained, infallible, authorized by the Deity to dictate, without appeal, the religion and the morals of the world. A Universal Church in which the Holy Ghost perpetually dwells, keeping it free from all error, and of which the traditions are of equal authority with Scripture; both being derived through plenary inspiration of God. No entrance into Heaven except for those who receive the sacraments. No escape from Hell except by obedience to the Universal Church's commands. No existence of religion outside of the Universal Church. Denial

* In Chapter IV. of the *Dogmatic Decree on the Church of Christ*, passed by the Œcumenical Council, and approved by the Pope, July 18, 1870, after defining the character of Apostolic teaching, it is added: "This apostolic teaching all the venerable fathers have embraced, and the holy orthodox doctors have revered and followed, knowing most certainly that this See of St. Peter ever remains free from all error, according to the Divine promise of our Lord and Saviour to the Prince of the Apostles."

And again, in the same chapter, "We teach and define it to be a doctrine divinely revealed, that when the Roman Pontiff speaks *ex cathedrâ*, that is, when in the exercise of his office of pastor and teacher of all Christians, and in virtue of his supreme Apostolic authority, he defines that a doctrine of faith or morals is to be held by the Universal Church, he possesses, through the Divine assistance promised to him in the blessed Peter, that infallibility with which the Divine Redeemer willed his Church to be endowed, in defining a doctrine of faith or morals; and, therefore, that such definitions of the Roman Pontiff are irreformable of themselves, and not by force of the consent of the Church thereto.

"And if any one shall presume, which God forbid, to contradict this our definition; let him be anathema."—*Catholic World* for September, 1870, pp. 856–8.

to the human soul (outside the Catholic priesthood) of the right to interpret Scripture. Subordination of scientific facts to the Church's doctrines. Finally, a solemn curse denounced against all who oppose or deny any canon promulgated by the Church.

Does it seem to you that TRUTH ought to have been powerless, for centuries, against prescripts such as these?—that, in all that time, against a Church styling itself infallible, she should have lost ground instead of making progress? One of the most powerful and cultivated intellects of the century, not Roman Catholic, seems to have taken refuge in that conclusion. In the essay from which I have quoted Macaulay says:

"We often hear it said that the world is constantly becoming more and more enlightened, and that this enlightening must be favorable to Protestantism and unfavorable to Catholicism. We wish that we could think so. But we see great reason to doubt whether this is a well-founded expectation. . . . As to the great question what becomes of man after death we do not see that a highly educated European, left to his unassisted reason, is more likely to be in the right than a Blackfoot Indian. . . . Nor is revealed religion in the nature of a progressive science. All divine truth is, according to the doctrine of the Protestant Churches, recorded in certain books. It is plain, therefore, that in divinity there cannot be a progress analogous to that which is constantly taking place in pharmacy, geology, and navigation. A Christian of the fifth century with a Bible, is on a par with a Christian of the nineteenth century with a Bible, candor and natural acuteness being, of course, supposed equal. . . . It seems to us, therefore, that we have no security for the future against the prevalence of any theological error that has ever prevailed in time past among Christian men." *

The gist of this is, that, under a system of revealed teach-

* *Macaulay's Essays:* vol. iii. pp. 305–307.

ings, there is no religious progress, nor any reasonable hope for the prevalence of spiritual truth.

Are you content to rest in a conviction thus hopeless? Are you content to labor in your vocation under such discouragement as this?

The triumphs, in our day, of art and science, especially in the production of material wealth, have been vast beyond all former precedent. In 1760 every species of thread was spun on the single wheel; water and wind were the chief inanimate motors; and the horse or the dromedary was the fleetest messenger, except when the intelligence it bore was occasionally anticipated by the beacon-fire on the hill-top, or by signal from the cross-bar and the pivoted arm of that clumsy expedient which was dignified, in those days, by the name of telegraph. Then came a sudden irruption of industrial inventions, fabulous in their results. Have you looked into that subject? If you consult the best English statisticians you will find that in the British isles alone, within little more than a century, the increased power obtained through labor-saving machinery equals the adult manual labor out of two worlds as populous as our own.*

Again, aside from industrial enterprise, there are the start-

* By English political economists the industrial inventions since 1760 are variously set down as furnishing a power equivalent to the unaided labor of from five hundred to seven hundred millions of adults. The mean of these—six hundred millions—may be assumed as near the truth. But as the average available manual labor of any given population is usually estimated as equal to that which might be performed by one-fourth of that population if all were working adults, it follows that the labor of six hundred millions of adult workers is equal to the manual power which resides in a population of two thousand four hundred millions, in other words, of nearly twice the present population of our globe.

Our statistics, in the United States, furnish no sufficient data for a similar calculation. The amount of mechanical power compared to population, though vast and ever increasing among us, averages less, doubtless, here than in England.

ling discoveries in the more abstruse departments of science, connected with such names as Faraday, Darwin, Tyndal, Hux ley.

Is the great, eternal law of progress to operate in every department of knowledge save one—the most important of all? Is everything to move on except religion? There has been a Galileo to enlighten our ignorance touching the orbit of the earth and the motion of the sun; a Newton to explain to us the career of planets and systems of planets throughout the heavens; a Harvey to detect the circulation of the blood; a Humboldt to unveil for us the Cosmos; a Bacon to organize the exploration of all fields of earthly knowledge. In every department of material and intellectual science, the advance has been from conquest to conquest. But in pneumatology is the end already reached? Has an investigator of religion no longer a legitimate vocation? Shall we say of its doctrines, as a Scottish philosopher did of the learned foundations of Europe that they are not without their lesson for the historian of the human mind: immovably moored to the same station by the strength of their cables and the weight of their anchors, they serve to mark the velocity with which, as it passes them, the rest of the world is borne along.

I thank God that I do not believe this. If it were true, life would be of little worth. How heart-sinking—how utterly unworthy—the conception that, under the Divine Economy, that grand privilege of progress to which man owes all he ever was or ever will be is denied to the science of the Soul, while inhering in every other!

It is not of the arcana of Theology that I am speaking; it is of man's soul, not of God's essence. I do not believe that we of this earth shall ever make progress in the literature of the planet Jupiter, or in the language spoken by the inhabitants of Saturn. There is what to man is the unknowable; and outside the sphere of the knowable, human progress cannot be. Except so far as God's works around us adumbrate their Author and His attributes, I do not think that by searching we can make progress in discovering the Creator's ways, or His thoughts, or His judgments; seeing that these are not as ours, but unsearchable and past finding out. When we press on in quest of such mysteries, the power of the highest intellect expires before it attains an object, as waves on a troubled ocean break and lose themselves in the vast expanse.

Evidence is scattered all over God's works of infinite intelligence, mercy, love. But when we seek to know what were the Deity's specific intentions in the original creation of man, for what purpose He permits evil and misery, *how* He himself exists—when we set about analyzing the divine hypostasis and the like—we come upon mysteries which it is not probable that, even in the next world, we shall have vision to penetrate or means to solve.

Macaulay's argument, then, may be admitted, so far as it applies to the abstruser portions of speculative theology; but only because abstruse theological doctrines are among the unknowable things.*

But as for Spiritual science, I firmly believe that we have the means of studying it, and therefore of advancing in its various branches. When we declare that Truth is mighty and will prevail, we must not except spiritual truth; for that is the mightiest of all. Why Calvinism, why Lutheranism, prevailed not, as against the Roman Church, may be explained without assuming that Christianity lacks the element of progress. To the wholesome truths which the Reformation put forth, it undoubtedly owed its half-century of progress. The hypothesis remains, that while Protestantism may have approached, in many respects, nearer to the truth than Roman Catholicism, it may, in other matters, have failed to meet the wants of the age, and may have made radical mistakes in opinion that have proved fatal to its advancement.

* Said Luther, preaching otherwise than he practised: "Let the Father's good will be acceptable to thee, O man, and speculate not with thy devilish queries, thy whys and thy wherefores, touching God's words and works."—*Luther's Table Talk*, p. 29.

The grand truth inherent in Protestantism, and through which, in the sixteenth century, chiefly came the wonderful impetus it received, is one that has stirred men's hearts ever since they began to think and to reason. Luther touched upon it: "Argue will I, and write, and exhort," he said, "but compel will I no one."* If he is not entitled to be called the Apostle of freedom in thought and speech, it is because, when men first emerge to the light, its effulgence is wont to blind them; and thus the world advances only step by step. If the Wittenberg Doctor had done nothing more than to demand, and to obtain, for the people the right to read in the vernacular the sayings and doings of Christ, instead of taking the Christian system, at second hand, from a privileged Order, that one deed would entitle him to the eternal gratitude of mankind. Luther was not tolerant, he was not consistent; but how outspoken and fearless was he, even when life was at stake! We cannot think of him without calling to mind the celebrated words: "I will go," he said, when on the arrival of the summons to appear before the Diet of Worms, faint-hearted friends augured for him the fate of Huss,—"I will go, if there were as many devils

* "—doch zwingen will ich Niemand." The expression occurs in his first sermon on his return from Wartburg. (*Luther's Works*, vol. xviii. p. 256.) Similar sentiments are found elsewhere throughout his earlier writings.

Hallam reminds us that we should be careful, in considering the Reformation as part of the history of mankind, not to be misled by the idea that Luther contended for freedom of inquiry and boundless privilege of individual judgment. (*Literature of Europe*, Boston Ed. 1864; vol. i. pp. 306-7.)

But I think we should not deny merit to those who may have advanced, if it be but a few steps, on the road to mental enfranchisement, because, clogged by the intolerant and dogmatical spirit of their age, they failed to go farther.

I shall have occasion also, before closing these remarks, to show, that Luther held, and boldly expressed, advanced ideas on the subject of literalism and plenary inspiration.

there as there are tiles on the roofs of the houses." He went, and the world will long remember the issue.*

---

§ 5. The Sin at Marburg and at Geneva.

Deep must be the regret felt by every friend of the fearless Wittenberger, in calling to mind that history was soon to present the reverse of the medal. Eight years later, Luther was summoned by Philip, Landgrave of Hesse, to another meeting; this time at Marburg; † not, as before, to face emperor, and nobles, and ecclesiarchs; but, in friendship to confer with a man as brave and honest as himself; a fellow-soldier in the good fight of faith, stout Ulrich Zwingli; who brought with him other of the Swiss Reformers. They differed on the doctrine of the Eucharist,‡ and the Landgrave hoped to recon-

* "Little monk," said the veteran commander Freundsberg, tapping him on the shoulder as he entered the hall—"little monk, little monk, thou art on a passage more perilous than any I have ever known on the bloodiest battle-fields. But if thou art right, fear not! God will sustain thee." Quaint and undaunted that monk stood before nobles of the Empire and dignitaries of the Church. When admonished that argument was unfit, and that the Diet wanted only a straightforward answer as to whether he would recant, he said they should have an answer that "had neither horns nor teeth" (die weder Hörner noch Zähne haben soll"); and it was that well-known one: "I am conscience-bound in God's Word, and cannot and dare not recant; since it is neither safe nor advisable to do anything against conscience. Here I stand; I cannot otherwise; God help me! Amen!"

† A town of Hesse Cassel, on the Lahn.

‡ Luther believed in the "real presence" of Catholicism; defending his opinion with his usual plump directness, in his treatise: *Dass die Worte Christi,* "das ist mein Leib," etc., *noch fest stehen;* and in his *Grosses Bekenntniss* (1528). He says (alluding to the text, Matthew xxvi. 26): "We are not such fools as not to understand these words. If they are not clear, I don't know how to talk German. Am I not to comprehend when a man puts a loaf of bread before me, and says: 'Take, eat, this is a loaf of bread;' and again, 'Take, drink,

cile this difference; but each held to his opinion. At the close Zwingli exclaimed: "Let us confess our union in all things in which we agree, and as for the rest let us remember that we are brothers." The Landgrave again earnestly urged concord. Zwingli, addressing the Wittenberg doctors, said: "There is no one on earth with whom I more desire to be united than with you." Then the noble Swiss Reformer, bursting into tears and approaching Luther, extended his hand. The obdurate German rejected it. "You have a different spirit from ours," was all he said.*

Ah, Martin Luther! Valiant wert thou in defence of the modicum of holy truth thou sawest; and, for that, honored forever be thy name! But at Marburg, like other disciples before thee, thou knewest not what spirit thou wert of. Quick

this is a glass of wine'? In the same manner, when Christ says, 'Take, eat, this is my body,' every child must understand that he speaks of that which he gives to his disciples."—*Luther's Works*, Walch's Ed. Halle, 1740-53, vol. xx. p. 918.

And again, in his *Larger Catechism*, Art. *Lord's Supper* (p. 554), he says: "A hundred thousand devils, with a pack of visionaries to boot, may come at me, asking: 'How can bread and wine be Christ's body and blood?' still I know that all the Spirits, and all the learned heads that can be lumped together, haven't as much wisdom as God's Majesty has in his least little finger."

Zwingli, on the contrary, regarded the words in question simply as a trope, like the other words of Christ: "I am the true vine: . . . ye are the branches" (John xv. 1, 5). "The bread," he said, "remains the same, but the dignity of the Lord's Supper gives it value."—HAGENBACH: *History of Doctrines*, vol. ii. p. 313 (New York Ed. 1862).

* It was in 1529. Two years later, Zwingli gave his life, on the battlefield, for the Protestant cause. One wonders what Luther's sensations may have been when the news reached him.

Since writing the above, I find, in a biography of Luther by one of his warmest admirers, the following: "When Luther heard of the death of the brave Swiss, on the sanguinary field of Cappel, fighting for the liberties of his country, there is no sympathy, but a grating harshness in the tone in which he received the sad news."—TULLOCH: *Leaders of the Reformation*. London, 1859, p. 62.

to condemn what to thy short-sight loomed up, though but a mote in another's eye, blind to the beam in thine own, when thou rejectedst the hand of thy gentle, weeping brother, who came to thee suing for peace as becomes a child of God, the Christian was dead within thee: it was that Evil Spirit of self-love, which thy fancy had so often personified as Demon, that ruled the hour. Heaven help those who, in this, are still following thy erring lead!

This radical error ran through the Great Reformer's life. While one cannot read his "Table Talk," * without warming under the blunt geniality of the man, nor without admiring the force of his rough-hewings, yet his unchristian asperity toward his opponents—alas! the spirit of his age among controversialists—is as directly opposed to the gentle teachings of his Master, as if the Wittenberg doctor had never looked into the Testament, or read the Sermon on the Mount.

We might excuse him, perhaps, considering how he was persecuted, for saying: "Seeing the Pope is Antichrist, I believe him to be a devil incarnate;"† we may find apology even for this: "He that says the Gospel requires works for salvation, I say, flat and plain, is a liar." ‡ But what shall we say of the terms he applies to one of the most distinguished scholars of the age, the intimate of Sir Thomas More, one who revived the

* Dr. Martin Luther's *Colloquia Mensalia, or his Divine Discourses at his Table:* gathered, with the scrupulous punctiliousness of a Boswell, from the mouth of Luther, by two of his most intimate friends and disciples (Lauterbach and Aurifaber), translated by Hazlitt, London, 1848.

Under an edict issued by the Emperor Rudolph II., 80,000 copies of this work (then to be found in almost every parish of the empire) are said to have been burnt.

† "Table Talk," p. 195. One of Luther's works is entitled: *Das Papstthum zu Rom vom Teufel gestiftet;* that is: *The Roman Papacy, an Institution of the Devil.* The expression quoted above is but one of a hundred (some much more abusive), which he "thundered," as his admirers were wont to express it, against the Church of Rome, its head and its clergy. The mace of steel was his weapon.

‡ *Table Talk*, p. 137.

study of the Scriptures in the original tongues, publishing, in 1516, the first edition of the Greek Testament from manuscripts —a man who, like himself, had been condemned as a heretic by Roman Catholic authority—what shall we say of his abuse of such a man, whose worst faults were timidity and conservative moderation? "Erasmus of Rotterdam," said Luther, "is the vilest miscreant that ever disgraced the earth. . . . Whenever I pray, I pray for a curse upon Erasmus." *

It is to be admitted, however, that Luther is not the exponent of that phase of early Protestantism which led men the farthest astray from the paths of charity and justice. A man, second only to himself in prominence as a Reformer, with more learning, and, in the sense of the schools, an acuter intellect than Luther—one more polished, too, and far more cold-blooded than the bluff and hearty Wittenberger—this man, John Calvin, sinned far more grievously than the other, not against light and knowledge—for the stern Genevan is not to be taxed with insincerity—but against the Spirit that can alone reform the heart of man—against that holy Spirit, without which the most eloquent master of all mysteries and all knowledge is but as sounding brass or a tinkling cymbal.

One of the forty-one heresies charged against Luther in Leo's bull of excommunication was that he (Luther) had declared it to be "against the will of the Holy Ghost to burn heretics." But Calvin was accessory to that very persecution unto death for opinion's sake which the other, at the outset of his career as a Reformer, had thus emphatically condemned.

That I may not be held to have made light assertion here touching an important episode in history which I had not carefully examined, I pray you to bear with me while I briefly recall the chief incidents connected with the burning as a heretic,

* *Table Talk*, p. 283. The immediate cause of this outburst seems to have been Erasmus' expression of opinion that the Epistle to the Romans, whatever it might have been at a former period, was not applicable to the state of things in the sixteenth century. (Same page.)

by the Protestants of Geneva, of a fellow Christian, in the year 1553. The story has been told by an eminent Protestant divine, with careful impartiality * and an exceeding minuteness of detail: and there are still extant numerous official, or otherwise trustworthy authorities by which to test the historian's accuracy.

---

§ 6. The Fortunes and the Fate of Servetus.

Michael Serveto (or, as he is usually called, Servetus) was born in the year 1509, in Villa Nueva, a town in the kingdom of Aragon which had, thirty-five years before, become part of the kingdom of Spain. He was of reputable birth; his parents being Catholic and his father an advocate in good standing and notary of the town. He was probably educated for the Church, in a Spanish Convent; but he emigrated from his native country at the age of nineteen, never to return to it. He was of feeble constitution, afflicted with hernia from his birth, and, ac-

* Mosheim's narrative bears, throughout, the impress of truth. Deeply feeling the delicacy of his task, he says, at the outset: "It is easier to pass unhurt between two fires burning close to each other than to relate, in such fashion that no one shall be offended or exasperated, the history of a man who had so many bitter enemies and strong friends. The deep emotions which arise when we look into such a history—emotions of pity, of love, of anger, of hatred—tend to mislead even the man who sets the strictest guard on his conscience. . . I approach this work with entire calmness and tranquillity of heart (mit einer völligen Gelassenheit und Stille des Herzens) and take with me the earnest resolve at once to put down all sentiment that might disturb that calm. . . . I deprecate but one thing—of all imputations the most shameful—that I shall knowingly pervert or suppress the truth." — Mosheim: *Geschichte des berühmten Spanischen Artztes, Michaels Serveto;* Helmstaedt, 1748, pp. 4, 5.

This history, which I believe has never been translated, extends, with its numerous accompanying documents, to 528 quarto pages, displaying an elaborate and exhaustive research rarely to be found outside of German literature.

cording to his own declaration, it was on account of his infirm health that he never married. He seems to have been earnest and studious from his youth up; and it is not improbable that incipient symptoms of heresy may have been the cause why, at so early an age, he left the place of his birth. It is certain that three years after his emigration he had already abandoned the Romish faith, and become imbued with the religious ideas that were to rule his life. These three years were chiefly spent in study at the University of Toulouse.

When but twenty-two years of age, to wit in 1530, he visited, at Basel, a noted Swiss Reformer, Johann Hausschein, better known under the Greek name he assumed, of Œcolampadius; frankly laying before him his creed. It appears to have been substantially as follows:

There is one God almighty, and none other beside him, single not complex, who through his Word and through the Holy Ghost, created all things. There is one only Lord, Jesus Christ, the Son of God, begotten by the eternal Word of the Father and given by God to men as Saviour and Redeemer: He prays to the Father for us; and through his prayers and by the agency of angels, we receive the Holy Ghost.*

Œcolampadius, the chief leader of the new religious movement in Basel and a man highly esteemed all over Switzerland, was by nature of mild and gentle character for that age; yet he was sorely tried by the eagerness, and what he must have

* MOSHEIM: *Geschichte des Michael Serveto*, p. 16. HOTTINGER: *Schweitzer Kirchengeschichte*, vol. ii. p. 94. Throughout Servetus' works, when he seeks minutely to define his idea of the nature and divinity of Christ, his expressions are not very intelligible: a common fault among the theologians of that age, to say nothing of our own.

Here is Calvin's definition of the Trinity: "There is in the Father a proper hypostasis, which is conspicuous in the Son; and thence, also, we may easily infer the hypostasis of the Son which distinguishes him from the Father. The same reasoning is applicable to the Holy Spirit. But this is not a distinction of the essence which it is unlawful to represent as any other than simple and undivided."—*Inst.*, Book 1, Chap. 13, § 2.

deemed the presumption, of a scarcely-bearded youth, who pressed upon him, a father in Israel, doctrines savoring of Arianism, and held argument with one of more than twice his own age, as man to man, on terms of frank equality. They parted, as honest men often do, mutually incensed; * the Spaniard protesting that he should ever recognize Christ as the Son of God; the Swiss insisting that if his opponent intended to be a Christian, he must acknowledge Christ to be the *uncreated and eternal* Son of God, of identical substance with the Father. It was the same dispute, unsettled yet, that had convulsed the Council of Nice, twelve hundred years before, between the advocates of the orthodox *Homoousian* and those of the heterodox *Homoiousian* doctrine.

A little knowledge of the world would have convinced Servetus that if his doctrines were thus harshly repulsed by a man of Œcolampadius' easy temper, they would be certain to create a storm of indignation among the Reformers generally. But not perceiving this, or, if he perceived it, undeterred by prudence and carried away by the conviction that he had a mission from God, the young Spaniard printed, in Strasburg in 1531, his work on the "Errors of the Trinity." †

* When Servetus, next year, went to Strasburg he complained to Bucer, a noted Reformer residing there, of Œcolampadius' harsh treatment. Bucer probably wrote on the subject to Œcolampadius: at all events there is a letter extant addressed by the latter to Bucer in which he exculpates himself in these words: "I will be mild in other things, but not when I hear Jesus Christ blasphemed."—RUCHAT: *Histoire de la Reformation de Suisse*, vol. iii. Book 7.

† *De Trinitatis Erroribus, Libri Septem.* As a specimen of the obscurity of definition to which I have referred, take the following from this work: "Christ was preformed in the Divine mind; he was a certain mode of existence which God constituted in himself, that he might make himself visible to us; namely by describing the effigies of Jesus Christ in Himself." (Erat Christus in mente divina præformatus; erat quidem modus se habendi, quem in se ipso Deus disposuit, ut seipsum nobis patefaceret, scilicet Jesu Christi effigiem in se discribendo.") Lib. vii. p. 110.

It had a large circulation, and an exasperating effect. Œcolampadius, writing to Bucer to exonerate his countrymen from all sympathy with such a heresy, adds that "he knew not how that beast had slipped into Switzerland." * And Bucer, usually temperate in language for a theologian of the sixteenth century, preached violently against Servetus, declaring "that the heretic ought to be disembowelled and torn to pieces." †

The Reformers felt the more outraged because the Catholics threw it up to them that this new Arianism of Servetus (as they called it) was the legitimate offspring of the Reformation. It became unsafe for the rash innovator either in Switzerland or in Germany. He took refuge in France, at first in Lyons, afterwards in Paris, where, for years, he studied the profession of medicine, obtaining a degree both in that science and in arts. He lectured, also, on astronomy and mathematics, and, as it appeared, not to obscure audiences; having had distinguished men among his hearers, one of these being the learned Peter Palmer or Palmerius, afterwards, fortunately for Servetus, a dignitary of the Roman Chúrch. Then he issued a medical work, got into serious trouble with the Paris faculty, and left Paris in consequence, in 1540. In 1542 he settled at Vienne, a town on the Rhone, some twenty-five miles south of Lyons; his chief inducement being that his former friend and patron, Palmier, was then Catholic Archbishop of the place. There, also, he found warm well-wishers in the Archbishop's brother, the Prior, Jean Palmier, in Rochefort, President of the medical faculty, and in a former intimate friend and fellow-student in Paris, Jean Perellus, the Archbishop's physician. In Vienne, he issued two works; a revised edition, with notes and emenda-

* *Epistola Zwinglii et Œcolampadii*, vol. iv. p. 801.

† Calvin is the authority for this. After Servetus' death, he wrote defending his conduct to a friend: "Is [he is speaking of Servetus] est, de quo fidelis Christi minister, et sanctæ memoriæ D. Bucerus, quum alioqui mansueto esset ingenio, pro suggestu pronunciavit: dignum esse, qui avulsis visceribus discerperetur."— *Calvini Epistola*, CLVI. ad Sulcerum, p. 294 (Ed. Amstelod. 1567, page 90).

tions, of that great thesaurus of ancient cosmical knowledge, by Ptolemy, which Humboldt characterizes as a colossal production; and a new edition of the Vulgate, with a preface and annotations.

Ten years he spent at Vienne, the most tranquil of his stormy life; his practice as physician daily increasing through the favor of influential friends, to whom, as he gracefully expressed it in the dedication of his *Ptolemæus*, his obligations were as great as were those of the students of geography to Ptolemy himself. During this time, he silently conformed to the rites of the Catholic Church; constrained thereto, doubtless, by a sense of the extreme rashness of alienating those benevolent patrons to whom he owed not his present easy circumstances only, but the protection of his life.

After a time, however, he became restless, accusing himself that, by such conformity, he was paltering with his conscience, and neglecting the work which God had laid upon him. He sought to renew, with Calvin, a theological correspondence which he had begun ten years before. Calvin's biographers state that in setting before the Genevese Reformer what he considered to be his (Calvin's) departure from true Christian doctrine, Servetus admonished him with much asperity; and this is doubtless true; for the Spaniard's zeal, like that of almost all the Reformers of that day, was mingled with arrogance. We may suppose it was for this reason that Calvin replied not a word to the other's repeated missives.*

* It ought not, however, in this connection, to be forgotten that Calvin, years before, permitted a spirit of the coarsest reviling against his opponent to break out even in his (Calvin's) commentaries on the Bible. On Genesis i. 3, his annotation is: "This alone is enough to refute the blasphemy of Servetus. That obscene dog barks that this was the origin of the Word when God commanded there should be light." In the Amsterdam edition of Calvin's works (9 vols. fol., 1671) will be found the original Latin, reading thus: "Latrat hic obscœnus canis hoc primum fuisse Verbi initium, quum Deus mandavit ut lux esset." Other passages (as the comment on St. John i. 1) contain similar terms of

Then Servetus resolved on the publication of his chief and most noted work;* one on which he had been laboring for years and which cost him his life. The idea which had formerly haunted him returned with resistless force. He was a soldier of Christ, called upon to take part (as he was wont to express it) in the great fight now being waged between Michael and the Dragon. Luther himself was not more zealous in his faith, nor more bold in expressing it. Servetus' preface exhibits his profound conviction that God had called him to bear witness before a benighted world. With a touching earnestness he implores the Son of God that he would reveal Himself to his servant, enlightening him, vouchsafing a holy spirit and words of power, and so directing thoughts and pen that the glory of His own divinity might be set forth and the very truth of Christian faith be illustrated. † Christ was banished from the world (he declares in his book) when the Nicean Council set aside the true doctrine touching His person, and proclaimed the dogma of a tripartite God. ‡

opprobrium. (Nec me latet quid oblatret hic canis, etc.) It needs a reference to such passages as originally written, to convince one that men of gravity and world-wide reputation, seeking sacred truths, could indulge, toward fellow-laborers, in spirit and language so utterly disgraceful.

* *Restitutio Christianismi.* It was printed, at Servetus' own cost (1,000 copies), by Balthazar Arnollet, in Vienne, and published early in the year 1553. This is said to be the scarcest work in the republic of letters. Catholics, Calvinists, Lutherans concurred in efforts for its destruction. It is doubtful whether more than a single printed copy remains, and that brought, at the Valleirian sale in 1784, the sum of 4,120 livres.

† "O Christe Jesu, fili Dei, . . . teipsum aperi servo tuo, ut manifestatio tanta vera patefiat. Spiritum tuum bonum et verbum efficax petenti nunc tribue, mentem meam et calamum dirige, ut divinitatis tuæ gloriam possim enarrare ac veram di te fidem exprimere."—Preface to the *Restoration of Christianity.*

‡ "Ab eo tempore est in tres res tripartitus Deus, fugatus omninc Christus, pessundata omnino ecclesia."—*Restitutio Christianismi,* Lib. I. p. 394.

Nor did the enthusiast conceal from himself that life was staked on the issue. In a letter to Abel Pepin, a Genevese divine, written some years before the publication of his work on the Restoration of Christianity, and used against him on his trial, he says: "I know of a surety that I shall die for this cause; but not on that account do I lose heart, desiring to become a disciple like unto my Master." *

In another part of this letter to Pepin is a sample of the imprudence of speech into which Servetus was occasionally betrayed. He bluntly tells the Genevese preacher, "Your gospel is without the one God, without the true faith, without good works. Instead of one God you have a three-headed Cerberus; instead of true faith you have a fatal dream; and good works you say are empty shows."

It does not appear, however, that in his works he permitted himself any expression so offensive to trinitarians, as the "three-headed Cerberus." His strongest printed expressions are a "chimera," a "mere imagination," and the like.

Scarcely had Servetus' book been issued, when a copy found its way to Geneva, where it produced no little excitement. A certain Frenchman, named William Trie, a convert from the Church of Rome, who had taken refuge in that city, seems to have been especially irritated thereby. He wrote, in March (1553), to a Catholic friend in Lyons, some have said at the instigation of Calvin, but of that I find no sufficient proof. He taunted his friend with the carelessness of the Church he himself had deserted, in tolerating, in Vienne, an arch heretic; and he gave Servetus' name and address, and the title of the new work of which he was the author. His friend held it a duty to bring the matter to the notice of the Archbishop of Vienne. Slowly and reluctantly, as it seemed, Servetus' Catholic friends in Vienne moved in the matter; alleging that there

* "Mihi ob eam rem moriendum esse, certo scio; sed non propterea animo deficior, ut fiam discipulus similis Preceptori." This letter, written in 1546, is given by Mosheim, copied from the official register of the trial.—*Geschichte des Michael Serveto*, p. 100.

was not sufficient proof that the well-known and much esteemed physician, Michael de Villa Nueva (for under that name he was known among them), was Servetus, and had written the book in question. Disappointed in his first effort, Trie procured from Calvin the private letters on theology which Servetus had addressed to him, and sent these, in the month of April, to Vienne. Even then the Catholic officials seem to have hesitated. Six weeks more elapsed ere Servetus was arrested; and this was done in a private way, his feelings being respected to the utmost. In prison he was assigned comfortable quarters; his servant was allowed to be with him; he was suffered to retain his money and other valuables and even permitted the range of the building. On his examination his book and his letters to Calvin were used as evidence against him, and he frankly confessed himself the author of both. A few days later and before sentence, he escaped from prison, probably by the connivance of his Catholic friends, including the Archbishop; and, after a fruitless search for him, which seems not to have been earnestly pressed, he was condemned as a heretic and burnt in effigy.

It was in the month of June that Servetus fled from Vienne, resolved to seek refuge and a livelihood as physician in Naples. Two roads were open to him; that by Piedmont, to which his objection probably was that he was then liable to be overtaken by a warrant issued for his apprehension by the inquisitors of Vienne; the other, by Geneva through Switzerland, which he selected, doubtless deeming it the safer route. He probably underrated Calvin's power among his fellow-burgesses, not knowing how narrowly a distinguished member of the City Council * had escaped a few years before. Nor is it likely he

* Peter Ameaux. He had spoken somewhat freely of Calvin's doctrines, especially of predestination and election, and his temerity cost him dear. Deposed from his office and cast into prison, he was fain to purchase his release by appearing as a penitent, waxlight in hand, confessing the sin he had committed and imploring forgiveness for his heresy.—*Geschichte des Michael Serveto*, p. 152.

had ever been informed, that in the previous month of November a decree had passed the Council of Geneva, declaring Calvin's *Institutes* to be a book "well and holily written, its doctrine to be the holy doctrine of God," and that "from this time forth no one shall dare to say aught against the said book or the said doctrine;" commanding all and several that they adhere to this.*

There was another document, which, had the poor fugitive seen it, would have warned him that of all places Geneva was the most dangerous for him to pass through. It was a letter, addressed by Calvin seven years before (to wit, in 1546), to his friend, William Farell (or Farellus), in which occurs this passage: "Servetus wrote to me lately, and to his letters added a large volume of his ravings, with braggart boastings that I should therein find things stupendous and hitherto unheard of. If it pleased me, he added, he would come hither; but I was

* I shall have occasion a few pages farther on to speak of the book here referred to and its doctrines. The decree from which I have quoted above is as well worth preserving, in its quaint old dress, as any Egyptian mummy in its cerements. Here it is, dated, it will be observed, Wednesday, November 9, 1552:

"Estans ouys in Conseil, et savans ministres de la parolle de Dieu, Maistre Guillaume Farel et Pierre Viret, et apres eux spectables maistre Johan Calvin et maistre Johan Trouillet, en leurs dires et reproches souvent debattues de l'Institution Chrestiene du dict monsieur Calvin, et le tout bien consideré, le conseil arresté et conclu que toutes choses bien oyes et entendu, a prononcé et declaré le dict livre de l'Institution du dict monsieur, estre bien et sainctement faict, sa doctrine estre saincte doctrine de Dieu; que l'on le tient pour bon et vrai ministre de ceste Cité, et que de l'ici a l'avenir personne ne soit ose parler contre le dict livre ou la dicte doctrine. Commandans aux pareilles et a tous se doive tenir a cela. Le Mequredi, que fut neufvieme de Novembre; l'an mille cincq cens cincquante et deux."

The original, on the records of the Council, can doubtless still be seen at Geneva. Castalio, a neighbor and contemporary of Calvin (if, as is usually believed, he was the author of *Contra libellum Calvini*, 1554), publishes it entire in that work.

not willing to engage my word. For if he does come, so far as my authority may prevail, he shall never go hence alive." *

Unknowing these things and hoping for better treatment from Protestants than Catholics, the unfortunate Servetus, after

* The authenticity of this extract has been sometimes called in question, probably because it has been confounded with another letter to Peter Viret, a minister of Geneva, which Bolsec (in his *De vita et moribus Calvini*, Book 3, p. 8) alleges that he saw and in regard to which the evidence *is* insufficient. The letter to Farell in Calvin's own, well-known hand, was found by the celebrated Grotius, in the year 1631, in a four-volume manuscript collection of letters from distinguished Protestants in Paris. (*Geschichte des Michael Servetus*, p. 130.) The Dutch historian Vytenbogaert, gives the extract in his *Kerkelyken Historie* (Book 2, p. 45), as follows: "Servetus nuper ad me scripsit, et litteris adjunxit magnum volumen suorum deliriorum, cum Thrasonica jactantia, me stupenda et hactenus inaudita visurum. Si mihi placeat, huc se venturum recipit: sed nolo fidem meam interponere. Nam si venerit, *modo valeat mea auctoritas, vivum exire nunquam patiar.*" The italics are my own. Vytenbogaert gives this extract on the authority of "een seer geleert, ende in dese Landen wol bekennt Personagie, anno 1631," who had inspected the letter in Paris. (P. 48.) "One can hardly doubt" says Mosheim, "that Grotius is here designated; he was an intimate friend of Vytenbogaert, and he lived in Paris in 1630 and 1631." (*Geschichte*, p. 131.) But, to remove all doubt as to the existence of this letter, we have Grotius' own words which I have verified. Speaking, in his theological works, of those who have written in favor of punishing heretics by the sword, he says: "Horum Calvinus autem is est qui antequam Servetus (is autem ipsius judicium super scriptis suis expetiverat) veniret Genevam, scripsit (exstat ipsius Lutetiæ manus) ad Farellum, si quid sua valeret auctoritas, effecturum ne vivus abiret."—GROTIUS: *Opera Theologica*, fol. Amsterdam, 1679, vol. iii. (Append. de Antichristo) p. 503.

It will be observed that Grotius not only states the fact that the letter to Farellus, in Calvin's own hand, was extant in Lutetia (Paris) and contained the threat against Servetus' life, but also alludes to another circumstance, to be gathered from the extract as given by Vytenbogaert, namely, that Servetus had solicited Calvin's opinion touching his (Servetus') writings.

Other authors testify to the same effect; but the above suffices.

secreting himself for sometime in Dauphiné, ran into the lion's mouth.

The precise period of his arrival in Geneva and the term of his residence there are uncertain : some alleging that he tarried in the city a single day only,* others that he lay hidden there, communicating with no one, for three or four weeks. Certain it is, that, on the eve of his departure, by vessel, up the lake, on his way to Zurich, he was, at the instance of Calvin,† arrested as a heretic and cast into prison. The property which the inquisitors of Vienne had respected was surrendered to the inquisitors of Geneva; it included a heavy neck-chain of gold, such as was usually worn in those days by men of his condition, several gold rings, and ninety-seven gold pieces. His place of confinement was a dungeon, assigned only to malefactors committed for capital offences. There he lay during two months and a half.

He was arraigned before the Syndics, judges of the Criminal Court. The charge against him was for heresy alone; his private character appearing to have been unblemished. In Geneva, as in Vienne, he admitted and justified his peculiar opinions, demanding permission to engage in public argument with Calvin, in open church, or before the larger council of the

* Principal Tulloch, who seems to have examined the authorities with care, thinks there is conclusive evidence that Servetus arrived at Geneva on a Sunday, wandered off, after dinner, into the church where his great adversary was preaching, was there recognized by some one who reported the fact of his presence to Calvin, and was arrested the same evening.—*Leaders of the Reformation*, London, 1859, p. 141.

† This will be admitted as beyond question by those who have looked carefully into the history of the case ; seeing that Calvin himself asserts it. In a letter written to his friend Sulcerus, dated September 9, 1553, speaking of Servetus, he says: "At length, driven hither by his evil genius, one of the Syndics, at my instigation, arrested him." The original reads: "Tandem huc malis auspiciis appulsum, unus ex Syndicis, *me auctore*, in carcerum duci jussit."—Epistola ad Sulcerum in Epistolis Calvini, No. 156, p. 294.

Servetus was arrested August 13, 1553.

two hundred, on the question whether his doctrine was in accordance with Scripture. This was denied him; and as a verbal discussion before the Court touching the true sense of the words *person* and *hypostasis*, and similar theological subtleties, had led to intemperance of language on the part of both controversialists, it was ordered that Calvin should set forth his argument in writing, to which Servetus should reply in like manner.

Two weeks had elapsed before Calvin had completed his paper. Therein he set himself to prove, and succeeded in proving, that many of Servetus' religious opinions were heretical; that is, were at variance with the teachings of his own Institutes, which Institutes, as we have seen, the Geneva Council had decreed to be "the holy doctrine of God." Then Servetus, having been furnished with writing materials, and with such books as he desired from Calvin's library and other sources, was called on for a reply. Some of Calvin's accusations he denied indignantly;* but stoutly defended his own actual opinions. All this caused great delay, during which the prisoner complained piteously to his judges of his miserable condition; eaten up by vermin, racked with pains from disease and from the cold and damp; without the means of cleanliness or even a change of linen; suffering other miseries, he adds, "about which it shames me to write." †

* For example, "that the human soul is mortal" and that "Jesus Christ derived but a fourth part of his body from the Virgin Mary:"—"things horrible and execrable," Servetus writes (September 22), "which if I had ever said in private or written in public, I should condemn my own self to death."—*Mosheim*, p. 419.

† "Les poulx me mangent tout vif, mes chauses sont descirées, et nay de quoy changer, ni pourpoint, ni chamise, que une mechante." This was September 15. Under date October 10 he writes: "Quant a ce que avies commandé, qu'on me fit quelque chose pour me tenir net, nen a rien estó faict et suys plus pietre que jamais. Et davantage le froyt me tormante grandament a cause de ma colique et rompure, la quelle mengeldre daultres pauretes, que ai honte vous escrire."—Original letters, given in *Geschichte des Michael Serveto*, p. 421.

The theological controversy could have but one issue; then the Public Prosecutor took up the case, and Servetus demanded the aid of an attorney, alleging that he was a foreigner, ignorant of the customs of their city. To this the prosecutor replied that the prisoner knew so well how to tell lies, he needed no counsel: and his demand was rejected accordingly.*

Aimé Perret, one of the principal members of the City Council, backed by a few equally tolerant spirits, sought to avert Servetus' impending fate; but the great authority of Calvin, who had determined on the heretic's death,† prevailed. Proposals to commute the punishment to banishment, or to perpetual imprisonment, were defeated; and after some weeks' delay, to give time for replies from various Swiss Churches which had been consulted on the matter,‡ the weary suspense of the prisoner was at last, on the twenty-sixth of October, broken by the announcement that he had just been condemned and would be executed the next day. For five or six weeks previously his urgent endeavors to procure a further hearing had been fruitless;§ yet he seemed to have been wholly unprepared for the terrible result. Weakened doubtless by his long

* De la Roche: *Memoirs of Literature*, vol. iv. p. 188. This author had access to the original papers in the trial.

† Under date August 20 (a week after the arrest of Servetus), Calvin wrote to a friend: "I hope that he will be sentenced to death; but the atrocity of his mode of suffering I desire to have remitted." ("Spero capitale saltim fore judicium; pœnæ vero atrocitatem remitti cupio").—*Calv. Epist. No.* 134, p. 290.

‡ Namely, the Churches of Zurich, Schaffhausen, Basel, and Berne. Though none of these Churches committed themselves on the subject of capital punishment for heresy, and though the Bernese expressed the hope that their brethren of Geneva, "would do nothing unworthy of a Christian magistracy," the gist of their replies was to encourage the prosecution.

§ "These three weeks," he wrote, October 10, "have I sought an audience—in vain. I implore you, by the love of Jesus Christ, not to refuse me the justice you would grant to a Turk."—*Mosheim*, p. 420.

and painful confinement, he was utterly overcome, shedding tears and uttering cries for mercy.

His death-sentence, after reciting his heresies, of which the principal seems to have been that, "contrary to the true foundation of the Christian Religion, and detestably blaspheming the Son of God, he said that Jesus Christ was not the Son of God from all eternity, but only since his incarnation"—went on to decree, in the name of the Trinity, that he should be bound and conducted to the spot called Champel, there fastened to a stake and burnt alive, along with his manuscripts and printed book, till his body was reduced to ashes.*

When they summoned the condemned, next morning, to execution, he begged to be beheaded, instead of undergoing the torture of fire; adding that if he had erred it was from ignorance, and with pure and good motive, and to further the glory of God. Farell, Calvin's friend and colleague in the ministry, † who had been appointed as his escort, told him, for sole answer, that his best plan was to recant and so gain pardon. Servetus replied that he had committed no crime, nor ever deserved death; but that he prayed God to forgive his accusers the sin they were committing against him. This grievously offended the other, who retorted sharply; and Servetus ceased to beg further mercy of man. This submission so far moved Farell

* "Au nom du Père, du Fils, et du sainct Esprit, . . toy, MICHEL SERVET condamnons a devoir estre lió et menó au lieu de Chapel et là devoir estre à un pilotis attachó et bruslé tout vif avec ton livre, tant ecrit de ta main qu'imprimé, jusqu'à ce que ton corps soit reduit en cendre."—*Mosheim*, p. 446.

† One of the most eloquent and violent among the Protestant divines of that day. He was the author of the celebrated *Placards*, written at Geneva, posted in an evil hour (during the night of October 24–5, 1534), on the walls of Paris, even in the palace of Francis I., and which, by the gross intemperance of their spirit, and the virulent abuse of their language, arrested for the time the cause of the Reformation in France, defeated the efforts of the gentle Margaret, the king's sister, to procure toleration for the new creed, and brought to torture and to death thousands of brave and good men.

that he sent to the Council praying that Servetus' punishment might be commuted to death by the axe; but the judges were inexorable, and the procession moved toward the small mount outside of the walls where the sentence was to be carried into effect. On the way Servetus exclaimed aloud, from time to time, "O God, save my soul! O Jesus, thou Son of the eternal God, have mercy upon me!"

"Mend thy last words," said his ghostly comforter: "if thou wouldst save thyself, call on Jesus, the eternal Son of God." But he could not be moved to this. When he approached the fatal spot and saw the stake, with fagots piled around it, he fell on his face, praying in silence.

Then Farell harangued the crowd: "You see here," he said, "how mighty is the power of Satan. This wretch, who is about to suffer death, is a very learned man; and perhaps, even, he may think that what he has done is right. But the devil has him in his coils, having taken entire possession. Take heed that a similar calamity overtake not yourselves."

When Servetus arose from prayer, Farell made a last effort to procure from him a confession that Christ was God's son from all eternity. But, in reply, he only cried out: "My God, my God!" "Can't you say something better than that?" persisted the preacher. "What better," replied the poor wretch, "than to call on God in my utmost need?" Then he entreated the bystanders to pray for him.*

At the very last, before he was committed to the executioner's hands, Farell exclaimed: "The eternal Son of God, say but that!" Not a word from the convict in reply! He was fastened to the stake by a strong chain about his body and a rope passed several times around his neck, the book which constituted his crime being bound to his loins.

When he saw the fagots kindled and felt the first touch of the flame, he cried out so piteously that the crowd around were

* Calvin (*Refut. error. Serveti*, p. 704) actually brings it up as an accusation against his victim that he asked the prayers of those whose faith he held to be false and heretical.

thrilled with horror. The fuel was green oak wood and his torture lasted a full half hour. Some of the spectators, urged by irresistible compassion, flung burning fagots over his body, the sooner to end his agony. His very last words, pronounced in a loud voice, were these: "Jesus, thou Son of the eternal God, take pity upon me." *

Thus perished, martyr to his religious opinions, a Protestant whom Mosheim declares to have been "one of the most thoughtful and learned men of his day." † Calvin caused his death, but is not responsible for his torture.‡ Nor should we

* These and many other details will be found in Mosheim's *Geschichte des Michael Serveto*, § xxxi. pp. 225–228.

† —"einer der tiefsinningsten und gelehrtesten Männer seiner Zeiten."—MOSHEIM: *Geschichte des Michael Serveto*, p. 230.

Science, too, owes a debt of gratitude to the Spanish physician. The author of the article "Circulation," in Rees' Encyclopedia, says: "The first ray of light was thrown on the circulation of the blood by a man (Servetus) whose name cannot be mentioned without feelings of compassion."

The passage to which the above refers will be found quoted, at length, in *An impartial History of Michael Servetus, burnt alive at Geneva for Heresie*, London, 1724, p. 67.

‡ When it seemed not unlikely that Perret and the other friends of moderation might carry the day and save Servetus' life, Calvin threatened, in that case, to leave Geneva and take up his abode elsewhere; whereupon his friend Heinrich Bullinger, hearing of such intention, thought it necessary to entreat him (by letter of September 14) not to desert a Church where so many good men were to be found; since "though swine and dogs" (the writer's paraphrase for heretics) "were more numerous than could be wished, yet we should bear much for the elect's sake, seeing that through many tribulations we must enter the Kingdom of God."—MOSHEIM, p. 231. HENR. BULLINGER, in Epist. Calvini, No. 157, p. 295. The text is: "Ne recesseris, oro, ab ea ecclesia, quæ tot habet viros excellentes. . . . Tametsi enim sunt porci et canes multo plures quam velimus, propter electos tamen multa sunt toleranda. Per multas tribulationes oportet nos ingredi in regnum Dei."

To console, under anticipated misfortune, a man who fears he shall not have the satisfaction of procuring the death of one who holds religious opinions at variance with his own, by reminding him that it is only

regard as feigned a zeal that errs only for lack of knowledge. We have no right to deny that, like Paul before his conversion, the Genevese Reformer verily believed that in persecuting those from whom he dissented he was doing God service. Certain it is, he boldly justified the deed.*

Nor he alone. Lamentable to relate, it was generally commended by the Protestants of that day as an act pleasing to God. Mosheim, speaking of the state of feeling among the Reformers, when the news of Servetus' death spread among them, says that while a few condemned the severity of the punishment, by far the greater number endorsed the deed and applauded, as worthy of immortal honor, Calvin's zeal for religion.† The mild Melancthon, himself, writing to Calvin a year after the martyrdom of Servetus, scrupled not to say: "The Church owes you now, and will owe you in future times, a debt of gratitude. . . . I affirm that your magistrates acted justly inasmuch as, by judicial sentence, they put to death that blasphemous man." ‡

through much tribulation we can reach Heaven, is a very peculiar and very sixteenth-century idea.

However—to the credit of the Genevese hierarchy be it said—as soon as it became known that Servetus was doomed to be burnt alive, Calvin and other preachers went in a body to the Council and sought to procure a commutation of the sentence to a milder form of death.—MOSHEIM, p. 217.

* "Am I guilty of crime," Calvin wrote, "because our Senate, at my instance (*meo hortatu*), revenged itself of his (Servetus') execrable blasphemies?" (execrabilis eius blasphemias ultus est.)—CALVINUS, *Responsione ad convitia Franc. Balduini*, p. 429.

† "Wenn der Haufe derer gezählet wird, die den Tod des Servet's bedauren, so ist er nur klein in Ansehen derer die sich über den Untergang eines so schädlichen Mannes freueten, und seinen Verfolger als einen um die Kirche unsterblich verdienten Eiferer lobeten."—*Geschichte des Michael Serveto*, p. 237.

‡ "Tibi quoque ecclesia et nunc et ad posteros gratitudinem debet et debebit. . . . Affirmo, etiam, vestros magistratus juste fecesse, quod hominem blasphemum, re ordine judicata, interfecerunt.—*Melancthon ad Calvinum*, *Oct.* 14, 1554. *Calv. Epist. No.* 187, p. 341.

Whether Luther would have coincided in this opinion must ever remain matter of conjecture; he died seven years before Servetus suffered. Twenty-five years previous to that event he had written against capital punishment for opinion; declaring that false teachers ought to be banished only.*

---

§ 7. Religious Toleration three hundred years ago.

In truth, as a general rule, the sixteenth-century Reformers rejected, in principle and in practice, the idea of religious freedom. Among all the noted theologians of the Reformation, I find but two who upheld man's right to liberty of conscience; Sebastian Castalio and Lœlius Socinus; neither to be ranked among the influential leaders of the Protestant movement.† Castalio, French by birth, and for several years professor of classical literature at Geneva (but banished thence in the year 1544 because of a quarrel with Calvin), was the more outspoken. Socinus, an Italian of noble family, and (as is well-known) an anti-trinitarian, timid by nature, spoke less openly.‡

* "Ego ad judicium sanguinis tardus sum, etiam ubi meritam abundat. . . Nullo modo possum admittere falsos doctores occidi: Satis est, eos relegari.—*Lutheri Epistolæ* (Ed. Aurifabri), vol. ii. p. 381.

† Since writing the above I am glad to find, in a recent work, evidence going to prove that Zwingli should be added to the list. Lecky (*Rationalism in Europe*, vol. i. p. 382, New York Ed.) quotes from Bossuet (*Variations Protestantes*, Book 2, Chap. 19) an extract from a Confession of Faith, written by the Swiss Reformer, just before his death, in which Zwingli describes that "future assembly of all the saintly, the heroic, the faithful and the virtuous," when Abel and Enoch, Noah and Abraham, Isaac and Jacob, will mingle with the sages and heroes of Greece and Rome, and when every upright and holy man who has ever lived will be present with his God. All honor to Ulrich Zwingli, gallant torch-bearer in a benighted generation! Bossuet, of course, adduces the sentiment as the climax of heresy.

‡ Beza (*Life of Calvin*, Book 8) speaks of these two as the chief supporters of freedom of opinion at that day. In the preface to a Latin

In a general way, religious liberty was unknown throughout Europe during the sixteenth century.

It is important to obtain a distinct idea of the stand taken by the Reformers of that day on the subject of mental emancipation. Luther had divested the Bible of its learned cerements and submitted it, in homely tongue, to the unlettered mass of his countrymen.* But in giving them the book, he denied to them the right of interpreting it.† He and his co-laborers in the ministry, declared that if any one, reading the translated Scriptures, derived therefrom, how sincerely soever, conceptions touching the nature of the Trinity or of the Divinity of Christ, or of the doctrines of the atonement, that differed from their own, such a dissenter was a detestable blasphemer, who ought to suffer death, or, at the least, banishment. How much worse was the decree of a single Pope than the dictation of a presbytery? How much better the City Council of Geneva than the Œcumenical Council of Trent—both assuming to decide, for the Christian world, what is "the holy doctrine of God."

Could such men conquer in spiritual strife? And because they did not, are we justified in concluding, with Macaulay, that there is no such thing as religious progress? I think not. The Protestantism of the sixteenth century failed, indeed, to establish itself as the one dominant religion of civilization. But, evincing the spirit it evinced, do you think it ought ever to have succeeded?

That question (you will perhaps remind me) concerns articles of religious faith as well as rights of private judgment.

translation of the Bible (1573) Castalio boldly asserts the principle of religious liberty.

* In ten years (from 1523, when Luther's translation appeared, to 1533), *fifty-seven* editions of the New Testament were printed, of which seventeen from the Wittenberg presses.

† "Whoso after my death shall contemn the authority of this school here at Wittenberg, if it remain as it is now, school and Church, is a heretic and perverted creature."—*Luther's Table Talk*, p. 339.

Undoubtedly. And though it be aside from my present purpose to engage in theological controversy—seeing that the world does not read folios nowadays, and that I propose to write but a single small volume,—yet it is useful to be reminded what the dogmas of that day were. And this the rather, because one finds, in the symbolic history of the time, all-sufficient cause, and a certain apology, for the denial of mental freedom to humankind. While the Reformers set up faith in doctrine, aside from works, as the one thing needful for the soul's salvation, they rejected another phase of faith essential to human improvement. They had no belief in human virtue; and, as a corollary, they considered man unfit to be trusted, especially in choice of a religion.

Suffer me, then, here briefly to reproduce, from the accredited text-books of early Protestantism, a few of the more important doctrines; sufficiently well-known, doubtless, to most students of your profession; but less familiar, probably, in their original form, to the majority of secular inquirers.

---

§ 8. Salient Doctrines of the Reformers.

> "The mournful record of an earlier age,
> That, pale and half effaced, lies hidden away
> Beneath the fresher writing of to-day."—Longfellow.

The sixteenth century was eminently the age of scholasticism. The public mind of Europe fed upon dogmas and confessions of faith, as eagerly as did that of America in Revolutionary days on political axioms and State constitutions. Lutheran and Calvinist and Catholic debated, at market and at board, in Diet and workshop, the exciting question of Papal infallibility, with the same absorbing zeal as did the Puritan a century later the vexed issue touching the right divine of kings. The early Protestants discussed free-will, and the real presence, predestination, and justification by faith, with a fiery earnestness that far outdid our warmest political strifes. We have much more toleration, but also much more indifference, in matters of religion, than these sturdy controversialists.

The fundamental and characteristic doctrines of the Reformation date from the patristic period. They derive chiefly from a man whose opinions, disseminated in the fifth century from the ancient capital of the Numidian kings, influenced with a power which no other schoolman ever exercised, the theology of the world throughout a thousand years, dating from the time he flourished.

St. Augustine seems to have deserved the character he bears, as one of the purest, kindest, and holiest of men; singular in his humility and severe in his self-discipline.* His "Confessions" have spoken to thousands of perturbed and penitent hearts, as they did, beyond question, to Luther in his Augustinian cell, and to Calvin during his precocious studies. "Luther," says Principal Tulloch, "nourished himself upon Scripture and St. Augustine." † Calvin's "Institutes" are based on Augustine's "City of God." In that great work, the monument of highest genius left to us from the ancient church, and generally

* In very early life led away by profligate companions, then attracted by the charm of classic poetry and æsthetics, afterwards, for nine years, a Manichæan; at the age of twenty-nine, weary of pleasure and philosophy, Augustine went to Rome, made the acquaintance of Ambrose, Bishop of Milan, and was by him converted to Christianity. The death of a saintly mother and of an illegitimate son, plunging him in deepest grief, drove him to a monastic life. His episcopate of thirty-five years was one long labor of benevolence. Courteous in bearing, he invited Pagans to his table. In a controversy with the Universalists of his day, he asserted that their error should be tenderly dealt with, since it originated in a desire to vindicate the goodness and mercy of God. While he condemned and combated the heresy of Donatus (founded on denial of the Church's infallibility), he protested to the Proconsul of Africa that, if capital punishment was inflicted on the Donatists, he and his clergy would suffer death at the hands of these turbulent heretics, rather than be instrumental in bringing them before the tribunals. —*S. Augustini Epistola*, No. 127, ad Procons. Africæ.

† *Leaders of the Reformation*, London, 1859, p. 10.

in the African bishop's voluminous lucubrations,* we find the source, not only of the Reformers' creed, but also, in later years, of the Jansenist heresy. His doctrine is tersely expressed in that saying of his: "He that made thee without thy aid, will He not save thee without thy aid?" Pity it is, that in reproducing, in exaggerated form, the worthy father's peculiar views, the sixteenth-century dialecticians failed to imitate his personal gentleness and charity.†

Luther led the forlorn hope against the old fortress of Papal infallibility, and it was the heavy cannon of his rough rhetoric that first effected a practicable breach. But, as regards the dogmatic history of the early Protestant movement, Calvin is the central figure. The chief work of his life, his celebrated "Institutes," ‡ officially set up by his fellow-townsmen of Geneva as a scheme of doctrine too holy to be questioned, won for him, in his own times, from Melancthon and from the Protestant world generally, the title, by excellence, of "THE THEOLOGIAN;" and even in our day it is accepted, by popular historians of the Reformation, not only as the most complete and methodical text-book of that movement, but as one of the most triumphant efforts of human wit. §

The chief characteristic of this work is its frank directness. It is free from all paltering and equivocation. Its author,

* The titles alone of St. Augustine's numerous works make a long catalogue.

† While full justice should be rendered to St. Augustine's kindly nature, one ought not to forget that the doctrines he taught led logically to intolerance and persecution.

‡ *Institutes of the Christian Religion* ("Institutio Religionis Christianæ"), by JOHN CALVIN. The translation which I have followed, made from the original Latin and collated with the author's last edition in French, is by John Allen, London, 1813. It has the reputation, deserved, I think, of being one of the most faithful extant.

§ Merle D'Aubigné says of this treatise, that it "is the finest body of doctrine ever possessed by the Church of Christ." And he adds: "This work, accomplished by spiritual force, far exceeds, in the importance of its consequences, all that has ever been done by the pens of the ablest

having assumed his premises, hesitates at no conclusions to which they logically lead. Even while he confesses predestination to be a "horrible decree," * he asserts it none the less boldly, as divine doctrine, on that account. Nor does he shrink from inculcating "abhorrence of ourselves,"† nor from such admissions as that grace is not offered to all men, that the most odious crimes are God's work, and the like. But let this fearless dogmatist speak for himself.

First, on the doctrine of human depravity:

"Let us hold this as an undoubted truth which no opposition can ever shake, that the mind of man is so completely alienated from the righteousness of God, that it conceives, desires, and undertakes everything that is impious, perverse, base, impure, and flagitious; that his heart is so thoroughly infected by the poison of sin that it cannot produce anything but what is corrupt; and that if, at any time, men do anything apparently good, yet the mind always remains involved in hypocrisy and fallacious obliquity, and the heart enslaved by its inward perverseness. . . . In vain do we look in our nature for anything that is good." ‡

He reiterates this sentiment again and again, apparently seeking, by sweep of condemnation, to leave no loophole for human self-respect. Witness this:

"Everything in man, the understanding and the will, the soul and body, is polluted. . . . Man is, of himself, nothing else than concupiscence." §

statesmen or the swords of the greatest warriors."—*History of the Reformation in the Time of Calvin* (New York Ed., 1865), vol. iii. pp. 170, 172.

Tulloch, with whom Calvin is no special favorite, admits him to be "the greatest Biblical commentator of his age," and characterizes his Institutes as "the charter of the great movement to which he was destined to give theological consistency and moral triumph."—*Leaders of the Reformation*, pp. 103 and 167.

* "Decretum quidem horribile fateor," are his words.—*Institutes*, Book 3, Chap. 23.

† *Inst.*, B. 2, C. 1, § 1.

‡ *Inst.*, B. 2, C. 3, § 19 and § 2.

§ *Inst.*, B. 2, C. 1, § 10.

Now and then one is tempted to infer that he deemed all human effort to reform the race but folly and waste of time. He says:

"Man cannot be excited or biassed to anything but what is evil. If this be so, there is no impropriety in affirming that he is under the necessity of sinning." *

This looks to the Deity as the author of evil; and Calvin meets the issue squarely. He scouts, as subterfuge which God himself rejects, the idea that sin and crime occur "by the permission and not by the will of God." He says that wicked men and the devil himself "can effect nothing but by the secret will of God." In illustration he adds: "God intends the deception of that perfidious king, Ahab; the devil offers his services for that purpose, and is sent with a positive commission to be a lying spirit in the mouth of all the prophets." (1 Kings xxii. 20–23.) . . . "Absalom, defiling his father's bed with incest, perpetrated a detestable crime; yet God pronounces that this was His work. . . . Whatever cruelties the Chaldeans exercised in Judea, Jeremiah pronounces it to be the work of God." †

But "while God, by means of the impious, fulfils his secret decrees, they are not excusable." ‡

Again, in the face of that sentiment, common to every creed, which prompts men, in hours of sorrow or peril, to invoke on themselves, or on those they love, the blessing of the Almighty, Calvin, true to his belief in human worthlessness, says: "God finds nothing in men which can incite him to bless them." §

He goes further still. It is a daring thing to speak of innocence that has never sinned, as steeped in pollution and hateful to its Maker; but that is among the corollaries of Calvin's favorite doctrine; and he courageously admits that it is; thus:

"We derive an innate depravity from our very birth: the denial of this is an instance of consummate impudence. . . . All children, without a single exception, are polluted, as soon

* *Inst.*, B. 2, C. 3, § 5.

† *Inst.*, B. 1, C. 18, § 4.

‡ *Inst.*, B. 1, C. 18, § 4.

§ *Inst.*, B. 3, C. 14, § 5.

as they exist. . . . Infants themselves, as they bring their condemnation into the world with them, are rendered obnoxious to punishment by their own sinfulness. For though they have not yet produced the fruits of their iniquity, yet they have the seed of it in them: their whole nature cannot but be odious and abominable to God." *

But his doctrine of predestination carries him even beyond this: that doctrine is thus stated:

"God elected whom he would, and, before they were born, laid up in reserve for them the grace with which he determined to favor them. . . . His foresight of our future holiness was not the cause of his choice. . . . The grace of God deserves not the sole praise of our election, unless this election be gratuitous: now it could not be gratuitous if, in choosing his people, God himself considered what would be the nature of their respective works." †

According to this Calvinistic theory even free will is denied to us; nor is God's grace offered except to a few of the favored among His creatures. "Man is not possessed of free will for good works unless he be assisted by grace, and that special grace which is bestowed on the elect alone in regeneration. For I stop not to notice those fanatics who pretend that grace is offered equally and promiscuously to all." ‡

After this, one can understand on what grounds he bases the assertion: "Conversion is entirely of God, because we are not sufficient even to think." §

Taken in connection with Calvin's idea of hell, and of the small numbers of the elect, this dogma predestines countless millions of the unborn, without any reference to their good or bad conduct in the future, or to their repentance, to eternal torments. Does this imply that the vast majority of the human race are hated by their Creator? Calvin, inexorable in his logic, confesses that it does. "Jacob and Esau," he reminds

* *Inst.*, B. 2, C. 1, §§ 5, 6, 8.
† *Inst.* B. 3, C. 22, §§ 2, 3.
‡ *Inst.*, B. 2, C. 2, § 6.
§ *Inst.*, B. 2, C. 3, § 6.

us, "are brothers begotten of the same parents, still enclosed in the same womb, not yet brought forth to light; there is, in all respects, a perfect equality between them; yet the judgment of God concerning them is different: for He takes the one and leaves the other. . . . The children being not yet born, neither having done good or evil, that the purpose of God according to election might stand, not of works but of him that calleth, it was said: 'Jacob have I loved, but Esau have I hated.'" * When one reads, in connection with this commentary, the strange story to which Calvin here refers,† one seems to hear the wail, throughout the universe, of millions on millions of outcast step-children, crying out, like rejected Esau, in vain: "Bless me, even me also, oh my Father!"

Referring elsewhere to this narrative and Paul's text, of which he makes frequent use, and to the fact that Jacob, "without any merit acquired by good works, is made an object of grace," Calvin does not scruple to add: "If we turn our attention to works we insult the apostle." ‡

One may conjecture the source whence came, to the Reformers, the idea that good works have nothing to do in effecting man's salvation. In the Augsburg Confession, after a complaint that "Catholic traditions obscure the commandments of God," it is added: "The whole of Christianity was thought to consist in the observance of certain holy days, rites, fasts, and vestments." § The feeling evidently was that this was but a Phar-

* *Inst.*, B. 3, C. 22, §§ 4, 5. The text wherein this doctrine is found (Romans ix. 11, 13) is here quoted literally; it is supported by Malachi i. 2, 3.

Another might have been at a loss to explain how Jacob, living seventeen hundred years before the time when Christ made atonement for the sins of mankind, could have been one of the elect; but Calvin overstrides the difficulty, telling us: "It ought not to be doubted that Jacob was ingrafted, with angels, into the body of Christ." (Dubitare mineme debeat Jacob cum angelis insitum fuesse in Christi corpus.") —*Inst.*, B. 3, C. 22, § 6.

† Genesis xxvii. 1–40.

‡ *Inst.*, B. 3, C. 22, § 11.

§ Augsburg Confession, Part 2, Article 5.

isaical making clean the outside of the cup and the platter. But if such was the original source, it was soon lost sight of in the mazes of theology. Calvin takes special pains to inform us that, aside from that faith which saves, the most virtuous life leads only to hell. He says that though what we call good men "may be esteemed worthy of admiration for their reputed virtue; though they are instruments used by God for the preservation of human society, by the exercise of justice, continence, friendship, temperance, fortitude, and prudence," yet if they "are strangers to the religion of the one true God," they "not only merit no reward, but are rather deserving of punishment, because they contaminate the pure gifts of God with the pollution of their own hearts.* . . . They who have no interest in Christ, whatever be their character or their actions or their endeavors, are constantly advancing, through the whole course of their lives, toward destruction and the sentence of eternal death." †

This is not an isolated expression of sentiment; the main idea breaks forth throughout the entire work. Here is an example: "The most splendid works of men not yet truly sanctified are so far from righteousness in the divine view that they are accounted sins. . . . The works of a man do not conciliate God's favor in his person." ‡

And here is another, showing that Calvin regarded this as the chief point of difference between the Reformers and their opponents: "There never was an action performed by a pious man which, if examined by the scrutinizing eye of divine justice, would not deserve condemnation. . . . This is the principal hinge on which our controversy with the Papists turns." §

* So incautious is the wording here, that one might almost suppose the author had conceived the idea that the best efforts of man to lead a purer life—to practise justice, continence, temperance, prudence—were deadly sins, inasmuch as this is but a culpable mixing up of Christian graces with the inevitable corruptions of the human heart.

† *Inst.*, B. 3, C. 14, §§ 3, 4.

‡ *Inst.*, B. 3, C. 14, § 8.

§ *Inst.*, B. 3, C. 14, § 11.

One is constantly reminded, in reading these sixteenth-century Reformers, of the incredible lengths to which the nature of their doctrines was wont to lead them; as, for example, to the declaration of Calvin that a part of this world only belongs to God. He (Calvin) says that the words of Jesus Christ, "I pray not for the world, but for them which Thou hast given me" * (John xvii. 9), afford proof "that the whole world does not belong to its Creator ("unde fit ut totus mundus ad suum Creatorem non pertineat"); only that grace delivers from the curse and wrath of God, and from eternal death, a few who would otherwise perish, but leaves the world in its destruction to which it has been destined. †

Another dismal corollary is this: Calvin did not believe that either love of God, or imitation of Christ, is efficient to salvation: we must seek to appease our Creator's anger—there must be fear, he thought—else all self-sacrifice—every offering of the heart—is to the Creator but abomination. These are his words: "No man can descend into himself and seriously consider his own character without perceiving that God is angry with him and hostile to him, and consequently he must find himself under a necessity of anxiously seeking some way to appease Him. . . . The beginning of the observance of God's law is an unfeigned fear of His name. If that be wanting, all the oblations made to him are not merely trifles, but nauseous

* It is remarkable, in connection with this verse from St. John, that, according to another evangelist, Jesus' last prayer on earth was for his murderers. See, as to John xvii., note on succeeding pp. 271,272.

† *Inst.*, B. 3, C. 22, § 7.

And if Calvin's earnestness is proof against the incredible, so is it also against the ridiculous. Who but himself would not have been deterred by inkling of the ludicrous from such comment on a scriptural metaphor as this? After quoting Christ's words, "The sheep follow the shepherd, for they know his voice," Calvin's comment is: "Now no man makes himself a sheep, but is created such by divine grace." ("Nemo, enim, se ovem facit, sed formatur cœlesti gratia.")—*Inst.*, B. 3, C. 22, § 8.

and abominable pollutions. Let hypocrites go now and, retaining depravity in their hearts, endeavor by their works to merit the favor of God." *

Here naturally suggest themselves the questions: If not by love of God, if not by leading a life of purity and benevolence, how, under this system, is man to appease an angry and hostile Creator? How is he to escape hell? The Reformer's answer is: By belief, not by acts. Those who have an assurance of election *are* the elect: but the elect, and the elect only, are saved by vicarious atonement made by the Son of God. †

This assurance that we are the favored of God is held by Calvin to be omnipotent to save sinners even though, after obtaining it, they indulge in gross sins. Witness the following passage, occurring in connection with his favorite illustration from Romans ix. 11, 13: "Rebecca, having been divinely assured of the election of her son Jacob, procures him the benediction by a sinful artifice; she deceives her husband, the witness and minister of the grace of God; she constrains her son to utter falsehoods; she corrupts the truth of God by various frauds and impostures." This, Calvin calls, "transgressing the limits of the word;" and he excuses her action: "for," says he, "as the particular error of Jacob did not annul the effect of the benediction, so neither did it destroy the faith which generally predominated in her mind, and was the principle and cause of that action." ‡

Every one knows that Calvin was one of the sternest of moralists, and we cannot rationally suppose that he really intended to palliate vice, or to excuse a vicious life. Observe, however, in what manner, led away by love of a dogma, he lays himself open, in the above passage, to the imputation of glossing over deliberate fraud and imposture, when such sins coëxist with belief in the atonement.

* *Inst.*, B. 3, C. 14, § 8.

† This doctrine will be found, a few pages farther on, graphically set out by the powerful pen of Luther.

‡ *Inst.*, B. 3, C. 11, § 31.

This doctrine of justification by faith alone is very concisely and lucidly set forth in the Augsburg Confession:

"Men cannot be justified before God by their own strength, merits, or works; but are justified freely, for Christ's sake, through faith, *when they believe that they are received into favor* and that sins are remitted on account of Christ who, by his death, made satisfaction for our sins. *This faith God imputes for righteousness.*" *

In the above I have italicized the words which prove that the faith which, according to this scheme of redemption, exclusively wins heaven, is a belief of our *personal* favor with the Almighty, resulting in our election and adoption by Him.

Let us now turn from the Genevese divine to his great German co-laborer.

We find, as between the two, great difference of character, indeed, but no essential variation in creed. One cannot doubt that, in a general way, Luther assented, verbally at least, to Calvin's system of divinity, as set out in the "Institutes;" since, while he refused the hand of brotherhood to Zwingli because of variance on a single doctrinal point, and even held it to be likely that the Swiss Reformer, after dying for the Protestant cause, would suffer eternal torments † because of disbelief in the "real presence,"—he remained in strict fellowship with Calvin throughout his life. Yet he might have said to the theologian of Geneva with more truth than he did to Ulrich Zwingli: "You have a different spirit from ours." Calvin's religion, like Jove's armed daughter, was the offspring of his brain; Luther's, of his heart. The two had this in common, that they ran the convictions which they had once assumed as

* *Augsburg Confession*, Part 1, Art. 4.

† "I wish from my heart Zwinglius could be saved, but I fear the contrary; for Christ has said that those who deny him shall be damned." LUTHER: in *Table Talk*, p. 324.

premises, to their legitimate conclusions, with unflinching temerity; but Luther's heart carried him into a region comfortable, genial, even jovial; while Calvin's brain tarried in a limbus, stern in every feature, icy cold, dreary, and, as regards the general fate of humanity, hopeless and implacable. If one would penetrate to the essence of Lutheranism, one must read Luther's own favorite Commentary on the Galatians.* He there summons up, indeed, the same abasing aspect of human nature,† that imparts so lurid a gleam to Calvin's writings; but the heartiness of the man and the unconventional sprightliness of his style break out over the saddening picture, lighting it up as the aurora borealis illuminates northern wastes. Permit me to recall to your recollection one or two of its more notable passages, in illustration.

The one idea (held, of course, in common with Calvin) that pervades the book and which constitutes, in fact, the corner-stone of Luther's entire doctrinal system,‡ is, that mankind,

* Luther thought his own best works to have been, his Commentaries on Deuteronomy, on Galatians, and on the four books of St. John.—See *Table Talk*, p. 21.

† It pervades his other writings also, and it was wont to break out in his conversation. "We have altogether a confounded, corrupt, and poisoned nature, both in body and soul: throughout the whole of man is nothing that is good."—*Table Talk*, p. 119.

So the other Reformers, for example Melancthon: "Anima, luce vitaque cœlesti carens, . . . sua quærat, non cupiat, non velit, nisi carnalia," etc.—*Loci Communes*, p. 18 (Ed. Augusti).

‡ "Luther arrived at the doctrine of the atonement through Christ wholly independently of works: this afforded him the key to the Scriptures, and became the main prop to his whole system of faith."—RANKE: *Hist. of the Popes*, vol. i. p. 186.

Luther himself took the same view of this tenet. He says: "All the other articles of our faith are comprehended in that of justification; and if that remain sound then all the rest are sound."—*Commentary on Galatians*, at chap. iii. verse 13. And again (same verse): "This is the principal article of all Christian doctrine, which the Popish schoolmen have altogether darkened."

So, in his preface to the Commentary on the Galatians, his chief com-

even down to the latest generations, steeped in sin through Adam's transgression, can be saved from an eternal hell only by a transfer of all human sins to Jesus Christ. Do you remember how vividly he sets this out?

"God sent his only son into the world and laid upon him all the sins of all men, saying: 'Be thou Peter, that denier; Paul, that persecutor, blasphemer, and cruel oppressor; David, that adulterer; be thou that sinner that did eat the apple in Paradise, that thief which hanged upon the cross; in brief, be thou the person who hath committed the sins of all men: see, therefore, that thou pay and satisfy them.' Here now cometh the law and saith: 'I find him a sinner and indeed such an one as hath taken upon him the sins of all men; therefore let him die upon the cross.' And so he setteth upon him and killeth him. By this means the whole world is purged and cleansed from all sins. . . . Therefore, where sins are seen and felt, there are they indeed no sins; for, according to Paul's divinity, there is no sin, no death, no malediction any more in the world, but only in Christ.* . . . But some man will say: 'It is very absurd and slanderous to call the Son of God a cursed sinner.' I answer: If thou wilt deny him to be a cursed sinner, deny also that he was crucified and died. . . . This is a singular consolation for all Christians, so to clothe Christ with our sins."†

It is curious to note how the man's intense perception of a

plaint against Catholicism is: "the infinite and horrible profanation and abomination which always hath raged in the Church of God, and even at this day ceaseth not to rage, against this only and grounded rock, which we hold to be the article of our justification."—*Preface*, p. 1.

* One might almost suppose, from such passages, that Luther held universalist doctrines. Very far from it. "God, in this world, has scarce the tenth part of the people; the smallest number only will be saved. . . . If now thou wilt know why so few are saved and so infinitely many damned, this is the cause: the world will not hear Christ."—*Table Talk*, pp. 41, 43.

† *Commentary on Galatians*, at chap. iii. verse 13.

single favorite doctrine like this led him on, step by step, until, like Aaron's rod before Pharaoh, it swallowed up all the rest. Speaking of "the phantastical opinions of the Papists concerning the justification of works," he says: "They do imagine a certain faith formed and adorned with charity. By this, they say, sins are taken away and men are justified before God. But what else is this, I pray you, but to unwrap Christ and to strip him quite out of our sins, and to look upon them, not in Christ, but in ourselves. Yea, what is this else but to take Christ clean away, and to make him utterly unprofitable to us." *

Again, he declared it to be blasphemy, inspired by the devil, to say that faith without works was dead, or to assert that faith, unfruitful of works, was not omnipotent to gain heaven for the believer. One would read with incredulity in these modern days, if the original was not still extant in proof, such a passage as the following:

"The perverters of the Gospel of Christ teach that even that faith which they call faith infused (*fides infusa*), not received by hearing nor gotten by any working, but created in man by the Holy Ghost, may stand with deadly sin, and that the wickedest men may have this faith. Therefore, they say, if it be alone it is idle and utterly unprofitable. Thus they take from faith her office and give it unto charity: so that faith is nothing, except charity, which they call the form and perfection thereof, be joined withal. This is a devilish and blasphemous kind of doctrine. . . . For if charity be the form and perfection of faith (as they dream), then am I by and by constrained to say that charity is the chief part of the Christian religion, and so I lose Christ, his blood and his benefits; and now I rest altogether in a moral doing even as the Pope, the heathen philosopher, and the Turk." †

Yet again: "The true doing of the law is a faithful and a

* *Commentary on Galatians*, at chap. iii. verse 13.

† *Commentary on Galatians*, at chap. iii. verse 11.

spiritual doing, which he hath not that seeketh righteousness by works. Therefore *every doer of the law and every moral worker is accursed;* for he walketh in the presumption of his own righteousness against God."*

This doctrine appears, without its Lutheran intensity, yet substantially the same, in the text-book of early Protestantism, the Augsburg Confession. We read there; "works cannot reconcile us to God, or merit remission of sins, grace and justi fication, but we obtain this by faith only." It is added: "Our divines teach that it is necessary to do good works, not that we may trust by them to merit grace, but in obedience to the will of God." And alluding to the accusations falsely brought against them "of prohibiting good works," they declare that they have "wholesomely taught all the modes and duties of life, what ways of life, what works in any calling, are pleasing to God;" while their adversaries "urged puerile and unnecessary works, such as certain holy days, certain fasts, fraternities, pilgrimages, worship of saints, rosaries, monasticism and the like." †

* In the English version which I have followed, the words I have italicized are not very strictly rendered; the original being even stronger than the translation, thus: "Ideo maledictus est omnis Legis operator, et *moralis Sanctus:*" literally "moral Saint." Luther might have been thinking of the morality of monkish austerity; at all events, his translator seems to have been afraid to follow him; seeing that *Saint* has been often regarded as the equivalent of *elect.*

† All the above quotations will be found in article 20, part 21, of the Augsburg Confession. I have followed the translation by the Rev. Henry Teal, M.A., London, 1842; who appears to have executed his task with critical care.

Considering that the Lutheran Church of America recently adopted a resolution that "this General Synod . . . maintains the divine obligation of the Christian Sabbath" (Annual Cyclopedia for 1868, p. 443), it is worthy of notice, in connection with the above dictum touching "puerile and unnecessary works," that in the Augsburg Confession (article 7 of part 2) the following plain words occur: "They who judge that, by the authority of the Church, the observing of the Lord's day, instead of the Sabbath day, was ordained as a thing necessary, do

Thus, though the Reformers taught that faith requires no works of us,* they not only inculcated, in their sermons, strict morality, but the chief leaders, as Luther, Calvin, Melancthon, Zwingli, illustrated, by their exemplary lives, the morals they taught.†

But it behooves us to bear in mind that a man's upright intention, or his good life, is one thing, and the tendency of the opinions he holds, or the doctrines he teaches, quite another.

greatly err. The Scripture which teaches that the Mosaic ceremonies since the revelation of the Gospel may be omitted, has abrogated the Sabbath. And yet, because it was needful to ordain a certain day, that the people might know when they ought to come together, it appears that the Church appointed the Lord's day,—which day seems to have pleased the more for this cause also, that men might have an example of Christian liberty and know that *neither the observance of the Sabbath, nor of any other day, was necessary*."—*Teal's Translation*, pp. 78, 79.

No human institution is more needed or more valuable than the setting apart one day in seven as a time of rest from worldly turmoil and of quiet for spiritual thought. Nevertheless it must be admitted that the views of the Augsburg Confessionists as to the religious obligation in this matter accord with the spirit of Christ's teachings (Mark ii. 27, etc.), and Paul's (Colossians ii. 16). They evince philological accuracy also, seeing that there *is* no Christian *Sabbath*. The Italians properly call Saturday, *Sabato;* while they term Sunday, *Domenica*, corresponding to our "Lord's Day."

* "Faith requireth no works of us, or that we should give anything unto God, but that we, believing the promise of God, should receive of him."—*Com. on Galatians*, chap. iii. v. 12.

† When some one drew, from Zwingli's belief in predestination, the practical inference that the elect could not be harmed, sin as they might, the Swiss Reformer's reply was, that "whoso argues thus furnishes proof that he himself is not among the elect."—See his *De Providentia Dei.*, Opera, vol. iv. p. 140.

In this work (Opera iv. pp. 79, 109, 113), Zwingli inculcates the doctrine of Predestination, running it out to all its logical consequences: asserting, for example, that the sin of Adam was originally included in God's plan; as also the scheme of redemption. This is Calvin's opinion also; he terms the exclusion of the fall of the first man from the divine predestination, a *frigidum commentum.—Inst.*, B. 3, C. 23, § 7.

Diderot taught atheism and openly avowed enmity to all religious ideas:* yet the sincerity of his enthusiasm in such tenets is beyond question, his works having been condemned to the flames, and himself to prison for teaching them. The sceptical D'Alembert, Diderot's co-laborer in the *Encyclopædie*, strongly expressed, in his correspondence with Voltaire, his disbelief in Christianity; yet his benevolence was proverbial and his life without a stain.† But because such writers have upright motives, or lead virtuous lives, are we thence to conclude that the belief in atheism is no injury to mankind, or that the world could do quite as well without religion?

These remarks have strictest application when, in the works of any author how estimable soever, we come upon such a passage as the following: "Thus you find how richly gifted is a Christian and baptized man, who, even if he wills it, cannot forfeit his salvation by how many sins soever, unless he is un-

* Diderot était un des ennemis les plus acharnés du Christianisme, et même de toute idée religieuse; il professait ouvertement le matérialisme et l'athéisme, et prêchait ces doctrines désolantes avec une sorte d'enthusiasme et de fanatisme.—BOUILLON: *Dictionnaire de Biographie Universelle*, art. "Diderot."

† "D'Alembert possédait des qualités qui l'ont fait aimer et estimer de tous ses contemporains; au plus vif amour pour la science, il joignait la bienfaisance et le désintéressement. . . . Il entretint avec Voltaire une correspondance suivie qui a été publiée après leur mort: tous deux y exhalent leur haine contre la religion chrétienne."—BOUILLON: *Dictionnaire de Biographie Universelle*, art. "D'Alembert."

"When D'Alembert's income amounted to 8,200 francs, he gave away one half. . . . The Bishop of Limoges said of him, during his life, 'His manners are simple and his conduct without a stain.' . . . He was the first mathematician of his day, and La Harpe says of him: 'I know D'Alembert well enough to be able to say that he was sceptical in everything except mathematics. . . . Himself tolerating all opinions, what he censured in the atheists was their intolerant arrogance. . . . Had it not been for his correspondence with Voltaire, the world would not have known except by implication what his opinions were. His published writings contain no expression offensive to religion."—*Penny Cyclopædia*, art. "D'Alembert."

willing to believe. For no sins have power to damn him save only the sin of incredulity." *

Finally, the evil tendency of such opinions is aggravated, in Luther's case, by his fatalist doctrines, pushed even to a distinct denial of man's free agency. Think of the practical effect—how deadening and discouraging to all virtuous effort—of such a passage as this: "The human will is placed between two, even as a beast of burden. If God mounts it, it wishes and goes as God wills. . . . If Satan mounts it, it wishes and goes as Satan wills. Nor is it free to run toward, or select, either rider: it is the riders themselves who contend which shall obtain and hold possession." †

Those who are familiar with the original documents will bear me witness that the foregoing brief synopsis of Protestant opinions in the sixteenth century, while it omits, for brevity's sake, many details, neither exaggerates nor extenuates the founda-

* This passage occurs in Luther's Treatise: *De Captivitate Babylonica*, 1520; the original reading thus: "Ita vides quam dives sit homo Christianus et baptisatus, qui etiam volens non potest perdere salutem suam quantiscunque peccatis, nisi nolet credere. Nulla enim peccata eum possunt damnare nisi sola incredulitas."

There are other passages of similar purport in Luther's works even more offensively expressed. In a letter to Melancthon (1521), quoted and excused by Archbishop Hare, occurs a well-known sentence: "Sufficit quod agnovimus per divitias gloriæ Dei Agnum, qui tollit peccata mundi; ab hoc non avellet nos peccatum, etiamsi millies, millies uno die fornicamur aut occidamus."

By an opponent of Luther the words "uno die" have been translated, incorrectly of course, "every day:" but even as it stands (however pure may have been the writer's intention) it would be a lack of candor to deny that it supplies, to evil-minded men, plausible apology for murder and incontinence.

† "Sic humana voluntas in medio posita est, ceu jumentum. Si insederit Deus, vult et vadit quo vult Deus, ut Psalmus dicit: 'Factus sum sicut jumentum et ego semper tecum.' Si insederit Satan, vult et vadit quo vult Satan. Nec est in ejus arbitrio ad utrum sessorem currere aut eum quærere, sed ipsi sessores certant ob ipsum obtinendum et possidendum."—LUTHER: *De Servo Arbitrio*, part I. sec. 24.

tion-doctrines on which rested the theological system put forth by the Leaders of the Reformation; to wit, the atonement, including justification by faith alone; the fall, the utter depravity of man, and predestination.

Such a synopsis was indispensable in treating the great historical problem to which I now revert.

---

§ 9. What Lesson does the History of the Reformation teach?

"Revealed religion is not in the nature of a progressive science. . . . We have no security for the future against the prevalence of any theological error that has ever prevailed in time past among Christian men."—Macaulay.*

Is that the lesson taught? Guardians of the Protestant faith, is that the Protestant reply?

If not, bestow, I pray you, dispassionate attention on the historical and statistical facts; and give your version of the explanation.

Three hundred years, observe!—from 1570 to 1870—and still, from a Protestant stand-point, retrogression, retrogression! At the beginning of that term, an overwhelming Protestant majority in Europe; at the end of the three hundred years, two Catholics there for every one Protestant. Among ourselves, at the present day, Protestants and Roman Catholics both increasing, indeed; but at a ratio of increase so different, in each sect respectively, that if it continues for a third of a

* Already quoted, with context, at page 44. Men, in the orthodox ranks, who have probably bestowed more thought on this subject than Macaulay, have reached conclusions similar to his.

"The same impediment which prevents the *formation* of Theology as a science, is also manifestly fatal to the theory which assert its *progressive development.*"—Mansel: *Limits of Religious Thought*, 4th Ed. London, 1859. (Bampton Lectures.) The italics are in the original.

century more, Roman Catholics will outnumber Protestants in the United States.*

How much longer are we to wait for the turning of the Spiritual tide? If we fight out this fight of faith on the same line, what reasonable hope is there that the tide will turn in our favor at all?

After a monition continued throughout so large a portion of civilized history—after so persistent a trial resulting in such miserable failure—ought we still to continue the strife, with front unchanged, hoping against hope in the future?

—Hoping against hope! For what a terrible thing would it be to conclude that it was Christ's very teachings, spiritual and ethical, which have been on probation for three centuries, in the most enlightened portions of the world, and that have lost ground throughout all that time, and are losing it still, against a Church that proclaims the Ultimate and the Infallible to be hers, and denies to the religious element in man alike liberty and progress!

Let us glance at the record, as a connected whole, in a trustful, and candid, and catholic spirit, ere we adopt a conclusion that might well cause thoughtful men to regard the future of our race with despair.

The Christian record consists of five narratives—four, by different Evangelists, of the doings and sayings of Christ, one of the doings of his disciples—and (aside from the Apocalypse) of twenty-one Epistles, two-thirds of these penned by Paul, who knew not the Great Teacher, nor believed in his teachings till after his crucifixion; the rest (with the exception of two or three pages),† written by the three chief among the

* See note on preceding page 31.

† "The Epistle of Jude is too unimportant to be a forgery; few portions of Scripture, with reverence be it spoken, could have been more easily spared." —*Dictionary of the Bible*, art. "Jude," (edited by WILLIAM SMITH, LL.D., American reprint, Boston, 1863.)

Twelve* whom their Master, at the commencement of his public labors, selected as special associates and co-workers.

Of the Evangelists, two certainly (Matthew and John) were Apostles who had daily opportunities, throughout three years, of personal intercourse with Jesus, while it seems likely that the two others also, Mark and Luke, may have known him, and heard, from his own lips, many of the discourses they recorded.†

Now, with these ancient‡ expositions of Christian history and doctrine all open before them, how did the Leaders of the Reformation proceed to construct for the world a system of dogmatic theology?

Substantially, by selecting portions of two epistles, both written by the only one of the New Testament authors as to whom we know that he never was acquainted with Jesus nor ever sat under his ministry; and by employing these as foundations and corner-stone of their entire spiritual edifice: the foundations being laid in the utter depravity of all human beings; their condemnation by their Maker, as criminals, to eternal torments; the impossibility of deliverance from these torments by any virtuous effort, how earnest and persistent

* "The three, Peter, James, and John, are with their Lord when none else are; in the chamber of death (Mark v. 37), in the glory of the transfiguration (Matthew xvii. 1), when he forewarns them of the destruction of the Holy City (Mark xiii. 3, Andrew, in this instance, with them), in the agony of Gethsemane."—*Dictionary of the Bible*, art. "John," vol. i. p. 1105.

† The "young man" mentioned Mark xiv. 51, is usually supposed to be Mark himself. In like manner, Luke is believed by many to have been one of the two disciples to whom Christ showed himself after death, on the journey to Emmaus; or, at all events, to have been one of the Seventy. See *Dictionary of the Bible*, vol. ii. p. 151.

‡ The narrative of Matthew is admitted to be the oldest of the Gospels, written, as some will have it, eight or ten years only after Christ's death, but more probably about the year 50; Mark and Luke appear to have written some ten or twelve years later, and John toward the close of the first century, perhaps about the year 90, or 95.

soever: and the corner-stone * being the escape to eternal happiness of a mere handful out of a vast multitude, † selected not because they were better than their fellows—did more good, were more useful in their day and generation—but because they had adopted two articles of faith; the first, that this minute fraction of human kind, and they alone, pre-elected of God, are saved from perdition by an actual transfer of their sins to one of the three persons of the Godhead, and by the terrible agonies suffered by that Holy Person; ‡ the second (equally important), that they themselves are among these God-elected few.

I think all careful and candid students of the Christian Scriptures will admit that had the two Epistles, to the Romans and to the Galatians, never been written, or never been included in the canon of the New Testament, the above dogmas would never have become the basis of Protestantism. I do not deny that if we select some six or eight chapters out of these two Epistles, shutting our eyes to the rest of the Christian Scrip-

* Luther evidently regarded as little better than outcasts all who dissented from the doctrine of imputed righteousness. "If the article of justification be once lost," said he, "then is all true doctrine lost; and as many as are in the world that hold not this doctrine are either Jews, Turks, Papists, or Heretics."—Argument to *Commentary on Galatians.*

And modern writers of authority among Protestants still take a similar view. "In our day we have lost sight of the cardinal doctrine of justification by faith. . . . The principle of justification by God's free grace, which delivered the Church from such deep darkness at the period of the Reformation, can alone renew this generation—in a word, bring back to God the world that has forsaken Him."—MERLE D'AUBIGNE: *History of the Reformation*, Book 3.

† Calvin puts it even more strongly; he speaks of professors of religion as "a great multitude in which the children of God are, alas! but a handful of unknown people, like a few grains on the threshing-floor under a great heap of straw." *Inst.*, B. 4, C. 1.

‡ "We may imagine what dreadful and horrible agonies Christ must have suffered while he was conscious of standing at the tribunal of God, accused as a criminal on our account."—*Inst.*, B. 2, C. 14, § 12.

tures, we may logically deduce from these some such scheme of redemption as the Reformers set up.

Had Luther and Calvin a right to make this exclusive selection? Beyond doubt Luther held to that opinion. With his usual fearlessness, he claimed the privilege to judge the entire record, holding fast to what seemed to him from the Lord and leaving the rest. Following the spirit of a Pauline text,* he says: "Doubtless the prophets studied Moses, and the later prophets studied the earlier ones, and wrote down in a book their good thoughts, inspired by the Holy Ghost. And though these good and true teachers and searchers sometimes fell upon hay, straw, and wood, and did not build of pure silver, gold, and precious stones alone, yet the foundation remains." †

He makes the distinction between the message and the messenger, saying elsewhere: "When I hear Moses enjoining good works, I hear him as I do one who executes the order of an Emperor or prince. But this is not to hear God himself." ‡

Nor must we imagine that Luther restricted his liberty of choice and rejection to the old Testament. One of the most outspoken of mankind, he sometimes lets us into the inner workings of his mind—a curious study. He advises those who find difficulty in reconciling other portions of scripture with his favorite texts from Galatians, to reply to an adversary after this wise: "Thou settest against me the servant, that is to say the Scripture, and that not wholly but certain passages touching the law and works. But I come with the Lord himself who is above the Scripture. . . . On Him I hold; Him I stick to and leave works unto thee. . . . Hold fast to this and lay it against all the sentences of the law and say: 'Dost

* 1 Corinthians iii. 13.

† The passage occurs in the Preface to Luther's *Commentaries on the four books of Moses:* ("Annotat. über die fünf Bücher Moses.")

The reader will find, in Breitschneider's work entitled *Luther und seine Zeit* (1817), pp. 97–99, the freer opinions of Luther about inspiration, brought together.

‡ See Walch's collection of Luther's works, vol. vii. p. 2044.

thou hear this, Satan?' Here he must needs give place, for he knows that Christ is his Lord and Master." *

We find a remarkable example of the bold manner in which Luther acted out these sentiments. James, as we have seen, was one of the most prominent among Christ's apostles. To him, whom he had trusted on earth, Jesus appeared after his death.† Paul, coming to Jerusalem and finding the disciples afraid of him—as not believing him to be a disciple—was brought by Barnabas to Peter and James, and by them accredited to the brethren. ‡ Afterward James reached the highest offices of trust in the gift of the early Christian Church. §

But this distinguished apostle, author of the epistle which bears his name, sets forth in that epistle doctrine diametrically opposed to Paul's justification by faith without works. He there teaches that faith alone cannot save, seeing that the devils also believe and tremble; finally declaring, "As the body without the spirit is dead, so faith without works is dead also." ‖

* *Commentaries on the Galatians;* on chap. iii. verse 10, last paragraph.

† All commentators are agreed that it is to this James that the text 1 *Corinth.* xv. 7, applies. The apparition seems to have been first specially to him; afterward to all the apostles.

‡ *Acts* ix. 27. With this text compare *Galatians* ii. 18, 19, where Paul, after stating that he saw Peter and abode with him fifteen days, adds: "But other of the apostles saw I none, save James, the Lord's brother."

§ A.D. 49, he was President of the Apostolic Council. Later he was formally appointed by the Apostles Bishop of Jerusalem. For his exceeding uprightness he was surnamed "The Just."—See SMITH's *Dictionary of the Bible*, vol. i. p. 924.

‖ *James* ii. 26. But the Apostle's statement of this doctrine runs through the last half of the chapter, verses 14 to 26. Abraham and Rahab are spoken of as having been justified by works: and James adds: "Ye see how that by works a man is justified, and not by faith only."—v. 24.

I do not allege that James meant to say that a man can *earn* justification by works; nor do I believe that he held to the doctrine of justi-

Now how does Luther deal with such a passage as this, from so eminent a source? Curtly enough. More logical or more candid than some of his commentators who have sought to reconcile the irreconcilable, he rejects the authority; declaring that James's entire contribution to the New Testament is but "an Epistle of straw." * Marvellous example of the effect which may be produced in an enthusiastic mind, when it dwells, with the partiality of love, on a favorite dogma! †

That the bold Reformer was entitled to the privilege here assumed, every friend of religious freedom will admit, whatever he may think of good Martin's discretion in the mode of exercising it. Far be it from me to deny to Luther, or to any honest, earnest seeker after truth, the right to judge for himself, as regards the Bible, between the gold and silver and the

fication as a reward of well-doing, but only as a consequent of good deeds.

* "Epistola straminea" is Luther's expression: it occurs in his preface to the New Testament. A writer in the *Dictionary of the Bible* (vol. i. p. 926), says: "Luther seems to have withdrawn the expression, after it had been two years before the world." I find no proof whatever of this. Carlstadt, a contemporary of Luther and the author of a work entitled *De Canonicis Scripturis*, reprehends Luther for his opinion about James (Hagenbach's *History of Doctrines*, vol. ii. note to page 241); but the great Reformer was not a man to shrink from an opinion once published, because an opponent attacked it.

† The Epistle thus summarily dealt with is filled with the noblest passages, and holds more strictly to the spirit of Christ's teachings than any other embraced in the Canon. Compare James i. 5; i. 26; ii. 8, 9; ii. 13; iii. 17; v. 1; v. 12; the last clause of v. 16, and other texts from this Epistle, with the words of Jesus. This apostle's strict adherence to his Master's doctrine may be partly due to the fact that his Epistle is the earliest in date; being written, as is usually calculated, about twelve years only after Christ's death.

James is, more preëminently than any other Apostle, the moral teacher of the New Testament. Where have we a more excellent definition of religion than he has given us? "Pure religion and undefiled before God and the Father is this, to visit the fatherless and the widows in their affliction, and to keep one's self unspotted from the world."

hay and straw which it may contain. Then, too, we must admit the great importance of the distinction which Luther sets up between the message and the messenger. We hear God through His works or his interpreters only; and that, as Luther reminds us, "is not to hear God himself."

This only I assert, that it was not the grand system of spiritual ethics taught by Jesus which was arrested in its progress for centuries, which failed to make headway against human claimants of infallibility, which lost more than half the ground it had gained, which cannot hold its own against the Roman hierarchy to-day—it was but an Augustinian commentary on some of the scholasticisms of St. Paul.

I find abundant proof of this assertion in the gospel record, taken as a whole. In its general aspect what do we find to be its essential features?

---

§ 10. Spirit and Teachings of Christianity compared with those of Calvinistic and Lutheran Theology.

"Scripture, as a witness, disappeared behind the Augsburg Confession, as a standard."—Tulloch.*

Men did well, after countless ages marked with fitful struggles only toward the light, to turn over a leaf in the world's chronology, and begin to date its years afresh, from the time when, at last, a Teacher spoke to its heart and to the affections there crushed and to the spirit of God there dormant; instead of addressing its fears, its superstitions, and its evil passions.

Ignorance or cynicism alone denies or overlooks the moral and spiritual progress of mankind. But to what is that progress due? To a spirit inherent in our race as is the vital principle in the bare-limbed, snow-clad forest-tree—a spirit that hardly manifested existence through the long, barren winter of human barbarism, but now, stirred to energy in this spring-time

* *Leaders of the Reformation* (London, 1869), p. 87.

of civilization, puts forth, of its kind, fresh, green leafage, to gladden the world.

How is this spirit named? When it stills, in the individual, or the nation, the fierce impulses of combativeness, and bids discard brutal force and substitute the mild appliances of reason, it is called PEACE. When it softens the asperity of human codes, and tempers indignation against the wrong-doer, we name it MERCY. When it seeks, in a neighbor's conduct, the good and not the evil; when it respects, in others, independence of thought and speech, and finds in honest difference of opinion no cause of offence; its name is CHARITY. When it attracts us to our fellow-creatures, of every tribe and tongue, impelling us to take them by the hand and do them good, we call it KINDNESS. By whatever name, under all its phases, a gentle spirit; eminently civilizing, humanizing; the herald of virtue, the dispenser of happiness.

As it happens that, while winter still lingeringly maintains dominion over earth, there sometimes intervenes a day of bright sunshine, harbinger of others, warmer and brighter yet, to come; so is it also with the changing seasons of the spiritual world. There have been gleams of premature brightness shed over an age still too wintry for their maintenance; there floats, sometimes, the faint fragrance of a summer yet afar off.

Of this there have been marked examples, far back in human history. In these we dimly recognize the divine efflation. But we recognize it as we do the remote star in the night-heaven. Star and sun shine upon us alike with celestial light; yet there is one glory of the sun, enlightener of the earth, and another of the pale, twinkling star. And never, in all the history of our race, has the gentle spirit of which I have spoken been heralded to humankind as it was, more than eighteen centuries since, in one of the Asiatic dependencies of the Roman Empire. A voice from Galilee, first heard by fishermen, its earliest teachings caught up by publicans and sinners, has reached, albeit through the din of controversialism, the entire civilized world.

Aside from parasitic subtleties of doctrine which have commonly enkindled zeal in the inverse ratio of their practical importance, what is the master-principle, pervading the entire code of Christian spiritualism and Christian morality,—giving it life and character, conspicuously distinguishing it from the Jewish and all other harsh systems of an austere Past?

It is, as to God, the regarding Him not as an implacable Sovereign, armed with the terrors of the Law, whose wrath is a consuming fire; but as a dear Father—his tender mercies over all his other works—who exacts not long prayer nor formal sacrifice; accepting, as most fitting service to Himself, the aid and comfort we may have given to His suffering creatures. And, as to man, it is the substitution, in all his affairs, whether international, legislative, litigant, executive, or social, of the law of kindness for the rule of violence. It is the replacement, throughout God's world, of war by peace, of severity by humanity: for contention the enthronement of meekness; and for hatred, of love.

We find, indeed, scintillations from such a spirit dating prior to the Christian era: in the Grecian schools of philosophy, especially from the lips of Socrates speaking through the transcripts of Plato; and even coming to us from an earlier school, in the moral code promulgated by the great sage of China, the contemporary of Pythagoras and of Solon. Confucius, twenty-four centuries since, forbade revenge of injuries, commended clemency, denounced self-righteousness, and declared that the very foundation of all law was this, that we should do as we would be done by.*

But what was subordinate injunction or incidental embellishment only in older codes is of the Christian system the soul and essence. Scarce a maxim but it colors; hardly a precept

* TELA: *Life and Morals of Confucius*, reprinted from the edition of 1691 (London, 1818); pp. 80, 82, 89, 92. But Confucius inculcated hatred of bad men, as of the slanderer, the reviler, the man wise in his own conceit, the fool who censures (p. 91). Compare with this, Matthew v. 43, 44.

to which it does not give tone. It is not one of many ministrant spirits, but the presiding deity. LOVE is the fulfilling of the Law.

It would be wrong to say that such a system was out of place eighteen hundred years ago, under a rule of legal vengeance and a code of retaliation. Even in those days, as long before, the still small voice in human nature, though commonly drowned by the clang of arms and the noisy conflict of rude passions, doubtless bore witness, when it could be heard above the tumult, in favor of the new philosophy; testifying to its justice, sympathizing with its kindly spirit. And to this steadfast ally within the citadel is to be ascribed its preservation amid the hostile elements around.

Yet one can hardly imagine anything more at variance with the temper of Christianity than the everyday thoughts and doings of men, not only at the period whence it dates, but long thereafter. And it is a thing very remarkable that the name was adopted and revered, age after age, while scarcely pretence was maintained of obedience to the gentle precepts that characterized it. The warrior-monk of Malta, after he had lost, amid luxury and license, every virtue except valor, called himself a Christian. The half-million of crusaders who six centuries since assembled at the call of Father Dominic, and marched forth, the cross emblazoned on their breasts, to exterminate the schismatic Waldenses—laid claim to the title of Christian pilgrims. Torquemada—he who during one brief inquisitoriate burned five thousand heretics,* and gave up ten times that number to torture or other punishment—caused the rack to be stretched and the martyr-fire to be kindled, by the authority of Christianity. Like the disciples demanding fire from heaven to consume the inhospitable Samaritans, these men knew not what manner of spirit animated Him, whom they vainly professed to follow and to serve.

* Variously estimated, by different writers, from two to eight thousand. I have assumed the mean, which I judge from the evidence to be under rather than over the truth.

Through these earliest and worst profanations of her name, Christianity is at length emerging. We have probably outlived the era of religious persecution unto death. You can speak of Roman Catholicism and I of Calvinism, without risk that either of us should be brought to the stake.

Under favor of this freedom, I may ask you dispassionately to reflect how far the theology taught by the Leaders of the Reformation conforms to, or diverges from, the religion of Christ. The subject should be approached—reverently, prayer fully, yes—but fearlessly also. The truth maketh free.

I admit, in advance, that a doctrinal system which, in various phases, has pervaded Christendom for fifteen hundred years, may rightfully demand to be respectfully dealt with by the historian, the statesman, the philosopher. We may rationally assume, too, that in a certain stage of mental development, such a system, like war, may have had its mission. Yet this theory does not bar the hypothesis that its days are numbered, or that its mission is already fulfilled. To everything there is a season. Like the dogma—as ancient as itself, and still nominally accepted by two hundred millions of people—that the Holy Ghost ever guides, exclusively and with unerring wisdom, the one only true and Catholic Church—the doctrine of innate and incurable depravity, supplemented by vicarious atonement, may be destined speedily to pass away.

If it shall appear that such a doctrine, though taught by Paul, conflicts with the sayings of Jesus, then we shall be relieved from the despairing conclusion that Christianity is losing ground, century by century. If it shall further appear that these favorite dogmas tend to retard the progress of civilization and to lower the standard of morality,* then we need not ac-

* In some of the succeeding pages, I shall speak, at large, of Plenary Inspiration. Meanwhile, if the doctrine of Luther suffice not, in the eyes of my clerical readers, to justify me in assuming it to be possible that a few of St. Paul's chapters are but straw instead of gold, let them be reminded what one of the most eminent and enlightened among the dignitaries of the English Church has left on record :

cept Macaulay's corollary that there is no progressive element in our religion, and no security, in the future, against any theological fallacy of the past.

In a brief address like this, it is impracticable to collate the writings of Calvin and Luther with the teachings of Christ. Text crowds on text; one would have to transcribe half the biography of the Testament.

And how unnecessary would be such a collation, if we of this generation could but examine that Testament uninfluenced by preconceptions!

Let us imagine Christendom to have known, until the present day, no Bible save Calvin's Institutes and Luther's Galatian Commentary. Let us suppose it to be receiving for the first time, now under the lights of the nineteenth century, the utterances of him whom it calls "Lord, Lord,"—to be reading the just-found words of Jesus, as the peasantry of Germany and England read them fresh from the pens of Luther and of Tyndale. Ah! small need would there be then of comment or studied comparison! The theology that rejoices in its orthodoxy to-day would melt away in a single year before the glow of the teachings by the sea and of the Sermon on the Mount.

Thus emerging to view, what a record would it be to us!—with first impressions undulled by formal iterations; with convictions still to be formed, not perverted from earliest childhood into antiquated grooves; its words fresh with their original meaning; no dogmatic gloss to dim its simple lessons; no obscuring commentary to cloud its priceless truths. Some things, no doubt, would startle us; others might cause us to

"I express myself with caution lest I should be mistaken to vilify reason; which is, indeed, the only faculty we have wherewith to judge concerning anything, even revelation itself: or be understood to assert that a supposed revelation cannot be proved false from internal characters. For it may contain clear immoralities or contradictions; and either of these would prove it false."—Bishop Butler: *Analogy of Religion*, part ii. chap. 3, p. 201. (London Ed., 1809.)

call in question the accuracy of the biographer's recollections. A portion of Luther's "hay and straw," we should detect; but the pure gold would be readily recognized; the grand foundation would remain.*

"Repent, for the kingdom of Heaven is at hand!"† These would be the first words of exhortation that met our eye. Next we should learn that the "gospel of the kingdom" was preached.‡ The gospel! That word would come to us in its etymological purity, § not overlaid by suggestions of catechism and faith-confessions. It would inform us that Jesus, the ANOINTED,‖ came a Messenger of Good Tidings.

Good tidings?—to us who had been hearing such as these? "Every thing in man, the understanding and will, the body and

* I may here advert to what I have touched upon elsewhere in this volume that, in a general way, I regard the three synoptical gospels—the earlier written—as much more reliable than the later biography of John; and I have therefore chiefly, though not entirely, trusted to them for Christ's teachings. The nearer (in time) to the Master, the more we find of the gold and the less of the dross.

It is remarkable that Justin Martyr, who usually refers to his authorities specifically, never quotes either of the Evangelists by name; but, instead, what he calls: *Memoirs of the Apostles.* The remarkable coincidences not only in incident, but often almost literal, between the three synoptical gospels seem to point to some common origin for these biographies; and it has been suggested that this common source may have been a Memoir or Biography, drawn up from the recollections of Christ's relatives, his Apostles, and other prominent disciples, soon after the crucifixion. This seems to me a reasonable hypothesis.

† Matthew iv. 17; Mark i. 15.

‡ Matthew iv. 23; Mark i. 14.

§ It would be superfluous, but that it is so often overlooked, to recall to the reader's memory that the word *gospel* (god-spell) derives from the two Anglo-Saxon words: *God*, good; and *spell*, history or tidings.

‖ The titles "The Christ" and "The Messiah" hardly recall to us now the fact, that both mean simply *The Anointed;* the former in Greek, the latter in Hebrew.

The disciples, soon after the crucifixion, "lifting up their voice to God with one accord," designated their Master (Acts iv. 27) as "Thy holy child Jesus, whom Thou hast anointed."

soul, is polluted.* . . . God finds nothing in men that can incite him to bless them." †

What good tidings, then? These—

"Blessed are the poor in spirit; for theirs is the kingdom of heaven. Blessed are they that mourn; for they shall be comforted. Blessed are the meek, for they shall inherit the earth. Blessed are they which do hunger and thirst after righteousness, for they shall be filled. Blessed are the merciful; for they shall obtain mercy. Blessed are the pure in heart; for they shall see God. Blessed are the peace-makers, for they shall be called the children of God." ‡

So, again, to ears accustomed to doctrine like this: "All children are depraved from their very birth; . . . their whole nature must be odious and abominable to God" §—how would sound the good tidings brought by another Teacher, guiding us from darkness to the "light of life"? ‖

"Jesus took little children in his arms and blessed them, saying: 'Of such is the Kingdom of Heaven:' and to his disciples he added: 'Except ye receive the Kingdom of God as a little child, ye cannot enter therein.'" ¶

Yet again: In the gospel from Geneva we had been accustomed to read: "The whole world does not belong to its Creator: . . . grace delivers from the curse and wrath of God a few, . . . but leaves the world to its destruction. ** . . . I stop not to notice those fanatics who pretend that grace is offered equally to all." ††

But how would our hearts warm within us when we found, in the Gospel from Galilee, invitation to all those who labor and are heavy-laden upon earth: "Ask, and it shall be given you; seek, and ye shall find; knock, and it shall be opened to you: for *every one* that asketh receiveth, and he that seek-

* See preceding page 73.

† See preceding page 74.

‡ Matthew v. 3–10.

§ See preceding pages 74, 75.

‖ John viii. 12.

¶ Luke xviii. 15–17.

** See the words of Calvin at preceding page 78.

†† See preceding page 75.

eth, findeth; and to him that knocketh it shall be opened. . . If ye, being evil, know how to give good gifts unto your children, how much more shall your Father which is in Heaven, give good gifts to them that ask Him?" *

Nor should we find the teachings that had come from Wittenberg to agree, any better than Calvinism, with the tidings from Nazareth, at last laid open before us; seeing that Luther had taught us in this wise: "To say that faith is nothing unless charity be joined withal, is a devilish and blasphemous doctrine. † . . . Every doer of the law and every moral worker is accursed." ‡

But in the new gospel we should find Christ saying: "When thou makest a feast, call the poor, the maimed, the lame, the blind; and thou shalt be blessed: they cannot recompense thee, but thou shalt be recompensed at the resurrection of the just." §

We should probably call to mind, too, that from Wittenberg we had heard: "He that says the gospel requires works for salvation, I say, flat and plain, is a liar." ‖

But when we open that gospel itself, how different the reading! "Whosoever shall do and teach the commandments, the same shall be called great in the Kingdom of Heaven." ¶

As we proceeded in the beautiful gospel-story, new surprises would meet us at every step.

That sinner of the olden time, was she, with her many sins, forgiven because she *believed* much? We should find the record to read—"because she *loved* much." **

And that other sinner, set in the midst for condemnation, was she bade to go and believe that a Holy Vicar bore her sins? Verily, no. We should learn that she was left uncondemned and bade to "go and sin no more." ††

That prayer of prayers (it would seem to us, Geneva-taught)

* Matthew vii. 11.

† See preceding page 83.

‡ See preceding page 84.

§ Luke xiv. 13, 14.

‖ See preceding page 51.

¶ Matthew v. 19.

** Luke viii. 47.

†† John viii. 10.

ought not to have read: "Forgive us our sins as we forgive them that sin against us;" * but thus: "Reckon it to us for righteousness that our sins are transferred to thy Son and that we are elected of Thee."

Then, again, when amid Christ's good tidings we heard of the great "joy in Heaven over one sinner that repenteth," the question would be sure to arise: "Why, when a sinner repents, should there be joy at all, if it be election, and not repentance, that has power to save?"

But chiefly would the wondrous narrative-teachings of Jesus be likely to arrest our attention; and what profound subject for thought should we find in them!

Suppose that, fresh from the Reformer's scheme of atonement, we came upon that noblest of parables, the story of the prodigal son. The father (we should read) bade bring forth the best robe and put it on him, and a ring on his hand and shoes on his feet. Was this advancement (typical of God's good-will to a sinner) due to the son's sudden adoption of a dogma, and to his certain belief that he was favored of his father and destined to happiness? "A thousand times, no!" (we should have to reply). It was due to the lost one's humility and repentance; to his sorrow for the past, and his resolution to lead an amended life of usefulness, even in a menial's place. "Father, I have sinned against Heaven and before thee, and am no more worthy to be called thy son; make me as one of thy hired servants."

Next, perhaps, reaching the parable of the man travelling into a far country, we might be reading how he called his servants and delivered to them his goods; how one servant improved the talents he had received and to him it was said: "Enter into the joy of thy Lord:" then how another servant left his talent unemployed, and was sent "into outer darkness." Straightway it would suggest itself to us that, unless we had

* There are two slightly variant versions: Matthew vi. 12, 14; and Luke xi. 4.

been misled by blind teachers, this parable ought to have stated that the one servant, who sought justification through the works he had done, was told that no man can be justified by works, and so, dismissed to "weeping and gnashing of teeth:" while the other, who trusted not to works, should have been informed that if he confidently believed that he had been elected to enter on the joy of his Lord, it should be unto him according to his belief.*

At last, it may be, urgent to have our doubts resolved, we might turn over the leaves, seeking some definite statement touching the fate of human beings after death. Matthew, in his twenty-fifth chapter, would supply our need.

For there we should find Jesus depicting a graphic scene, typical of the effect which man's doings in this world produce on his state in the next.

When the King says to those on his right, "Come, inherit the Kingdom," he assigns the reasons for his choice. "I was an hungered and ye gave me meat; I was thirsty and ye gave me drink; I was a stranger and ye took me in, naked and ye clothed me; sick and in prison and ye visited me." And when they who were thus addressed disclaimed having rendered him service, the reply is: "Inasmuch as ye did it unto the least of these, my brethren, ye did it unto me." Could we construe this except to mean that we best serve God when we do good to the lowliest of his creatures; and that if we spend our lives here in such good deeds, then when Death summons us to another phase of life, our state there will be a happy one? Yet,

* The passages that would be sure to startle our supposed Genevan catechumen are without number, and will occur to every candid searcher of the record. The parable that closes the Great Sermon is, perhaps, one of the most striking. "Whoso heareth these sayings of mine *and doeth them*, shall be likened to a wise man building his house on a rock. But every one that heareth my sayings *and doeth them not*, is like a foolish man, building on the sand." Not the hearing, not the believing aside from works—the *doing* is the rock-foundation. Everything else is a structure on sand, that shall be swept away.

if we still retained our Calvinistic proclivities, would it not seem to us that the words of the King ought to have been: "Come, inherit the Kingdom; for I have elected you of free grace to enter it, without reference to your works on earth, whether they have been good or whether they have been evil."

But who, according to Christ, were to go into "everlasting fire," *—whatever the words thus rendered may mean—at all events, who were to suffer instead of enjoying? They who, wrapt up during their earth-life in selfishness, failed to minister to their fellow-creatures. But unless, by this time, we had no longer the fear of Calvin before our eyes, how should we receive such a declaration? With incredulity, doubtless, or with a feeling that the sentence of the condemned should have been couched in some such terms as these: "Depart, ye cursed, to dwell for ever with the devil and his angels, for so from the foundations of the world was it determined, or ever ye were born or had done good or ill. That my purpose according to election might stand, not of works but of Him that calleth, I select as seemeth good to me: I take one and leave the other. These, on my right hand, have I loved; but you have I hated." †

* Christ's more usual and favorite paraphrase for the condition of evil-doers hereafter is "outer darkness, where shall be weeping and gnashing of teeth" (Matthew viii. 12; xxii. 13; xxiv. 51; xxv. 30; and Luke xiii. 28); words seeming to typify an utter eclipse of the soul and grievous mental sufferings. In the body of this volume I shall give reasons for believing that these words of Jesus aptly describe the future state of those whose lives here have not fitted them for light and happiness in a higher phase of being.

I recommend those who have the habit of dogmatizing on the subject of eternal punishment and assuming that the Hebrew *Sheol* and the Greek *Hades* have, in our Authorized Version, been correctly translated, to read the article "Hell" in Dr. Smith's "Dictionary of the Bible." They will find that the writer, after giving the result of much critical research, says: "Respecting the condition of the dead, whether before or after the resurrection, we know very little indeed. . . . Dogmatism on this topic appears to be peculiarly misplaced."

† See, for Calvin's words on this subject, preceding page 76.

Do you tell me that this is impious? I agree with you; it is the very climax of impiety. But it is John Calvin's impiety, not mine. And it is an impiety which seems secretly to have shocked the modern world's sense of right and wrong: for the last three centuries have given their verdict against it.

Yet, withal, there is a power and a subtile fascination * about the Genevese theology, terrible as Gustave Doré's conceptions of Dante's "Inferno." When I turn from Calvinism to Christianity, I feel as one awaking from some frightful nightmare—some dream of an arid desert peopled with phantom-shapes of demons and monsters—and coming face to face with the calm loveliness of a bright, genial spring-morning; the song of birds in my ears, the odor of dew-fed flowers stealing over my senses.

It is for you, guides of the Protestant Church, to say whether the facts adduced sustain the proposition which I have already advanced and which I here repeat: It was not the grand system of ethics taught by Jesus which was arrested in its progress for

* It is beyond doubt that it had strange attraction for the European mind in its state of transition during the sixteenth century. "About the year 1540 a little book was published, entitled *Of the Benefits of the Death of Christ*, which, as a decree of the Inquisition expressed it, 'treated, in an insinuating manner, of justification, depreciated works and meritorious acts and ascribed all merit to faith alone.' It had incredible success and rendered the doctrine of justification, for a time, popular in Italy; but it was finally so rigidly suppressed by the Inquisition that not a copy is now known to exist."—RANKE: *History of the Popes*, vol. i.

A significant expression, well worth pondering in connection with the hold which, in these rude days of public wrong and private outrage, this doctrine obtained on the human mind, occurs in the Augsburg Confession. Speaking of justification by faith without works, the Confessionists say: "This entire doctrine is to be referred to the conflict of the terrified conscience; nor without that conflict can it be understood."—*Article* 20.

A doctrine of fear, not of love. "What if God, willing to show his wrath and to make his power known," &c., is Paul's expression.—Romans ix. 22.

centuries; which failed to make headway against human claimants of infallibility; which lost more than half the ground it had gained; which cannot hold its own against the Roman hierarchy to-day:—it was an Augustinian commentary on some of the scholasticisms of St. Paul.

You will judge, also, whether I have made good this other proposition: It is not a fair inference from the history of the Reformation and the reverses to Protestantism therein recorded, that Christianity is not in the nature of a progressive science; or that we have no security for the future against the prevalence of any theological error that has ever prevailed in time past among Christian men.

---

§ 11. Effect on Morality of certain Favorite Doctrines of the Reformers.

But it is not alone the divergence of some early Protestant doctrines from Christ's teachings, extreme as it is, that arrests one's attention. It is also the effect on civilization and human progress of the doctrines themselves. I intreat your attention to this branch of the subject, urgent in its importance.

—Urgent, for many reasons. It is far short of the truth to say that the material progress of the world in the last hundred years has exceeded that obtained in any ten previous centuries. Yet I am sure it must have occurred to you that the advance in morality has not kept pace with that in all physical arts and sciences. Especially in this new country of ours, liable as it is to the excesses and the shortcomings of youth, improvement in human actions and affections, as compared with improvement in mechanical agencies, lags lamentably behind. Intemperance, partially checked from time to time, is yet a terrible power in the land.* Vast wealth and stintless luxury—

* Special Internal Revenue Commissioner Wells, whose labors in connection with financial reform have made his name favorably known all over the country, states, in his Report to Congress for the year 1867

heralds of ruin that go before the decline and fall of nations—are so swiftly and so widely extending their baneful influence over our people, that Christ's warning comes to us with tenfold force: "How hardly shall they who have riches enter into the Kingdom of Heaven!" Public morality is at a lower ebb than it was a quarter of a century ago: our legislative bodies are less pure, our public service generally more stained with venality. Nay, the very source whence our political system springs—the election precinct itself—has become subject to invasions of corruption that have waxed, year by year, more frequent and more shameless. But public immorality reacts on private morals. The vice-diseases which originate in politics, if they assume a malignant type, cannot, by any sanitary cordon, be confined to politics; they are sure to infect, first our business marts, then the home-circle itself.* Never has there been a time when a great reformatory agency was more pressingly needed among us than now.

I do not say this discouragingly; for I feel no discourage-

that, during that year, the sales of persons retailing spirituous and malt liquors reached the sum of $483,491,865. This, however, included *all* their sales which, in many instances, extended to other articles, such as sugar, flour, tobacco. As the tax was much larger than that imposed on ordinary dealers, it is not likely that any one would return himself as a retailer of liquors unless he sold sufficient of the article to warrant payment of the increased tax. Mr. Wells (in a letter to me of February 10, 1871) says: "I think you would be safe in saying that a third part of the sales returned was for liquors."

This would give *upward of a hundred and sixty millions of dollars*, as the sum annually paid by the people of the United States over the counter to retailers, *for glasses of liquor alone:* averaging, probably, seventy or eighty glasses a year for every man, woman, and child in our country.

How past human calculation the amount of vice and misery which so enormous a sum, thus expended, represents!—as little capable of estimate the amount of good it *might* represent, if spent for the education of youth and the instruction of the people.

* I witnessed a memorable example of this during a five years' residence, under the old régime, in the kingdom of Naples.

ment. The great stream of human progress flows ever onward, even if we, for the time, are found in one of its side-eddies. He, without whom no sparrow falls, if He fosters the less will care also for the greater. In His own good time the needs of the soul will surely be supplied as bountifully as the wants of the body.

But if we take note of God's economy, we shall observe that he effects these objects in our world, not by miracle or direct interposition, but mediately, through meliorating agencies, under general law. And, as He usually acts upon us here through human agencies, men, though they cannot arrest God's law or change its influence, have a certain power to quicken or retard its operation. They quicken that influence when they call the attention of their fellows to its inevitable action and to its power for good. They retard its action when they weaken the faith of mankind in its existence, or assert that God arbitrarily suspends it. And this last is what zealous men—in a matter most gravely affecting morals,—have assumed to do for centuries, and continue to do at this very day.

If there be one universal law, patent wherever man is found, it is that every act, good or bad, entails its appropriate result, be it beneficial or injurious to the actor. So far as we know anything of God, by observation of His works, He does not permit this law, or any other natural law, to change or to be suspended.*

Men, conscious of evil-doing, have, in all ages, striven to evade the operation of this great law; seeking out many inventions whereby, in the matter of sin, the consequence might be detached from the cause. But this cannot be done, any more than the sun can shine and no light follow, or a field be sown in tares and wheat spring up as the result.

A sin can be repented of. A sinful life can be amended. A man, sorrowing over the evil he has done, may learn to do well.

* I shall speak at large of the universal reign of law and the mistakes men have made when they imagined its suspension, in another part of this book.

A sinner may be cured of sin, as one who is sick may be cured of a disease. Thus, and thus alone, can the consequences of sin be averted. When the cause ceases, then only ceases the effect.*

Any attempt to persuade men that the effect of sin can cease while the sin remains is of exceedingly immoral tendency—of tendency much more immoral than would be the striking, from a statute against murder, of its penal clause. For it would be as if we deceived a man under temptation to kill, by telling him that the law against murder contained no penalty or that its penalty could be annulled, while in fact the penalty in force was death. Does it mend matters that we add: "What, then? Shall we continue to murder because there is no penalty? God forbid!" God *has* forbidden, and under a penalty. If you blind men's eyes to the penalty, little avails it that you repeat to them, "God forbid!"

Happily for the world, there are men (though Calvin denies this), in whom the hunger after the Right † is so strong that they need no other incentive to virtue. Yet, in the masses at the present day, the hope or the fear of consequences chiefly decides action. Thus legislators do not consider it safe to trust the control of mankind to moral precepts without penal law.

Upon the same principle the world is agreed that it will not do to leave out of view a future state of reward and punishment. ‡ Of all demoralizing doctrines I know of none more

* "Cessante causâ cessat effectus" is one of the oldest of legal maxims.

† Matthew v. 6.

‡ I by no means assert, however, that the fear of Hell and the hope of Heaven are the foundation-motives on which Christ's system of ethics rests, or which lie at the basis of the noblest morality. See, as to that subject, the concluding chapter of this book. It is indispensable to distinguish between what may be put forward as chief motive at this age of the world and what may be man's basic motive in a more advanced stage of civilization. Nor will the time ever come when it will cease to be important that we should clearly know, and deeply ponder, the natural consequences of our acts.

thoroughly vicious in tendency than this, that character and conduct in this world do not determine our state of being in the next.

And, on the other hand, I know of no more powerful incentive to morality, at this stage of human progress, than a profound conviction that, by an inevitable law, our well-doing in this stage of existence decides our well-being in that which is to come.

That sagacious and kindly man, Bishop Butler, following the lights of analogy, and from the seen deducing the unseen, has some wise words in this connection. While he abstains from anything beyond supposition as to how and in what manner, in the next world, sin will entail suffering, he suggests "that future punishment may follow wickedness in the way of natural consequence, or according to some general laws of government already established in the universe." *

I shall give my reasons, farther on, for believing that Butler here touches a great truth; that God's laws for the soul are not restricted to earth-life; and that His creatures, still under

* BUTLER: *Analogy of Religion*, part ii. chap. 5, § 2 (p. 232 of London Ed., 1809). A page or two previously occur these sentences: "The divine moral government which religion teaches us implies that the consequence of vice shall be misery, in some future state, by the righteous judgment of God. . . . There is no absurdity in supposing future punishments may follow wickedness of course, as we speak; or in the way of natural consequence from God's original constitution of the world; from the nature which He has given us and from the condition in which He places us; or in a like manner as a person rashly trifling upon a precipice, in the way of natural consequence, falls down; in the way of natural consequence breaks his limbs, suppose; in the way of natural consequence of this, without help, perishes. Some good men may perhaps be offended with hearing it spoken of as a supposable thing that the future punishments of wickedness may be in the way of natural consequence: as if this were taking the execution of justice out of the hands of God. But they should remember that when things come to pass according to the course of nature, this does not hinder them from being His doing, who is the God of nature."—pp. 230, 231.

these laws after the death-change, will find them in the Great Beyond as on this little planet, unchanged and unchangeable.

Does not such a conception (involving no earning of heaven, no arbitrary consignment to hell) commend itself to our better nature as in accordance with the attributes of "the Father of lights, with whom is no variableness, neither shadow of turning?" *

And what have we had in Hebradom and in Christendom for tens of centuries to replace it?

In the childhood of the world—at all events when it was three thousand years younger than it is to-day—a strange rite was instituted, at the alleged command of God, among the Hebrews. Sins were treated as if they were tangible and movable objects that could be detached from the sinner by a High Priest, and sent away, as worn-out garments or cumbrous rubbish might be, on a beast of burden. † This typical action might have been well enough, in that age of ceremonies, if there had been any true principle underlying it. But it was founded on an error of the gravest character. We cannot *scape* sins by a shifting of them from ourselves to another living being, any more than we can evade the fever that consumes us, or the plague that threatens life, by transfer of either to friend or foe. God's immutable law is against it. He has made it impossible to detach effect from cause.

Paul, "an Hebrew of the Hebrews and as touching the law a Pharisee," ‡ continued, after he became a Christian, to cherish the ancient Jewish idea that sin is gotten rid of by sacrifice,

* James i. 17.

† "The scape-goat shall be presented alive before the Lord, to make an atonement with Him. . . . Aaron shall lay his hands upon the head of the live goat, and confess over him all the iniquities of the children of Israel, and all their transgressions in all their sins, putting them upon the head of the goat, and shall send him away by the hand of a fit man into the wilderness: and the goat shall bear upon him all their iniquities unto a land not inhabited."—Leviticus xvi. 10, 21.

‡ Philippians iii. 5.

and that only thus man can atone (that is, reconcile himself,*) with an offended God. He seems to have forgotten, if he had ever read or heard, what Christ said to the Pharisees: "Go ye and learn what that meaneth, 'I will have mercy and not sacrifice.'" †

—Mercy, not sacrifice. Mercy for repentance, showing itself in an amended life; mercy for every human creature who forsakes evil courses and learns to do well; rest to the heavy-laden; comfort to the mourner, burdened with the memory of past misdeeds. Such—so charitable, hopeful, loving—is the plan of reformation and salvation put forth by the Great Master, gently seeking out those who are soul-sick: such the Gospel, coming to us with healing under its wings, from the shores of the Galilean sea. Its tidings are eminently promotive of morality, encouraging, humanizing, civilizing: for it presents to erring man the strongest of all inducements to resist temptation and to follow wisdom's pleasant and peaceful paths.

How different the influence on the world's morality of the scheme of redemption imagined by Paul and intensified by the Leaders of the Reformation! Calvin and Luther exhorted, indeed, to virtuous actions, inculcated the exercise of Christian graces; yet, in the same breath, they took pains to instil the idea that deeds of virtue, even the highest, and Christian graces the most eminent, are no atonement for past sins, cannot appease God's wrath or awaken God's mercy; and that such good deeds and graces do not influence, by one hairbreadth, man's chance of happiness or of misery in the world to come. No word of pardon or comfort for the penitent mourner; no hope of heaven to be reached through purification of life. They took special pains to deny that our well-doing here worked for us well-being hereafter. For well-doing they substituted what they thought to be well-believing. They set up faith in a sin-

* Atonement; at-one-ment; a pacifying or appeasing of a person offended, so as to make him *at one* with the offender.—*Bishop* BEVERIDGE.

† Matthew ix. 13.

gle mysterious dogma as the one shining, redeeming, immaculate merit of mankind.

Yet faith in any tenet is not a merit at all. Love for truth is a merit; eagerness to learn is a merit; painstaking research is a merit; but (these duties being religiously fulfilled) the *result* of such research—belief in any dogma, true or false—has not, attached to it, one whit more of merit or demerit than have far-seeing eyes or dull ears. Belief in truth is a blessing, sometimes a priceless blessing; misbelief is a misfortune, often of grievous character: for just practice is based upon just opinions. But belief in the highest truth is not a virtue; honest misbelief in the worst error is not a crime.* Nor, in admitting this, have we reached the full measure of the folly which sometimes springs from zeal without knowledge. The result of sincere inquiry—belief in this or in that doctrine—is not, in any sense, under human control. Man, at the bidding of his fellow, can no more add an article to his creed than a cubit to his stature.

Tell me, if you can, how I should set about believing that God, who never disconnects good and evil actions from their consequences in this world, has seen fit to disconnect them in the next. Tell me, if you can, how I am farther to obtain belief that God, passing by human deeds which men *can* control, selects as worthy of eternal happiness, a certain phase of faith in the unseen, which the creature from whom it is exacted can no more have, or not have, by any conceivable effort of his, than he can arrest the rising of the sun, or hasten the coming on of night. Explain to me, if you know how, by what process of volition I am to produce in my own mind such a belief. Reason and conscience within me alike reject it. Shall I do violence to them? He is false to God who is false to the sense

* William of Orange, writing in 1578 to the Calvinist authorities of Middleburg in behalf of the Anabaptists, struck the true note: "You have no right to trouble yourselves with any man's conscience, so long as nothing is done to cause private harm or public scandal."—BRANDT: *Historie der Reformation*, vol. i. pp. 609, 610.

he has received from God, enabling him to distinguish the Right from the Wrong.

I know of nothing you can say in reply, except what was said of old: "Nay but, O man, who art thou that repliest against God?" I answer that it is not against God, nor yet against Christ, that I am replying. I am replying against Calvin and Luther's conceptions of God, as I and all men have a right to do. I am replying against him whom, as guide in this matter, the Reformers preferred to Christ—against Paul: and that not wholly, by any means; but only against him in some of his doctrinal moods.* I am not more thoroughly convinced that Paul was inspired when he penned that wonderful thirteenth chapter of his first Epistle to the Corinthians, than I am that inspiration was supplanted by vain philosophy in other portions of his writings. I think he sometimes felt this himself. He seems to have induced, and to have shared Luther's opinion about the stubble that is sometimes mixed with the gold.†

It avails nothing to bid me believe unworthily of God, because Paul, now and then, sets me the example; or to arraign me for presumption because, according to best light, ‡ I decide for myself what is worthy and what is not. In this twilight world of ours where all are fallible, we ought not to place the

* At other times his teachings on this very subject harmonize with those of Christ. "God will render to every man according to his deeds: to them who by patient continuance in well-doing seek for glory and honor and immortality, eternal life; but unto them that are contentious and do not obey the truth, . . . tribulation and anguish." —Romans ii. 6–9.

† "Other foundation can no man lay than that is laid, which is Jesus Christ. Now if any man build upon this foundation gold, silver, precious stones, wood, hay, stubble; every man's work shall be made manifest: for the day shall declare it."—1 Corinthians iii. 11–13. I have already alluded to this text, preceding page 94.

‡ "The spirit of man is the lamp of God, wherewith he searcheth the inwardness of all secrets."—Proverbs xx. 27. But the translation is Bacon's: *Advancement of Learning*, Book I.

candle that gives light to the house under a bushel, merely because its rays reach not as far as those of the sun. I claim for head and heart, such as they are, the right to judge. And, in my own case as to this matter, their judgment accords with the tender-and-true poet of America, when he says:

> "I may not look where cherubim
> And seraphs cannot see;
> But nothing can be good in Him
> Which evil is in me.
>
> "The wrong which pains my soul below
> I dare not throne above:
> I know not of His hate—I know
> His goodness and His love." *

There is one other doctrine, universally accepted by the early Protestants, to the effect of which on human progress I invite your attention.

The ideas of these stern theologians touching the inborn corruption of our race were carried, as we have seen, † to a fearful extent. They regarded man as a being so desperately wicked, of nature so utterly debased and degraded, that his best-show-

* WHITTIER: *The Tent on the Beach;* Boston, 1868, p. 140.

† Preceding pages 73 to 75. Other passages might have been added, showing how deeply rooted this tenet was. The third of the celebrated ninety-five theses, nailed in 1518 by Luther on the gate of the Wittenberg church, reads thus: 3. "Works of men, let them be as fair and good as they may, are yet evidently nothing but mortal sin." Later he wrote: "Original sin lives and does all other sins and is the essential sin: one which does not only sin an hour or any given time; but wherever and as long as the person lives, there, too, is sin."—LUTHER: *Werke*, vol. xi. p. 396.

The warm-hearted Melancthon, even, who used to call his nursery "God's little church" (ecclesiola Dei), gave in his adhesion: "The soul, lacking celestial light and life, . . . seeks nothing, desires nothing, save carnal things."—MELANCTHON: *Loci Communes* (Ed. August.), p. 18.

Zwingli, somewhat more lenient, spoke of original sin as a disease. "Originale peccatum non est peccatum sed morbum."—ZWINGLIUS: *De peccato originale*, Opera, vol. iii. p. 628.

ing actions are but veiled varieties of original sin, and his noblest thoughts mere offshoots of innate depravity. Nor did they restrict this anathema to the unbeliever: they held that all actions whatever—even those performed by the most religious—must be included. "There *never was an action performed by a pious man*" (Calvin says), which, in the eye of God, did not "deserve condemnation." *

Another phase of the doctrine reaches far in its influence: for it teaches not only that all men and women, from earliest infancy up, are, in their whole nature, "odious and abominable to God," † but that they are irreclaimable also. "Man cannot" (says the Genevan Reformer) "be excited or biassed to anything but what is evil." ‡

Calvin might well have confessed of this tenet, as he did of predestination, that it was a "horrible decree." For it is a virtual announcement that there is, in human nature, no element of moral progress. It is the drawing of a pall across the future of our race in this lower world. It is a declaration to the reformer and to the philanthropist that their hopes for humankind are baseless, and their best efforts profitless and vain.

But nothing so takes from man his manhood as the persuasion that he *cannot* do what he ought. It discourages, demoralizes. Even in worldly enterprises of mere material character, it works disappointment and defeat. Would young Napoleon's Italian army have effected the wonders it did, if he had preached

* See preceding page 73.

† Preceding page 75.

‡ Preceding page 74. At first sight this seems irreconcilable with another sentiment of Calvin (*Inst.*, b. 1, c. 1), reading thus: "There is no other faith that justifies save that which is connected with charity; but it is not from charity that it derives its power to justify." The explanation undoubtedly is, that (according to Calvin) even the charitable deeds of pious men spring from corrupt motive, and therefore deserve condemnation.

But Luther (preceding page 83) declares that to say "faith is nothing except charity be joined withal," is a "devilish and blasphemous kind of doctrine."

to his soldiers their cowardice and impotence, instead of inspiring them with wholesome confidence in themselves?

And, in other far nobler fields, consider its evil sway. When Oberlin commenced his half-century of humanitarian labor in a benighted Alsacian valley, would he have had courage to proceed, for a day, if he had taken to heart Calvin's abasing assumption that man cannot be moved to an impulse that is good?

Or shall we accept the doctrine that there *is* nothing good in holy ministerings like these? Shall we read the history of our race, bearing with us the conviction that not a virtuous action there recorded; not a noble deed of patriotism, self-sacrifice, mercy, generosity; no fervent devotion of love; no sublime martyrdom for opinion's sake; no consecration of life to the relief of suffering humanity; not the purest aspiration above the mists and the misbeliefs of a dim present, nor the most exalted endeavor to bring about a bright and happy future for humankind—in a word, that nothing grand or illustrious which has been endured, attempted, enacted, by God's creatures in this world of His, from the earliest dawn of society down to the present day—is other than a vile fruit of hypocrisy,* a phase of pollution, at the very best a vain shadow † that is worthless—ay, damnable!—in God's sight?

The worst of human errors is to identify God with evil—to regard Him as a Spirit of Wrong: the next worst is to identify man with evil—to look upon him as an outlaw, past saving. God deliver us from the setting up of devil to worship, and of hopeless depravity to believe!

Better—if Calvin's Stygian creed were truth—to burn at

* "Let hypocrites go now and, retaining depravity in their hearts, endeavor by their works, to merit the favor of God."—Quoted, with context, on preceding page 79.

† Both Luther and Melancthon called the virtues of the Gentiles "mere shadows" (virtutum umbræ), and held that Socrates, Cato, and others were virtuous only from ambition.—HAGENBACH, *History of Doctrines*, vol. ii. p. 256.

once every record of the detestable Past. To what purpose the perusal of a long series of abominations?

One finds, in Calvin's "Institutes," good cause for belief that a main object of this Reformer was to inculcate humility: a praiseworthy intention. But humility and self-abasement are as wide apart as vain-glory and self-respect. Humility looks up, with hope; self-abasement looks around, with despair. There is no nobler lesson than that taught in Christ's parable of the Pharisee, supercilious in his self-righteousness, and the Publican standing afar off and imploring mercy. Paul has set out the true basis of humility: "What hast thou that thou didst not receive? Now, if thou didst receive it, why dost thou glory as if thou hadst not received it?"* All that we have, all that we are, is but a gift: if humble we should not despise, if precious we should not parade it. But we should recognize it; and we may recognize it with joy and gratitude. What justice and Christ's injunction alike forbid is that it should inspire us with that pride which leadeth to destruction. We ought to receive it humbly; we ought to use it unostentatiously: but when we have done our very best, we should not, like the leper of old, go around crying out: "Unclean, unclean!"

And when one of the elect, self-installed, thus cries out, the heart—even if he be unconscious of the truth—is seldom in the words he utters. The belief in innate depravity, coupled with the belief that one is a favorite of God—selected, with a handful more, by Him, out of countless myriads of his creatures. to share, by exclusive appointment, His glory forever—such a belief is practically incompatible with genuine humility. I do not doubt Calvin's earnest desire to be humble; yet his life was a life of spiritual pride. With what haughty arrogance did he look down on Servetus! He inveighed against the overbearing assumption of the Catholic hierarchy: was there humility in the Genevan theocrat's own tyrannic rule?

It is probable that Calvin took himself seriously to task, pain-

* 1 Corinthians iv. 7.

fully searching out every sin, dealing harshly with many of his own spiritual shortcomings. Yet even this may be carried to an extreme little conducive to that humble charity which seeketh not her own and vaunteth not. The evil effects of a persistent habit of self-introspection are often as great as those which result from the opposite extreme of self-neglect. It is a duty to care that the body be hale and that the spirit be prepared for another world; yet mainly to occupy one's time and thoughts with every petty detail connected with the condition of one's health, physical or spiritual, is an unwholesome practice, which nourishes selfishness and fosters a spirit of exaction. We become, as it were, all the world to ourselves, and our thoughts and emotions gradually contract, in proportion. Nothing does a man so much good, physically and spiritually—nothing so chastens a haughty, worldly spirit—as, in a measure, to forget one's self—to feel and to think for others.

The true lesson taught by history, as regards man and his attributes, is this: There is just cause for surprise and gratulation that, considering the terrible influences brought to bear, by vitiating circumstance and demoralizing doctrine, on the nature of man, his nature should still exhibit the eminent and progressive spirit which, ever and anon breaking away from evil training and ancient prejudice, bids us rejoice that we belong to a race—erring and frail and sinful, indeed—but in which there still inheres, as Christ has told us, an earnest of the "Kingdom of God."

Such a race gradually discards its fanaticisms. Into the creed of the modern world are entering, one by one, such tenets as these: Fear, distrust, despair, are abject influences. Terrorism, domestic, political, or religious, is of all governments the worst: it dwarfs and debases the race. A child habitually distrusted is exposed to the most baneful of all temptations. A man without hope and trust and self-respect is shorn of half his strength.

Nor does the Genevese Reformer seek to deny this. Nothing that can be said of the disheartening influence of his creed is stronger than his own words. Hear his confession: "God generally manages his disciples, that is to say all the faithful, in such a manner that whithersoever they turn their views throughout the world, nothing but despair presents itself to them on every side." *

GOD so manages? Seek the true solution in the lines:

> "As one who, turning from the light,
> Watches his own gray shadow fall;
> Doubting, upon his path of night,
> If there be day at all." †

How has Calvin's gray shadow fallen, for centuries, athwart the Christian world!

But let us turn from the shadow to the light: nor, because the leaders of the Reformation have sectarianized men's conceptions of faith, let us forget its value. Christ employed the strongest metaphors to express its potency. ‡ And very surely—the word being accepted in its comprehensive sense—one can hardly exaggerate faith's power for good: it can remove mountain-difficulties from the path of human progress. Thus, faith in noble effort; faith in our common nature; in its capabilities: in its progress. Faith in the Good and the Beautiful—in the good that is felt, not seen; in the beautiful that must be conceived before it can be realized. Faith, too, in the economy of the world: tranquil assurance that all is well and wisely ordered by a Wisdom that sees deeper than ours. Faith, again, reaching farther still: faith that progress in knowledge and goodness ends not here, but continues in another phase of being where there are many mansions, to be occupied by those who shall be fitted to enter therein.

And if Paul, in his dogmatic vagaries, did mislead the early Protestants, nobly has he elsewhere supplemented, in this very connection, some of the highest teachings of Jesus. Far be-

* *Institutes*, B. iii. C. 14, § 4.

† WHITTIER: *Among the Hills*, p. 80.

‡ Matthew xxi. 21; Luke xvii. 6.

yond even Faith and Hope, first among Christian graces, embracing in its generous scope Peace and Mercy and Charity and Friendship, ruling in Heaven as on earth, is Love.

But who, in terms more glowing than the great Apostle of the Gentiles, has spoken the praise of that glorious spirit, the very soul animating the system of morals and civilization set forth by Christ? Can we ever forget the words?

Though I speak with the tongues of men and of angels; though I have the gift of prophecy and understand all mysteries and all knowledge; though I have all faith, so that I could remove mountains; though I bestow all my goods to feed the poor; though I give my body to be burned; and have not love, I am nothing. "Love suffereth long and is kind; love envieth not; love vaunteth not herself, is not puffed up, doth not behave herself unseemly, seeketh not her own, is not easily provoked, thinketh no evil; rejoiceth not in iniquity but rejoiceth in the truth; beareth all things, believeth all things, hopeth all things, endureth all things. . . . And now abideth Faith, Hope, and Love, these three; but the greatest of these is Love." *

In tendency and influence how immeasurably far from this gracious spirit, "gentle and easy to be intreated, full of mercy and good fruits," was the spectre, mysterious and austere, whose outcry led astray the chief among the Protestant Fathers! Some men cannot hear the voice of God except in the thunder. † Think of Calvin's scheme of the world! A vale of

* I have followed Tyndale, the virtual patriarch of our authorized version of the Testament, in his translation, according to its original sense, of an important word (*agapé*). A writer in Smith's *History of the Bible* (vol. iii. p. 1676), adverting to King James' fifteen instructions to the Bible translators, of which instructions the third was to the effect that "the old ecclesiastical words were to be kept" (as *Church* instead of *Congregation*)—adds: "To this rule is probably due "Charity" in 1 Corinthians xiii." I prefer *not* to follow King James in this matter.

† "Videor mihi non verba sed tonitrua audire"—were St. Jerome's words, after meditating the Pauline dogmas of Predestination and Election.

tears hé deemed it—a vale of tears or of impious license, lugubrious and loathsome, thronged with a depraved multitude, myriads on myriads of whom—all but a chosen few—are to their Creator but as disinherited children, outcast and forsaken; suffered to wander, for a brief season, shrouded in moral darkness, along the broad road that leads to destruction, and then consigned, by the divine fiat, to the scorching flames of a bottomless pit, the smoke of their torment ascending forever and ever! *

I make no argument against the horrors of such a scheme, imputed to a God of Love. The generation that clings to it must die out in its superstitions, and we must look to the next for clearer heads and better hearts.

---

§ 12. Corroboration from History.

This must be very briefly dealt with: for I have already transgressed the limits which I had originally set for myself in addressing you.

Hallam, Sir William Hamilton, † and others have spoken in

* The theologians of that age were wont to elaborate the picture: "Alas, misery and pain, they must last forever! O eternity, what art thou? O, end without end! O death which is above every death; to die every hour and yet not to be able ever to die! . . . Give us a millstone, say the damned, as large as the whole earth, and so wide in circumference as to touch the sky all round; and let a little bird come once in a hundred thousand years and pick off a small particle of the stone not larger than the tenth part of a grain of millet, and after another hundred thousand years let him come again, so that in ten hundred thousand years he might pick off as much as a grain of millet; we wretched sinners would ask nothing but that when this stone has an end, our pains might also cease: but yet even that cannot be!"—Suso: *Büchlein der Weisheit*, chap. xi., "Vom immerwährendem Weh der Hölle."

† Hamilton: *Discussions*, p. 499, etc. Hallam: *Literature of Europe*, vol. i. *passim*.

strong terms of the dissolute manners which followed the Reformation in Germany. But I think too little weight has usually been given to the fact that a certain license is inseparable from all great moral revolutions. Tulloch takes a temperate view of the matter: "Such an awakening as this, in the very nature of the case, soon began to run into many extravagant issues. In the first feeling of liberty men did not know how to use it temperately; and Anabaptism in Germany, and Libertinism in France, testified to the moral confusion and social license that everywhere sprang up in the wake of the Reformation. We can now but faintly realize how ominous all this seemed to the prospects of Protestantism. It appeared to many minds as if it would terminate in mere anarchy." *

It is well known how this state of things embittered Luther's last days. And we have abundant evidence that, at times, he distrusted his own system. "As he and his Catherine were walking in the garden one evening, the stars shone with unusual brightness. 'What a brilliant light!' said Luther as he looked upward; 'but it burns not for us.' 'And why are we to be shut out from the kingdom of Heaven?' asked Catherine. 'Perhaps,' said Luther with a sigh, 'because we left our convents.' 'Shall we return, then?' 'No,' he replied, 'it is too late for that.'" †

Six years after Luther's death happened a noteworthy thing. Amsdorf, one of his dearest friends and fellow-laborers in Wittenberg, pending a public discussion held in 1552 with Major, an advocate for the necessity of good works, maintained that "*good works were an impediment to salvation.*" The result is very remarkable: Major renounced his doctrine, lest he should be looked on as "a disturber of the Church." ‡

A distinguished Protestant divine acknowledges that the Wittenberg Reformers were so engrossed by polemics that they

* Principal TULLOCH: *Leaders of the Reformation* (London, 1859); p. 173.

† Quoted by Tulloch, p. 75.

‡ MOSHEIM: *Ecclesiastical History* (London, 1804); vol. iv. p. 39.

had to neglect "the advancement of real piety and religion;" and that none of them attempted to give a regular system of morals. *

This, however, was attended to by Calvin; not, like Luther, too tender-hearted to frame a moral and ecclesiastical government in accordance with his estimate of human kind. Within meagre and barren limits, because of that estimate, were his efforts pent: but what he thought he could do, he did. Body and soul were corrupt—incurably, beyond earthly agency for good: yet external decorum goes for something. The cup and the platter must ever remain full of extortion and excess, but the outside could be made clean: that was within human power, and common decency required that it should be done. Phylacteries, fair with the words of the law, could be deferentially worn, their breadth determined by imperative rule. Tithe of mint and rue could be paid to public opinion; tombs could be built and sepulchres garnished; though weightier matters, judgment and mercy and faith in man, were unattainable. To the eye things could be made white and beautiful even if dead men's bones and all uncleanness must needs abide beneath. Coercion could effect all this; and the iron will of the rigid Genevan determined that it should.

In 1536 Calvin and his co-worker, Farell, drew up a confession of faith in twenty-one articles, of which one gave the clergy the right of excommunication; and they procured from the Council of Two Hundred a proclamation, in which these were declared to be binding on the whole body of the citizens. Five years later a Consistorial Court was appointed, of which Calvin appears to have assumed the permanent presidency; † and for

* "The number of adversaries with whom the Lutheran doctors were obliged to contend gave them perpetual employment in the field of controversy, and robbed them of that precious leisure which they might have consecrated to the advancement of real piety and virtue. . . . . None of the famous Lutheran doctors attempted to give a regular system of morality."—MOSHEIM: *Ecclesiastical History*, vol. iv. p. 24.

† TULLOCH: *Leaders of the Reformation*, p. 119. HENRY: *Life of Calvin*, vol. i. p. 469 (Translation by Stebbing).

its government and that of the Council he drew up a code of laws, ecclesiastical and moral, which were sworn to by the people.* This Court had but one direct weapon—excommunication: like the Spanish Inquisition which forbore shedding blood, it turned over the culprit, when anathema was deemed inadequate penalty, to the civil authority for punishment, even unto death.

History records no more striking example of tyranny, with authority intimately united of Church and State; with sway, social as well as religious and political, sumptuary and domestic as well as social.† Its redeeming point was, that it put down open profligacy and reformed dissolute manners.

This is what a friendly biographer has to say: "A marvellous change, in the course of a short time, was wrought upon the outward aspect of Geneva. A gay and pleasure-loving people, devoted to music and dancing, the evening wine-shop and card-playing, found themselves suddenly arrested in their usual pastimes. Not only were the darker vices of debauchery, which greatly prevailed, punished by severe penalties, but the lighter follies and amusements of society were laid under imperious ban, all holidays were abolished except Sunday; the innocent gayeties of weddings and the fashionable caprices of dress, were made subjects of legislation: a bride was not to adorn herself with floating tresses, and her welcome home was not to be noisy with feasting and revelry. The convent bells which had rung their sweet chimes for ages across the blue waters of the Rhone, and become associated with many evening memories of love and song, had been previously destroyed and cast into cannon." ‡

The details, attested by official records, are alternately ludicrous and horrible.

* On the 20th of November, 1541.

† "From his cradle to his grave the Genevese citizen was pursued by its inquisitorial eye."—*Calvin in Geneva;* Westminster Review for July, 1858.

‡ *Leaders of the Reformation*, pp. 107, 103.

At betrothals, marriages, or baptisms, it was illegal to present the guests with nosegays fastened with wire-ribbon (*canetilles*) or gold cord or jewelled band. At a marriage-feast or other friendly entertainment it was unlawful to set on the table more than a single course of meat including fish, and such course was limited to five dishes only: while for dessert the law allowed no pastry except a single tart for every ten persons.* The character of personal ornaments, the mode of cutting hair and the length it might be worn, the fashion of dress, were all prescribed: slashed breeches, for example, being prohibited. †

There was no novel-reading in those days; but the favorite substitute for our romances, Amadis de Gaul, was peremptorily interdicted; nay the preachers of Geneva, less tolerant than the curate and barber when they made a bonfire of Don Quixote's library, ‡ burned every copy of that work on which they could lay their hands.

Mere childish indiscretion incurred legal penalty: the lightest jest was a criminal offence. A young girl in church, singing to a psalm-tune the words of a song, was ordered to be whipped. Three children were punished by the authorities because, instead of going to church, they remained outside eating

* "—et q'au dit dessert q'ouai patisserie ou pièce de four, sinon une tourt seulement, et cela en chacune table de dix personnes." The word now spelt *tourte* is sometimes used for a fruit or pigeon pie. Under Calvin's law there was temptation to make huge pasties.

Principal Tulloch tells us that, while travelling in Switzerland, he visited Geneva and sought out Calvin's grave. A plain stone, with the letters "I. C." on it, was shown to him as marking the spot; and the old man who conducted him thither seemed (he says) to have little idea of the Great Reformer except as "the man who limited the number of dishes at dinner."—*Leaders of Reformation*, pp. 120, 147.

† "We saw," said Calvin, "that through the chinks of those breeches a door would be opened to all sorts of profusion and luxury."—Quoted by TULLOCH, p. 136.

‡ "It is the best book of the kind ever composed," cried the barber, "and ought to be pardoned as an original and model in its way."

"Right," said the curate, "and for that reason he shall be spared for the present."

cakes. A man, hearing an ass bray, said "he's singing a pretty psalm;" * and for that offence was banished from the city. Another swore "by the body and blood of Christ;" and thereby incurred a fine and exposure in the market-place, hands and feet in the stocks.

But all this is as nothing, compared to the tragedies that intervened. The ecclesiastical legislator who believed that, from the hour of birth, children are polluted, and that their nature ever remains odious and abominable to God, framed his laws accordingly. It would be incredible, were it not recorded by Calvin's warmest admirers, that in 1568 a girl—a mere child—for having struck her parents, *was beheaded!* And that a lad of sixteen, only for a *threat* to strike his mother, was condemned to death. †

Order reigned in Geneva!—at what sacrifice of human suffering and crushing of human hearts they only know who still, perhaps, look back from the bright mansions of a better world on the gloom and the terrors of their earthly prison-house.

I might turn from the Continent of Europe to that marvellous little island whence we of North America chiefly derive our ancestry, especially to its northern portion; there to find the same tree bearing its appropriate fruit. But space fails me; and another has already exhausted that field. ‡ The Presbyte-

* "Il chante un beau psaume."

† The above facts are given in Paul Henry's *Leben Johann Calvins, des grossen Reformators;* Hamburg, 1844: translated by Hibbert, London and New York, 1854: vol. i. p. 361, of translation.

Partisanship can hardly go farther than did that of Henry; who finds in these terrible cruelties only "great beauty in the earnestness with which parental authority was defended." Yet Henry's is generally considered the best biography of Calvin extant.

‡ One of the hardest students of our age, Henry Thomas Buckle, in the fragment he has left us of a stupendous work, has a chapter, with elaborate references, devoted to the influence of the Presbyterian polity on the Scottish nation in the seventeenth century. So far as the condition of a country can be predicated upon its theological literature and

rian polity of the Scottish Kirk, within a century after Calvin's death, embodied almost all the worst features of the Genevan tyranny: the same despairing views of life and death; the same abject fear of offending the Creator by innocent pleasures, and incurring hell-fire by wholesome, light-hearted gayety; the same repression of human affections, the same domiciliary inquisitions, the same assumption of the right to excommunicate, and even to inflict, for breaches of church discipline, the torture of

its Church records alone, we have it there before us, and may read it with much instruction and profit: it justifies all, and more than all, that I have briefly condensed into the text above. Yet many of Buckle's strictures on Scottish character and intellect, even in the rude seventeenth century, being founded on too narrow a basis, are hasty and exaggerated. Underneath the religious profession of this people, how earnest soever, lay a deep vein (almost left out of view by Buckle) of strong, shrewd sense, and often of daring humor, which protested alike against theological dogmatisms and clerical assumption. The indications of this temper of mind come to the surface occasionally only during the period covered by Buckle's authorities; but the temper existed, nevertheless; and, a century later (the eighteenth), it found fearless expression through a child of the people, echoing their social talk and unrecorded protests. Robert Burns was none the less the idol of his countrymen because of such racy heresies as stamp his addresses *To the Unco Guid* and *To the Deil.* Of this last--a familiar remonstrance with Presbyterianism's Prince of Darkness—how homely but scathing the satire! And how charmingly imbued with charity the rebuke launched against the cruel spirit of the Kirk's theology, in its concluding stanza:

"But fare-ye-weel, auld Nickie-ben,
O wad ye tak a thocht an men'!
Ye aiblins micht—I dinna ken—
Still hae a stake.
I'm wae to think upo' yon den,
E'en for your sake."

'or those to whom the old dialect of Scotland is more or less of an wn tongue, I here subjoin a prosaic—a *very* prosaic—paraphrase inimitable lines:

e you well, Old Nick! Oh, if you would but take thought and your ways! you might perhaps—who knows?—have a chance l. For your own sake, it is a grief to me, the thought of that den of yours!"

the scourge and of the branding-iron.* In compensation, also, there was the same unflinching war waged against profligacy and dissolute conduct. One marked difference, however, deserves notice. Whereas the Genevan lawgiver inculcated submission to kings, however bad,† the Scottish preachers were democratic, to the verge of rebellion:‡ defending the people against every despotism except their own, and claiming that the ministers of the Kirk (their commission derived directly from God) had the sole right to demand implicit, unreasoning obedience. Subjugators of the conscience, enemies of toleration, they were sturdy friends of political freedom.

But, resisting temptation to enlarge on this and cognate examples from European history, let us proceed to inquire whether this plant of Calvinism, when transferred to another hemisphere, essentially varied in its type or in its productions.

Let us pass from the sixteenth to the seventeenth century and cross the Atlantic with the Puritans.

A grand, old race!—the stuff that heroes and empire-founders are made of. What they thought right they did, and seldom asked whether it was pleasant to do it. They were estimable but they were not amiable. They were men and women to trust to in the hour of trial; but to deal with in daily life! Right glad may we be that we did not live among

* "On the 22d October, 1648, the Kirk Session of Dunfermline ordered that a certain Janet Robertson 'shall be cartit and scourged through the town and markit with an hot iron.'"—CHALMERS: *History of Dunfermline*, p. 437, quoted by Buckle.

† "The Word of God requires us to submit to the government, not only of those princes who discharge their duty to us with becoming integrity and fidelity, but of all who possess the sovereignty, even though they perform none of the duties of their station. . . . The seditious thought must never enter into our minds that a king is to be treated according to his merits."—CALVIN: *Inst.*, B. iv. C. 20, §§ 25, 27.

‡ See, for sundry illustrations, the chapter of Buckle's work already referred to.

them in the days when such as Hester Prynne walked about with that scarlet letter on their breasts. *

In the Colonial character, the theology of the *Institutes* was a pervading element, for good and for evil. The best virtues of the New England pioneers were those of stout, self-sacrificing seekers after liberty. The hardihood that broke away from Papacy in Rome, cast loose also from intolerant Prelacy in England. Nor did they heed the cost of voluntary exile. Calvin's dismal view of God's world toughened them as settlers. Not expecting ease, comfort, social enjoyment, the amenities of life—regarding these, indeed, with suspicion, as effeminacies used by the Evil One for baits to ensnare the unwary—hardship and suffering were what they looked for; and when, in their rude frontier life, they encountered these, they met them, as God's normal allotments to His Saints, with iron fortitude. They were hard on themselves and on others, as befitted believers in universal depravity.

These acerbities seemed to assort with their condition. But the followers of the Pilgrims brought to Plymouth rock a fatal element, relic of human barbarism, however cherished by the Reformers—a crime against the deathless soul—religious persecution. Laws that stain their statute-books, deeds that blot their annals, are traceable to the same source as the edicts and the inflictions of the Genevese Consistorial Court.

"I approve," said Calvin, "of civil government which provides that the true religion which is contained in the law of God be not violated and polluted by public blasphemies." †

The New England offspring of this sentiment, is a law enacting that whoso affirms works, not faith, to be the mode of salvation; or opposes infant baptism; or purposely leaves the church when infants are about to be baptized; shall suffer ban-

* "A capital A of two inches long, cut out in cloth of a contrary colour to their cloaths," etc.—*General Laws and Liberties of Massachusetts*, chap. xxviii, § 1.

† *Institutes*, B. iv. C. 20, § 3.

ishment:* and that whoso denies the infallibility of any portion whatever of the Bible, shall, for the first offence, "be openly and severely whipped by the executioner," and, for the second, may be put to death. †

Speaking of those, who imagine to themselves some other method than the Scriptural one of approaching God, Calvin had said: "They must be considered not so much misled by error as actuated by frenzy;" and again: "These persons are guilty of detestable sacrilege." ‡

Strictly in the spirit of these doctrines were framed the Puritan laws against "a cursed set of hereticks lately risen up in the world which are commonly called Quakers." § They provided, as punishment of a Quaker on the first conviction, twenty stripes; on the second, the loss of an ear if a man, if a woman to be severely whipped; on the third, *whether man or woman*, to have the tongue bored through with a red-hot iron: Quakers returning to the colony after banishment, to suffer death. ‖

We have no record that the boring of men's and women's tongues with a red-hot iron was ever carried out. But Bishop,

* Banishment of Baptists under this law occurred throughout several years of the Colonial history.

† *Ancient Laws and Charters of Massachusetts Bay*, published by order of the General Court, Boston, 1814; pp. 120, 121.

The preamble of these "Acts against Heresy," is a curious specimen of logic. It recites that "although no human power be Lord over the faith and consciences of men, yet because such as bring in damnable heresies . . . . ought duly to be restrained," it is enacted, etc.

The law above cited making it, at the option of the Court, a capital offence to "deny by word or writing any of the books of the Old or New Testament to be the written and infallible Word of God," enumerates these books by title from Genesis to Revelations, including, of course, that epistle of James which Luther rejected. The Wittenberg doctor, had he been a colonist of Massachusetts Bay, might have lost his life for his opinions.

‡ *Institutes*, B. i. C. 9, § 1.

§ The words of the preamble to the laws against Quakers.

‖ Laws cited · pp. 121–126. Their date is A.D. 1656–7.

in his *New England Judged*, has left it on record that three Quaker men had each his right ear cut off; * that "Patience Scott, a girl eleven years old, was imprisoned for Quaker principles; and that, when her mother, Catherine Scott, reproved them for a deed of darkness, they whipped her ten stripes, though they allowed her to be otherwise of a blameless conversation and well-bred, being an English clergyman's daughter." †

The death, by hanging, of three Quaker men and one Quaker woman, executed because, after banishment, they returned to the colony, is well known. They died with eminent fortitude, willing martyrs to freedom of conscience, on Boston Common.‡

Some of the terms of Puritan indictment, against men thus tried for their lives, sound strangely to-day. It was charged against William Leddra that he "had refused to take off his hat in court, and would say *thee* and *thou*." "Will you put me to death," he asked, "for speaking good English and for not putting off my clothes?" §

The poor excuse made by their executioners was a declaration, spread on the records of the Court, that "they desired their lives absent rather than their deaths present." The apology usually offered to-day for these legal killings is that the Quakers who landed at Boston were disturbers of public peace and decency, as well as heretics. But their principles were emphatically of peace, simplicity, and non-resistance: nor is it true that they made any disturbance whatever until some of their property had been destroyed and their personal liberty

* Their names were Holder, Copeland, and Rous.

† Quoted by Hutchinson: *History of Massachusetts*, vol. i. p. 184.

‡ Marmaduke Stephenson, William Robinson, } Executed October 27, 1659.
Mary Dyar, " June 1, 1660.
William Leddra, " March 14, 1661.

Four only, be it borne in mind; and we have no list of the five thousand whom Torquemada handed over to the flames: but Torquemada never talked about liberty, civil or religious.

§ Chandler: *American Criminal Trials;* Little & Brown, Boston, 1841: vol. i. p. 46.

violated. The first two Quakers who set foot in the colony, Mary Fisher and Ann Austin, were seized on shipboard, their books burnt by the hangman, they themselves closely imprisoned for five weeks and then thrust out of the colony.* During the same year eight others were sent back to England. These (and far worse†) infractions of the freedom of the

* They arrived in July, 1656.

† It was a crime to afford them hospitality, or even to direct them on their way. In 1660, at one court, seven or eight persons were fined as high as ten pounds for entertaining Quakers; and Edward Wharton, for piloting them from one place to another, was whipped twenty stripes and bound over for his good behavior. See, for particulars of these and other persecutions of this sect, Hutchinson's *History of Massachusetts*, vol. i. pp. 180 to 189.

In the legal records of these days we find darker shades. In 1662, three women, Anne Colman, Mary Tomkins, and Alice Ambrose (convicted under the law against "vagabond Quakers") were sentenced to be tied to a cart's tail, stripped from the waist up and whipped, with ten stripes in each town, through *eleven* towns, to wit, Dover, Hampton, Salisbury, Newbury, Rowley, Ipswich, Wenham, Lynn, Boston, Roxbury, and Dedham—*a hundred and ten* stripes, in all. "One of the nipples of Anne Colman's breast was split by the knots of the whip, causing extreme torture." (*Criminal Trials*, already quoted, vol. i. p. 54.) This was in the dead of a New-England winter, the warrant bearing date December 22, 1662. No wonder that warrant was eventually executed in three towns only; the humanity of public sentiment rising in protest against legal brutality.

One reads with more sorrow than surprise some of the extravagances which followed these indecent cruelties. In 1665 Lydia Wardell, a respectable married woman, entered stark naked into the church in Newbury, where she formerly worshipped, "and was highly extolled for her submission to the inward light that had revealed to her the duty of thus illustrating the spiritual nakedness of her neighbors." In the same year, Deborah Wilson, a young married woman of unblemished character, made a similar display in the streets of Salem, for which she was condemned to be stripped from the waist upward, tied to a cart's tail, and whipped.—*Criminal Trials*, vol. i. pp. 54, 55.

How fervid, in those mistaught old times, the zeal among persecutors and persecuted alike! Now that we have knowledge to guide it, how has the fervor died out!

citizen, preceded the clamorous testimony borne by Quakers against colonial rule.

The Calvinism of those days forbade even to tolerate toleration. The bravest champion of man's right to worship God as conscience bids—the noblest apostle of soul-freedom among them all *—was compelled to flee the colony under cloud of wintry night; owed his life to heathen hospitality; and when this future lawgiver of Rhode Island embarked at last to found a settlement where God alone should be judge of human religions, it was in an Indian canoe, with five followers only. Yet the offence for which Roger Williams was banished the jurisdiction, † was not that his own creed was heretical, but that he was guilty of granting to others the same right to choose a creed which he claimed for himself.

Little more than a century after this America had a Constitution in which all laws respecting an establishment of religion, or prohibiting the free exercise thereof, were forbidden. So fast, despite dwarfing creeds, grows the spirit of man in a new and a free country.

Other Calvinisms, too, we have outgrown. The counterpart of laws under which children were beheaded in Geneva, are found on the records of Plymouth and Massachusetts Bay Colonies. "If any child or children above sixteen years old, and of sufficient understanding, shall curse or smite their natural father or mother, he or they shall be put to death:" the only exception being unless it shall be proved that the parents

* I scarcely remember a parallel case, except one—among the Hindoos. A Brahmin once suffered martyrdom under a Mussulman prince, for preaching the doctrine of his sect, that "all religions if sincerely practised, are acceptable to God." "In the whole annals of suffering for righteousness' sake," says the narrator, "I know of no martyrdom more glorious than this."—BRUCE: *Scenes and Lights in the East.*

† A warrant enforcing his banishment to England had issued against him (January, 1636) at the time he fled from Salem, and wandered for three winter months, "not knowing what bread or bed did mean," ere he reached the friendly cabin of Massasoit, chief of Pocanoket.

"have been very unchristianly negligent in the education of such children," or else that the children "have been forced thereunto to preserve themselves from death or maiming."

This refers to both sexes: the next section applies to boys only: "If any man have a stubborn or rebellious son of sufficient years of understanding (viz.), sixteen years of age, which will not obey the voice of his father nor the voice of his mother, and that when they have chastised him he would not hearken unto them," the parents shall bring him before the magistrates, and testify that he is stubborn and rebellious, and "such a son shall be put to death." *

A girl of sixteen, because she struck her mother—a boy of that age, if denounced to the magistrates by his parents on the general charge that he was stubborn and rebellious—was to be hanged! And this, in our own country, little more than two hundred years ago!

That no executions took place under this law, or under the clause of the other law according to which a denial that the Bible was infallible became a capital offence—is due to this, that the Puritans were men before they were Calvinists, and that their hearts were more merciful than their doctrines.

None the less, the theocracy of the first two New England colonies, patterned after that of Geneva, was a despotism, fatal to progress.

Fatal—because it was founded on the ancient, mischievous error of retributive justice: an error of which the tendency is to retard the moral advance of the world.

Take any great social reform that now enlists philanthropic zeal, whether of law, or education, or prison discipline—whether in lunatic asylums or in temperance labors, or in the struggle against the great sin of great cities—take any such enlightened movement that is made in our modern day, to civilize mankind

* Laws cited; pp. 59, 60. The date is A.D. 1646. The laws of New Plymouth had the same two sections for the capital punishment of children cursing or striking parents, and of disobedient sons.—*Laws of Plymouth Colony*, p. 245.

—look into its organization, and ask its conductors what is its governing principle: you will learn that it is based on the belief that man's better nature can be confidently appealed to; that love is stronger than fear, and gentle influences more humanizing than penal rigors. This accords with Christ's religion; but it runs directly counter to the Genevese theology. When reforms, thus administered, are carried out, it is done despite the chilling and deadening tendencies of Calvinism.

The world owes the Reformers a vast debt, but not for their theology. It owes it—

Because they maintained that the succession of ecclesiarchs who, for a thousand years, had ruled the Christian world from Rome, were not infallible.

Because they exposed many corruptions which had crept into the Church over which these ecclesiarchs presided.

Because they denied the merit, and the saving power, of many empty ceremonials; of ascetical austerities, of monkish seclusions; of fasts, pilgrimages, celibate vows; and of pardons said to be of God, yet purchased with silver and gold.

And, generally, because they shook, to its foundation, an ancient system of ecclesiastical rule which debarred religious progress, which habitually employed religious persecution, and which, as a whole, had outlived its utility.

But we owe them far more than this. The inestimable boon which the Reformers bestowed on mankind was the disenthrallment of the Christian Record, till their day locked up in the Latin of the Vulgate; and, even in that secluded form, prohibited, as we have seen, by express canon, to all but the priesthood.

Their theology will die out, but the results of that great gift will endure forever. The gift will finally prove an antidote to the theology.*

* I would not be understood as denying that the theology, though it ran much closer to downright Antinomianism than Catholicism ever did, was yet, in its day, a certain progress. Luther as theologian, for exam-

What are the fair inferences from the summary of historical events and religious doctrines given on the preceding pages?

The Protestantism of the Reformation failed to make head against the Catholicism of Rome—

1. Because its foundation-principles were derived from two of the epistles of St. Paul, not from the teachings of Christ.

2. Because the theology of the Reformers is not (any more than Romanism) in the nature of a progressive science.

3. Because that theology is not a fitting agent, at this age of the world, to correct the manners of the day, or work out the civilization of mankind.

And, finally, the history of the reverses which overtook the Reformers, after their first half-century of success, is not to be accepted as proof that Christianity, though a revealed religion, is devoid of that element of progress which inheres in material science.

This last inference is negative only: but I advance another step. I assert that Christianity, wisely studied as a revealed religion, *is* in the nature of a progressive science; and, if you will follow me a few pages farther, I hope to show you good cause for the assertion.

---

§ 13. Christianity, shorn of parasitic Creeds, a Progressive Science.

"A Christian of the fifth century, with a Bible, is on a par with a Christian of the nineteenth century with a Bible; candor and natural acuteness being, of course, supposed equal."—Macaulay.

While I utterly dissent from the opinion which Macaulay

ple, advanced beyond Tetzel. He never, indeed, shook himself free from the primitive idea of indulgences; but he held that these were granted by God for the sake of Christ's sufferings, and could not be granted by priests for the sake of money. He spiritualized the idea; but it was a false idea that he spiritualized.

here expresses I can readily imagine by what process he reaches such a conclusion.

He means, of course, that his fifth-century Christian should have had the privilege of reading the Bible, and of finding it written or printed in a language with which he was familiar: conditions which existed not, for the body of the laity, until a thousand years after the fifth century. But he means, doubtless, much more than this. He assumes, probably, that his nineteenth-century Christian believes in the plenary inspiration of the Bible, as sole source of spiritual knowledge, word for word as translators have given it; and, further, in the miraculous character of the "signs and wonders," narrated in the four Gospels.

No doubt many Protestant professors of Christianity do still hold to such beliefs; and no doubt such beliefs do, in a measure, put the professing Christian of to-day on a par with the Christian of centuries long past.

If I thought that such beliefs were to continue for generations still to come, I should admit that Macaulay had plausible ground for his hopelessness in religious progress, and that Roman Catholicism had as fair a prospect of becoming the religion of Christendom as Protestantism has. But I feel assured that these old-time doctrines are passing away. Whenever they disappear, then Christianity will overcome not only the errors which preceded the Reformation, but those of the Reformation also: and then the Christian—not as Roman Catholic, not as Protestant, but as CHRISTIAN—will have a future before him of religious peace and religious development.

Infallibility, whether of man or book; disbelief in the universal reign of law, and misbelief that the Great Lawgiver arbitrarily suspends his own laws; these are the lions in the way that arrest the Christian pilgrim's progress.

—Infallibility, whether of man or book. These last words are, in strictness, unnecessary. For God makes no books. Nor can any book be said to have been written by His dictation. However it may have been in Eden, God shows Himself not, in this world, to man. He does not walk in the garden in the cool of the day; nor does His voice reach His creatures here, in exhortation or in reproof.

Then, as God himself does not write history, any more than He dictates works on science or treatises on art, all history, sacred or profane, must come to us written by man; in other words, it must come to us transmitted through a fallible medium. We cannot change this, and we ought not to forget it. It occurs according to the nature of things; or, otherwise expressed, by God's ordination.

We can, indeed, imagine God making a Pope, or an Evangelist, infallible; but, in either case, it is a man. God has not told us that Pius IX., from the date of his election by a College of Cardinals, became infallible; neither has he told us that Matthew was so, while engaged in writing or dictating his gospel. And although the Pope claims infallibility, neither Matthew nor any of his co-evangelists set up any such claim.* It was set up, for them and for a few other writers, nearly fifteen hundred years ago. The Œcumenical Council which assembled at Carthage in the year 397, proclaimed the infallibility of the author of every book which they then decided to include in the canon of the Bible, and Pope Innocent I. confirmed their decision: this decision all orthodox Protestants accept. In like manner the Œcumenical Council which assembled at Rome in the year 1870 declared the Pope to be, like all his official predecessors, infallible: this declaration all orthodox Roman Catholics accept. But orthodox Catholic and Protestant alike accept these canons of infallibility from men, not from God.

The Church of Rome has given to Protestantism an immense advantage by the error she made in reaffirming the infallibility of the Pope. But Protestantism will lose that advantage if she clings to a remnant of Catholicism that is quite as untenable:

* "Forasmuch as many have taken in hand to set forth in order a declaration of those things which are most surely believed among us . . . it seemed good to me also . . . to write, etc.," are Luke's modest words.—Luke i. 1-3.

the plenary inspiration of every writer in the Bible. It is just as fatal a mistake to declare one man, or one set of men, infallible as another.

This mistake connects itself with disbelief in the uniform prevalence of law. For there is no law governing the world which is better entitled to be called universal, or which is more palpable, than that all men are fallible, and are left by God to the guidance of that judgment, ever liable to error, which He has given them.

It is the more difficult to imagine any suspension of this law, because the gift of infallibility to one man would not only render his own reason useless, but would give him a despotic right over the reason of his fellows: the right which the Pope claims to-day.

In so far as men act upon the belief that any author, or any ecclesiarch, is an infallible teacher, just to that extent is freedom of conscience disallowed and trodden under foot. But freedom of conscience is an indispensable condition of religious progress.

I am speaking here not as doubting that Christ was an Inspired Teacher, nor as denying the probability that his biographers, in recalling and recording the sayings of their Master, may have had spiritual aid: * I am speaking of the doctrine that every word of every book included in the Scriptural Canon of the Latin Church and translated under instructions from King James, is direct speech of God, and therefore to be held as literal and infallible truth.

That doctrine should, in my judgment, be rejected, not only because it is untenable, † but because of its practical effect. The

* I admit inspiration, but not *plenary* inspiration; I admit revelation, but not revelation free from liability to error: both inspiration and revelation occurring under law. Of this, in the next section, a few pages farther on.

† My limits, of course, forbid detailed discussion of this aspect of the doctrine. It takes for granted the infallible integrity of numberless custodians through dark ages; and the infallible accuracy alike of copyists and translators—of those translators of our Authorized Version

worship of words is more pernicious than the worship of images. Grammatolatry is the worst species of idolatry. We have ar-

who, in the original preface to that work, vindicated a common practice of theirs (namely, the translating one word of the original by various English words), partly by the childish plea that it would be unfair to choose some words for the high honor of being the channel of God's truth, and to pass over others as unworthy. It assumes that no interpolation was possible: yet every well-read divinity student knows (to select a single example) that one of the most important texts in the first Epistle of John (v. 7: "For there are three that bear witness in Heaven, the Father, the Word, and the Holy Ghost, and these three are one")—is a forgery of the fifteenth or sixteenth century; being contained in *four* only out of a hundred and fifty manuscripts of that epistle. (Smith's *Dictionary of the Bible*, i. 1115.) And this is but one of many disputed passages; as ii. 23, in the same epistle.

Then what multitudes of other questions arise! Was it through the special inspiration of God that Paul, in most of his epistles, but especially in Corinthians and Thessalonians, makes repeated references to himself; to his labors, persecutions, example, care of the Church; and again to his own holy and blameless conduct (1 Thess. ii. 10), humility (2 Cor. iii. 1), tenderness (1 Thess. ii. 2), consistency (2 Thess. iii. 7–9): while Peter and James and John, the chief apostles of Christ, make no personal allusions, in their epistles, to their own merits or doings or sufferings? Had the individual idiosyncrasy of the respective authors nothing to do with this?

Again: in reading John's Gospel, are we not to make allowance for the fact that it was written thirty or forty years later than the others, by an aged man who had lived to witness and participate in scholastic controversy? Are we to believe that God inspired that author to repeat four times in his gospel (xiii. 23; xix. 29; xx. 2, and xxi. 20), that he himself was the disciple whom Jesus loved, while neither of the other three evangelists allude to the fact at all?

Then there are the trivialities, quite natural in a letter to an intimate friend, but certainly not like divine dictation. Was Paul inspired of God when he wrote to Timothy (2 Tim. iv. 13, and 1 Tim. v. 23) to bring him a cloak he had left at Troas, and to take a glass of wine now and then, because of failing health?

Surely we must discriminate. The gold and silver come to us from the deep mine. Are we to believe that the hay and the stubble are produced from the same profound source?

But this note is already too long.

rived at an era in which literalism is destroying faith. That was foretold long ago. "The letter killeth."

I shall be told, of course, that it is eminently dangerous to dispense with an infallible standard. I know that many of you sincerely believe this. But the world is gradually reaching the conclusion that the danger is precisely in the opposite direction. Science sets up no infallible standard: if she did, there would be an end to all scientific progress. But if we separate theology from the rest of human studies, asserting that the rules which prevail in other branches of knowledge have no application in this, the tendency is to discredit religion in all philosophic minds. The assertion of infallibility was the worst enemy of Christianity in the sixteenth century: it is her worst enemy still.

Take note of a few of the difficulties thence arising. There are numerous discrepancies, alike in narrative and doctrine, to be found, as you well know, between the different gospels. These do not at all affect the substantial truth of the narrative, nor the general scope and spirit of Christ's teachings: the pure gold—all that is truly valuable—remains. And, rationally viewed, they afford evidence that there was no collusion between the evangelists—no concerted plan of deceit. So far, then, they go to prove the authenticity of the record. But if, unwisely zealous, you set up the claim of infallibility, you lose all this vantage ground. The slightest variance becomes fatal. Such variances can be adduced, and have often been adduced, as proof that the entire superstructure is treacherous, and crumbles whenever its foundations are probed.

Truth is ever strongest without artificial support. We ought not to ascribe to ourselves faith—or any grade of belief deserving the name of faith—in Christianity, if we do not believe that, in herself, she is mighty and will prevail. That was a suggestive vision of Luther's, in the old fortress of Coburg. He wrote thence to Chancellor Bruek: "I was lately looking out of a window when I beheld a wonderful sight. I saw the stars and God's fair firmament, but nowhere any pillars on which the Master-builder had poised this lofty frame: yet the heavens did not fall in, and the firmament stood quite fast. But there are some who search for such pillars, and would anxiously grasp and feel them; and, because they cannot, fear and tremble lest the heavens should fall." *

Fears puerile as these pervaded men's minds in what we are wont to call the olden time, but what we ought to call the world's youth. † They believed that unless they erected the pillars of the Infallible and the Miraculous, the heaven of Christianity would fall in and the world be involved in heathen darkness. If Christ were yet on earth, he would address all such proppers-up: "Oh ye of little faith!"

They had this apology, however, that the element of true faith was lacking in their day. As they could not appreciate the essential excellence of the system they sought to prop, so neither could they discern its intrinsic power. It is not for us to deny that the pillars may, in the past, have had their temporary use.

For there is a time to every purpose under the heaven. Obedience is fitting in childhood. We cannot always give a young child the reasons for our bidding. He must learn to obey, to a certain extent, without reasons. And so it may have been in the childhood of the world. The fiction of infallibility, enforcing blind assent, may have been in place one or two thousand years ago. It is out of date to-day. When we become men, we put away childish things.

Akin to the dogma of infallibility is the doctrine that God, on certain occasions, has worked miracles; in other words,

* LUTHER: *Briefe*, vol. iv. p. 128.

† "And, to speak truly, *Antiquitas sæculi juventus mundi.* These times are the ancient times, when the world is ancient, and not those which we account ancient *ordine retrogrado*, by a computation backward from ourselves."—BACON: *Advancement of Learning*, Book I.

that he has occasionally suspended, for a time, the laws of the universe, in attestation of some divine truth.

Having treated the subject at large elsewhere,* I shall not here reproduce my arguments. This is the less necessary because not only is the modern scientific world almost unanimous in asserting the unbroken prevalence of law, but Protestant divines are gradually assenting to the view that what have been called miracles were but the results of laws not known, or imperfectly known, to the witnesses.

This (held in early days, by some of the ancient Fathers, † asserted in the last century hypothetically by Bishop Butler, ‡ and more positively by Archbishop Tillotson § and by Locke ‖), has been brought prominently forward in our own day both by lay and ecclesiastical writers of reputation and position.

A volume by the Duke of Argyll, on the changeless rule of

* *Footfalls on the Boundary of Another World*, by the author of this volume: Lippincott & Co., Philadelphia, and Trübner & Co., London, 1860: Book i. Chap. 3, pp. 70–91 (of Amer Ed.). In proof that the subject of ultramundane phenomena attracts public attention, it may be stated that this work, in the United States and in England, has had a circulation of about twenty thousand copies.

† St. Augustine (himself virtually a Spiritualist, see next section, § 14) held that a miracle was a thing occurring not against nature, but against what we know of nature. "Portendum ergo fit, non contra naturam, sed contra quam est nota natura."—*De Civitate Dei*, lib. xxi. cap. 8. This was written about A.D. 420.

‡ BUTLER: *Analogy of Religion*, London, 1809, part ii. chap. 2. He leaves it in doubt whether we ought "to call everything in the dispensations of Providence not discoverable without Revelation, nor like the known course of things, miraculous."—(p. 194.)

§ TILLOTSON: Sermon clxxxii. He there says: "It is not the essence of a miracle (as many have thought) that it be an immediate effect of the Divine power. It is sufficient that it exceed any natural power that we know of to produce it."

‖ LOCKE: *A Discourse on Miracles*. His words are: "A miracle I take to be a sensible operation which, being above the comprehension of the spectator and, in his opinion, contrary to the established course of nature, is taken by him to be Divine."

law * (reaching its fifth edition in fifteen months), is a noteworthy example. The ground there taken as to miraculous suspension of law, may be gathered from the following excerpts.

"The idea of natural law, the universal reign of a fixed order of things, has been casting out the supernatural. This idea is a product of that immense development of physical sciences which is characteristic of our times. We cannot read a periodical or go into a lecture-room without hearing it expressed. . . . We can never know what is above nature, unless we know all that is within nature. . . . No man can have any difficulty in believing that there are natural laws of which he is ignorant. . . . There is nothing in religion incompatible with the belief that all exercises of God's power, whether ordinary or extraordinary, are effected through the instrumentality of natural laws brought out, as it were, for a Divine purpose. . . . Christianity does not call upon us to believe in any exception to the universal prevalence and power of law." †

Another example, as eminent, is to be found in a sermon preached before the University of Oxford, during the annual meeting of the British Association for the promotion of science, by the present Bishop of Exeter. ‡ The Bishop there said:

"One idea is now emerging into supremacy in science, a supremacy which it never possessed before, and for which it

* ARGYLL: *The Reign of Law;* Strahan & Co., London, 1866; reprint by Routledge & Sons, New York, 1869. In the preface the author informs us that he withholds a chapter on *Law in Christian Theology*, among other reasons, because it is "inseparably connected with religious controversy." It is matter of regret that so acute a mind "shrank from entering" (as the Duke himself expresses it) this important field.

† Work cited: pp. 3, 14, 22, 25, 51, 53, of American reprint.

‡ On Act Sunday, July 1, 1860. The preacher was then known as the Rev. Frederick Temple, D.D., head-master of Rugby School and Chaplain in Ordinary to the Queen: still better, perhaps, as one of the leading authors of *Essays and Reviews.*

still has to fight a battle; and that is the idea of law. Different orders of natural phenomena have in time past been held to be exempt from that idea, either tacitly or avowedly. The weather, the thunder and lightning, the crops of the earth, the progress of disease, whether over a country or in an individual,—these have been considered as regulated by some special interference. . . . But the steady march of science has now reached the point when men are tempted, or rather compelled, to jump at once to a universal conclusion: all analogy points one way, none another. And the student of science is learning to look upon fixed laws as universal. . . . How strikingly altered is our view from that of a few centuries ago is shown by the fact that the miracles recorded in the Bible, which once were looked on as the bulwarks of the faith, are now felt by very many to be difficulties in their way; and commentators endeavor to represent them, not as mere interferences with the laws of Nature, but as the natural action of still higher laws belonging to a world whose phenomena are only half revealed to us." *

Still another name, no less eminent in physical science than in sacred learning, may here be adduced. The late Baden Powell, in his contribution to *Essays and Reviews*, has this passage: "The modern turn of reasoning adopts the belief that a revelation is then most credible, when it appeals least to violations of natural causes. Thus, if miracles were, in the estimation of a former age, among the chief *supports* of Christianity, they are at present among the main *difficulties*, and hinderances to its acceptance." †

* This sermon will be found in an Appendix to the Second Edition of the American reprint of "Essays and Reviews," which was published under the title of *Recent Inquiries in Theology*, Walker, Wise, & Co., Boston, 1861.

The *Westminster Review* says of this volume: "The social and official position of the authors, their learning, their abilities, and their sincerity, courage, and earnest, reverential spirit, entitle them to an un prejudiced and considerate hearing."

† *On the Study of the Evidences of Christianity*, by BADEN POWELL, M.A., F.R.S., etc., Savilian Professor of Geometry in the University of

Similar opinions show themselves in the American Churches, and are even heard from the pulpit, though chiefly, it is to be admitted, from the pulpit of the more heterodox sects. The Rev. James Freeman Clarke, a representative of the Unitarian faith, says: "If I considered the wonderful works of Jesus as violations of law, I should also say that they were essentially incredible." *

In truth, thoughtful and dispassionate minds, on both sides of the Atlantic, are reaching the conviction that the old dogma of miraculous suspension of law is rapidly undermining modern faith in the gospels. It is creating, in millions of souls, doubt or disbelief that the signs and wonders ascribed to Jesus occurred at all. Rénan is one of the ablest exponents of this latter opinion. I shall by and by † lay before you my reasons for believing that this opinion of his is false and mischievous; yet, none the less, it is spreading far and wide.

But the doctrine of the miraculous not only tends to subvert faith; it contains also a *non sequitur*. It assumes that the possessor of spiritual gifts, in other words the person through whom occur phenomena which transcend our experience, is an infallible teacher of morals and religion. Test this doctrine. Suppose the moral and spiritual doctrines of the gospel, instead of being the religion of love and peace and charity they are, to have been made up of injunctions to hate our enemies, to make war on our neighbors, never to forgive an offending brother or to have mercy on a repentant sinner; to trust to violence for the civilization of the world, to adopt polygamy, to make slaves of all men whose skins were darker than ours; to murder all men whose creed differed from our own: should we still believe in its divine character, because of signs and wonders narrated? If, as in St. Paul's case, a voice from Heaven called to us; and if this voice, instead of arraigning us that

Oxford. See *Recent Inquiries in Theology*, p. 158. The italics are in the original.

* *Steps of Belief*, by J. F. CLARKE, Boston, 1870: p. 128.

† In the concluding section of this address.

we persecuted for opinions' sake, commanded us to do so, would that voice be to us sufficient warrant to reënact the horrors of the Spanish Inquisition ?

I know what must be your answer: *No* phenomenon, mundane or ultramundane, can make wilful murder a virtue, or prove that we ought *not* to do unto others as we would that they should do unto us. We must fall back at last, you see, on our inner sense of uprightness and justice.

The obligation to do good, the obligation to shun evil, cannot be changed according to any objective occurrences, seeming ever so marvellous, that may be presented to our senses. Right and wrong are eternal, and must be judged by that which is eternal as themselves. God has provided for this. His kingdom is within us. The nearest approach to the infallible upon earth is the still, small voice of the human conscience.

Do not understand me as denying that the highest character of spiritual gifts should attract our attention to the doctrines with which they are associated. A believer in the value of such gifts, I admit this. Yet, after all, our final judgment on any system of spiritual ethics cannot rationally be made up without reference to its doctrinal character and its consistency; and ought not to be determined by outside phenomena. Internal evidence of any such system is far superior to external; and nothing can properly be accepted as a rule of action until it has been subjected to that light within, which is from God.*

* I have set forth this argument elsewhere; and may be pardoned for here reproducing, from a former work, a single paragraph:

"Let us suppose that, from some undeniably spiritual source, as through speech of an apparition or by a voice sounding from the upper air, there should come to us the injunction to adopt the principle of polygamy, either as that system is legally recognized in Turkey, or in its unavowed form, as it appears in the great cities of the civilized world. In such a case what is to be done? The world is God's work. The experience of the world is God's voice. Are we to set aside that experience, proclaiming to us, as it does, that under the principle of monogamy alone have man's physical powers and moral attributes ever maintained their ascendency, while weakness and national decadence

This inner sense, like every other divine gift, can be strengthened and developed. The conscience of the world is educated from age to age. It is more trustworthy now than it was three hundred years ago; it will doubtless be far more trustworthy three hundred years hence than it is to-day From generation to generation it becomes more capable of appreciating the grand truths of Christianity and of discarding the errors and superstitions that have overlaid these, and that have thus, in a measure, covered up their beauty from our sight. Hence moral and religious advancement.

I trust you will think that I am justified in deducing, from the above considerations, this result: Though the Christianity of Orthodoxy, loaded down by extrinsic dogmas, has failed by the way, and has seemed, for centuries past, bereft of power to advance; yet the temporary burden is likely soon to be removed. And whenever it is, the Christianity of Jesus will be found to contain the element of progress, and will gradually become the religion of civilized men.

Of this we may the more reasonably entertain a confident hope, seeing that while we are discarding old burdens, we are also obtaining new lights and fresh aids. A few words in explanation of this last allegation shall conclude these remarks—remarks which, for some years past, I have greatly desired to lay before you.

follow in the train of polygamy, whether openly carried out, as in Deseret and Constantinople, or secretly practised, as in London and New York? Are we to give up the certain for the uncertain?—the teachings of God, through His works, for the biddings of we know not whom? The folly and danger of so doing are apparent."—*Footfalls*, p. 42.

§ 14. Spiritualism necessary to confirm the Truths, and assure the Progress of Christianity.

"The need was never greater of new revelation than now."—Emerson.

And now, Leaders of our Protestant Church, if you have given me your attention throughout the foregoing preliminary matter, let me ask your dispassionate judgment on a subject vital to religious advancement, and which, because I have nowhere found it distinctly stated or fully considered, I have made the staple of this volume. It does not embrace discussion of disputed doctrines—we have had enough of that—but relates rather to a study of the great principle upon which doctrines should be received—to the *leges legum*, as Bacon might have phrased it—to the laws underlying spiritual teachings and to the manner in which spiritual researches should be conducted.

The state of religious feeling in the days of the Reformation was peculiar. The two great divisions of the Christian Church agreed in this, that the Scriptures—more strictly, perhaps, the books comprising the New Testament—are the foundations of a just faith. The Roman Catholic branch has affirmed, however, that within its Church the same inspiration which produced the Gospels and Epistles has continued, even to the present day, an infallible guide to religious truth; while the orthodox part of the Protestant branch, repudiating this, has assumed that all inspiration and all spiritual gifts and revelations similar to those of Christ's time, have been withheld by God from succeeding ages.

It was natural that the Reformers, protesting against the infallibility of the Pope, should reject also the claim of the Church of Rome to an exclusive, divinely-directing influx, emanating from the Holy Spirit. But they were not satisfied to deny the exclusive character of such ultramundane influence: for some reason, certainly not derived from the Gospel itself nor from patristic authority, they rejected it altogether.

I think that, in this matter, the Roman Catholic Church (aside from her exclusive pretensions) and the Ancient Fathers are nearer to the truth than our Protestant Churches are.

The chief reason for scepticism in the spiritual gifts of the present day is the idea that powers of this character are supernatural, coupled with the application to all such modern phenomena, of that other idea put forth by Rénan: "Till we have new light we shall maintain the principle of historical criticism, that a supernatural relation cannot be accepted as such—that it always implies credulity or imposture." *

Let us beware! Rénan's premises admitted, there follow logically his conclusions, cold and disheartening as they are. Thus: The signs and wonders alleged to have been wrought through Christ are miraculous, but we cannot accept the miraculous: therefore these signs and wonders did not occur at all. His explanation is: "Jesus was a thaumaturgist against his will. . . . His reputation as a miracle-worker was imposed upon him, and he did not resist it very much. . . . The miracles of Jesus were a violence done him by his time, a concession which the necessity of the hour wrung from him. So the exorcist and the miracle-worker have fallen; but the religious reformer shall live forever." †

This author does not seem to realize the direct corollary from his words. What reverence, what respect even, can we retain for a Teacher who lends himself to imposture?

But are we reduced to this alternative?

No. The signs and wonders may have been phenomena, of a

* RENAN: *Life of Jesus* (Wilbour's translation); p. 45. German Rationalists concur in this view. "We may summarily reject all miracles, prophecies, narratives of angels and demons, and the like, as simply impossible and irreconcilable with the known and universal laws which govern the course of events."—STRAUSS: *Life of Christ*, Introd.

† *Life of Jesus;* pp. 235, 236, 238.

spiritual character indeed, but occurring under law. There may be intermundane as well as mundane laws.

This explanation would be more generally admitted (since it is evidently the height of presumption to assert that we know *all* the laws of the universe), but for a difficulty which occurs to many. Natural laws are not only invariable but are also continuous. The effects of natural laws do not show themselves for fifty or a hundred years and then cease for tens of centuries. These results may, indeed, manifest themselves more powerfully or more frequently at one age of the world than another, as a particular geological stratum may attain in one locality vast development, while in another it shrinks into petty proportions. But the action of law is perpetual from generation to generation, suffering no interregnum.

Thus, if the extraordinary manifestations of power ascribed in the Gospels and in the Acts of the Apostles to Christ and to his disciples did occur under certain spiritual laws,* the same laws must be in operation still: and powers analogous to those which resulted from these laws eighteen hundred years ago ought to be traceable in history, and may be confidently looked for in our own day.†

—Analogous powers: not necessarily powers to the same extent; yet powers exhibiting sufficient similarity to mark their common origin. Observe, then, I pray you, how the matter stands.

There are two theories, directly at variance. The first is that the spiritual gifts of the Apostolic age were isolated phenomena, showing themselves during a single century only of the world's existence. If so, they did not occur under law, since

* That is, if they did *substantially* occur. Not believing in human infallibility, I admit that the biographers, even if spiritually aided in their recollections of the past, were liable to errors in detail—to misconception and mistake; as all biographers are.

† The analogous case, noticed in the Preface to this work, of an astronomer predicting the existence of a planet, before that planet had been observed, will here, probably, suggest itself to the reader.

all human experience is opposed to the idea that God makes laws, as men might, to last a hundred years and then to be repealed: therefore they must be regarded as miraculous. But if, in the progress of science, the belief in the miraculous is melting away, the ultimate result will be disbelief in the alleged miracles of the Gospels; and we shall fall back on Rénan's conclusion that Christ countenanced fraud.

The second theory is that there have existed from all time laws regulating intercourse between this world and the next—laws under which certain men and women, more or less favored, have occasionally exercised spiritual powers and gifts; that there occurred an extraordinary development of such powers in the first century, of which the effect was to attract public attention to the teachings of a system, the innate beauty and moral grandeur of which were insufficient to recommend it to the semi-barbarism of the day; that the existence of such spiritual gifts is traceable throughout the history of the last seventeen hundred years; and, finally, that similar gifts and powers show themselves among us at the present time.

The manner in which the evidences of Christianity are affected by these two theories, respectively, is worthy your special notice.

Under the first we are driven to maintain the Roman Catholic and orthodox Protestant belief in the Exceptional and the Miraculous. If, defeated by scientific progress, we fail to sustain this dogma, then the wonderful works of Christ and his disciples take their place beside the labors of Hercules, and other tales of heathen mythology. In that case the gospel biography of Christ must needs weaken the authority of his doctrines.*

Under the second theory, if history sustains it, and if phenomena occurring daily under our eyes confirm its truth, the result is precisely the reverse. For in that case we have the

* Speaking of the miracles of Christ, a modern American divine says: "If such narratives do not strengthen our faith in the religion, they weaken it. If not proofs of its truth, they are burdens upon it." —BULFINCH: *Evidences of Christianity*, p. 142.

evidence of our senses in proof that the marvellous powers ascribed to Jesus, and the spiritual gifts alleged to have been enjoyed by his disciples, were natural and are credible; that, in fact, we have no more reason for rejecting them than for denying the wars of Cæsar, or the conquests of Alexander. Thus *the alleged spiritual manifestations of our day*, if they prove genuine, *become the strongest evidences to sustain the authenticity of the gospels.*

There is another view to take of this matter. To act upon the ignorance of the first century it needed works which that ignorance looked upon as miracles. To act upon the apathy of our day it needs phenomena acknowledged to be natural, yet of an intermundane character. The need is as great now as it ever was. When we boast of our civilization as compared with the rudeness of the sixteenth century, let us be reminded that in those days tens of thousands gave their lives for their religious opinions, while in these, men will scarcely give their time to think about them. There are not, it is true, many open scoffers at religion among us—the age of Voltaire and of Holbach is past—but there are millions who belong to the vast sect of INDIFFERENTS. There is but too much truth in what one of the acutest minds of our own country declared, when addressing the senior class in the Divinity School of Harvard College in Cambridge:

"It is my duty to say to you that the need was never greater of new revelation than now. From the views I have already expressed, you will infer the sad conviction which I have, I believe, with numbers, of the universal decay, and now almost death, of faith in society. The soul is not preached. The Church seems to to tter to its fall, almost all life extinct. . . . I think no man can go with his thoughts about him, into one of our churches, without feeling that what hold the public worship had on men is gone, or going. It has lost its grasp on the affection of the good and the fear of the bad.*

* EMERSON: *Miscellanies*, Boston, 1856. Bishop Butler bears similar testimony in his day. In the Advertisement to his *Analogy of Relig*

Here it is worthy of remark that the better class of sceptics, in our day, regret their own lack of faith. An English author of a careful and critical inquiry into the origin of Christianity is a type of this class. He speaks of Christ and the ethical system he taught with reverence; but reaches the conclusion that the historical evidence for miracles and a Divine mission is insufficient. One sees that he deplores the conviction to which his reason had brought him; for in his concluding reflections he says:

"It is impossible to disguise the momentous consequences of the rejection of the divine origin of Christianity—that a future state is thereby rendered a matter of speculation instead of certainty. If Jesus was not seen after he was risen, we no longer see immortality brought to light: the veil which Nature has left before this mysterious matter still remains undrawn. . . . With respect to one of the subjects most interesting to man we return into the position in which the whole race stood for four thousand years, and in which a great part has remained ever since."

Again: "Whilst it was thought that Jesus had brought the guarantee of Heaven for man's immortality, we persuaded our-

ion (A.D. 1736), he says: "It has come, I know not how, to be taken for granted by many persons, that Christianity is not so much as a subject of inquiry; but that it is now at length discovered to be fictitious. And, accordingly, they treat it as if, in the present age, this were an agreed point among all people of discernment."

Strong evidence of the indifference evinced at the present day in England to established forms of religion is to be found in the 'English Census of 1851.' That document informs us that while at that time there were in England and Wales church-buildings capable of seating *ten millions two hundred thousand* persons, it was ascertained by actual enumeration that the attendance (averaging morning, afternoon, and evening services) was but *three millions six hundred and thirty-two thousand* (3,632,022). In other words, each clergyman preached, on the average, to a congregation which filled little more than one-third of the seats. And, strange to say! the smallest average attendance was found to be in the churches in which the seats were free.

Further details from this census will be found in the body of this work.

selves that this was necessary to man's improvement and happiness. We were mistaken; no such guarantee has been given; it is wise to acquiesce and to conclude that happiness and improvement are best promoted by our present ignorance. . . . The withdrawal into obscure remoteness of the future eternal life may leave men more free to appreciate the advantages of their present sphere. . . . Yet it must be owned that there are states in which all such reasonings are felt to be insipid, and in which the human mind feels a deeper want." *

Finally this author seeks comfort by "indulging the thought that a time is appointed when the cravings of the heart and of the intellect will be satisfied, and the enigma of our own and the world's existence be solved." †

These remarks undoubtedly present the frame of mind prevailing among a large proportion of intelligent sceptics; especially among leading scientific men. *Simple theism, shut out from the cheering warmth of spiritual revealings, is ungenial and unsatisfactory.*

All this, I admit, does not make out my case. As men knowing the world, you will doubtless concede the danger from that easy-going scepticism which "hopes it may all come out right, and that, in the Unknown Dark, we may find something good in store for us." You may further admit the vast importance it would be to Christianity if God would give to His

* As witness the tone of deep sadness which, especially in poetic temperaments, pervades the thoughtful hours of those who find nothing fairer to bound this checkered earth-life—no more auspicious prospect in the Great Future—than the dreary vacancy of dreamless sleep.

"The cloud-shadows of midnight possess their own repose,
For the weary winds are silent and the moon is in the deep;
Some respite to its turbulence unresting Ocean knows;
Whatever moves, or toils, or grieves, hath its appointed sleep.
Thou in the grave shalt rest—"

SHELLEY: *Stanzas, April,* 1814.

† HENNELL: *An Inquiry concerning the Origin of Christianity*, London, 2d Ed., 1841: pp. 481, 483, 485, 489.

creatures of to-day the species of evidence which He did not refuse to the incredulous Thomas. But you will remind me that to make out the importance, or the apparent necessity, of a thing is not to demonstrate its existence.

The consciousness of this gave rise to the present volume. To the body of the work I refer you for direct evidence that immortality *is* brought to light now, among us—that the apostolic gifts *are* reproduced at this day and are not restricted to the Roman Catholic Church. Meanwhile a few words touching the historical testimony in the case may be of service.

We must refuse to the Old Testament not only all claim to inspiration, in any sense, but also all credence as ancient history, if we deny that, from the earliest ages, the two worlds have been, from time to time, in communication. Cut from its pages all that relates to such intercommunion; and there would remain, of its narrative, but a lifeless and unintelligible residue.

As to the New Testament, we find neither in gospels nor epistles, a word to indicate the cessation, in the future, of spiritual gifts: so far as there is expression on the subject, it sustains the belief in their indefinite continuance.

Take a few examples:

Christ, when he appeared after death to the eleven, said: "These signs shall follow them that believe. In my name shall they cast out devils; they shall speak with new tongues. . . . They shall lay hands on the sick and they shall recover." * Again, in the immediate prospect of death, Jesus said: "He that believeth on me, the works that I do shall he do also; and greater works than these shall he do." †

No limitation as to time, observe; not to the apostles then living, nor to the disciples of that day, are these promises re-

* Mark xvi. 17, 18. Some commentators have cast doubts on the authenticity of the closing verses of Mark's Gospel (xvi. 9–19); but these verses are quoted, without question, by Irenæus (iii. 10, 6), are found in three out of four of the uncial manuscripts and have uniformly been retained in the Canon.

† John xiv. 12.

stricted: nothing to show that they do not extend to all who shall believe in his teachings, "even to the end of the world," as in another promise of spiritual aid he expressed it.

Nor were such powers, even at that day, exclusive. The seventy enjoyed them.* And when the disciples saw a certain man who followed them not, casting out devils in Christ's name and forbade him, Jesus reproved them, saying: "Forbid him not: for there is no man that shall do a miracle † in my name

* Luke x. 17.

† In prosecuting such an inquiry as the present, the student is constantly reminded of the urgent necessity for a modern revision, at least of the New Testament. The word above translated *miracle*, is dunamin, accusative of *dunamis*, which, in the best lexicons, we find interpreted: "potency, power, faculty, efficacy." We do not say "do a power," or that would have been the literal translation. The true meaning is, undoubtedly, "exercise a power" or "gift;" and withal a spiritual gift or power. such as Christ himself possessed. King James' translators believed spiritual gifts to be miraculous; and so they here make Christ declare them to be miracles, without the slightest authority, in the Greek text, for doing so.

In the Gospels *dunamis* is, twice at least, translated *virtue*, as we sometimes use the word in the sense of energy, physical or moral. Speaking of Jesus healing the sick, Luke (vi. 19) says: "The whole multitude sought to touch him, for there went virtue (*dunamis*) out of him, and healed them all." Think of saying "there went miracle out of him"! And again (Mark v. 30), when Jesus was touched by the woman who was cured of an issue of blood, he felt (so the translation reads) "that virtue (*dunamis*) had gone out of him." Jesus, it appears, was physically conscious of this wonderful power. But when the attribute of the miraculous is ascribed, it is by sheer assumption; prompted, probably, by the third instruction given by King James to his translators. (See preceding page 125.)

To the spirit of the same instruction it is doubtless due that, in one passage at least, the word miracle is arbitrarily supplemented, where there is no corresponding word whatever in the Greek text. It will be found at Mark vi. 52. "For they considered not *the miracle* of the loaves; for their heart was hardened." The literal translation is "for they thought not of the loaves:" the words "the miracle" being purely gratuitous. This and similar errors are corrected in Griesbach's text.

that can lightly speak evil of me: he that is not against us is of our part." *

More striking still is this: At the very close of Christ's ministry on earth, just before he crossed the brook Cedron into the garden where he was betrayed, he said to his apostles: "I have yet many things to say to you, but ye cannot bear them now. Howbeit when he, the Spirit of truth, is come, he will guide you into all truth; for he shall not speak of himself, but whatsoever he shall hear, that shall he speak." †

May not this be fairly construed as a promise of spiritual progress; an assurance of constant advance by the aid of the spirit of truth—medium of perennial revelation between Heaven and earth? Is it not a declaration, too, that Jesus' own teachings, while here, were not a finality; neither, indeed, could be: seeing that even the Twelve he had selected and taught throughout three years were not prepared to receive what yet remained to be said? The Christian world has strangely overlooked this text and the fair corollaries therefrom.‡

The Acts are filled with passages in proof of the continuance, throughout the Apostolic age, of spiritual powers and gifts. There came a multitude bringing sick folks to the Apostles, "and they were healed every one." § "By the hands of the Apostles were many signs and wonders wrought among the people." ‖ "Stephen, full of faith and power, did great wonders and miracles (dunameōs) among the people." ¶ "Special miracles" (dunameis) were wrought through Paul. ** Peter raised Dorcas †† and Eutichus ‡‡ from the dead. A certain

* Mark ix. 39, 40.

† John xvi. 12, 13. There are many similar promises, where this spirit is called the Comforter; as John xv. 26; xiv. 26; xvi. 7.

‡ It is a mere assertion, unwarranted by Scripture, that these promises were restricted to the writers of the gospels and epistles, eight only in number: or, as others would have it, to the Seven Churches and during the apostolic age alone.

§ Acts v. 16. ‖ Acts v. 12. ¶ Acts vi. 8.

** Acts xix. 11, 12. †† Acts ix. 37, 40, 41. ‡‡ Acts xx. 9, 10, 12.

man (Philip, the evangelist) "had four daughters that did prophesy." * And so on.

To all the disciples, soon after Christ's death, came, on the day of Pentecost, the gift of tongues.† The same gift appeared among the Gentiles also.‡

But as to spiritual gifts, various in character, Paul's testimony is the most distinct and comprehensive. He declares that, in the churches, then including numerous converts, there are diversities of gifts; besides the words of faith and wisdom, he enumerates the gifts of healing, working of miracles (dunameōn), prophecy, discerning of spirits, divers kinds of tongues.§ He himself rejoices in the possession of such gifts,‖ and, in the same text in which he enjoins charity, he bids us desire spiritual gifts, especially the gift of prophecy.¶ To deny that this last behest is addressed to us is virtually to assert that all the precepts contained in Paul's epistles were intended for the Seven Churches only, and have no application to the present generation of men. Paul's express words are: "There are diversities of gifts, but the same spirit. But the manifestation of the spirit is given *to every man* to profit withal." **

Passing on from the first century and coming upon the Ecclesiastical, or Patristic "miracles," we enter an oft-trodden field, familiar to those who have followed an English Doctor of Divinity, writing in the middle of the last century, through a celebrated "Inquiry" into that subject.†† I think a dispassionate student rises from the perusal of Middleton's book, and of the best modern commentaries thereon, with the conviction

* Acts xxi. 9. † Acts ii. 1–4. ‡ Acts x. 45, 46.

§ 1 Corinthians xii. 4–11 and 28–30. But read the whole of chapters xii. and xiv., in proof of the great importance which Paul attached to that matter.

‖ 1 Corinthians xiv. 18. ¶ 1 Corinthians xiv. 1, and xii. 31.

** 1 Corinthians xii. 4, 7.

†† Middleton: *Free Inquiry into the Miraculous Powers which are supposed to have subsisted in the Christian Church from the Earliest Ages.* London, 1749.

that the concurrent testimony of the Fathers for the alleged spiritual gifts of the early centuries are inadequate evidence of these, *as miracles*, but all-sufficient proof to establish (in a general way) their occurrence, if we regard them as natural phenomena. To that testimony I can but briefly advert.

Irenæus (a pupil of Papias and of Polycarp, both of whom sat under the teachings of St. John) was Bishop of Lyons A.D. 177. We have but fragments of his works; but he is quoted a hundred and fifty years later, by Eusebius (writing A.D. 325), who says, in his *Ecclesiastical History*, that Irenæus "shows that even down to his times, instances of divine and miraculous power were remaining." He quotes textually from Irenæus, thus: "Some most certainly and truly cast out devils. . . . Others have the knowledge of things to come, as also visions and prophetic communications; others heal the sick by imposition of hands, and restore them to health. . . . Even the dead have been raised and have continued with us many years. . . . It is impossible to tell the number of gifts which the church throughout the world has received from God." *

To the same effect testify Justin Martyr † and Theophilus, Bishop of Antioch, both contemporary with Irenæus; Tertullian, flourishing toward the close of the second century; Origen and Minutius Felix, in the beginning of the third century; and Cyprian, pupil of Tertullian, about the middle of the same. Arnobius and his disciple Lactantius, writing in the fourth century, may be added to the list. ‡

* EUSEBIUS: *Ecclesiastical History*, book v., chap. 7. He states that the extracts are taken from the second book of Irenæus' *Refutation and Overthrow of False Doctrine* ("Adversus Hæreses").

† "Justin Martyr, who is supposed to have written his first Apology within fifty years after the days of the Apostles, says: "There are prophetical gifts among us to this day, and both men and women endowed with extraordinary powers by the Spirit of God."—Quoted by Dr. MIDDLETON, in his *Free Inquiry*, p. 10.

‡ See Middleton's *Inquiry*, pp. 11–19; where are given extracts from the writings of each, with references to the original authorities

St. Augustine, whom Calvin and Luther copied so closely, and who was Bishop of Hippo A.D. 395, may be called the Spiritualist of his age. In his celebrated *City of God* he has a long chapter filled with minute details of numerous miracles wrought in his day. At the outset he says: "They ask me, 'Why do the miracles which, as you say, were performed in former times, not occur to-day?'" And his reply is: "At this very day a multitude of miracles do occur; the same God who caused the signs and wonders which we read of, works similar prodigies still by such persons as He sees fit to select." He attests, as having happened under his own eye, most of the miracles which he relates, and says that, did space permit, he could add many more of his own knowledge.*

Of another St. Augustin, the apostle of the English, who landed in Great Britain A.D. 596—who became Archbishop of Canterbury and is said to have baptized ten thousand persons in a single day—we read that he had the reputation of miraculous powers in the restoration of sight and even of life.

I might go on to speak of the St. Gregory of the third century (surnamed *Thaumaturgus* from his wonderful powers), of St. Martin, and many others deemed equally gifted; and I might add abundant proof that the faithful Roman Catholic continues to believe in the reality of Ecclesiastical miracles up to the present day. But it needs not further particulars.

Middleton discredits these patristic powers and gifts, concluding that "they were all contrived, or authorized at least, by the leading men of the Church for the sake of governing with more ease the unruly spirit of the populace." † For this scepticism his chief motive seems to be that "the belief and defence of these miracles . . . gives countenance to the modern impostures of the Catholic Church." ‡ He takes pains

Speaking of the gift of tongues, Middleton says: "If the testimony of Irenæus can be credited, many were endowed with it in his days, and heard to speak all kinds of languages in the Church."—*Inquiry*, p. 117.

* *City of God* ("De Civitate Dei") book xxii., chap. 8.

† *Inquiry*, p. 109. ‡ *Inquiry*, p. 176.

to remind us "how naturally the allowance of these powers to the earlier ages will engage us, if we are consistent with ourselves, to allow the same also to the later ages:" * evidently looking not so much to the amount of evidence that can be found for the alleged facts, as to the theological results of admitting their truth.

So also Bishop Douglas, who in his *Criterion*, assuming to show how "the true miracles recorded in the New Testament are distinguished from the spurious miracles of Pagans and Papists," † concludes that we are warranted in rejecting the latter—that is, the Ecclesiastical miracles—"as idle tales that never happened, and the inventions of bold and interested deceivers." ‡

Protestants generally, except those who evince Puseyite proclivities, § take the same ground. Locke, doubtless correctly, states the chief prompting motive: "I think it is evident that he who will build his faith or reasonings upon miracles delivered by Church historians, will find cause to go no farther than the Apostles' time, or else not to stop at Constantine's." ‖

But this Protestant scepticism leads far. The more sweeping among the arguments employed against "Papist miracles"

* Preface to *Inquiry*, p. xix.

† DOUGLAS (Bishop of Carlisle): *Criterion by which the true Miracles*, etc. (as above) 1754. See title-page. This is virtually a reply to Hume's celebrated argument.

‡ *Criterion*, p. 26.

§ As JOHN HENRY NEWMAN, in his *Essay on the Miracles recorded in the Ecclesiastic History of the Early Ages*, Oxford, 1843. This was written while he was still a Protestant. The gist of his argument is: "If our Lord is with his disciples 'alway, even unto the end of the world;' if he promised his Holy Spirit to be to them what he himself was when visibly present, and if miracles were one special token of his presence when on earth; . . . surely we have no cause to be surprised at hearing supernatural events reported in any age."—p. 78.

This may savor of Roman Catholicism; but it savors equally of logical inference.

‖ LOCKE: *Third Letter on Toleration*, c. x. p. 269.

by such writers as Middleton and Douglas will be admitted, by dispassionate readers, to be equally valid against the "signs and wonders" of the Gospels and the "spiritual gifts" of St. Paul.

I speak here of wholesale arguments. It is to be admitted, of course, that many of the narratives coming to us from patristic times are apocryphal, and others obviously obscured by superstition. Where there is genuine coin there also will counterfeits be found.* To St. Anthony, a stout believer in the Devil, Satan (according to his biographer) appeared, usually as "a spirit very tall with a great show," "who vanished at the Saviour's name; it burnt him, and he could not bear it;" with other similar tales.†

It is to be admitted, further, that some of these early ecclesiastical gifts, unlike those of Christ's day, were often committed, not to the principal champions of the Christian cause, but "to boys, to women, and above all to private and obscure laymen not only of an inferior but sometimes also of a bad character."‡ This only proves, however, that they were in a measure dependent, like magnetic power, on certain physical conditions. The modern examples among us confirm this. Nevertheless, the highest order of spiritual gifts appear to attach themselves only to those who are, in a correspondent degree, morally and spiritually elevated. Hence, doubtless, the unexampled preëminence of Christ's powers.

To arrive at any just conclusion on such a subject we must examine and test each narrative on its separate merits. It is a question to be determined, as the fall of aërolites has been, by facts, not by closet speculations. Even Middleton admits

* Matthew xxiv. 24; Mark xiii. 22—"they shall seduce the very elect."

† St. Athanasius: *Life of St. Anthony; passim.*

‡ Middleton: *Inquiry*, p. 25. But as to women, it is certain that spiritual gifts attached to both sexes in Christ's day. See Acts xxi. 9; ii. 17, 18; and xvi. 16, 17.

that "the testimony of facts may properly be called the testimony of God himself." *

It was after a careful examination of this testimony, as it is found among us, that the narratives which follow were written. There you will find my reasons for the conviction that God has not left us without present witness touching the great truths of our religion; that we, like the Apostles when they beheld the risen Christ, may see immortality brought to light; that the "Spirit of truth," to-day as of yore, is present "to guide us into all truth;" becoming the medium between spirits in the next world and men in this.

I believe that this spirit (divulging what reason tests and accepts but could not have originated) has been the origin of all religions. This was Bishop Butler's opinion, thus expressed: "There does not appear the least intimation in history or tradition, that religion was first reasoned out: but the whole of history or tradition makes for the other side, that it came into the world by revelation. Indeed the state of religion in the first ages of which we have any account seems to suppose and imply that this was the original of it among mankind." †

But if revelation be the origin of all human religions, it cannot be a phenomenon restricted to a single century, or showing itself up to a certain period of man's history, and then disappearing, to be seen no more. It must be a guiding influence for all time; a permanent element of civilization and of spiritual progress; as essential to vital religion among us who live now as it was to the Jews of eighteen hundred years ago.

To deny that this revelation comes from God is to deny that the Book of Nature has God for its author. But like everything else in this world, it comes to us *mediately* not *directly*, from Him: and so only must we receive it. Thus it aids Reason, not dethrones it: it appeals to Conscience, not coerces it. If everything that claims to be revelation were to be accepted as such, we should have to admit the whole Koran. Because

* *Inquiry*, p. 10.

† *Analogy of Religion* (Ed. of 1809), pp. 195, 196.

men, by God's universal law, are fallible, and because the holiest truths reach us only through fallible men, Reason and Conscience, God-given guides, must sit in judgment on all alleged revelations—humbly, reverently indeed, but fearlessly also; for perfect love casteth out fear.* A captious spirit is especially out of place in such connection; yet it is our right, and our bounden duty, to prove all things, spiritual pretensions included.

If the general view I have here offered you of this subject be correct, then it will not suffer denial that, as clergy, most of you have hitherto too much restricted the circle of your duties. Overlooking what Christ said about the Spirit of truth, which was to teach men, after his death, what he had left untaught, you have omitted to inquire whether there is a present revelation; and, if so, how far it is trustworthy—what are its character and claims. If, as Middleton said of spiritual gifts coming to light in earlier ages, these are still sometimes committed to children and to persons of indifferent character, this makes more imperative the duty to sift and to discriminate.

Many of your number are, probably, deterred from entering on this task by the idea that the (alleged) phase of modern revelation is anti-Christian in tendency. If, after a varied experience of sixteen years in different countries I am entitled to offer an opinion, it is, that if such spiritual communications be sought in an earnest, becoming spirit, the views presented will, in the vast majority of cases, be *in strict accordance with the teachings of Christ*, such as we may reasonably conceive these to have been from the testimony of his evangelical biographers. They touch upon many things, indeed, which he left untouched; but the spirit is absolutely identical. They breathe the very essence of his divine philosophy.

I speak here of those ideas as to which, in all trustworthy

* "There is no fear in love; perfect love casteth out fear."—1 John iv. 18.

spirit-messages, there can scarcely be said to be variance of sentiment. As to side-issues and non-essentials, it would seem that the same variety and uncertainty of opinion exist in the next world as in our own.

The following may be taken as the great, leading principles on which intelligent Spiritualists unite:

1. This is a world governed by a God of love and mercy, in which all things work together for good to those who reverently conform to His eternal laws.

2. In strictness there is no death. Life continues from the life which now is into that which is to come, even as it continues from one day to another; the sleep which goes by the name of death being but a brief transition-slumber from which, for the good, the awakening is immeasurably more glorious than in the dawn of earthly morning, the brightest that ever shone. In all cases in which life is well-spent, the change which men are wont to call Death is God's last and best gift to his creatures here.*

3. The earth-phase of life is an essential preparation for the life which is to come. Its appropriate duties and callings cannot be neglected without injury to human welfare and development, both in this world and in the next. Even its enjoyments, temperately accepted, are fit preludes to the happiness of a higher state.

4. The phase of life which follows the death-change is, in strictest sense, the supplement of that which precedes it. It has the same variety of avocations, duties, enjoyments, corresponding, in a measure, to those of earth, but far more elevated;

* Contrast, with this, the conception of early Protestantism, on the same subject. Luther regarded death as the expression of God's wrath. Said he: "It were a light and easy thing for a Christian to suffer and overcome death, if he knew not that it were God's wrath. . . . An heathen dieth securely away; he neither seeth nor feeleth that it is God's wrath, but meaneth it is the end of nature."—*Table Talk.*

Christian's weary bundle that dropped from his shoulders as the pilgrim neared the cross, was as nothing compared to the terrible burden, borne day by day through life, of such a belief as that.

and its denizens have the same variety of character and of intelligence; existing, too, as men do here, in a state of progress.* Released from bodily earth-clog, their periscope is wider, their perceptions more acute, their spiritual knowledge much greater, their judgment clearer, their progress more rapid, than ours. Vastly wiser and more dispassionate than we, they are still, however, fallible; and they are governed by the same general laws of being, modified only by corporeal disenthralment, to which they were subjected here.

5. Our state here determines our initial state there. The habitual promptings, the pervading impulses, the life-long yearnings, in a word the moving spirit, or what Swedenborg calls the "ruling loves" of man—these decide his condition on entering the next world: not the written articles of his creed, nor yet the incidental errors of his life.†

* This view of our next state of existence, expressed in general terms, occurs in the religious literature of modern times, antedating Swedenborg's writings. To select an eminent example, we find Bishop Butler (A.D. 1736) saying: "There appears so little connection between our bodily powers of sensation and our present powers of reflection that there is no reason to conclude that death, which destroys the former, does so much as suspend the exercise of the latter or interrupt our *continuing* to exist in the like state of reflection which we do now. . . . Death may not, perhaps, be so much as a discontinuance of the exercise of these powers, nor of the enjoyments and sufferings which it implies. So that our posthumous life, whatever there may be in it additional to our present, yet may not be entirely beginning anew, but going on. . . . For aught we know of ourselves, of our present life and death, death may immediately, in the natural course of things, put us into a higher and more enlarged state, of life, as our birth does; a state in which our capacities and sphere of perception and of action, may be much greater than at present."—*Analogy of Religion*, Part 1, chap. i. pp. 33, 34 (of London Ed. of 1809).

† "The sin that practice burns into the blood,
And not the one dark hour that brings remorse,
Will brand us, after, of whose fold we be."

TENNYSON: *Idyls of the King.* Vivien.

6. We do not, either by faith or works, *earn* Heaven, nor are we sentenced, on any Day of Wrath, to Hell. In the next world we simply gravitate to the position for which, by life on earth, we have fitted ourselves; and we occupy that position *because* we are fitted for it.*

7. There is no instantaneous change of character when we pass from the present phase of life. Our virtues, our vices; our intelligence, our ignorance; our aspirations, our grovellings; our habits, propensities, prejudices even—all pass over with us: modified, doubtless (but to what extent we know not), when the spiritual body † emerges, divested of its fleshly incumbrance; yet essentially the same as when the death-slumber came over us.

8. The sufferings there, natural sequents of evil-doing and evil-thinking here, are as various in character and in degree as the enjoyments; but they are mental, not bodily. There is no escape from them except only, as on earth, by the door of repentance. There as here, sorrow for sin committed and desire

* One finds the germ of these ideas in writings of twenty-three hundred years ago. The wisest of Grecian philosophers—representative of the Spiritualism of his age—propounded it. Socrates (Plato being interpreter) says: "Since the soul is immortal, it requires our anxious care, not only for this interval which we call life, but always." . . . The soul "can have no other refuge nor safety from evil except in remaining as good and wise as possible. For it descends to Orcus with nothing else but the results of its mode of discipline and education, which are said to be either of the greatest advantage or injury to the departed." . . . Then, as to the soul of the evil-doer, he adds: "It strays about involved in utter perplexity, until a certain period has elapsed, on the expiration of which it is of necessity carried into an abode suitable to it. But the soul that has led a pure and well-regulated life, having the gods for associates and guides, proceeds to inhabit a region adapted to those like itself."—*Phædo*, § 57, Stanford's translation.

Let us translate *Orcus*, "intermediate state;" and, for "the gods," let us read "advanced spirits;" and we have here, substantially, an important tenet of modern Spiritualism and of Swedenborgianism.

† 1 Corinthians xv. 44.

for an amended life are the indispensable conditions-precedent of advancement to a better state of being.

9. In the next world Love ranks higher than what we call Wisdom; being itself the highest wisdom. There deeds of benevolence far outweigh professions of faith. There simple goodness rates above intellectual power. There the humble are exalted. There the meek find their heritage. There the merciful obtain mercy. The better denizens of that world are charitable to frailty and compassionate to sin far beyond the dwellers in this: they forgive the erring brethren they have left behind them, even to seventy times seven. There, is no respect of persons. There, too, self-righteousness is rebuked and pride brought low.

10. A trustful,* childlike † spirit is the state of mind in which men are most receptive of beneficent spiritual impressions; and such a spirit is the best preparation for entrance into the next world.

11. There have always existed intermundane laws, according to which men may occasionally obtain, under certain conditions, revealings from those who have passed to the next world before them. A certain proportion of human beings are more sensitive to spiritual perceptions and influences than their fellows; ‡ and it is usually in the presence, or through the medi-

* Matthew xiii. 58; Mark vi. 5, 6.

† Matthew xviii. 3.

‡ Those who, in modern phrase, are termed *mediums* are probably to be included in the class called by Reichenbach *sensitives*; persons capable of distinguishing odic incandescence in a *perfectly* dark chamber. He thinks that nearly half the human race belong to that class, though the power of many among them is so weak as to be hardly appreciable. He found *all* natural somnambulists to be sensitives; also all who are subjects of artificial somnambulism.—*Der Sensitive Mensch*, Stuttgart, 1854; vol. ii. pp. 549, 555, etc. He found that the gift, or attribute, of sensitiveness was usually hereditary; inherited sometimes from the father, more frequently from the mother, occasionally from both.—pp. 522–526, where lists are given. Children sometimes possess it so strongly as to be alarmed by luminous appearances at night.—p. 121.

um, of one or more of these that ultramundane intercourse occurs.

12. When the conditions are favorable, and the sensitive through whom the manifestations come is highly gifted, these may supply important materials for thought and valuable rules of conduct. But spiritual phenomena sometimes do much more than this. In their highest phases they furnish proof, strong as that which Christ's disciples enjoyed—proof addressed to the reason and tangible to the senses—of the reality of another life, better and happier than this, and of which our earthly pilgrimage is but the novitiate. They bring immortality to light under a blaze of evidence which outshines, as the sun the stars, all traditional or historical testimonies. For surmise they give us conviction, and assured knowledge for wavering belief.*

13. The chief motives which induce spirits to communicate with men appear to be—a benevolent desire to convince us, past doubt or denial, that there *is* a world to come; now and then, the attraction of unpleasant memories such as murder or suicide; sometimes (in the worldly-minded) the earth-binding influence of cumber and trouble: but, far more frequently, the divine impulse of human affection, seeking the good of the loved ones it has left behind, and, at times, drawn down, perhaps, by their yearning cries. †

14. Under unfavorable or imperfect conditions, spiritual communications, how honestly reported soever, often prove vapid and valueless; and this chiefly happens when communi-

Reichenbach's researches in this field were continued, with astonishing industry, through ten years, and were, at an early day, highly appreciated by Liebig (Preface to *Sensitive Mensch*, p. xxiii.) and by Berzelius (*Jahresbericht*, 1846, p. 819). See, for Reichenbach's earlier observations, *Untersuchungen über die Dynamide*, Braunschweig, 1850.

* If we think of the "dark seasons" that overcome the most orthodox professors, and consider how many persons, pious and strictly nursed in faith, have been overtaken by Giant Despair and led captive to Doubting Castle, we shall not find fault with the adjective *wavering*, as employed above.* See preceding page 127 as to Luther's doubts.

† "Si forte fu l'affettuoso grido."—DANTE: *Inferno*, canto 5.

cations are too assiduously sought or continuously persisted in: brief volunteered messages being the most trustworthy. Imprudence, inexperience, supineness, or the idiosyncrasy of the recipient may occasionally result in arbitrary control by spirits of a low order; as men here sometimes yield to the infatuation exerted by evil associates. Or, again, there may be exerted by the inquirer, especially if dogmatic and self-willed, a dominating influence over the medium, so strong as to produce effects that might be readily mistaken for what has been called possession.* As a general rule, however, any person of common intelligence and ordinary will can, in either case, cast off such mischievous control: or, if the weak or incautious give way, one who may not improperly be called an exorcist—if possessed of strong magnetic will, moved by benevolence, and it may be aided by prayer, † can usually rid, or at least assist to rid, the sensitive from such abnormal influence. ‡

In all this there is no speculative divinity. And I admit the probability that if, through spiritual source, you were to inquire whether the theological guessings, touching the essence of the Godhead, of Arius or of Athanasius come the nearer to the truth, you might get no reply, or perhaps the answer: "We are uninformed as to that matter;" with the remark added, it may be: "We do not entertain such discussions here."

Are they not, in this, wiser than we? Up through the mists and horrors of the persecution-ridden Past, the common-sense convictions are reaching us that we have no conceivable means of settling any such controversy; and, again, that, if we

* Dr. John F. Gray, whose experience entitles his opinion to great consideration, and others, believe that what some call demoniac possession, may be explained, in very many if not in all instances, by purely human agency; for example, by mesmerism.

† Mark ix. 29; Matthew xvii. 21.

‡ The Rev. James Freeman Clarke has become convinced as to the reality of possession.—*Steps of Belief*, Boston, 1870, pp. 132, 133.

had, its settlement would not influence, by a hairbreadth, the morals or the welfare of man.

Further than this, I have never, out of thousands of communications, received one that denounced any sincere religious opinion, whether Catholic or Protestant, Mahommedan or Hindoo. It is to be conceded, indeed, that, in these modern revelations, certain orthodox deductions from a portion of the epistles, entertained by Calvin and Luther, find no countenance. But, in the preceding pages, I have taken some pains to set forth the grounds for my belief, that until these deductions are abandoned, there will be no religious progress; and that, so long as they are proclaimed from your pulpits, the Church over which you preside will stand still or lose ground.

I am sorry to believe that the failure of modern Spiritualism to indorse the doctrines of vicarious atonement * and original depravity, will cause many of your number, in advance of evidence, to condemn its influence, and reject its claims to be heard. Yet if a Wise Man of old speak truth, "He that answereth a matter before he heareth it, it is folly and shame unto him." †

* Throughout this address I have taken the tenet of the atonement in its doctrinal sense, as the Reformers held it; deeming that to be the honest way of putting it. There *is* a sense in which such a dogma is equally true and important. Christ came, as he himself said, "a light into the world," that whoso accepted his teachings "should not abide in darkness" (John xiii. 46, 47). In inculcation of these teachings, replete with spiritual light, he spent his life; and in attestation of them he sacrificed it. If we act out the spirit of his teachings in daily walk, we reconcile our ways with the eternal laws of our being, and may be said to be *at one* with the Great Author of these laws. In this sense we may declare that Christ died for humankind, and that through his interposed agency—his mediation—our race is redeemed from error, and from the sufferings error entails here and hereafter. But this is not what Luther meant when, in his *Commentary on Galatians*, he spoke of one of the Persons of the Godhead accursed for our sake; nor is it what the orthodox Protestantism of our day means, when it preaches vicarious atonement.

† Proverbs xviii. 13.

Others may be staggered at the outset, by the nature of its claims. The "gift of tongues," perhaps, may seem to them an incredible absurdity. Yet if it is not incredible nor absurd in the second chapter of Acts, or the fourteenth chapter of first Corinthians, at what time did it change its character?

Baden Powell deemed it an actual phenomenon, occurring under law at the present day.*

So, again, of prophecy. It may seem to us beyond belief that what is yet to be should ever be disclosed to fallible creatures. Yet in all ages, back to the days of Abraham and Melchizedek, certain men have been honored and trusted as possessors of prophetic power. Is it incredible that the greatest of all earthly Teachers should have been heralded, more or less distinctly, by the ancient prophets, as the Anointed of God, who was to call mankind from darkness to light? Bunsen admits this. †

* The sermons of the Rev. Edward Irving, a clergyman of the Church of Scotland, created, about the year 1825, an unprecedented excitement in London. In 1830 appeared, in his Church, the Apostolic gift of unknown tongues. Baden Powell, alluding to this, says:

"*At the time* the matter was closely scrutinized and inquired into; and many perfectly unprejudiced and even sceptical persons themselves witnessed the effects and were fully convinced—as indeed were most candid inquirers at the time—that after reasonable or possible allowance for the influence of delusion or imposture, beyond all question *certain extraordinary manifestations did occur*. . . . Yet no sober-minded person did for a moment believe that they were *miraculous*, . . . but that they were in some way to be ascribed to natural causes, as yet, perhaps, little understood."—BADEN POWELL: *Recent Inquiries in Theology*, p. 122. The italics are in the original.

† In his *Gott in Geschichte.* He there says that the power of sight, in the old Hebrew prophets, reaching beyond ordinary prediction, rose to the character of a true world-survey (sich zur wahren Weltanschauung erhoben hat); and he adds: "They had the power of prophecy in common with the Pythoness, . . . and with many clairvoyants of our own century."—pp. 149 and 151.

Bunsen regarded this power as a natural gift, consistent with fallibility. Yet his commentator in *Essays and Reviews* (Dr. Williams), seems to regret the admission of prophecy as an actual phenomenon. "One would wish," he says, "Bunsen might have intended only the power of

Orthodoxy regards Baden Powell and Baron Bunsen as ultra-sceptical authorities. Does it not occur to you that modern spiritual phenomena which men so able and so little disposed to superstition admit as realities, may be worth looking into?

I remind you, in conclusion, that, aside from phenomenal evidence of this character, you have no *certain* proof, such as Thomas had, of the existence of another world. It is not sceptics alone who have alleged this and bewailed it—like Shelley:

> "Who telleth a tale of unspeaking death?
> Who lifteth the veil of what is to come?
> Who painteth the shadows that are beneath
> The wide-winding caves of the peopled tomb?"

The most eminent divines have admitted a lack of certainty as to a life to come, in the absence of testimony from the senses. Examples abound, but I have space here for two only. Butler, in his *Analogy of Religion*, confesses: "I do not mean to affirm that there is the same *degree* of conviction that our living powers will continue after death as that our substances will." *

And Archbishop Tillotson, in an argument against the *real presence*, says: "Infidelity were hardly possible to men, if all men had the same evidence for the Christian Religion that they have against transubstantiation; that is, the clear and irresistible evidence of sense." †

Hundreds of thousands feel assured to-day that they *have* had this "clear and irresistible evidence" for immortality. Think of such a living conviction! Consider how it stands out above all that wealth, fame, and every earthly good-fortune can

seeing the ideal in the actual, or of tracing the Divine Government in the movements of men."—*Recent Inquiries in Theology*, p. 70. Why this regret? I think Bunsen's the correct view.

* *Analogy of Religion*, p. 17. Italics in original.

† *Sermons*, 8th Ed. London, 1720, Sermon xxvi.

bestow—the blessing of blessings, which the world can neither give nor take away!

I think if we only realized in what deep earnest millions on millions have longed, with a longing past expression, for some sure token of another life, we should better conceive the sacred duty of investigation. With transcendant interests at stake, can we neglect such a duty without risk that, like the unbelievers in Gamaliel's day, we may haply be found fighting against God?

Thus I have sought to show—

That Protestantism has steadily lost ground for three centuries past, and is losing it still.

That this retrogression seems to be caused by its adherence to certain so-called orthodox dogmas which the intelligence of the world has outgrown; perceiving them to be contrary to God's eternal laws, promotive of intolerance, injurious to morality, and arrestive of religious progress.

That Christianity, divested of alien scholasticisms which its Author never taught, is a progressive science, destined to become the religion of Civilization.

That if we admit miracles, we must deny the uniform reign of law and thus come into direct conflict with modern science: but if we recognize the reign of law and admit that the spiritual powers and gifts of the first century existed under law, then, as law is continuous as well as uniform, spiritual phenomena of a similar character ought to be found still occurring.

That, in point of fact, the teachings of Christ have been supplemented, as he promised they should be, by revealings bringing truths and comfort from that higher sphere of being toward which we are all fast hasting: and that this happens not miraculously, but in accordance with intermundane laws which it behooves us to study.

And, finally, that such modern revealings, bringing immortality to light, are essential to arrest the growing scepticism of the present day.

If what has been said should induce the earnest thinkers of your profession to study intermundane laws, the foregoing pages will not have been written in vain. But as laws dimly discerned can only be explored in the phenomena they govern, I have sought, in the chapters which follow, to lighten, for you and for others, the labor of such study, by bringing together, in narrative form, some of the more salient and suggestive of the phenomena in question; attested, I venture to affirm, by evidence as strong as that which is daily admitted, in our courts of justice, to decide the life or death of men.

ROBERT DALE OWEN.

NEW HARMONY, INDIANA,
October 1, 1871.

THE DEBATABLE LAND.

BOOK I.

TOUCHING COMMUNICATION OF RELIGIOUS KNOWLEDGE TO MAN.

CHAPTER I.

OF HUMAN INFALLIBILITY.

"The mortalest enemy unto knowledge, and that which hath done the greatest execution upon Truth, hath been a peremptory adhesion unto authority."—Sir Thomas Browne: *Vulgar Errors.*

"Conscience is the supreme interpreter, whom it may be a duty to enlighten, but whom it can never be a duty to disobey."—Temple: *now Bishop of Exeter.*

I propose to investigate a class of phenomena that have been regarded, by turns, as miracles, feats of magic, arts of necromancy; signs and wonders, mighty works, spiritual gifts; occult forces, mysterious agencies, spiritual manifestations.

Not as a topic of curious research; not as a theme of speculative inquiry. I have selected this disparaged subject because it brings one face to face with the great questions of the world.

Of late years many earnest and thoughtful minds have been led to recognize, in certain strange incidents of the above class, when rationally interpreted, beneficent agencies of eminent power and vast practical importance: influences urgently needed, in this age of the world, to quicken waning faith in a life to come, and to afford, in support of public and private morals, helps more cogent than those which conventional creeds commonly supply.

But the value of these phenomena, as religious and reformatory agencies, rests, at the outset, on their claim to be spiritual; and that again intimately connects itself with the solution of a problem than which no more important one can engage the attention of man: Do the denizens of the next world * ever intervene in the concerns of this? Have they the power, and do they occasionally exert it, to affect, for good or evil, the lives and the fortunes of human kind? In fine, has God vouchsafed, or denied, to us here upon earth, intercourse on certain conditions with the spiritual world?

An overwhelming majority among all sects of Christians holds that spiritual intervention has been; while the most numerous of these sects teaches that it still is, albeit restricted within the limits of a single church. A small minority, but one that is rapidly increasing, believes that intermundane laws have always existed, and now exist, under which occasional intercourse between the two worlds is possible; and that, in point of fact, such intercourse occurs at this day, unrestricted to favored church or sect, in various phases throughout the world.

Let us consider how this last belief adapts itself to the wants of the age, what relation it bears to the intellectual and religious tendencies of the times, and what position it is entitled to hold among the creeds of Christendom.

Wherever religion has existed, the human mind has been wont

* I here refrain from touching on the analogical evidences for a future state, having discussed that matter elsewhere; (*Footfalls on the Boundary of Another World*, Book IV. Chap. I., pp. 476–503.) The subject has been ably treated by Isaac Taylor, in his *Physical Theory of Another Life:* London, 1839; pp. 64–69.

to occupy itself with the inquiry how far, and in what mode, God has imparted spiritual knowledge to men: a sceptical portion of society (specially active all over Europe in the eighteenth century) doubting or denying that He has ever imparted it.

The current opinion of the past has been that He has imparted it directly; and if directly, then infallibly, seeing that we cannot rationally impute error to God. Thus all spiritual communication or influence has been, almost by the common consent of Christendom, interpreted as actual speech of the Deity, or Divine intromission immediately emanating from one of the Persons of the Godhead. Hence knowledge spiritually communicated has been regarded as the equivalent of knowledge free from all error. Hence, also, derives the claim of all dominant religions, Hindoo, Mahometan, Roman Catholic, even Protestant, to be the organs of infallible truth and the depositories of spiritual authority, by right divine; authority which it is impious to question and incurring eternal punishment to disobey.* Even individuals believing themselves spiritually favored have given in to this idea. "It came to me from the Lord," was a common expression of Swedenborg.

But the tendency of the civilized mind is unmistakably opposed to the idea of direct divine interposition. We witness a thousand beneficent agencies around us; and, unless we are atheists, we ascribe these to God. Yet we see that every one of them is mediate. There has been no direct gift. To us of modern times there have been granted, under the divine economy, facilities for acquiring and perpetuating knowledge unimagined by our remote ancestors. But God did not invent for us the telescope to detect planets and suns which these ancestors had never seen, nor the microscope to penetrate the minute mysteries of an invisible world. He did not reveal to men

* Exceptions are to be found throughout the doctrinal history of the Dark Ages. The votaries of Black Magic believed that spiritual knowledge came to them, not from the Lord, but, in illicit form, from the Devil, or other Mephistophelian agency.

sensible signs to represent human thoughts, the pen to perpetuate these thoughts from generation to generation, the printing-press to enlighten the intellectual world. He is the author of all these blessings, but indirectly only; they come to us from Him, but they come to us through our fellow-creatures.

All analogy, then, fortifies the idea not only that God's agency in man's favor is ever mediate, but also that His aid is given on certain conditions. And these conditions involve, on our part, thought, research, reflection, industry, enterprise. There is a great truth in a homely proverb: "God helps those who help themselves." We can perceive His design that we should search out what is to benefit us; that we should earn what we receive. Among God's eternal laws one of the chief is the law of progress; but throughout the entire physical world we see that it is by man's head and hands this progress is worked out, not by miraculous intervention.

Some of the soundest intellects of former centuries, from the seen inferring the unseen, have reached, or approached, the conclusion that every exercise of God's power, alike in the physical and in the spiritual realm, is effected through the instrumentality of means: in other words, mediately under law.* And surely there suggest themselves, in connection with man's nature and with his position in a world where evil exists, and with his career in that world, the strongest reasons in favor of this intermediate action. Though we can but dimly discern those things which go to make us the beings we are, yet we

* Bacon, whose mind ranged over all subjects, sublunary and spiritual, takes this ground: "God worketh nothing in nature but by second causes; and if they would have it otherwise believed, it is mere imposture."—*Advancement of Learning.*

And we find a distinguished divine of the last century asserting the credibility of such a view. "The visible government which God exercises over the world is by the instrumentality and mediation of others. And how far His invisible government be or be not so, it is impossible to determine at all by reason. The supposition that part of it is so, appears, to say the least, as credible as the contrary."—BUTLER: *Analogy of Religion*, Part II. Chap. V.

perceive that man takes delight in progress, and that his moral and intellectual wants find full satisfaction only in a progressive state. We perceive, also, that if there is to be progress, there must be the worse and the better—the worse in the past, the better in the future; in other words there must, as a general rule, be comparative evil behind us, and comparative good to come. Thus only do we obtain a glimpse toward a rational theory of evil, and of the reasons which may underlie its permission. For, though we may desire unmixed good in worldly affairs and unmixed truth in spiritual revealings, both are unreasonable wishes. Witness our consciousness that our best happiness consists in sustained efforts, from darkness to approach the light; from evil gradually to attain unto good; and from error to climb the pleasant paths of truth, as these open to more and more excellent knowledge. Finality is stagnation; a paradise for the sluggard only.

We perceive, further, that all human powers dwindle if they are not fitly used, and that judgment itself, if not habitually called into exercise, is liable to deterioration and decay.*

But to beings thus constituted and existing in such a world, an infallible revelation, direct from its Creator, would be a gift utterly unsuited to their nature, at variance with everything we see around us, and involving a conception that is disproved, as far as the unseen can be disproved, by all the lessons of analogy. It would be a finality where all else is

* "A world in which men should be exonerated from the duty, or forbidden the right, to bring the judgment into play—to sift, by the strict dictates of conscience, good from evil, the right from the wrong, would be a world disgraced and degraded. If such a principle were fully carried out, it would at last become a world lacking not only the exercise of reason, but reason itself. Use, to an extent which it is difficult to determine, is essential to continued existence. That which ceases to fulfil its purpose finally ceases to be. The eyes of fishes found far in the interior of the Mammoth Cave of Kentucky, shut out forever from the light of day, are rudimental only."—*Footfalls on the Boundary of Another World*, p. 41.

profluent; therefore, an anomaly in a progressive world: avowedly so, indeed, since its friends admit, as to their religion, that as there has been no scientific formation, so there can be no progressive development.* It would be an element alien and discordant in a world to the inhabitants of which God has given reason to prove all things, and conscience to hold fast that which is good. It would tend to narrow, in a lamentable manner, the field of action in which man's intellectual faculties and moral sentiments can have play. As regards the highest of avocations—the study of spiritual science—its inexorable effect would be to deaden Reason and to silence Conscience.

Beyond all this, there is a cogent influence which goes to determine the tide of public opinion that is setting in against the old doctrine of infallibility. The line of human progress is from the less to the more of liberty. Despotisms give way to limited monarchies; limited monarchies tend to republicanism. And more especially is the sentiment of the present day adverse to mental absolutism and spiritual coercion. But infallibility entails and justifies tyranny, alike of mind and body.

It justifies it logically, even mercifully. If a man be the possessor of infallible religious truth, to miss which is to sink into Hell, and to accept which is to attain Heaven, such a man ought to be—he is, by right divine—a despot. If he loves his kind and can control them, it will appear to him an imperative duty, by argument if he can, by force even to death if he must, to put down all opposing doctrines. When, in Italy, during the fifteenth century, the plague thrice decimated the population, it was a popular belief that this frightful pestilence was caused by wholesale poisoners (*avvellenatori*) whose diabolical arts caused the death of hundred-thousands. If this idle suspicion had been just, who would have raised his voice against the punishment of such criminals? Would not Italy and the

* See Prefatory Address to the Protestant Clergy, Motto to section 9, and foot-note to motto.

world have been gainers by their deaths? But what was the offence committed against the perishing body, compared to his who poisons the deathless soul?

If a Church conscientiously believes that she holds and teaches the one infallible religion, must she not, as to all heretics, necessarily take this view? In the eyes of devout Romanists, were not the Albigenses and the Vaudois just such poisoners? When the massacres which followed the night of St. Bartholomew had done their work, were there not tens of thousands of spiritual poisoners less to be found throughout France?

The horrors of the Inquisition are chargeable, not to the Inquisitors (except such as were hypocrites), but to the doctrine underlying their creed, which vindicates and sanctifies the mental despotism they have exercised.

But a world that is waxing, age by age, more liberty-loving and more humane—a world that is learning obedience to Christ's injunction that we judge not lest we in turn be judged—a world that, with all its faults, is gradually becoming more gentle and charitable and kindly—in other words, more Christian—such a world instinctively rejects a doctrine that logically leads to wholesale murders for honest opinion's sake. It is rapidly reaching the conclusion that a God of Goodness and Mercy never has granted, and never will grant to any man, or to any Church, a gift of infallibility which would entitle its possessor to punish and exterminate other men and other Churches, because they did what conscience enjoined, and believed what their reason taught them.

But the spirit of the age, we shall be told, effectually protects us from such outrages on religious freedom. No doubt. The civilized world of to-day will not suffer the believers in infallibility to be consistent in carrying out their doctrine. What then? In proof that the world has outgrown that doctrine we find the strongest of all evidence, namely this: that, because of the progress of humane ideas, its appropriate exercise has become insufferable.

In view of considerations so numerous and so cogent, one

might be led to expect the immediate downfall of a doctrine fraught with barbarity. Its ultimate downfall is certain; yet its hold is still strong on the human mind, and there are grave difficulties in the way of its abolition. Men are wisely loath to pull down an old house, how dilapidated soever, until they see their way to some better shelter wherewith to replace it.

During the latter portion of the last century, millions, deserting the venerable mansion of Catholic infallibility, tried the shelter of Materialism. It proved blank and cheerless, and, after a brief sojourn, a large portion of these millions, as we have seen,* returned to the ancient stronghold they had left. They preferred to be submissive Catholics, and believers in a life to come, rather than to enjoy religious liberty shrouded with doubts of a future existence. And they had found, outside of their Church's teachings, no certainties touching the realities of another world—neither in Rationalism nor in Protestantism.

Not in Rationalism; for Rationalism not only rejected all revelation of a spiritual character coming to us directly from God, but denied also, or had never seriously considered, spiritual revealings of a mediate character, coming to us from those whom we shall recognize as our fellow-creatures by and by, when death shall have ushered us among them.

And not in Protestantism; because, in Catholic eyes, her chain of evidence touching the infallible appears manifestly composed in part of fallible links. Its first links, indeed, she borrowed from Romanism, agreeing with her in this, that the New Testament in the original tongues contained infallible narratives and teachings, infallibly recorded. But by her own showing, this infallible revelation, long existing in detached portions, was committed, for unenlightened centuries, to the custody of fallible men; was translated by fallible men, at first into Latin, after a thousand years more, into modern tongues; was gradually separated by fallible men from apocryphal matter; was finally adopted, more than three hundred and fifty

* See Prefatory Address, section 2.

years after the crucifixion, by a Catholic Œcumenical Council, and a Catholic pope,* who announced the books that should be included in the canon; authenticating the whole as the Word of God;† and, finally, has been interpreted, and is interpreted

* Lecky, a writer whose researches touching this matter seem to have been thorough, speaking of "the Fathers of the fourth century," says: "It is quite certain that they were not, in the ordinary sense of the word, Protestants. It is quite certain that there existed among them practices, forms of devotion, and doctrinal tendencies, which may not have been actually Roman Catholic, but which at least hang upon the extreme verge of Catholicism, and inevitably gravitated to it."—*Rationalism in Europe*, vol. i., p. 169.

† A few memoranda may here be acceptable to the reader.

As to the translations of Scripture. To the zeal and learning of Jerome (Hieronymus), the best scholar not only of his age, but of many succeeding centuries, the Christian world owes the first reliable Vulgate of the New Testament. His translation, as St. Augustine called it, or revision (emendatio) according to his own more modest expression, was made at the instance of Pope Damasus, from A.D. 382 to 385. Up to that time there had been innumerable translations, some partial, some assuming to be complete—"almost as many forms of text as copies" Jerome himself says:—("tot sunt exemplaria quot codices."—*Praef. in Evv.*) Jerome's version, though many exclaimed against it as a dangerous and profane innovation, gradually came into favor; was, substantially, for a thousand years, the Bible in common use; was declared by the Council of Trent (1546) to be the authentic edition;—"statuit et declarat ut hœc ipsa vetus et vulgata editio . . . pro authentica habeatur;") and is the real parent of all the vernacular versions of Western Europe, especially the English, Wycliffe's translation being an almost literal rendering of it. It guided the German edition by Luther, and from him the influence of the Latin passed to our Authorized Version.

As to the Scriptural canon, the New Testament authors, believers in the speedy end of the world, had evidently no idea that their writings would ever be collected in a volume. An orthodox Protestant authority says: "The writings of the New Testament themselves contain little more than faint, perhaps unconscious intimations of the position which they were destined to occupy." . . . "The canon grew silently under the guidance of an inward instinct, rather than by the force of external authority."—*Smith's Dict. of Bible*, Article "*Canon of Script*

to-day, by fallible churches who differ grievously in their several constructions of its meanings. Nor have Protestant

ure." Books, which finally came to be deemed apocryphal or spurious, held doubtful places for a time. The epistles of Barnabas and Clement, the Shepherd of Hermas, the Apocalypse of Peter, are all more or less quoted or referred to by the Fathers. The epistle to the Laodiceans was frequently interpolated in Jerome's Vulgate. Some books that are now lost had currency in early apostolic days, as the Gospel according to the Hebrews, that according to the Egyptians, and (in the Marcion Canon) the "Gospel of Christ." Some now found in our own canon, as the Apocalypse, the second and third epistles of John, the epistles of James and Jude, but especially the second epistle of Peter, were more or less questioned, and were omitted by various councils. Gradually the canon approached its present form. The Council of Hippo (A.D. 393) accepted nearly all; and, twelve years after Jerome's Latin version had appeared, the Council of Carthage (A.D. 397) admitting Hebrews, completed the Testament as we now have it. A decree of Pope Innocent I., confirming their selection, finally decided the canon of the Latin Church.

In all this there seems to have been very good judgment exercised. Jerome was probably the most trustworthy translator of the Patristic age. And as to the canon, the gold appears to have been substantially separated from the alloy. One finds nothing of value in the extracts remaining of the lost books; and one cannot read the other rejected Scriptures without a conviction that they were utterly unworthy of admission. The noble purity of the Parthenon is not more impressive when compared with some whimsical abortion of the Cinque-cento, than are the grand simplicity and intrinsic power that speak from the synoptical gospels, when set side by side with the childish crudities that disfigure, for example, the Arabic story called "The Infancy," or the bungling narrative enriched with a familiar talk between Satan and Hades, that has been saddled on poor Nicodemus. It is apparent that internal evidence chiefly governed. Thus we may ascribe to the Council of Carthage sound discretion in her selection.

But judgment in translating, discretion in selection, is one thing, and infallibility altogether another. The Romish Church affirms that the translator was selected, and the final canon determined, each by the action of an infallible Pope; one can understand that: but how orthodox Protestantism can seriously assert that her chain of infallible testimony touching our present Bible as the unalloyed Word of God, is unbroken

churches retained the promised spiritual gifts—the miraculous stamp of the Infallible.

This being the Catholic view, can we wonder that wanderers from the Roman fold, when they found nothing but dim uncertainty in a heretic world, returned repentant to St. Peter's arms?

This will occur again and again; a numerous class will go on believing in the Infallible; the Catholic Church, surviving reverse after reverse, may continue to grow and prosper for generations still, as during this very century she has grown and prospered, her professors outnumbering more than three to one the members of all other Christian sects,* unless

from Christ's day until ours, must remain a mystery to all who are guided by sound principles of evidence.

To us, readers of the Authorized Version, there are superadded difficulties that complicate the situation. King James, as director of that translation, and whom the translators address as "that august person, enriched with singular and extraordinary graces," that had appeared "like the sun in his strength," sent to each translator fifteen instructions, including a command that "the old ecclesiastical words should be kept." Was the pedant-king infallible? Yet his instructions undoubtedly determined the translation of many all-important words, *Hades* and *dunamis* included. Whenever a modern revision is conscientiously executed, the first of these words will not be rendered *hell*, nor the second *miracle*.

* The successes and reverses of Protestantism as against Catholicism, and the ascendancy still maintained by the latter, have been set forth at length in the Prefatory Address prefixed to this volume, section 2, and to which, if he has not read it, I beg to refer the reader.

And see note, there given, in proof that, in Europe, the Catholic Church (including the Greek and Eastern) numbers nearly *two hundred and twelve million* votaries (211,899,500); while the Protestants amount to but a trifle over sixty-eight millions (68,028,000): in other words, that *less than one-fourth of the Christians in Europe are Protestants;* also that the Catholic Church agrees, in essential doctrine, with the Greek and other Eastern Churches, except on one point: the latter attributing to Œcumenical Councils the infallibility which by the former is ascribed to the Pope—both believing, therefore, in the existence, at the present day, of human infallibility.

there be found outside of infallibility conclusive evidence touching a world to come. Men can cheerfully dispense with the dogmatic mysteries which have formed part of all infallible creeds; they can be thoroughly happy and contented, though the inscrutable enigma of the Divine Hypostasis remain forever unsolved; but they cannot be happy, they cannot be contented, in ignorance of the Great Future; they cannot dispense with faith in immortality.

So universal, so deep-rooted in man's heart is this sentiment, that, if the sole alternative be between Roman Catholicism and Materialism, Catholicism will be the popular choice. In other words, the masses will resist the tendency of the age to discard the doctrine of a direct revelation from God, unless it can be shown that spiritual knowledge, including proof of immortality, can come to man, like physical knowledge, mediately, in virtue of natural law.

I think the reader who may have followed me to this point will begin to perceive why I attach so much importance to the phenomena of modern Spiritualism. If these prove genuine, then we can obtain, outside of Infallibility, conclusive evidence of another world. If these are realities, then we have found proof that spiritual knowledge may be received, like earthly knowledge, intermediately; namely, through beings who were once like ourselves.

And thus the harmony of the Divine Government will be illustrated in one of its most important relations to man. For it will appear that, without violation or suspension of the great law of mediate agency, God brings immortality to light; affording man perennial aid in educing conceptions of the next world, as He has guided him, from discovery to discovery, in the arts and sciences of this.

CHAPTER II.

OF MEDIATE SPIRITUAL REVEALINGS.

"Religious dogmatism is losing all hold of the most living and earnest intelligence everywhere. . . . A second Calvin in theology is impossible. Men thirst not less for spiritual truth, but they no longer believe in the capacity of system to embrace and contain that truth, as in a reservoir, for successive generations. They must seek for it themselves afresh in the pages of Scripture and the ever-dawning light of spiritual life, or they will simply neglect and put it past as an old story."—TULLOCH.*

"It needs no diviner to tell us that this century will not pass without a great breaking up of the dogmatic structures that have held ever since the Reformation or the succeeding age."—SHAIRP. †

"We are arrived visibly at one of those recurring times when the accounts are called in for audit; when the title-deeds are to be looked through, and established opinions again tested. It is a process which has been repeated more than once in the world's history; the last occasion and greatest being the Reformation of the sixteenth century: and the experience of that matter might have satisfied the most timid that truth has nothing to fear, and that religion emerges out of such trials stronger and brighter than before."—FROUDE: *Criticism and the Gospel History.*

"Daughter of Faith, awake, arise! illume
The dread Unknown, the chaos of the tomb!"—CAMPBELL.

IF the views set forth in the preceding chapter be just, the present aspect of religion throughout Christendom may be thus sketched.

Infallibility is still the ruling element, counting its nominal votaries by hundreds of millions.

* *Leaders of the Reformation*, London, 1869, p. 169.

† *Culture and Religion*, by J. C. SHAIRP, Principal of the United College of St. Andrews (reprinted from the Edinburgh Edition, New York, 1871); p. 128. A noteworthy book.

There is a manifest tendency, however, in the present age, to discredit the supernatural,* including, under that term, not only miracles and infallible revelation, but all ultramundane agencies of a spiritual character: and this sceptical element has rudely shaken both the plenary infallibility of Catholicism and the limited infallibility of Protestantism.

But the inroads of this rationalistic tendency are constantly repelled by a popular conviction, that to abandon infallibility is to surrender also all assurance of another and a better world. Thus, one of the most powerful of human instincts attracts and attaches millions to the infallible school.

So long as these were the only two elements engaged, there was, substantially, but a single alternative offered to the seeker after religious truth—the choice between infallibility (in one or other of its phases), on the one hand, and some one among the various shades of Unbelief, on the other.

But within the last quarter of a century there has emerged to public view in distinct form, from that phenomenal field where Science has won all her victories, a third element; namely the belief in the epiphanies † of Spiritualism; in other words, in intermediate spiritual revealings, with no claim to infallibility save this, that they supply positive proof of a life to come.

It is evident that if there be such proof to be found, outside of direct infallible revelation, and if that proof is derived from actual phenomena, then the belief in such phenomena, as it gradually spreads, will take a prominent place among religious

* This tendency is fully and ably illustrated in two modern works by LECKY: *Rationalism in Europe* (New York Ed. 1866); and *European Morals* (New York Ed. 1870).

† This is one of those ecclesiastical terms which, through restricted usage, come to lose, for the careless reader, their original signification. Usually employed to designate the Church festival commemorating the Magian journey to Bethlehem, one almost forgets that the word, derived from *epiphaneia*, means simply an appearance or phenomenon, and is strictly appropriate in designating spiritual manifestations.

creeds. To deny that this belief is entitled to such a place is virtually to assert that it matters little whether man obtains positive assurance of a life beyond the grave or not.

Such a belief has the elements of a universal creed; or rather it is fitted to inspire into all creeds an active principle—a living spirit; while, at the same time, it effectually defeats the claim which any one Church may set up to sole religious authority in virtue of her possession of spiritual powers and gifts which, she asserts, are to be found nowhere save within her divinely-favored precincts.

Infallibility cannot object to such a belief that it neglects the one thing needful, or fails to bring immortality to light; for no religion professed by man can supply, as spiritual researches do, proofs patent to the senses, and potent to convert mere hope of another world into certainty of its existence.

Rationalism cannot object to it that it contravenes the doctrine of law; for its phenomena occur strictly under law: nor yet that it assumes the existence, in spiritual matters, of that direct agency of God which the naturalist finds nowhere in physical affairs; for its revealings come to man mediately only: nor yet that it is dogmatic, or exclusive, or intolerant, as Infallibility is; for its adherents adduce experimental evidence, open to all men and gleaned after the inductive method, for the faith that is in them: nor, in fine, that it ignores progress, as Infallibility does; seeing that it is ever freshly vivified and cheered by the ceaseless illumings of spiritual life.

Still less can the Bible student object that he finds no Scriptural warrant for such a belief. If there be one distinct promise made by Jesus to his followers, it is, that spiritual signs should follow those who believed in his words;* that they should do the works that he did, and greater works also;† that his apostles could not bear the whole truth, so that he had to leave many things unsaid; and that, after his death, that spirit which pervaded his life—the spirit of truth—should still bring

* Mark xvi. 17, 18; and other texts. † John xiv. 12.

comfort, communicating with them, even to the end of the world; * mediately teaching them what he had left untaught. † So also Paul. Can injunction be more positive than his to seek after spiritual gifts? ‡

These are strong claims. Against them will, of course, be set up the popular objection to all things novel. Why now, at this age of the world? Why not sooner, long ago, centuries since? In reply one might suggest that the Atlantic has always been there, though thousands of years elapsed ere a Columbus adventured its passage. One might ask when the diurnal motion of the earth, when the circulation of the blood, when the fall of aërolites, was first accepted as truth by science. But I rest not the case in generalities like these. I believe that Spiritualism, in its present phase, could not have been the growth of an age much earlier than our own.

—In its present phase. In distorted form it has appeared, from time to time in past ages, to the terror and the unutterable suffering of the world. The holiest things are the most deadly when they are profaned.

"Ye cannot bear them now." In these words we may find the clue to the late appearance of modern Spiritualism. Certain debasing superstitions had to disappear before the world was worthy of it. The letter, which killeth, had itself to die, and the spirit which giveth life had to replace it, before the wiser and the better portion of those who have gone before us could find such sympathy as would attract them to earth, and meet such reception here as would justify their efforts to enlighten us.

Take a notable example of the letter which killeth: the old belief in the personal existence of a Great Spirit of Evil,

* Matthew xxviii. 20.

† John xvi. 12, 13. If any one objects to the words used above—"*mediately* teaching them"—let him refer to the text, where he will find the remarkable expression: "he shall not speak of himself, but whatsoever he shall hear, that shall he speak."—v. 13.

‡ 1 Corinthians xii. 31, and xiv. 1, 2.

roaming the world in search of whom he might devour; the earliest and crudest of the various human fantasies that have been suggested by the perception of evil in the world, coupled with a desire to explain the cause of its existence. In the exordium to that sublimest among ancient Oriental fragments of philosophy, the Book of Job, occurs a brief narrative which modern critics begin to treat as mere allegory. Not so the theological mind of past times. To our ancestors, if they accepted the Bible at all, it was literal truth. They believed that Satan, just returned from going to and fro on the earth, presented himself one day, among the Sons of God, to the Lord; and that, being allowed after some conversation with the Almighty, to afflict Job, he destroyed that good man's substance and slew his children. They believed that, on another day, the Devil, again by God's permission, "smote Job with sore boils" from head to foot.

So, in the New Testament also. The belief of the orthodox, even to-day, is that the Devil, taking Jesus up, set him, first on a pinnacle of the temple, then on an exceeding high mountain whence all the kingdoms of the earth may be seen; there seeking worship from him: while less literal Christians regard this as a parable only, informing us that Christ was tempted as we are, yet without sin.

Now, so long as a belief in a personal devil pervaded Christendom, spiritual agency assumed forms that were hideous in proportion to the hideousness of the belief that engendered them. Faith which, in its purity, has power to remove mountains, can also, in its perversion, pile them up, Pelion upon Ossa. In spiritual matters, *to a certain extent*, we receive what we expect: sympathy being a ruling element. Whether we fearfully deprecate, or recklessly invoke, a Spirit of Evil, spirits of truth will not answer to our call. They have still enough of human nature about them to decline communication with those who take them for devils.

In ages of the world when the popular mind was imbued with the notion that there exists around us a hierarchy of malign intelligences, headed by the Prince of the Air, whose agency, tolerated by God, is unceasingly exercised to instigate man to evil, and that these are the only disembodied beings with whom man is permitted to commune, the portals of the Spiritual seldom opened except to give exit to frightful errors and delusions. In those days that subtle power (*dunamis* was the Evangelists' term for such), corresponding doubtless, in a measure, to Reichenbach's *sensitivity* * and now spoken of among us as *mediumship*, rarely gave birth save to monstrosities, such as are usually known under the names of Sorcery and Witchcraft: superstitions only the more dangerous and horrible because there was a small amount of reality underlying the terrible phantom-shapes they assumed.

There was, in Jesus' day and long before, as there still is, a certain spiritual condition which may be termed possession. It was a disease usually induced, in some sensitive organizations, by deluding opinions or impotence of will; its slender basis of reality being a mental influence usurped by departed spirits of a degraded order, while its vast mediæval superstructure was reared by imagination running wild under the terrors of a pernicious faith. This disease was aggravated by harshness, diffused by persecution, intensified by torturings. It could be cured, like other phases of lunacy, only by charitable judgment, and gentle firmness; but believers in remedies

* For a new occasion I originate a new word. By *sensitivity* I designate that gift or faculty possessed by Reichenbach's Sensitives, and to which, elsewhere in this volume, I have alluded. A careful perusal of the German naturalist's works on this subject, namely *Untersuchungen über die Dynamide*, Brunswick, 1850, and *Der Sensitive Mensch*, Stuttgart and Tübingen, 1854, has convinced me that he has fully made out both the existence of a new power or faculty possessed by a certain portion of mankind, and the importance of studying it. The former of these works has been translated into English by Dr. Ashburner (London, 1850). Reichenbach's works, though they created, at the time they appeared, considerable excitement throughout Germany, and some stir among us, have never attracted the attention which they deserve, and which, some day, they will obtain.

so reasonable as these are, with one illustrious exception, but of modern times. The unutterable woes and atrocities * which followed directly or indirectly, partly from the belief in a devil, partly from the abnormal influence referred to, exemplify the great truth that from the same source may proceed healing or pestilence, happiness or misery, just as its waters are kept pure by enlightened care, or adulterated by the frenzy of ignorance.

The eminent exception above referred to seems to have been little noted or understood by those who are wont to seek mysteries and miracles, rather than law-governed spiritual phenomena, in the Gospels.

Among the thousand illustrations of the notorious persistence with which men and nations professing Christianity have directly contravened the spirit of its Founder, is the popular belief in witchcraft, cropping out, more or less frequently,

* In an interesting chapter on Sorcery and Witchcraft, LECKY says: "Tens of thousands of victims perished by the most agonizing and protracted torments, without exciting the faintest compassion. (?) . . . In almost every province of Germany, but especially where ecclesiastical influence predominated, the persecution raged with a fearful intensity: seven thousand victims are said to have been burnt at Trèves. . . . In France decrees were passed on the subject by the Parliaments of Paris, Toulouse, Bordeaux, Rheims, Rouen, Dijon, and Rennes, and they were all followed by a harvest of blood. The executions which took place in Paris were, in the emphatic words of an old writer, 'almost infinite.' . . . In Italy a thousand persons were executed in a single year in the province of Como; and in other parts of the country the severity of the inquisitors at last created an absolute rebellion: etc."—*Rationalism in Europe*, vol. i. pp. 28–31.

This persecution was by no means exclusively Catholic. In Luther's *Table Talk*, under date August 25, 1538, we find this: "The talk falling on witches who spoil eggs, etc., Luther said: 'I should have no compassion on these witches; I would burn all of them.'"—p. 251. And Calvin, in remodelling the laws of Geneva, left those which condemned witches to the stake unaltered.

In accordance with such opinions we find that, in England and Scotland after they became Protestant, witches were pursued at times, especially during the seventeenth century, with an almost insane fury.

throughout fifteen Christian centuries,* the popular abhorrence of supposed witches, and the incredible cruelty with which these poor wretches have been treated.† We have every reason to conclude that Christ himself did not believe in a personal devil. When he used the word devil or Satan he commonly employed it ‡ to designate either error or wickedness in man, or else a

* There were believers in witchcraft, among Christians as well as Pagans, at least as early as the middle of the third century (MIDDLETON, pp. 85-87); and there are instances of witch-burning less than a hundred years old: the two latest examples being, probably, one in Seville, Spain, in 1781, and (strange to say!) one in Glaris, Switzerland, in 1783—just eighty-eight years ago. Men still alive might have witnessed these.

† Readers who have the heart to go through the sickening details will find such, in authentic form, scattered over Pitcairn's *Criminal Trials of Scotland.* It seems scarcely credible now that, in that country of strong hearts and strong prejudices, less than a single century ago (in 1773) the Divines of the Associated Presbytery passed a resolution declaring their faith in witchcraft and deploring the growing scepticism on that subject.—MACAULAY: *History of England*, vol. iii. p. 706.

‡ The rare examples in which any of the Evangelists ascribe to Christ expressions which might bear a different interpretation may, in virtue of his uniform silence touching all diabolical compacts or seductions, properly be interpreted metaphorically (as "I beheld Satan, as lightning, fall from Heaven,"—Luke x. 18); or as simply meaning physical or moral evil; thus, of the woman "who had a spirit of infirmity and was bowed together," he says: "Ought not this woman, . . . whom Satan hath bound, lo, these eighteen years, be loosed from this bond on the Sabbath day?"—Luke xiii. 16. It will surely not be held, that Christ thought, or that we ought to think, that whenever we have rheumatism, or similar infirmity, it is the devil's doing.

But, beyond this, the hypothesis remains that the biographers of Jesus, how upright soever yet misled by the spirit of their age, may occasionally have mistaken the import of their Master's words; as, at other times (for example, Luke ix. 54), some of the Apostles grievously misconceived the spirit of his teachings. If we would form a candid and enlightened judgment of these marvellous teachings, we must take them as a grand, connected whole, not stumble over incidental expressions at variance with their general tenor, and very liable to have been misinterpreted.

debased condition in spirits. Thus, to Peter: "Get thee behind me, Satan;" * and, of Judas Iscariot: "One of you is a devil." † Thus, again, in the case of the man "possessed with the devil," his words are: "Come out of the man, thou unclean spirit!" ‡ Not a word of reproach to the afflicted; not a hint of suspicion that the maniac had made a compact with any Prince of Darkness: he assumes, simply, that a spirit or spirits of a degraded order had obtained control, or possession, of the unhappy creature; and, by virtue of the power with which he himself was gifted, he compelled them to go out of him.§ Yet again, when he warned his disciples against snares and evils to come, the warning was not touching a devil who should tempt them to sell their souls to him for worldly wealth or diabolical powers to injure, but touching false prophets who should show signs and wonders, thereby seducing even the wisest. ‖ It was a warning against wicked men, not against fallen angels—a warning inculcating the much-needed lesson that signs and wonders themselves are not infallible tests of moral truth.

Thus, eighteen hundred years ago, Christ saw, and habitually acted on, all that there is of truth underlying witchcraft, sor-

* Mark viii. 33. † John vi. 70. ‡ Mark v. 8.

§ It is quite evident that if we reject, as delusion, modern examples of possession and exorcism—in other words, if we deny that inferior spirits from the next world may sometimes, through the weakness or credulity of man, obtain a certain control over the human will and the human thoughts; and if we deny, further, that, in such case, a strong, magnetic volition may free the sufferer from such control—then we must accept one or other of these alternatives:

Either the numerous minutely-detailed relations scattered over the gospels, touching the "casting out of devils" by Christ and his disciples, are all pure fables, throwing suspicion upon the entire narrative:

Or else they refer to miracles, occurring in the first century by suspension of law, and never to occur again; a conclusion which modern civilization, enlightened by science, rejects.

That is to say: the enlightened portion of society must either discredit the gospel biographies, or accept the fact that possession may occur, and may be cured, in our day.

‖ Mark xiii. 22.

cery, magic, the black art, or by whatever name imaginary compacts with Satan may have been called. He knew that spirits of low character, occasionally obtaining control over men and women, do cause what we may call spiritual disease; and he instructed his Apostles and the Seventy how to cure it; though their power to exorcise was inferior to his.* When he found others, not of his disciples, following the same practice, he approved their doings.†

What thousands of lives might have been saved, ‡ what countless torturings of soul and body averted, had the Christian world, in this, caught the spirit, and followed the example, of Christ!

But it is only in modern times that eclectic searchers after truth, through the study of vital magnetism and spiritual manifestations, have come practically to believe, on this subject, what the Gospels have been teaching, unheeded, or misinterpreted, to fifty generations of men.

Somnambulism, as I shall have occasion to show by and by, is allied to mediumship and is governed, in a measure, by the same laws. Among these laws we find, by experience, the rule that a dogmatic frame of mind imbued with false doctrine, whether orthodox or sceptical, tends to produce abnormality in the ideas received or communications obtained. Here is an example which I translate from an accredited work on Animal Magnetism, by M. Lamy-Sénart, a pupil of the Marquis de Puységur, the first observer of Somnambulism.

"A patient who had become under my care a lucid somnambule was, with my permission, magnetized by another person, who readily cast her into a magnetic sleep. But this magnetizer believed in the Devil and his influence; and he could not help thinking of this every time he magnetized. The first day the patient was restless in her sleep; the second she saw a black

* Matthew xvii. 19, 20.

† Mark ix. 38, 39.

‡ Averaging the statistics given in various histories of witchcraft, it would seem that the number of those who have suffered death for this imaginary crime exceeds thirty thousand.

man; the third two presented themselves, with horns; the fourth they used threatening expressions to her. On the fifth day it was still worse; they seemed to sit beside her. She rose, terrified and screaming, thinking they had assaulted her; rushed out of the room and into the court-yard, followed by her magnetizer, who succeeded at last in awaking her. She suffered cruelly, complained of a great weight on her breast, her respiration was difficult, and she passed a frightful night." *

This narrative is very suggestive. Though we cannot doubt that imposture, spurred on by hate or malice, was an occasional element in witch-trials; † and though we know that many a confession, wrung forth by torture, was recanted before the sufferer was led to the stake; yet the general rule is to be found outside of these incidents.

A condition analogous to somnambulism—trance in some of its phases—not infrequently supervenes, without magnetization, in persons of sensitive temperament or secluded habits, especially when inordinately excited. Taking this and the phenomenon of obsession or possession into account, and reflecting on the probable power of such influences in a rude age when the conception of the Devil and his agency was far more vivid and influential,—more constantly present to the mind of the masses—than the conception of God and his providence, can we wonder that accusers and accused should frequently have been moved, by honest illusion—the former to accusations that they were diabolically tormented, the latter to confessions that they had visited the witches' Sabbath and witnessed its abominations?

* *Bibliothèque du Magnétisme Animal*, Cahier iv. p. 6. See, for a beatific vision, similarly suggested, *Footfalls on the Boundary of Another World*, p. 142; note.

† It is a mistake to suppose that imposture supplies the chief explanation of the witch-mania. Hume, writing of witchcraft in Scotland, remarks: "Among the many trials for witchcraft which fill the record I have not observed that there is even one which proceeds upon the notion of a vain or cheating art, falsely used by an impostor to deceive the weak and credulous."—*Commentaries on the History of Scotland*, vol. ii. p. 556.

Without some such clue as the above, how shall we explain the fact that judges so clear-sighted as Sir Edward Coke and Sir Matthew Hale recognized the reality of this alleged crime against man's allegiance to God?—that a jurist so eminent as Blackstone declared it to be a "truth to which every nation in the world hath, in its turn, borne testimony?" *—that Sir Thomas Browne, physician, philosopher, and scholar, testified in court to the same effect; that among divines Baxter, Wesley, and a host of other worthies set forth elaborate evidences of its existence, and arguments for its condign punishment; and that, in our own country, less than a hundred and eighty years ago, thirteen women and six men were hanged and one octogenarian died under horrible torture, all for the alleged crime of witchcraft? †—these executions taking place among a people earnest,

* *Footfalls on the Boundary of Another World*, p. 30; note.

† A terrible summer for Salem village and its vicinity was that of 1692!—a year of worse than pestilence or famine. Bridget Bishop was hanged in June; Sarah Good, Sarah Wildes, Elizabeth How, Susanna Martin, and Rebecca Nurse in July; George Burroughs, John Procter, George Jacobs, John Willard, and Martha Carrier in August; Martha Corey, Mary Easty, Alice Parker, Ann Pudeator, Margaret Scott, Wilmot Reed, Samuel Wardwell, and Mary Baker in September: in which last month Giles Corey, eighty-one years of age, was pressed to death under a board loaded with heavy stones; not heavy enough, however, to crush out life, until a day or two of lingering torture had intervened. Sarah Good's daughter Dorcas, between three and four years old, orphaned by her mother's execution, was one of a number of children who, with several hundred other persons, were imprisoned on suspicion of witchcraft: many of these sufferers remaining in a wretched condition (often heavily ironed) for months, some upwards of a year; and several dying during the time. A child of seven, Sarah Carrier, was called on to testify, as witness against her mother.

Some of the condemned, especially Rebecca Nurse, Martha Corey, and Mary Easty, were aged women who had led unblemished lives, and were conspicuous for their prudence, their charities, and all domestic virtues. "The question," says a painstaking, modern historian of Salem witchcraft, "arises in every mind, why did not their characters save them from conviction, and even from suspicion? The answer is to be found in the peculiar views then entertained of the power and agency of Sa-

conscientious, practical, and if piety according to the Calvinistic acceptation of the term entitle to election, worthy to be called "the very elect."

There is another popular error, treated of at large in the preceding pages, of which we must rid ourselves, ere spiritual communications can be sought or accepted without danger. It is the mistake of supposing that because a message or a lesson comes to us from a denizen of the other world, it must, on that account, be infallibly true. Death procures for us higher powers and clearer perceptions; it opens to us a wider horizon and discloses to us much which we can but dimly surmise here below: but it does not confer on us infallibility. There is doubtless, in the next world, a more elevated range of thought and of sentiment, but there is the same variety of character as here; there is diversity of opinion, too, though probably not to the same extent as among us. All this is proved by comparing,

tan. . . . Our fathers accounted for the extraordinary descent and incursions of the Evil One among them, in 1692, on the supposition that it was a desperate effort to prevent them from bringing civilization and Christianity within his favorite retreat, and their souls were fired with the glorious thought that, by carrying on the war with vigor against him and his confederates, the witches, they would become chosen and honored instruments in the hand of God for breaking down and abolishing the last stronghold of the Kingdom of Darkness."—UPHAM: *Salem Witchcraft*, Boston, 1867: vol. i. pp. 393, 394; and vol. ii. p. 373.

The evils and miseries growing out of this mental epidemic are not to be measured by the number of actual sufferers, whether on the scaffold or in loathsome prison. "It cast its shadows," says Upham, "over a broad surface, and they darkened the condition of generations. . . . The fields were neglected; fences, roads, barns, even the meeting-house, went into disrepair. . . . A scarcity of provisions, nearly amounting to a famine, continued for some time. Farms were brought under mortgage or sacrificed, and large numbers of people were dispersed. One locality in Salem village . . . bears to this day the marks of the blight. . . . The ruinous results were not confined to the village, but spread, more or less, over the country." —*Salem Witchcraft*, vol. ii. pp. 380, 381.

one with the other, various communications, which we may have ascertained, from the attendant circumstances, to be unquestionably ultramundane. Many Spiritualists, like their fellow-religionists of other persuasions, who do not accept that phase of belief, have this important truth still to learn, and for lack of having learned it, are often lamentably misled. Belief in infallibility is equally mischievous, whether held by Calvinist, by Episcopalian, or by Spiritualist. It is almost as unsafe for a dogmatic infalliblist, as for a confirmed devil-fearer, to engage in spiritual research. It is not desirable that the belief in Spiritualism should spread, except in proportion as the belief in Infallibility dies away. Here we may discern another reason why the appearance of spiritual phenomena, in their modern or normal phase, as a universal religious element, has been so long delayed.

The lesson taught by a thousand warnings from the past is unmistakable; and it is of vital moment that we heed it. It is dangerous for men and women who are confirmed in certain old superstitions, or who believe in their own possession of infallible truth, to put themselves in the way of communings with a higher sphere of being: they cannot bear them yet. We seek aid or enlightenment from another world in vain, unless we enter the spiritual school, not only in a reverent spirit, but in a fit frame of mind. We must seek ere we find: and we must seek in that catholic temper which is willing to put to the proof all things, and to accept truth, wherever found. It is not given to dogmatism, shut up in its contracted shell, to distinguish the still, small voice; it hears but the echo of its own delusions. Except we be converted from wisdom in our own conceit—except we draw near to the shrine as little children—the spiritual voices, in their purity, will not reach our ears.

It is with the teachings of Spiritualism as with the praying of men: they are but mockeries, unless approached in a becoming spirit.*

* The effect of levity in spiritual researches is not so fatal as that of dogmatic superstition: none the less its tendency is to preclude all

But, for the reasons above set forth, even able searchers, earnestly and reverently prosecuting inquiries into the character of modern Spiritual revealings, if still haunted by the idea of Satanic agency, may be led into a grievous error, the very opposite of that which sets up all Spiritual messages as Gospel truths.

A noteworthy example is before me, in a well-known European journal.* I find therein an editorial, entitled *Tables Tournantes*, in which the writer, after alluding to the fact that "the marvels of magnetism, or rather of Spiritualism, as the Americans call it," seem to be "again coming into fashion," quotes from one of the most respectable of the Parisian journals, as follows:

"It will be remembered," says the *Courrier de Paris*, "that a certain number of French and foreign prelates thought it their duty, about a year ago, to interdict the practice of table-moving. Their motive, or alleged motive, was that this practice brought men into dangerous communication with the spirits of darkness. The fact is, that most of the spirits that manifested themselves through the tables or under the floor, when questioned as to their identity, answered, 'demon,' 'devil,' or at least, 'damned.' †

"One of the most eminent and enlightened members of our

valuable or satisfactory results. If we enter a church as we would crowd into a comic theatre, or kneel in prayer-meeting as we would sit down to a game at cards, the exercises in either case will probably not tend much to edification. Spiritualism is not intended to make sport for graceless idlers at an evening party: and if to them it furnish but platitudes, inanities—buffooneries even—what is this but the natural result of misplaced merriment and thoughtless irreverence?

Yet even at such disadvantage, it has happened, from time to time, that Frivolity was startled out of her heedlessness—the poet's line being realized—

"And fools, who came to scoff, remained to pray."

* *Le Nord*, published at Brussels; No. 185, of date July 4, 1857.

† My experience is the reverse of this. Throughout the many hundred sittings at which I have assisted, no such replies were ever elicited

hierarchy, the Lord Bishop of Rennes, had thought it his duty, for his own personal edification, to institute some experiments with the tables; but he reached a result which caused him to abandon the practice. It was as follows:

"The Bishop, the Vicars-General, and his Canons having assembled at the Episcopal palace, interrogated a table as to the fate and the sufferings of a young and generous missionary who had recently suffered martyrdom in China. The Bishop had with him, as a relic, a fragment of the bloody shirt of this devoted and unfortunate soldier of the faith. Was this the talisman that operated? We cannot tell. Suffice it that the table set about relating, in its language ("en sa langue," meaning, probably, by raps), and with a most startling fidelity, the whole history of the agonies and tortures of the courageous missionary; all circumstances well-known to most of the assistants. The Bishop, on his part, was so much struck by it, that, interrupting the proceedings, he cried with a loud voice: 'To know all that, thou must be the Devil. Well! if thou art the Devil, by the omnipotent God, by Jesus Christ crucified, I adjure thee, I summon and command thee, to break thyself in pieces at my feet.'

"Instantly the table made a great spring; and, falling back obliquely, broke off two of its legs, dropping at the feet of the Lord Bishop of Rennes.

"It is not our intention," adds the *Courrier*, "either to explain or to call in question the incident we have related. Only let our readers be assured that we have invented nothing. The fact has been certified to us by witnesses the most respectable and the most trustworthy. And, for the rest, it is well-known that we are not among the number of those who lend themselves to the circulation of fables, or would put forth a profane jest at the expense of the revered name we have just cited."

This anecdote may call forth a smile, but it has its serious aspect. The Bishop, convinced from the manifestations that an occult intelligence is communicating, takes it for granted that because that intelligence accurately discloses a variety of facts connected with the martyrdom of a missionary, it must be Satan himself:* thereupon he addresses it as such. But they who assume, in advance, the question they propose to investigate, are in no fit frame of mind to enter upon such investigation at all. Nor will any intelligent Spiritualist be surprised at the issue of the episcopal experiment: the case thus prejudged, some such result might have been predicted.† For there are recorded cases of analogous character. There occurred a century and a half ago at Epworth parsonage, the paternal home of the celebrated John Wesley, loud knockings and other strange disturbances continued for two months, and which Dr. Adam Clarke, in his biography of the Wesley family, regards

* This is in accordance with the tests of Demon agency set forth in the *Roman Ritual*, and with the practice of the Catholic Church. Among the signs of possession there designated, is the "disclosing of distant and hidden things." "Signa autem obsidentis dæmonis sunt: Ignota lingua loqui pluribus verbis, vel loquentem intelligere: distantia et occulta patefacere," etc.—*Rituale Romanum* (Mechliniæ, 1856), p. 514, Cap. "De Exorcizandis obsessis a Dæmonio."

But every well-informed student of vital Magnetism knows that clear-sight (clairevoyance) and far-sight (vue à distance) are phenomena of frequent occurrence during somnambulism; to say nothing of mediumship. To regard these as Satanic powers is no whit more rational than to declare, as men did five hundred years ago, that the experiments of the laboratory are unlawful. In Chaucer's tale of the Chanon Yeman, chemistry is spoken of as an elfish art, conducted by aid of spirits: a superstition of Arabian origin, Warton says.—*Warton's History of English Poetry*, vol. i. p. 169.

† Those who have assisted frequently and under various circumstances at such sittings, know well that the table—meaning, thereby, the invisible intelligence which manifests its presence by rappings, tiltings, raising of the table and other sounds or movements—often exhibits, in the most unmistakable manner, human emotions; and none more plainly than indignation (as by violent jerkings or stampings), when the phenomena are treated with ridicule, or ascribed to Satanic agency. That this frequently occurs under circumstances which preclude all possibility of trickery, any careful and persevering observer may readily ascertain for himself. I have myself witnessed it, on various occasions.

as Spiritual manifestations connected with the death of Mrs. Samuel Wesley's brother in India. * Emily Wesley writing the details to her brother John, after declaring that a month's experience had thoroughly convinced her that trickery was impossible, adds: "As for my mother, she (at first), firmly believed it to be rats, and sent for a horn to blow them away. I laughed to think how wisely they were employed who were striving half a day to fright away Jeffrey (for that name I gave it) with a horn. But whatever it was, I perceived it could be made angry; for from that time it was so outrageous, there was no quiet for us after ten o'clock at night. . . . It was more loud and fierce, if any one said it was rats or anything natural." †

It "could be made angry," Emily Wesley said. So, probably, could the spirit addressed by the French Bishop, when mistaken by him for the devil. Or that spirit might have departed and another suddenly taken its place. Abundant facts indicate (though, in advance of experience, one might reject such an idea) the frequent agency of a somewhat singular class of spirits; as imps, we might say, of frolic and misrule; not wicked, it would seem, or, if wicked, restrained from inflicting serious injury, but, as it were, tricksy elves, sprites full of pranks and levities—a sort of *Pucks*,—"*esprits espiègles*," as the French phrase it; or as the Germans, framing an epithet expressly for this supposed class of spirits, have expressed it, "*poltergeister*." ‡

Whether the Rev. Charles Beecher, a Congregational clergyman of our own country, has had any experience similar to that

* *Memoirs of the Wesley Family*, by ADAM CLARKE, LL.D., F.A.S.; London, 1843; vol. i. pp. 288, 289. That, also, was Mrs. Wesley's final opinion. All the details will be found in these Memoirs, pp. 245–291.

† *Memoirs of the Wesley Family*, vol. i. pp. 271, 272.

‡ *Footfalls on the Boundary of Another World*, p. 212. For examples of the agency of such spirits see Book iii. chap. 2 of that volume.

of the Lord Bishop of Rennes, I know not. Certain it is, he reaches the conclusion that all modern spiritual revealings come through the Powers of Darkness, and that "we are entering on the first steps of a career of demoniac manifestations, the issues whereof man cannot conjecture."* A similar mistake was mode in Jerusalem eighteen hundred years ago. When the people witnessed the "signs and wonders" wrought by Jesus, they "were amazed and said, 'Is not this the son of David?' But when the Pharisees heard it, they said, 'This fellow doth not cast out devils but by Beelzebub, the Prince of the devils.'" †

It does not seem to have suggested itself to the Pharisees, nor to Mr. Beecher, that all analogy is opposed to such an explanation of spiritual phenomena. In this world God does not, indeed, shut his creatures away from earthly influences tending to deception and to error. But the good is the rule; the evil (often good in disguise) is but the exception. If it enter into God's economy to permit evidences and influences to come over to us from a higher phase of being, are we to believe that He excludes from these all that is true and good, and suffers only deceptions and false teachings, emanating from the devil and his angels, to reach us? Is this the doing of a Father, whose "tender mercies are over all his other works"? If, in very deed, such were the Divine plan, then—adopting the lines of a modern poet—

> "Then God would not be what this bright
> And glorious universe of His—
> This world of wisdom, goodness, light
> And endless love proclaims—He is."

If we listen to sober reason, she teaches us that, as from this world, so from the other, there are richly furnished to us the elements of truth and the means of happiness. If we fail to

* *Review of Spiritual Manifestations*, read before the Congregational Association of New York and Brooklyn, chap. vii. (p. 65 of London Ed. 1853).

† Matthew xii. 23, 24.

interpret the revealings from Heaven or to avail ourselves of the teachings from earth, it is not by the Divine fiat except so far as this, that God has made wisdom and peace obtainable only through virtuous exertion, and that He has interposed no ægis to protect man from the natural results of his inexperience and of his misconceptions.

The following table may be useful in exhibiting, in a general way, the main varieties of religious opinion throughout the Christian world; and the position which, according to the preceding views, modern Spiritualism occupies among them:

CHIEF PHASES OF RELIGIOUS BELIEF IN CHRISTENDOM.

I. School of *Secularism*, namely:

a. Radical: Materialists * denying a Hereafter.

b. Conservative: Sceptics, doubting a Hereafter.

II. School of *Infallibility*, namely:

a. Pure: Catholics, including Greek and Eastern Churches.

b. Mixed: Main body of Protestants.

III. School of *Spiritualism*, namely:

a. Exclusive: Orthodox Quakers and Swedenborgians, retaining element of infallibility.

b. Universal: Modern Epiphanists, † rejecting element of infallibility.

In elucidation of the above table I offer a few remarks.

* I here employ the term *materialist* in its popular sense, to mean a person who believes the soul to be merely a quality appertaining to our vital existence here, which can have no existence separate from the body, and which ceases to be as soon as earthly life is extinct.

Whether, in scientific strictness, materialism must be taken to mean a doctrine which is inconsistent with the immortality of the soul, I need not here stop to inquire.

† For a new occasion I may be allowed to coin an appropriate word. *Spiritual Epiphanist* accurately designates a believer in spiritual appearances or manifestations.

(I.) I employ the term *Secularism*, rather than that of *Rationalism*, as more correctly designating the creed of those who believe it to be the part of wisdom that we restrict our attention to secular affairs and physical studies, and that we refrain from the investigation of religion, seeing that man can find no solid ground for any spiritual belief. Rationalism is not so much a creed as a cast of thought.*

The age of radical Secularism is passing away: it has, at the present day, no distinguished leader; and probably never will have again. If a second Calvin is impossible, so also is a second Voltaire.

On the other hand, conservative Secularism, seeking religious rest but finding none, is steadily increasing. It includes within its ranks some of the most eminent scientific men of our day, large numbers from the medical and legal professions and among politicians; together with some worthy and respected divines.† Especially among English artisans and working

* Lecky defines it to be "a bias of reasoning which has during the last three centuries gained a marked ascendency in Europe. . . . It leads men on all occasions to subordinate dogmatic theology to the dictates of reason and of conscience, and, as a necessary consequence, greatly to restrict its influence upon life. It predisposes men, in history, to attribute all kinds of phenomena to natural rather than miraculous causes; in theology, to esteem succeeding systems the expressions of the wants and aspirations of that religious sentiment which is planted in all men; and, in ethics, to regard as duties only those which conscience reveals to be such."—*History of Rationalism in Europe*, vol. i. pp. 16, 17 (of New York Ed.).

† A few years since I had a long, quiet conversation with a Bishop, who is held in deservedly high estimation by the orthodox body of Christians to which he belongs. He introduced the subject of modern Spiritualism, and I asked him in what light he regarded its phenomena. He answered frankly and satisfactorily. Evidences of infidelity, he said, were multiplying among us: he had lately heard a professor of Harvard College express the opinion that three-fourths of the scientific men of our day are unbelievers, and that scepticism is beginning to intrude among the clergy. He told me that he himself, a few weeks before, had visited the death-bed of an aged brother in the ministry; a

classes generally, this passive phase of irreligion has, of late years, made rapid strides.*

man who had devoted a long life, with rare faithfulness, to the duties of his profession. As they spoke of the evidences of Christianity a shade of sadness passed over the dying man's face: "Ah! Bishop," he said, "the proof, the proof! If we only had it!"

These and similar experiences had led the Bishop to believe that the evidences of a future life which satisfied our ancestors are insufficient to convince some of the most honest and able of their descendants. Looking around for the remedy, he had asked himself if it would not, in God's good time, be vouchsafed. "I look anxiously," he added, "to Spiritualism and its phenomena for the answer."

* The British government, alive to a sense of the important aid which civilization may derive from accurate statistics, employed, in making out the Census of 1851, a staff of forty thousand persons, and obtained, incidentally much valuable information on religious matters. The results are condensed in an official Report on *Religious Worship* made, in 1853, to the Registrar-General. The Reporter states (p. 58) that while among the upper classes in England and Wales "a regular church-attendance is now ranked among the recognized proprieties of life," it is the great body of the people who chiefly absent themselves from public worship. He goes on to say, as to artisans and other workmen: "From whatever cause,—in them or in the manner of their treatment by religious bodies—it is sadly certain that this vast, intelligent, and growingly important section of our countrymen is thoroughly estranged from our religious institutions in their present aspect. . . . Probably the prevalence of *infidelity* has been exaggerated, if the word be taken in its popular meaning, as implying some degree of intellectual effort and decision; but, no doubt, a great extent of negative, inert indifference prevails, the practical effects of which are much the same. There is a sect, originated recently, adherents to a system called "Secularism;" the principle tenet being that, as the fact of a future life is (in their view) at all events susceptible of *some* degree of doubt, while the fact and the necessities of a present life are matters of direct sensation, it is therefore prudent to attend exclusively to the concerns of that existence which is certain and immediate—not wasting energies required for present duties by a preparation for remote, and merely possible, contingencies. This is the creed which probably with most exactness indicates the faith which, virtually though not professedly, is entertained by the masses of our working population."—*Report on*

(II.) Except in restricting the attribute of infallibility to the Church speaking through Œcumenical Councils, and in steadily rejecting the supremacy of the Roman Pontiff,* the variations in doctrine between the Greek and Latin branches of the Catholic Church are non-essential; consisting chiefly in this, that, while admitting church traditions, the seven sacraments, a mild phase of original sin, and an intermediate state, the Oriental Churches scruple about a Purgatory with flames and the efficacy of private masses for the dead,† and (dropping the *filioque* of the Council of Constantinople) hold that the Holy Ghost proceeds from the Father only.

With variances in doctrine so inconsiderable, the Greek and Roman Churches, after their eight centuries of separation, might, in a tolerant age like this, have united their two hundred and eighty millions of believers in one vast, harmonious body, had the present Pope but pursued a conciliatory line of policy. A few timely concessions to the spirit of the age would, at this juncture, have incalculably strengthened the Papal influence. But this was not to be. In December, 1867, the Austrian Government passed a law declaring freedom of religious opinion, with liberty of the press; and granting to all

Religious Worship made by HORACE MANN, barrister of Lincoln's Inn, to the Registrar-General, under date December 8, 1853.

For a statement, from the same Census, of the average attendance at church or chapel, as ascertained on a particular Sunday all over England and Wales, showing how small that attendance is, *especially in free-seated churches*, see note on preceding page 159.

* As to the tenets of the Greek Church, Mosheim says: "The Holy Scriptures and the decrees of the first seven Œcumenical Councils are acknowledged by the Greeks as the rule of their faith. It is received, however, as a maxim established by long custom, that no private person has a right to explain, for himself or others, either the declarations of Scripture, or the decisions of these Councils; and that the Patriarch, with his brethren, are alone authorized to consult these oracles and declare their meaning."—MOSHEIM: Eccl. Hist. iii. 483, 484.

† Thus incurring the anathema of Rome: "Si quis dixerit Missæ sacrificium . . . non pro defunctis offerri debere: anathema sit."—Concil. Trident: cap. ix. can. 3.

sects the right of establishing schools and colleges and of teaching their own tenets there. This was followed, in May, 1868, by another statute, legalizing civil marriage, and transferring from the ecclesiastical to the civil authorities the general supervision of public instruction. This enlightened policy proved deadly offence at Rome. The Pope delivered an Allocution (June 2, 1868), in which he took occasion to "reprove and condemn those abominable laws," as in flagrant contradiction to the Catholic religion, the power of the Apostolic See and "natural right itself;" and went on to declare the said laws null and void. Austria replied that the Holy See was extending its strictures to objects not within its jurisdiction; and added: "We shall none the less persevere in the way we have begun." A powerful empire virtually lost by this!

Then followed the Council of the Vatican. To this the Patriarchs and Bishops of the Greek Church were, indeed, invited; but the invitation was coupled with the odious reminder that their Church, in seceding from that of Rome, had been seduced "by the infernal arts and machinations of him who plotted in Heaven the first schism;" in plain terms, that they —the said Patriarchs and Bishops—were, so long as they remained insubordinate to Papal authority, the spiritual agents of the Devil.

Protestants, too, were exhorted to return to the ancient fold; but what availed exhortation or invitation to them from an Ecclesiastical Sovereign who, as we have seen,* set out by announcing that he himself was infallible and that all the dogmas he might dictate were "irreformable;" following this up by a recurse denounced against all who should prosecute scientific researches beyond the limits of Roman Catholic permission.

But for these capital errors, the "Holy Catholic Church" might not only have reclaimed the Eastern branch, but possibly have added twenty millions more to her adherents; thus massing three hundred million souls under her ecclesiastical

* See preceding page 42.

standard: for one of the Protestant sects has recently made certain advances (which have been favorably met) to the Oriental branch of Catholicism.

In the year 1867, the Pan-Anglican Synod caused to be transmitted, through the Archbishop of Canterbury, to the Patriarchs and Bishops of the Greek Church, a Pastoral Letter, setting forth the faith of the Anglican Church and expressing, in general terms, a wish to harmonize and a hope "that there may be 'one flock and one shepherd.'" This being received favorably and with profound respect, by the Prelates of the Greek Church,* was followed up, in the Convocation of Canterbury, assembled July 4, 1868, by a Report declaring the object to be, not a submission of either Church to the other, nor a modification of their respective services so as to conform, but "simply the mutual acknowledgment that all Churches which are one in the possession of a true Episcopate, one in sacraments and one in their creed, are, by their union in their common Lord, bound to receive one another in full communion in prayers and sacraments as members of the same household of faith." The Convocation, accepting this Report, instructed its President to open negotiations with the Eastern Patriarchs and Metropolitans, with a view to the establishment of such relations.

A movement among ourselves in sympathy with this and resembling the Tractarian agitation which originated at Oxford in 1833,† has already produced considerable excitement. Its

* The Rev. Mr. Williams, an English clergyman, stated, at a meeting of the "Eastern Church Company" held in 1867, that he had conversed with the Patriarchs of Constantinople, Antioch, and Jerusalem, who had expressed their entire approbation of the union; that the Patriarch of Antioch proposed to establish a school with a Professor of English, as preparation for it, and that the Metropolitan of Scio had declared to him his conviction that the time for such a union had arrived.—See *Schem's Ecclesiastical Almanac*, 1869, pp. 23, 24.

† Lecky says of the English Tractarian movement: "It produced a defection which was quite unparalleled in magnitude since that which

character may be gleaned from a pamphlet-volume of sermons delivered three years since by Dr. Ewer, Rector of Christ Church, New York; in which the ground taken is that the Episcopal Church always has been a branch of the one Holy Catholic Church,* infallible † and blessed with Apostolic succession: denying, however, the supremacy of the Roman Pontiff, holding each branch of the Catholic Church, Latin, Greek, or Anglican, to be independent; and admitting that extrinsic abuses had overtaken the Church of Rome. The title of Dr. Ewer's second sermon, *The Anglican Church not Protestant*, sufficiently marks the position which its author assumes.

The later developments from Rome evidently destroy all hope of Catholic union except between the Greek and Anglican Churches; and thus, by lack of temper and judgment on the part of her most powerful branch, the School of Infallibility has lost the golden opportunity of a gigantic union. Is there not a great truth underlying the text that God maketh the wrath of man to praise Him?

I have already ‡ noticed an enlightened movement in the Anglican Church; a movement opposed to Literalism: opposed to the doctrine of the Miraculous; opposed, in a general way, to the dicta of the Infallible School. It is steadily gaining ground and has evidently the virtual support of the British Government. Its leaders have all maintained their official

had taken place under the Stuarts; and which, unlike the former movement, was altogether uninfluenced by sordid considerations."—*Rationalism in Europe*, vol. i. p. 174.

* Dr. Ewer appeals to the Apostles' Creed, forming part of the Evening Service of the Episcopal Church, wherein we read: "I believe in the Holy Ghost, the Holy Catholic Church, the Communion of Saints, etc." In that which is occasionally substituted for it the words are: "I believe in One Catholic and Apostolic Church."

† "The very infallibility of the Bible demands the infallibility of the Church; the two stand or fall together."—*Sermons on the Failure of Protestantism and on Catholicity*, by the Rev. Ferdinand C. Ewer, S.T.D., Rector of Christ Church, New York: sermon ii. p. 34.

‡ See preceding page 150.

standing and one of its ablest exponents has become Bishop of Exeter.

The six or seven million Jews scattered over the world must be included in the School of Infallibility.

Of the more liberal class of Protestants many, retaining their denominational position, but rejecting infallibity, have become Spiritualists. So also have not a few Catholics. But the largest accession to the ranks of the Spiritualists has been from the School of Secularism.

(III). Two hundred years ago there sprang up a remarkable sect. The people called *Quakers* were the Spiritualists of the seventeenth century. Their Luther was George Fox, and their Calvin was Robert Barclay, a man of some distinction, who was appointed Governor of New Jersey.* Barclay's "Apology" was as much the acknowledged text-book for the Quakerism of his day, as was Calvin's "Institutes" the code of sixteenth-century Protestantism.

The fundamental doctrine of this people was that an inward, saving light, or spirit of truth, promised by Christ, and emanating immediately from God, is the supreme rule of faith: this light, or spirit, coming to all men who resist it not, and moving them to virtue and good works.† To the Heathen and the Gen-

* In 1682; but he served by deputy only.

† The *Apology* (A.D. 1675), comprehending fifteen Propositions (Theses Theologicæ), and copious commentaries thereon, was originally written in Latin, but afterward translated by its author into English, and by others into French, German, Spanish, and Dutch. I quote from an American reprint of Barclay's English version, Philadelphia, 1805:

"The testimony of the Spirit is that alone by which the true knowledge of God has been, is, and can be only revealed. . . . By the revelation of the same Spirit He hath manifested Himself all along unto the sons of men, both patriarchs, prophets, and apostles; which revelations of God, by the Spirit, whether by outward voices and appearances, dreams, or inward objective manifestations in the heart, were of old the formal object of their faith, and remain yet so to be."—*Proposition* ii., p. 17.

tiles of old, as to us of to-day, this personal revelation has been given; and all who have acted up to the light within, even though they had never heard of Christ, are thereby justified and saved.*

Barclay alleges that this inward light never contradicts either natural reason or Scripture; the teachings of Christ and his apostles being a declaration by the Spirit, and to be reverenced accordingly. Nevertheless, the light within is, to each man, the primary law, while the Scriptures are to be esteemed a secondary rule only.†

A singular element pervaded this faith. It ignored the lively, the humorous, the esthetic; it forbade, not plays and dancing alone, but music, whether vocal or instrumental. It interdicted all games, sports, pastimes; even laughter and jest; holding the fear of God to be the proper recreation of man; and restricting "lawful divertisements" to visiting, reading history, speaking soberly of past or present events, gardening, geometrical and mathematical studies, and the like. Adopting Calvin's sumptuary principles, it enjoined grave simplicity and strict economy in dress, and declared that for Christian women to plait their hair or wear ornaments was unlawful.‡

* "Both Jew and Gentile, Scythian or Barbarian, of whatever country or kindred, . . . may come to walk in this light and be saved."—pp. 209, 210. "The outward knowledge of Christ's death and sufferings . . . we willingly confess to be very profitable and comfortable, but not absolutely needful unto such from whom God himself hath withheld it."—*Prop.* vi., p. 123.

† "The Scriptures of truth . . . are only a declaration of the fountain, and not the fountain itself, therefore they are not to be esteemed the principal ground of all truth and knowledge, nor yet the adequate primary rule of faith and manners: nevertheless, as that which giveth a true and faithful testimony of the first foundation, they are and may be esteemed a secondary rule."—*Prop.* iii., p. 81.

‡ "Games and sports, plays, dancing, . . . consist not with the gravity and godly fear which the Gospel calls for."—pp. 550, 556. "As to their artificial music, either by organs or other instruments or voice, we have neither example nor precept for it in the New Testament."—p. 422. "Laughing, sporting, jesting, etc., is not Christian

The first outbreak of Quakerism was powerful: despite bitter persecution, it spread rapidly and to remote regions. But, for many years, it has been stationary or declining; the total number of Quakers throughout the world not exceeding a hundred and twenty-five thousand: of whom four-fifths inhabit the United States.*

This phase of Spiritualism has its strong points and its weak ones: in virtue of the first it made way and prospered; by reason of the last it suffered arrest and decay.

It asserted, in unqualified terms, liberty of conscience for all men; † it declared that the Scriptures are not a finality; it subordinated the old-written Word to the Spiritual revealings daily vouchsafed to mankind: daring opinions these; a noble stand for the day in which they were announced. But it fell, in a measure, into the old error of the infallible; for it held that the light within, guided by which the Evangelists

liberty nor harmless mirth."—p. 529. "The fear of God is the best recreation."—p. 554. "Lawful divertisements" are "for friends to visit one another; to hear or read history; to speak soberly of the present or past transactions; to follow after gardening; to use geometrical and mathematical experiments, and such other things."—pp. 554, 555. "Christian women ought not to use the plaiting of hair or ornaments, etc.; for the Apostle (1 Peter iii. 3, 4) condemns the use of them as unlawful."—p. 549.

* In an elaborate paper (published 1869) in the *Westminster Review*, entitled "The Quakers," and evidently written by one friendly to the sect, the writer says: "At the present time there are not more than 14,000 Quakers in Great Britain, and 3,000 in Ireland; and they have at no time exceeded 60,000. There are scarcely any to be found on the Continent of Europe.

Adopting their own estimate, as given in Schem's *Ecclesiastical Year Book* (for 1860, page 82), there are 100,000 Quakers in the United States; chiefly in Pennsylvania (23,000), Indiana (20,000), Ohio (14,000), and New York (10,000).

The total throughout the world seems to fall short of 125,000.

† "The forcing of men's consciences is contrary to sound reason and the very law of nature. . . . The conscience of man is the seat and throne of God, of which God is the alone proper and infallible judge."—*Apology*, pp. 503, 511.

and Apostles wrote, and which comes to-day to every man who will seek and receive, is a direct revelation from God; therefore, in all its teachings, unerringly true. Hence great confusion of ideas. For truth must always be consistent with itself: but if, at any time, the light within assent not to every word of Scripture, then one or other must be at fault; and this discordance, in point of fact, does happen.

Thus the alternative presented itself, to Quaker teachers, either to admit that the Scriptures are not infallible, or else to assume as to every man who dissented from any portion whatever of the written Word, that he had not received the true light. But this last, making man the arbiter of his neighbor's conscience, is a direct denial of religious liberty—in other words, it subverts the very foundation of the original Quaker faith.

The practical result has been that the orthodox portion of the Society of Friends, clinging to the literal infallibility of the Biblical Record and directly violating not only the great tenet of their founders, but the express words of Jesus, "Judge not, that ye be not judged"—now disown all those who "deny the divinity of Christ or the authenticity of the Scriptures." They require their members to believe that Jesus Christ was miraculously conceived; that we have remission of sins through his blood, that he was a sacrifice for the sins of the world and now sits, as Mediator between God and Man, at God's right hand.*

But, of course, a Spiritual kingdom thus divided against itself cannot stand. And its decay has been hastened by the undue importance it attached to trifles, and its narrow-minded condemnation of innocent gayety and wholesome amusements. Many of the liberal or Hicksite branch of the Society have become Spiritualists.

In the eighteenth century, Spiritualism appeared under the

* Article *Quakers*, American Cyclopedia, vol. xiii. This article was furnished to the Cyclopedia as an authorized exposition of orthodox Quaker doctrine at the present day.

form of *Swedenborgianism.* From Quakerism to Swedenborgianism was a great advance.

Fox and Barclay did not recognize communion with the spirits of the departed, rigidly adhering to the doctrine of agency direct from God: they still held to the old Miltonian idea of angels created such and of a personal Devil; believed in a day of judgment on which, by the fiat of their Creator, one portion of mankind was consigned to happiness, another to misery; regarded the next phase of existence as a life without variety of duties or of enjoyments, and without progress—a life with but one avocation for each of its denizens—the constant exercise of worship for the good, the perpetual endurance of torment for the wicked.

But Emanuel Swedenborg taught that men, in this world, can have communion with spirits in the next, which communion is reliable and valuable or mischievous and misleading, according as men are sensual and worldly-minded or the reverse; like attracting its like from the world of spirits: * that there are no angels, created such, whether good or bad, and of course no fallen angels, nor any Satan, Prince of Hell; self-love being the only Devil: † that men carry with them to the next world

* To the Rev. Arvid Ferelius Swedenborg said, "that every man might have the same spiritual privileges as himself, but the true hindrance is, the sensual state into which mankind has fallen." To his friend Robsahm: "A man lays himself open to grievous errors who tries, by barely natural powers, to explore spiritual things." Wilkinson, one of his best biographers, sums up his views on this subject thus: "The reason of the danger of man, as at present constituted, speaking with spirits, is, that we are all in association with our likes, and being full of evil, these similar spirits, could we face them, would but confirm us in our own state and views."—WILKINSON: *Emanuel Swedenborg, a Biography*, London, 1849: pp. 156, 225.

† "There does not exist, in the universal heaven, a single angel who was created such from the first, nor any devil in Hell who was created an angel of light and afterwards cast down thither: but all the inhabitants, both of Heaven and Hell, are derived from the human race. . . . The falsity of evil and Satan are one."—SWEDENBORG: *Heaven and Hell*, London Ed. of 1851, pp. 136, 33. "There is no par-

the leading characteristics which distinguished them here; * that Heaven is reached, not by faith nor by baptism, but by a pure love of truth and goodness; † that love toward God and the neighbor comprises all Divine truth; ‡ that there exists an intermediate state, which men enter very soon after death, where they have free liberty of choice either to walk in the paths which lead thence to Heaven, or to follow those which conduct to Hell: § that God rewards no one with Heaven, nor consigns any one to Hell; each spirit being attracted to one region or to the other, according to its ruling loves, just as men and women in this world are drawn by their dominant desires, some to virtuous associates, others to the companionship of the wicked: ‖ that all sufferings in the next world are self-inflicted; self-love and worldly-mindedness ruling there and constituting Hell and its flames: ¶ and, finally, that the duties and occupa-

ticular Devil that is Lord in Hell; but self-love is so called."—SWEDENBORG: *Divine Providence*, London Ed. of 1857, p. 302.

* "The ruling affection or love of every man remains with him after death, and is not extirpated to eternity."—*Heaven and Hell*, p. 167.

† "Heaven is not imparted to any one by baptism, nor yet by faith. . . . All reach Heaven who have loved truth and good for their own sake."—*Heaven and Hell*, pp. 147, 157.

‡ "Love to the Lord and love toward the neighbor comprehend in themselves all divine truths."—*Heaven and Hell*, p. 10.

§ "The world of spirits is stationed in the midst between Heaven and Hell. . . . All are left to their liberty such as they enjoyed while in the world. . . . Spirits that are good walk in the ways which tend toward Heaven; while spirits that are evil walk in the ways that tend toward Hell."—*Heaven and Hell*, p. 312.

‖ Swedenborg expressed himself on this subject to Robsahm thus: "When men first come into the spiritual world, no one thinks of anything but the happiness of Heaven, or the misery of Hell. Soon the good spirits come to him and instruct him where he is; and he is then left to follow his own inclinations, which lead him to the place where he remains forever."—*Emanuel Swedenborg, a Biography*, p. 102.

¶ "Not any, the smallest portion, of the punishments which spirits undergo comes from the Lord; but all of it from evil itself. . . . Self-love and the love of the world . . . reign in the hells and also

tions of Heaven are not restricted to a single rite, but are manifold and various, it being a world of activity, of progress, and of uses;* and that human affections, alike to God and to his creatures, are transferred thither, graciously to blossom and expand into more than earthly beauty and purity, and to make the happiness of that genial paradise for evermore.†

Grand conceptions these! wonderful conceptions, to have come to us from the frigid North, through a government Assessor of Mines, ‡ more than a century ago. Golden conceptions which, had they been laid before the world unmixed with dross and in a lucid, concise, practical manner, might already have worked no small revolution in Christian creeds. But what has been their fate?

Though Swedenborg was a man of distinction, highly connected, in favor with his government, invited to the royal table and regarded with respect, in his own country, both by ecclesiastics, nobles, and men of science, § yet, at the outset, Quakerism (re-

constitute them. . . . Infernal fire, or the fire of Hell, is the love of self and of the world."—*Heaven and Hell*, pp. 285, 289, 298.

* "The occupations that exist in the Heavens . . . are innumerable and vary, also, according to the offices of the various societies. . . . Every one, there, performs some use; for the Lord's kingdom is a kingdom of uses."—*Heaven and Hell*, p. 181.

† "All delights flow from love. . . . The delights of the soul or of the spirit all flow from love to the Lord and toward the neighbor. . . . In proportion as these two loves are received . . . the soul is turned away from the world toward Heaven."—*Heaven and Hell*, p. 185.

‡ Swedenborg, eminent as a man of science, discharged during thirty-one years, the office of Assessor of the Board of Mines, under the Swedish government. In 1747, giving himself up to spiritual studies, he resigned the office; but King Frederick, in consideration of his services, continued the full salary during his life.

§ Swedenborg was a son of the Bishop of Westrogothia, and was brother-in-law of the Archbishop of Upsal and of Lars Benzelstierna, Governor of a Province. He was ennobled by Queen Ulrica Eleonora in 1719; and was a member of the Academies of Sciences of Stockholm and St. Petersburg. In a letter written from London, in 1769, to a

stricted as was its sphere of influence) was a brilliant success compared to Swedenborgianism. During Swedenborg's life he does not seem to have made even a single hundred proselytes; * and his voluminous folios obtain but a passing notice, here and there, in symbolic history. † Even now, when three or four generations have passed, the adherents of the Swedish seer, avowed and unavowed, do not equal in number those of George Fox: ‡ a mere handful, one may say. During a century of existence the Church of the New Jerusalem hardly exerted a perceptible influence on the religious opinions of the four hundred millions inhabiting Christendom. It is chiefly during the last twenty years—and in great part through modern Spiritualism—that the fundamental truths taught by Swedenborg have been gradually coming to win the ear and the respect of the civilized world.

friend who had asked particulars touching himself and his family connections, he says: "I am in friendship with all the bishops of my country, who are ten in number, and also with the sixteen Senators and the rest of the Peers. . . . The King and Queen themselves, and also the three Princes, their sons, show me all kind countenance; and I was once invited to dine with the King and Queen at their table."—Letter in London Ed. of 1851 of *Heaven and Hell*, pp. 51, 52.

* And, in Swedenborg's own opinion, his system seems to have been as unpopular in the next world as in this. When General Truxen asked him how many persons he thought there were in the world who favored his doctrine, he replied "that there *might perhaps be fifty*, and in proportion the same number in the world of spirits."—*Swedenborg, a Biography*, by Wilkinson, p. 236.

† HAGENBACH: *History of Doctrines*, vol. ii. pp. 391, 393, and a few others.

‡ Through the kindness of the Secretary of the late General Conference of American Swedenborgians, I have (under date January 1, 1871) the following: "The number of professed Swedenborgians—that is, persons who openly and publicly proclaim themselves believers in the doctrines taught by Swedenborg—in this country is not, so far as I can learn, more than 5,000. In Great Britain there are about 5,000 more, and in other parts of the world about 1,000. It is our conviction, however, that ten times this number accept Swedenborg's fundamental doctrines, but, for various reasons, say little or nothing about it."

The dross was the retarding element. Swedenborg fell deep into the old, old error—the worst of drosses—the time-honored delusion of Human Infallibility. He regarded himself as a Spiritual Ambassador from God to man; the One specially selected from the human race to that holy office, by the Almighty; the first and sole interpreter of the Word of God, whom the angels themselves dared not instruct in biblical knowledge, seeing that he was taught and illuminated directly by the Deity himself.*

The Bible—or the Word, as he usually called it †—he regarded as a species of spiritual palimpsest, the original meaning covered up from the apprehension of mankind, hid in wisdom among the angels, and the visible text which overlies it, a series of Celestial Mysteries, not at all to be interpreted as it reads in Scripture; ‡ and to which, since the words were first penned,

* He wrote (1769) to Dr. Hartley: "I have been called to a holy office by the Lord himself, who most graciously manifested himself in person to me, his servant, in 1743." He adds that "God also opened his sight to the view of the spiritual world and granted him the privilege of conversing with spirits and angels."—*Emanuel Swedenborg* (by Wilkinson), pp. 74, 75. Elsewhere, speaking of his own communion with God and with the spiritual world, he says: "This has not been granted to any one since the creation of the world as it has been to me."—Work quoted, p. 206.

Again, he says: "I have discoursed with spirits and angels now for several years; nor durst any spirit, neither would any angel, say anything to me, much less instruct me, about anything in the Word; but the Lord alone, who was revealed to me, and afterward continually did and does appear before my eyes as the Sun in which He is, even as He appears to the angels, taught me and illuminated me."—*Divine Providence* (published 1764), p. 135.

† "But Swedenborg rejected, as not directly revealed by God, certain portions of the Old Testament; and, of the New Testament, he accepted the four Gospels and the Apocalypse only, as forming a portion of the 'present Word.'"—*Emanuel Swedenborg*, a Biography, pp. 139, 141.

‡ One cannot look into some of Swedenborg's works, especially his *Arcana Cœlestia*, without amazement at the character of the Scriptural interpretations that run through them; and one is forced to the conclusion that these must be accepted, if accepted at all, for a single reason,

no living creature ever held the secret key, till it was entrusted by the Creator of the Universe to a Swedish philosopher.* No candid student of Swedenborg doubts his sincerity. Beyond question, he believed his "Arcana Cœlestia" to be written under the unerring dictation of God.

This capital error—greatest among all religious fallacies of the past—here produced, as so radical an error always produces, its legitimate results. Not—strange to say! in the character of the man; it bred in him no arrogance; he retained his modest simplicity to the last: the fatal influence was on his system; sapping its cogency, neutralizing the virtue of its fine gold.

From another superstition, also, Swedenborg failed to shake himself free: he believed, if less rigidly than Calvin, in the original depravity of mankind.† Hence his doubts whether any of his fellow-creatures were worthy to enjoy the spiritual intercourse which he felt to have been granted, throughout a quarter of a century, to himself. Hence, too, his belief that the wickedness of hell was incurable and its punishments without end.

Again, some of the dogmas which he imagined to have re-

borrowed from one of the old Grecian schools—because "the Master said it." Take three or four examples, selected at hap-hazard out of tens of thousands. *Cows* signify "good natural affections" (*Divine Providence*, No. 326). A *horse* means "the understanding of the Word of God" (*True Christian Religion*, Nos. 113, 277, etc.). *Ishmael to beget twelve princes* denotes "the primary precepts which are of charity" (*Arcana Cœlestia*, No. 2089). *Joseph sold to Potiphar* is to be interpreted to mean "the alienation of Divine truths by scientifics" (*Arc. Cœlest.*, No. 4790). And so on.

* Speaking of his mission as interpreter of the Word, Swedenborg thus expresses himself: "The laws of Divine Providence, hitherto hid in wisdom among the angels, are now revealed."—*Angelic Wisdom concerning the Divine Providence*, London Ed., 1857, p. 70.

† "Every man has hereditary evil, and therefore he is in the concupiscence of many evils. . . . A man, from himself, cannot do good. . . . Thence it is that in man there is no health, or nothing sound, but that he is one entire mass of evil."—*Divine Providence*, p. 277.

ceived from God, were of a character to retard the acceptance of the truths he taught. While he rejected the idea of the Trinity,* or of a Son of God, † he held that Jehovah himself descended and assumed humanity on our earth, for the purpose of redeeming mankind, of reducing hell to subjection, and of re-organizing Heaven: seeing that He could not save His creatures from damnation in any other way. ‡ Orthodoxy and Rationalism, of course, alike repudiate this heretical and illogical conception.

But the worst results from Swedenborg's master-error were connected with that lack of charity which ever follows the insidious illusion of infallibility. Despite his equable and gentle character, despite his own tenet that men are not saved by faith, he was occasionally betrayed into the harshest intolerance. Speaking of those "who are called in the world Socinians and some of them Arians," he says: "The lot of both is . . . that they are let down into hell among those who deny God. These are meant by those who blaspheme the Holy Ghost, who will not be forgiven either in this world or in that which is to come." §

* "Scarcely any remains of the Lord's Church are left. This has come to pass in consequence of separating the Divine Trinity into three persons, each of which is declared to be God and Lord. Hence a sort of frenzy has infected the whole system of theology."—SWEDENBORG: *True Christian Religion*, London, 1858, p. 4.

† "The idea of a Son born from eternity, descending and assuming the humanity, must be found to be altogether erroneous. . . . The production of a God from a God is a thing impracticable. It is the same thing whether we use the terms begotten by God or proceeding from Him."—*True Christian Religion*, p. 83.

‡ Swedenborg's doctrine as to the incarnation is this: "Jehovah himself descended and assumed the humanity." This he did, "that he might accomplish the work of redemption, which consisted in reducing the hells to subjection and in bringing the heavens into a new, orderly arrangement. . . . God could not redeem mankind, that is deliver them from damnation and hell, by any other process than that of assuming the humanity."—*True Christian Religion*, pp. 81, 84.

§ *Angelic Wisdom concerning Divine Providence*, p. 231.

Even worse than this is the cruel spirit, aggravated by the assumption of false premises, in which he speaks of those whom he ought to have commended and hailed as spiritual brethren. We have it under his own hand, as divinely revealed to him, that the Quaker worship is so execrable and abominable that if Christians but knew its true character, "they would expel Quakers from society and permit them to live only among beasts." * And this—think of it!—from one who deemed himself the penman of God!—the recipient and inditer of truth unmixed with error!

* In Swedenborg's diary, under date October 29, 1748, he says: "The secret worship of the Quakers, sedulously concealed from the world, was made manifest. It is a worship so wicked, execrable, and abominable, that, were it known to Christians, they would expel Quakers from society, and permit them to live only among beasts. They have a vile communion of wives, etc." Again, October 28, 1748: "They are indomitably obstinate in their aversion to having their thoughts and doings made public. They strove with me and the spirits who desired (but in vain) to know their secrets."—See *Emanuel Swedenborg, his Life and Writings*, by WILLIAM WHITE, London, 1867, vol. i. p. 386, 387.

The poison of intolerance, in its most malignant type, still works among a bigoted portion of Swedenborg's followers. The (London) *Intellectual Repository* is the accredited organ of *orthodox* Swedenborgianism. Its editor (sixteen years since, however,) after stating his opinion that "spirits, even the highest angels, have nothing to tell us in relation to doctrine and life but what is revealed in the Word," goes on to say: "We therefore conclude that it is not only dangerous, but impious, to seek to have communion with spirits, especially in regard to anything of doctrine and life." But he does not stop here. He tells us that there is good reason for the command "so often repeated to the Children of Israel, to *put those to death* who had familiar spirits and who were necromancers, or as in the Hebrew text, 'asked inquiries of the dead.'"—*Intellectual Repository*, vol. for 1855, pp. 460, 461. Anything worse than this we may search the records of modern theology in vain to find.

Such is one phase of this religious movement. There is a second, directly opposed to the first. Thousands will unite with me in the acknowledgment that some of our best and most enlightened friends are *liberal* Swedenborgians.

One reads such passages as these with deep regret that a man so eminently wise in many things should have strayed, in others, so far from charity and common sense. Yet perhaps it was best. The state of society in the middle of the last century may have been such that men could not then safely be trusted to seek, through communion with the spirit-world, proofs of its existence and information touching its character and pursuits.

May we, living in the eighth decade of the nineteenth century, be trusted in this matter? Can we bear the many things, promised to us from the spiritual sphere, which Christ's apostles were not yet able to bear, and which our ancestors, of one or two centuries since, evidently were unfitted to receive? If it appear that normal spiritual communion, like adult suffrage, is upon us, the fact of its advent will, to a certain extent, be evidence that the world is not wholly unprepared for its reception.

The character of that reception, too, adds vastly to the evidence for its timeliness. One would think the world must have been an hungered for the proofs of immortality which Spiritualism has brought to light. The new faith has overrun, not our country alone, but every portion of the civilized world.* At this day, less than a quarter of a century from

* Judge J. W. Edmonds, formerly of the Supreme Bench of New York, has had more experience among Spiritualists, and a wider correspondence on Spiritualism all over the world, than any one else with whom I am acquainted. Writing to me in February last, he says: "I have received letters on the subject, during the last twenty years, from all parts of the United States, from England, Ireland, Scotland, France, Germany, Russia, Spain, Italy, Greece, the East Indies, Cuba, Jamaica, Brazil, Guatemala, Australia, New Zealand, the Sandwich Islands, the Ionian Islands, Malta, Algiers, and other places that I cannot now recall." And he mentions having received a letter and book (published in London, 1865) from an English lady who had spent ten or twelve years travelling all over Europe, and in Asia and Africa. From her book he extracts the following:

what may be regarded as its inception,* its believers, private and avowed, probably outnumber, ONE HUNDREDFOLD, the aggregate to which either of its spiritual predecessors—Quakers or Swedenborgians—ever attained. The number of those who accept, more or less unreservedly, its phenomena, may be safely assumed to exceed, in the United States, seven millions and a half,† and in the rest of Christendom at least as many more.

One might have to double this last amount, reaching thirty millions, to include all in the Christian world whose scepticism in what is called the Supernatural—but what *is* the law-governed Spiritual—has been, chiefly by this movement, more or less shaken or removed.

The constant increase in the number of Spiritualists is by no means confined to this country. In London, ten years ago,

"There is scarcely a city or a considerable town in Continental Europe, at the present moment, where Spiritualists are not reckoned by hundreds if not by thousands; where regularly-established communities do not habitually meet for spiritual purposes: and they reckon among them individuals of every class and avocation, and intellects of the highest order."—*Scepticism and Spiritualism, or the Experience of a Sceptic;* by the authoress of *Aurelia.*

* March 31, 1848. See *Footfalls*, p. 288.

† Judge Edmonds, in a letter to the "Spiritual Magazine" of London, dated May 4, 1867, estimated the number of Spiritualists in the United States, five years ago, at *ten millions.* In a recent letter to myself he has reiterated the conviction that he had good authority for such a calculation: adding that he feels assured it is under, rather than over, the truth. With less extended opportunities of judging than he, and to avoid chance of exaggeration, I put the number at three-fourths of that amount only: my own opinion being, however, that this is an under-estimate.

Those who the most deprecate the influence of modern Spiritualism are the most ready to confess how far that influence has spread. "The countless hosts of modern necromancers" is the expression employed by a religious Quarterly of the day (in a review of Dr. BUSHNELL'S *Nature and the Supernatural*) to designate the Spiritualists of the United States.—*Theological and Literary Journal* for April, 1859, p. 535.

there was but a single spiritual paper; to-day there are five,* advocating, for the present, different phases of spiritual belief. There cannot, of course, be sceptics in immortality, or secularists, among those who admit the phenomena of Spiritualism. But, for the time, there are those who are termed Christian Spiritualists, and others, calling themselves Radicals, who look upon Christ but as one of the ancient philosophers, with no claim to distinction as a teacher beyond Socrates, Seneca, and a host of others.

I am convinced that this schism is temporary only. Spiritualism is the complement of Christianity. Spiritual phenomena are the witnesses of Christianity. All thoughtful believers in the epiphanies of Spiritualism will be Christians as soon as they learn to distinguish between the simple grandeur of Christ's teachings, as embodied in the synoptical Gospels, and the Augustinian version of St. Paul's theology, as adopted in one form by the Church of Rome, and in another indorsed by Calvin and Luther: a system associated with infallibility and known, among Protestants and Romanists alike, as Orthodoxy.

Spiritual Epiphanism is spreading as fast, probably, as the world can bear it—as fast as its wisest friends desire; and it is spreading, as they think, in manner the most desirable: not as a sect—nor ever, I trust, to become such—not as a separate Church, with its prescribed creed and its ordained ministers and its formal professors. It spreads silently through the agency of daily intercourse, in the privacy of the domestic circle. It pervades, in one or other of its phases, the best literature of the day.† It invades the Churches already estab-

* Namely, the *Spiritual Magazine*, the *Spiritualist*, the *Christian Spiritualist*, *Human Nature*, and the *Medium and Daybreak:* the first three representing Christian Spiritualism; the two latter advocating Spiritualism in connection with what are usually termed radical doctrines.

† Writing this in January, 1871, I call to mind that, within the last four or five weeks, six stories of apparitions, all seriously and earnestly narrated, have appeared in one or other of Harpers' periodicals: one

lished, not as an opponent but as an ally. Its tendency is to modify the creed and soften the asperities, of Protestant and Romanist, of Presbyterian and Episcopalian, of Baptist and Methodist, of Unitarian and Universalist. Its tendency is to leaven, with invigorating and spiritualizing effect, the religious sentiment of the age, increasing its vitality, enlivening its convictions.

I would not be understood, however, as expecting that Spiritualism will effect all this except in measure as its rich mines are wisely worked; nor as asserting, in a general way, that we of the present age are worthy recipients of its revealings. There are millions of men and women among us who lack the judgment needed to prosecute spiritual research, just as there are millions more who have not the culture necessary to exercise judiciously the right to vote. In either case there is but one remedy: the millions must be educated up to the occasion.

Spiritual manifestations are more inevitable than universal suffrage; for a majority, if it see fit, can limit the elective franchise: but no majority, be it ever so large, can summon, or can exclude, the most important among the epiphanies of Spiritualism. If dreams do, sometimes, supply warning or prophecy; if material objects are, occasionally, moved before our eyes by powers not of this world; if houses really are what is termed haunted, without human agency; if the spirits of those whom we call dead do, at times, reveal themselves by influence, or by intelligent sounds, or by actual apparition as did Christ to assure his disciples of immortality—what power

leading to the detection of a murder; three others (supplement to *Harper's Weekly* of December 24, 1870, p. 846) from the pen of Florence Marryat, daughter of the celebrated novelist: one of these last having been witnessed by Captain Marryat himself, and all, the writer says, being "strictly true and well authenticated." But no periodicals of our country are conducted with better judgment, nor with stricter regard to the demands of public sentiment, than those issued by the Harpers.

have we weak mortals, who must sit still and see winds and waves fulfil their mission, to control the agency of disembodied spirits? Shall we set about considering whether we shall accept the epiphany of the rainbow or the apparition of the Aurora Borealis?

If the belief in the phenomena called Spiritual be a delusion of the senses, it will come to naught; if it be of God we cannot arrest its advent. We may receive it unwisely, interpret it ignorantly, treat it with distrust or with levity; or we may examine its phenomena in a patient and catholic spirit of inquiry, in manner suited to its sacred claims: that is all. And it is inexpressibly important that it find us with our lights burning. If we seek it, darkling; if we meet it, insensible to its high character; it may prove a bane instead of a blessing.

That the Spiritualists of our day need wise advice and prudent cautions; that some of them run into extravagance and misconceive alike the objects of spiritual research and the fitting mode of conducting it; that their ranks have been invaded by thousands of waifs and strays, possessed by vagrant and fantastic opinions—is but what happens in all great revolutions of opinion, political or religious; is but that which befel the German Reformers of the sixteenth century and the French Revolutionists of the eighteenth. The wild waves of freedom, as some one has suggested, occasionally cast their blinding spray beyond legitimate bound. But time brings counsel.

Nor is it reasonable to expect that Spiritualism's best fruits should be obtained in their maturity, at this early stage of their culture; much less do I assume here to produce them. If, even, by length of experience and profundity of research, I had become fully competent to set forth all the conditions necessary to obtain the surest and most useful results from the manifestations of Spiritualism, it would require a volume to contain a detailed statement of these conditions, properly evidenced and illustrated. But, though I have faithfully expended the leisure which fifteen years of active life left me, in this study, I am far indeed from being thus competent: nor do I believe that any man living yet is. Such knowledge must come, like all important knowledge, through the labors of many and the gradual unfoldings of time.

Such hints and warnings as seemed to me the most important I have already given; as that the Spiritualist must beware of the temptation to imagine that he is obtaining revealings direct from God, or from any person of the Godhead, or from any other infallible source. Let him rest satisfied if he obtain sure proof of immortality: that is the pearl of great price, to become the possessor of which no efforts are too arduous, no pains too great. For the rest he must trust to general precepts and advices, tested and approved by reason and conscience. Every profound student of Nature becomes convinced that infallible teachings touching the details of human conduct and earthly affairs do not enter into the economy of the universe.

Especially should the Spiritualist be on his guard against seeking worldly wealth and profit through spiritual revealings. The very attempt tends to attract spirits of a low order. The medium who submits to it incurs grave dangers; while the votary puts himself in the sure road to delusion and disappointment.* A medium who is true to his high trust will refuse to enter a path thus perilous and misleading.† If, some-

* But that space fails me I could adduce numerous examples in proof of this.

† An anecdote, in this connection, may be worth relating. In the spring of 1858, we had several sittings in my apartments in the Palazzo Valli, Naples, with the celebrated medium, Mr. Home; at which sittings the Count d'Aquila (or, as we usually called him, Prince Luigi, third brother of the then reigning King of Naples), at his own suggestion, assisted; no one else except my family being present. It was thought by some that, in case of a revolution, the Prince's chance to succeed his brother on the throne was good; and he asked Mr. Home to obtain for him an answer to a question which, though cautiously worded, evidently looked to the succession. "I know," said Mr. Home, in reply, "that your Royal Highness will pardon me for saying that such an

times when all human effort has failed, spiritual aid or advice in such matters is volunteered, it should, even then, be received with great caution. Money-changers are out of place in the spiritual temple. Man's destiny is to earn his bread by industry, not by divination.

Still another warning is greatly needed. The most experienced Spiritualists believe that no one, though actuated by the purest motives, can abandon himself to influences from the next world, exclusively and throughout a long term of years (for instance as Swedenborg did), without risk of serious injury and without imminent danger of being, more or less frequently, misled. Secularism is lamentably in error when she teaches that it is the part of wisdom to live here without taking thought, or seeking to fit ourselves, for a hereafter: but, on the other hand, it *is* true that earth-life and its duties are an indispensable preparation for our next phase of being. Each world, like each age of man, has its own sphere with appropriate duties, to be fulfilled with reference the one to the other, but not to be interchanged. If, in infancy, dreaming constantly of manhood and its privileges, we neglect the culture and pursuits which pertain to childhood, we shall suffer for it in our adult years; and it is doubtful whether any development in the next world can fully compensate for neglected opportunities of improvement and of usefulness in this. If, while here, we do not habitually avail ourselves of such opportunities, it may be assumed as certain that we shall die at last, like hermits after a barren life in the desert, utterly unfitted for our future homes.

Again: Exclusive devotion to meditations, or to spirit-

inquiry ought not to be made of the spirits. It is their office to supply us with spiritual knowledge, not to satisfy curiosity about worldly concerns."

"You are quite right, Mr. Home," replied Prince Luigi, "and I thank you for speaking so plainly."

A reproof and a reply which, considering the circumstances, were equally honorable to the medium and to the Prince.

influences, connected with the next world, gives birth, in Spiritualism as in Theology, to a vague and heavy literature, in which common sense has small part. Nevertheless slurs against the current effusions of Spiritualism come with a bad grace from those, standing afar off, who have never lifted a finger to sift profitable from worthless, or done aught, in any way, to purify or improve what they condemn.

The space I allotted to this branch of the subject is exhausted; and perhaps I have said enough toward marking the importance of this phenomenal movement, and assigning to Spiritualism itself definite character and fitting place among the religious beliefs of the day. Though not a sect, it is doubtful whether any sect, exerting peaceful influence only, ever spread with the same rapidity, or made its mark during so brief an existence, on the hearts of so considerable a fraction of mankind. Already it begins to assert its position. Though its truths are disputed still, yet, except by the ignorant or the hopelessly bigoted, they are not despised. The idea is daily gaining ground that its occult agencies may richly repay earnest research. The essential is that the entire subject should be studied in its broad phase, as one of the vital elements of an enlightened Christian faith.

CHAPTER III.

OF INSPIRATION.

"That perfect silence where the lips and heart
Are still, and we no longer entertain
Our own imperfect thoughts and vain opinions,
But God alone speaks in us."—LONGFELLOW.

"There does not appear the least intimation in history or tradition that religion was first reasoned out: but the whole of history and tradition makes for the other side, that it came into the world by revelation. Indeed the state of religion in the first ages of which we have any account, seems to suppose and intimate that this was the original of it among mankind."—BUTLER.*

THE subject of Inspiration, like that of the signs and wonders of the Gospels and of the spiritual gifts commended by Paul, has usually fallen into very injudicious hands. Its would-be friends have done it far more harm than its opponents. The rationalistic spirit of the age is disposed to reject it; and the chief reason for this is the extravagance, and the exclusive character, of the claims put forward in its behalf by theologians.

Protestant Orthodoxy claims that it is an exceptional and miraculous gift of God, granted to man during one century only of the last eighteen; and then granted only to the Author of

* *Analogy of Religion*, part ii. chap. 2; pp. 195–6 (of London Ed. of 1809). See, in corroboration, pp. 139, 140. See also, on the same subject, preceding page of this volume, 169.

our religion and to eight others; namely, to the four Evangelists and to St. Paul, St. James, St. Peter, and St. Jude.*

Roman Catholic Orthodoxy claims that this miraculous gift of God has been granted throughout the whole of the last eighteen centuries; but, during the last seventeen of these, only to one ecclesiastical jurisdiction; namely, to the Holy Catholic Church.

Both Orthodoxies, though differing on so many other points, agree in claiming for Inspiration that it is a direct gift of God and the source of unmixed, unerring truth.

Loaded down by claims so unphilosophical as these, we need not wonder that Inspiration is rejected as a fallacy by many of the most earnest and thoughtful minds of the day. When Science fully awakes to the fact that there may, as part of the cosmical plan, be intermundane as well as mundane phenomena, much of this growing scepticism will be dissipated. Before this can happen, however, we must discard the orthodox definition of Inspiration, and adopt one more in accordance with the enlightened spirit of the age; somewhat, perhaps, in this wise:

It is a mental or psychical phenomenon, strictly law-governed; occasional, but not exceptional or exclusive; sometimes of a spiritual and ultramundane character, indeed, but never miraculous; often imparting invaluable knowledge to man, but never infallible teachings; one of the most precious of all God's gifts to His creatures, but, in no case, involving a *direct* message from Him—a message to be accepted, unquestioned by reason or conscience, as Divine truth unmixed with human error.

To this it may be added, in accordance with Bishop Butler's

* It may, however, properly be added that Protestantism claims that the majority of a certain Œcumenical Council was inspired by God *in one of its acts;* namely, the Council of Carthage when, at the close of the fourth century, it established the Canon of Scripture. For, unless this be admitted, there is no sure proof that the Bible, as now canonically constructed, is a miraculously inspired volume.

views, that Inspiration is the source not of one religion alone, but, in phase more or less pure, of all religions, ancient or modern, that have held persistent sway over any considerable portion of mankind. And just in proportion to the relative purity of this source, welling up in each system of faith respectively, is the larger or smaller admixture of the Good and the True which—modern candor is learning to admit—is to be found, in certain measure, even in the rudest creed; as Lowell has it:

"Each form of worship that hath swayed
The life of man, and given it to grasp
The master-key of knowledge, reverence,
Enfolds some germs of goodness and of right." *

Among those who adopt this broad view of Inspiration as a universal agency, there are two different opinions touching its origin: one class of reasoners (including many students of vital magnetism) tracing it to a peculiar condition of the mind, while others seek its source in some occult intelligence outside of the individual, and operating upon him. My own conviction is, that there is truth in both theories. Inspiration is a phenomenon sometimes purely psychical, correlative with clearsight (clairvoyance), and appertaining to the department of Mental Science; † sometimes produced by influences from the next world, and to be referred to Spiritualism.

* It is a cheering sign of the times when a clergyman of one persuasion issues a series of sermons, in which he recognizes and sets forth the excellence of Churches other than his own, prefaced with the remark that "a good man's home is the more delightful as he calls to mind that the world is full of good homes; and that millions are as happy as he." The Rev. THOMAS K. BEECHER (of Elmira, New York), has done this, in a small volume entitled *Our Seven Churches* (New York, 1870): including, among the seven, the Church of Rome.

† Andrew Jackson Davis, the well-known author of *Nature's Divine Revelation*, is often quoted as having written that work under dictation of spirits. But he himself declares—correctly, no doubt—that it was

Among the ancient philosophers there were those who, more or less distinctly, detected its existence; some in one of its forms, some in the other. I have space but for a single specimen of each.

The most illustrious example comes to us from One who has not inaptly been called the Father of Moral Philosophy, and who was the Spiritualist of the age in which he lived. In regard to Inspiration, Socrates, unless Plato has belied him, adopted the spiritual theory.

Among the celebrated Dialogues of Plato is one in which the interlocutors are Socrates and Ion, an Athenian declaimer or rhapsodist who had been in the habit, in his public harangues, of introducing copious and beautiful illustrations of Homer. Alluding to the great success these had obtained, and to the fact that, when he attempted to illustrate other poets, all his efforts failed, Ion asks of Socrates an explanation of this distinction. Socrates replies:

"I will tell you, O Ion, what appears to me to be the cause of this inequality of power. It is that you are not master of any art for the illustration of Homer; but it is a Divine influence which moves you, like that which resides in the stone called magnet by Euripides." *

Socrates, then, in further explanation, adds: "The authors of these great poems which we admire do not attain to excellence through the rules of art, but they utter their beautiful melodies of verse in a state of inspiration and, as it were, possessed by a Spirit not their own."

Then he inquires of Ion: "Tell me, and do not conceal

written in a state of clairvoyance, or as he phrases it, in "the superior condition." The distinction between clearsight and mediumship is important.

* It is noteworthy that, twenty-two centuries since, a philosopher detected the connection between magnetism (though only in its terrestrial phase) and that state of mind which frequently gives birth to inspiration. How much Reichenbach's experiments would have interested Socrates!

what I ask. When you declaim well and strike your audience with admiration; whether you sing of Ulysses rushing upon the threshold of his palace, discovering himself to the suitors and pouring his shafts out at his feet; or of Achilles assailing Hector; or those affecting passages concerning Andromache, or Hecuba, or Priam—are you then self-possessed? or, rather, are you not rapt and filled with such enthusiasm by the deeds you recite, that you fancy yourself in Ithaca or Troy, or wherever else the poem transports you?"

ION. "You speak most truly, Socrates."

The sage then gives his explanation. "You, O Ion, are influenced by Homer. If you recite the works of any other poet, you get drowsy and are at a loss what to say; but when you hear any of the compositions of that poet, your thoughts are excited and you grow eloquent. . . . This explains the question you asked wherefore Homer and no other poet inspires you with eloquence: it is that you are thus excellent not by science but through Divine inspiration." *

The expression (ascribed, as above, by Plato to Socrates), "you are influenced by Homer," is very remarkable: it embodies the cardinal doctrine of Spiritualism.

The philosopher had the best of all reasons for adopting this view of the case; namely, his own personal experience. This leads me to speak of

* "*Ion*," or of Inspiration. I have here followed the translation adopted by G. H. Lewis in his "History of Philosophy," series i. The above extracts and many others in corroboration, may there be found. The authenticity of this dialogue, as written by Plato, is admitted on all hands. It contains, of course, only a narration of Socrates' opinions, not an indorsement of them by the narrator. Yet they seem to have been substantially shared by Socrates' illustrious pupil. An enlightened church historian says: "Plato's speculations rested on a basis altogether historical. He connected himself with the actual phenomena of religious life and with the traditions lying before him. . . . It still continued to be the aim of original Platonism to trace throughout history the vestiges of a connection between the visible and invisible worlds."—NEANDER: *Church History* (Bohn's Ed.), vol. i. p. 26.

The Genius, or Demon, of Socrates.*

For particulars touching the noted Guardian Spirit or Demon (*Daimonion*) of Socrates, we are indebted to the same eminent authority through which most of the opinions spoken but not set down by the martyr-philosopher himself, have reached us.

Though alluded to elsewhere in Plato's writings,† the most direct and reliable account of this spirit-voice and its warnings is to be found in the "Apology," written immediately after the death of Socrates. In this paper, the only strictly authentic record we possess of that philosopher's defence before his judges, Plato, who was present at his trial, may surely be trusted as having reproduced, with fidelity, the statements made, and the arguments employed, on that memorable occasion, by the master he loved.

Among the charges preferred against Socrates had been set out his pretence of communicating with a familiar spirit. In connection with this, and alluding to the fact that he had taught in private, not delivered orations in popular assemblies, Socrates said to his judges:

"The cause of this is what you have often and in many places heard me mention: because I am moved by a certain divine and spiritual influence, which also Melitus, through mockery, has set out in the indictment. This began with me from childhood: being a kind of voice which, when present, is wont to divert me from what I am about to do, but which

* It need hardly be stated that *Demon* is here employed, as usual in Grecian mythology, in the sense of a divinity below the great gods. Thus in Cooke's *Hesiod:*

"Holy demons, by great Jove designed
To be on earth the guardians of mankind."

† As in the *First Alcibiades*, § 1. Also, at length, in the *Theages*, §§ 10, 11.

To the same subject Xenophon alludes in his *Memoirs of Socrates*, Book i., § 1: where he says that those who neglected the warnings of Socrates' Genius "had no small cause for repentance."

never urges me on. This it was which opposed my meddling in public politics." *

Another allusion to the same subject, more solemn, pronounced in the immediate prospect of death after a majority of his judges had passed sentence upon him, is as follows:

"To me, O my judges, a strange thing has happened. For the wonted prophetic voice of my guardian deity, on every former occasion even in the most trifling affairs, opposed me if I was about to do anything wrong. But now, when that has befallen me which ye yourselves behold—a thing which is supposed to be the extremity of evil—neither did the warning of the God oppose me when I departed from home this morning, nor yet while I addressed you, though it has often restrained me in the midst of speaking. What do I suppose to be the cause of this? . . . That which has befallen me is not the effect of chance: but this is clear to me that now to die and be freed from my cares is better for me. On this account the warning in no way turned me aside." †

The sincerity of the philosopher when he said this cannot rationally be doubted. He must be a stubborn or a thoughtless sceptic who assumes the ground that a man like Socrates, about to die because he would not purchase life by desisting from teaching what he felt to be good and just, would, at such a moment, swerve a hairbreadth from the strict truth. ‡

According to what rational canon of evidence can we reject such testimony as this? The most candid among modern his-

* *Apology*, § 19.

† *Apology*, §§ 31, 33. See also, as to that matter, PLUTARCH, *De Genio Socrates*, c. 20; and APULEIUS, *De Deo Socratis*.

‡ Seldom in any age, by sage or martyr, has nobler sentiment been uttered than by Socrates on his trial, in reply to the charge of impiety: "If it is your wish to acquit me on condition that I henceforth be silent, I reply that I love and honor you, but that I ought rather to obey the gods than you. Neither in the presence of judges nor of the enemy is it permitted me, or any other man, to use every sort of means to escape death. It is not death but crime that it behooves us to avoid · crime moves faster than death."

torians of philosophy admit that the proof is conclusive.* Lewis, who will certainly not be accused of superstition or credulity, alluding, in his History of Philosophy, to Socrates' belief that he was warned, from time to time, by a Divine voice, says: "This is his own explicit statement; and surely, in a Christian country, abounding in examples of persons believing in direct intimations from above, there can be little difficulty in crediting such a statement." †

To what extent Socrates owed his views on immortality and a future life to his Guardian Spirit we can never know; nor is it likely that he himself could have determined. He seems to have regarded that influence as one sent to warn rather than to teach. Yet it would be strange if, twenty-three centuries ago, he had groped his way, unaided, to truths which we scarcely recognize to-day. Take, in addition to the foregoing, the following example:

"When does the soul attain to the truth? For when it attempts to investigate anything along with the body, it is plain that it is then led astray by it. . . . The soul reasons most effectually when none of the corporeal senses harass it; neither hearing, sight, pain or pleasure of any kind; but it retires as much as possible within itself, and aims at the knowledge of what is real, taking leave of the body and, as far as it can, abstaining from any union or participation with it." ‡

* As STANLEY, in his *History of Philosophy*, London, 1856. He there says: "We have the testimony of Plato and Xenophon, contemporary with him, confirmed by Plutarch, Cicero, and other reliable authorities, to say nothing of Tertullian, Origen, and others of the Ancient Fathers, that Socrates had an attendant Spirit, which warned him of danger and misfortune."—Chap. vi. p. 19.

† G. H. LEWIS: *Biographical History of Philosophy*, London 2d Ed., 1857, p. 141.

‡ *Phædo*, § 10. I have followed Stanford's translation.

It is worth noting, however, that Socrates (if he be correctly reported), following out this idea, strayed, as many noble souls have strayed, into the barren regions of asceticism and abstraction; forbidding use, lest abuse should follow. He sought wisdom through deliverance "from

Here we have the germ of the apneumatic or psychical view of Inspiration. Cicero, in a later age, enlarged on this. The following remarkable passage, literally translated, is from his "Tusculan Questions."

"What else do we do, when from pleasure, that is from the body, when from common affairs which minister to the body, when from public duties, when from all business whatever, we call off the soul—what, I say, is it that we then do, other than to recall the soul to itself and to self-communion, and to lead it in a great degree away from the body? But to segregate the soul from the body, can it be anything else than a learning how to die? (nec quidquam aliud est quam emori discere?) Wherefore, believe me, we should lay this to heart, and disjoin ourselves from our bodies; that is, we should accustom ourselves to die (disjungamusque nos a corporibus; id est, consuescamus mori). And thus, while we remain on earth, it will be as if we approached celestial life; and when at last we are released from earthly bonds, the exit of the soul will thereby be less retarded." *

The "accustoming ourselves to die" is somewhat fanciful; yet the expression is, in a measure, borne out by some of the phenomena of Vital Magnetism. When artificial somnambulism deepens into what French magnetizers call *extase*—that is, profound trance—the bands which connect soul and body seem to be greatly loosened; a strong desire sometimes shows itself in the subject to escape from earth to a brighter world; and if, through inexperience or inadvertence of the operator, this deep

the irrationality of the body;" thought we should "study to live as though on the very confines of death;" and advises "to use reflection alone and unalloyed, endeavoring to investigate every reality by itself and unmixed, *abstaining as much as possible from the use of the eyes*, and in a word of every part of the body, as confounding the soul and, when united with it, preventing its attainment to wisdom and truth."—*Phædo*, §§ 10, 11, 12.

He did not recognize the essential value and uses of earth-life, nor the importance of teachings through the senses.

* *Tuscul. Quæst.*, lib. i. § 31.

trance is too much prolonged, death may actually ensue. I was told, in Paris, that several such cases had occurred; but the names of the parties, as may be supposed, were kept secret. An instance in which a somnambule* had a narrow escape is related by a French magnetizer, author of a curious work on the "Secrets of the Future Life." He had two lucid somnambules; one a youth named Bruno, the other, Adèle, a woman in humble circumstances ("simple ouvrière comme moi," he says of her), not a professional medium nor ever taking money for the exercise of her gift, but who had been, from infancy, a natural somnambulist.

One day he had magnetized both simultaneously, desiring to compare their impressions and to satisfy his doubts whether there was danger in carrying the state of *extase* too far. He brought Bruno into magnetic relation with Adèle, telling him to observe what became of her. While occupied during some time with the young man, he (Bruno) suddenly cried out: "I've lost sight of her; awake her; there's but just time." Alarmed, the magnetizer turned his attention to Adèle whom, for a quarter of an hour, he had left to herself. I translate the rest from his own words: "In that short time her body had become almost icy cold; I could detect neither pulse nor respiration; her face was of a yellowish green, the lips blue, the heart gave no sign of life. A mirror which I approached to her lips remained undimmed. I magnetized her with my utmost force, hoping to revive her; but, during five minutes, without any effect whatever. Bruno and several persons who were assisting at the sitting added, by their terror, to my discomfiture; and, for a moment, I thought all was over and that the soul, in very deed, had left its body. I begged all present to pass into the next room, so as to recover my energy; but, though hope still lingered, I felt powerless. Throwing myself on my knees, I im-

* I adopt, from the French, the term *somnambule*, to designate a patient under the influence of artificially-induced somnambulism; restricting the meaning of the more usual word *somnambulist* to a natural sleep-walker.

plored God not to suffer that soul, a victim of my doubts, to pass away. After a brief period of anguish, I heard the low words: "Why did you recall me? It was all but done, when God, touched by your prayer, sent me back." *

The author adds: "I entreat those who might be tempted to risk a similar experiment to desist. A more terrible spectacle cannot be witnessed; and the issue, in their case, might be less fortunate than in mine."

On a previous occasion, Adèle being in the state of *extase*, there had appeared to her, and conversed with her (as she believed), her mother and two deceased brothers. The following conversation between her and her magnetizer then ensued:

"Ah, how I should like to be with them! Let me go; I shall soon be in Heaven."

"Very generous of you! And what shall I do with your body?"

"Have it buried, or disposed of as you please."

"And the officers of justice, what am I to say to them?"

"Tell them, I'm gone." †

That there is, during magnetic sleep, a modification of the normal relations between soul and body, is further attested by the insensibility to outward sounds and to pain, even the most acute, which sometimes supervenes. ‡ One cannot read the

* CAHAGNET: *Arcanes de la Vie Future dévoilés*, Paris, 1848; vol. i. pp. 117, 118. This work went to press in December, 1847, some months before even the name of "Rochester Knockings" had been heard among us. Yet Cahagnet registers full details of communications made to his somnambules by eighty different spirits of the departed; and the identity of several among these he considers positively proved.

† Work quoted: vol. i. pp. 90, 91.

‡ As early as the year 1846, there was performed at Cherbourg (the well-known French port in the Department de la Manche), a surgical operation of the most painful character, affording proof that the phenomena above alluded to are real. The official record of this operation, signed by fifty-two witnesses present, was published in the *Journal de Cherbourg*, and in the *Phare de la Manche* of September 25, 1846. This *procès-verbal* was drawn up from notes taken on the spot by M.

best works on Magnetism without coming upon strong reasons for the belief that, in the profound magnetic trance, there is a certain recession of the soul from its earthly minister and an approach to that stage of existence, soon to come, when what St. Paul calls the "natural body" will be wholly discarded.

Another phenomenon is now proved beyond reasonable denial; namely, that, during this partial segregation of the soul from physical impressions and worldly concerns, its native powers, less subjected, it would seem, to the earth-clog that habitually weighs upon them, exhibit clearer perceptions and higher knowledge. This occurs when, as Socrates expressed it, the soul "retires within itself," or, as Cicero phrases it, when we "recall the soul to itself, and to self-communion;" whether this be done artificially (as by magnetic passes), or whether it happen in a more normal condition of the body, by natural idiosyncrasy.

The most modest and cautious of writers on Vital Magnetism, Dr. Bertrand,* has well defined this state, when artificially superinduced: "The somnambule," he says, "acquires new perceptions furnished by interior organs; and the succession of these perceptions constitutes a new life, differing from that which we habitually enjoy: in that new life come to light phases of knowledge differing from those which our ordinary sensations convey to us." †

I myself have, on many occasions, verified this phenomenon of what may be called double-consciousness, ‡ attended by exal-

Shevrel, advocate and member of the Municipal Council of Cherbourg; and to its scrupulous accuracy the signatures of the witnesses testify.

I should here give this *procès-verbal* but for its length, and for the fact that enlightened physicians no longer deny the reality of this phenomenon.

* Member of the Faculty of Medicine of Paris, and formerly a pupil of the Polytechnic School.

† BERTRAND: "Traité du Somnambulisme," Paris, 1823; pp. 469, 470.

‡ An interesting case of *natural* double-consciousness, continued throughout fifteen years, is related by the Rev. Dr. Plumer, in Harpers Monthly for May, 1860, page 807. It is suggestive.

tation of intelligence in the abnormal state. But others can speak, as to this, from a much wider range of experience than I. A physician with whom I am intimately acquainted—one among the best known and most successful in New York—and his wife, having, before the advent of Spiritualism, taken a deep interest in magnetic phenomena, experimented for about two years with an American sempstress, moderately educated, with rather more than the average mental capacity of her class. He told me that Marian awake and Marian in magnetic sleep were two persons as far apart by perceptions, intelligence, judgment, as could well be imagined. One day when we were talking of magnetism and its effects, he told me that the girl had made commentaries upon medical and philosophical subjects, evincing great profundity and acuteness. On many other subjects she was equally clearsighted.*

While adverting, in connection with the subject of inspiration, to such phenomena as the above, occurring under the operation of a special agency, I bear in mind that the world has

* But here is a supplement to such experience. Dr. Bertrand, speaking of somnambules whose power of clear-sight *in detecting disease* had been satisfactorily verified, relates the following conversation which he had with one of them:

"Do you see your heart and the blood flowing from it?"

"Yes."

"Can you perceive that it is divided into two cavities?"

"Yes, I see one on the right and one on the left."

"Then tell me, is the blood of the same color on both sides?"

"Yes," she answered in a decided tone, "and to prove to you that it is, you may bleed me here or here (touching first her right arm then her left), and you will find the same blood."

"This reply," says Bertrand, "plainly showed that this woman imagined there were two cavities in the heart, from one of which flowed the blood to supply the right side of the body and from the other to supply the left."—*Traité du Somnambulisme*, p. 73.

In all such cases there is the chance of what magnetizers call "imperfect lucidity." It will not do, as Socrates recommended, to abstain from the use of our eyes.

recognized them, in this special form, for less than a century.* But the analogy between these and the various phases of intellectual and psychical exaltation, religious ecstasy, involuntary hypnotism, spontaneous trance, is so close that one cannot reasonably deny the connection of one with the other. Most of the spiritual gifts enumerated by Paul come to light, in persons of sensitive temperament, during magnetic sleep, and showed themselves during such strange, epidemical excitements as produced the alleged possession of the Ursuline Nuns of Loudun † (1632 to 1639), and brought out pseudo-miracles among

* Somnambulism, in the form now known to magnetizers, was observed for the first time, by the Marquis de Puységur, on his estate of Buzancy, near Soissons, on the fourth of March, 1784.

† *Histoire des Diables de Loudun, ou de la Possession des Religieuses Ursulines*, Amsterdam, 1670. At page 235 of this work is a curious document; namely, the certificate of *Monsieur* (Gaston, brother of Louis XIII., then King of France), who visited Loudun in May, 1635, to inquire into the character of the alleged possession. He certifies that he had *perfect proof of its reality;* namely, that the possessed nuns *obeyed his mental orders;* in other words, read unexpressed thoughts. He says: "Ayant desiré d'avoir un signe parfait de la véritable possession de ces filles, avons concerté secrettement et à voix basse avec le Père Tranquille Capucin, de commander au Démon *Sabulon*, qui possédoit actuellement la Sœur Claire, qu'il allât baiser la main droite du Père Elizée, son exorciste; ledit Démon [meaning, of course, the nun herself] y a ponctuellement obéi, selon notre desir; ce qui nous a fait croire certainement que ce que les religieux travaillans aux exorcismes desdites filles nous ont dit de leur possession est véritable."

But this phenomenon of thought-reading is familiar to magnetizers. I myself instituted, in the years 1856 and 1857, a series of careful experiments to verify it, keeping strict minutes. By reference to these I find that I propounded 216 questions and obtained about *ninety-three per cent* of pertinent answers, through a medium (not professional) and of but moderate powers. Many of the answers extended to several lines; and, apart from their strict relevancy, were beyond the mental capacity of the medium. The following may be taken as an average example; both questions being asked mentally:

Q. "Can you tell me whether spirits have the power of prophecy?"

A. "To some extent."

the Prophets (Trembleurs) of the Cevennes* (1686 to 1707). The mantic fury of the Pythoness was evidently of magnetic character. Numa, in the Arician grove; Mahomet, in the cave of Hira; may have been unconsciously under spiritual or somnambulic influence. Peter's vision, when he saw Heaven opened and a certain vessel descending; Paul's trance, "whether in the body or out of the body" he could not tell; bear, unmistakably, more or less resemblance to many hundred cases of *extase* that have appeared in Paris, in London, and elsewhere, during the present century. All such manifestations belong to one great class of phenomena.

The simplest and most usual form of Inspiration is what is usually called the inspiration of genius; its results appearing in eminent literary efforts, in masterpieces of art, possibly in some of our most wonderful scientific discoveries and mechanical inventions, more evidently in the highest order of musical composition. All this is sometimes ascribed to native organization duly cultivated.† But aside from the confessedly

Q. "What are the limits?"

A. "Perceiving more than men, one element of prophetic power is greater."—Extracted from sitting of April 11, 1857.

A concise and pertinent reply, not so much to the words, as to the sense of my mental question. But I did not for a moment imagine, as Prince Gaston did, that the Devil had anything to do with it. It purported to come from a dear, deceased friend.

For further references on the subject of the Ursuline Nuns of Loudun, see note on page 103 of *Footfalls on the Boundary of Another World.*

* Sometimes called *Camisards* or *Camisars.* They were French Protestants who took arms to resist persecution under the revocation of the Edict of Nantes.—See *Histoire des Camisards*, by M. de Court de Gébelin, 1760. Also *Clavis Prophetica*, or a key to the prophecies of Monsieur Marion and the other Camisars, London, 1707: *Nouveaux Memoires pour servir à l'Histoire des Camisars*, London, 1708; *Examin du Théatre Sacré des Cevennes.* For other references see *Footfalls*, note on page 103.

† See, on this subject, Mr. Galton's interesting work on *Hereditary Genius.* I do not assert that in the department of what are called the exact sciences—as, for example, in the researches of Galileo and in those, still more inestimable, of Newton—we are justified in assuming

powerful influence of a large and well-formed brain—the best of patrimonies—genius may owe its triumphs to agencies that are invisible, like attraction, except in their effects.

Great poets from the earliest times have had a dim feeling that they were aided from above, and were wont to invoke the assistance of unseen Powers—may we not say (as Socrates said), with reason? When a poem by a Greek schoolmaster, dating from the far past, still invites translation by our ablest scholars, calling forth the same admiration to-day with which it was greeted almost three thousand years ago; when a few dramas by a comparatively illiterate man * are found, after three centuries have elapsed, to have furnished, to the Saxon tongue, one fourth of its household words; † does it not suggest the probability of aid from a higher sphere of being? The wondrous character of these results, bewildering the world, has provoked sceptical speculations touching their authors; as if the effect were out of proportion to its reputed cause. Professor Wolf of Berlin, ‡ in a celebrated work, denies to Homer

that spiritual aid was granted. Even if we do not subscribe to the poet's lines,

> "Nature and Nature's laws lay hid in night,
> God said 'Let Newton be!' and all was light"—

we cannot but admit that the scientific clearsight of England's greatest physicist was almost beyond parallel. Still it was of mathematical character—strictly material, not spiritual—and may have been but hereditary aptitude, appearing in eminent degree.

* "It is a strong argument in favor of Shakspeare's illiterature, that it was maintained by all his contemporaries, many of whom have bestowed every other merit upon him, and by his successors who lived nearest to his time: and that it has been denied only by Gildon, Sewell, and others down to Upton, who could have no means of ascertaining the truth."—*Life of Shakspeare* prefixed to Chalmers' edition of his Plays, 8 vols., London, 1823, p. 14.

† In BARTLETT'S *Familiar Quotations* (American edition, 1867), out of 391 pages of noted passages from various English authors, 94 pages are devoted to Shakspeare alone.

‡ Frederick Augustus Wolf, one of the founders, and afterward one of the Professors, of the University of Berlin. The work alluded to

the authorship of the Iliad and Odyssey, even casting doubts on his existence, and taking the ground that these immortal poems were the joint production of many successive rhymers and rhapsodists. So, too, in the case of Shakspeare, a cultivated and most industrious writer spent her life, and may be said to have lost it, in collecting and giving to the public what she believed to be proof that the pupil of the Stratford free-school was, in no sense, entitled to the authorship of the plays that have enchanted the world under his name. *

So, again, in regard to the most celebrated among painters: his contemporaries regarded him, and his biographers speak of him, though he died at the early age of thirty-seven, with a sort of reverence, as of a divinely-inspired personage. Vasari commences his life thus: "The large and liberal hand with which Heaven is sometimes pleased to accumulate the infinite riches of its treasures on one sole favorite . . . is exemplified in the instance of Raphael Sanzio." Again he says that such as Raphael "are scarcely to be called simple men; they are rather, if it be permitted so to speak, entitled to the appellation of mortal gods." And, further on, he speaks of this painter as one of those "who by some special gift of nature or by the particular favor accorded to them by the Almighty, are performing miracles in the art." †

We have, so far as I know, no record of Raphael's domestic life, nor any collection of his familiar letters. These might

above, *Prolegomena ad Homerum* (Halle, 1795), created much excitement in the literary world and called forth many replies.

* *The Philosophy of the Plays of Shakspeare Unfolded*, by DELIA BACON: Boston, 1857.

The story of this intellectual, untiring, and eccentric writer is one of the saddest episodes in the history of literary enterprise. Her peculiarities and her fate—insanity supervening as the result of utter disappointment—are recorded in HAWTHORNE'S *Our Old Home;* chapter entitled *Recollections of a Gifted Woman.*

† VASARI: *Lives of the Painters* (Foster's Translation, London, 1851), vol. iii. pp. 1, 2, 58.

have disclosed his own consciousness of the Inspiration that marks the artistic temperament.

We *have* direct evidence of this kind, however, in the case of two of the world's most renowned musicians.

Beethoven, speaking of the source whence came to him the spirit of his wonderful masterpieces, said to "Bettina": "From the focus of inspiration I feel compelled to let the melody stream forth on all sides. I follow it—passionately overtake it again; I see it escape me, vanish amid the crowd of varied excitements—soon I seize it up again with renewed passion; I cannot part from it—with quick rapture I multiply it in every form of modulation—and at the last moment I triumph over the first musical thought—see now! that's a symphony." *

Even more striking is the following, from a letter written by Mozart to an intimate friend: "You say you should like to know my way of composing, and what method I follow in writing works of some extent. I can really say no more on this subject than the following; for I myself know no more about it and cannot account for it. When I am, as it were, completely myself, entirely alone and of good cheer—say travelling in a carriage, or walking after a good meal, or during the night when I cannot sleep; it is on such occasions that my ideas flow best and most abundantly. *Whence* and *how* they come I know not; nor can I force them. Those ideas which please me I retain in memory, and am accustomed, as I have been told, to hum them to myself. If I continue in this way, it soon occurs to me how I may turn this or that morsel to account, so as to make a good dish of it; that is to say, agreeably to the rules of counterpoint, to the peculiarities of the various instruments, and so on. All this fires my soul, and, provided I am not disturbed, my subject enlarges itself, becomes methodized and defined; and the whole, though it be long, stands almost complete and finished in my mind, so that I can

* GOETHE: *Briefwechsel mit einem Kinde.*

survey it, like a fine picture or a beautiful statue, at a glance Nor do I hear, in imagination, the parts successively; but I hear them, as it were, all at once (gleich alles zusammen). What a delight this is I cannot tell! All this inventing, this producing, takes place in a pleasing, lively dream. Still the actual hearing of the entire whole is after all the best. What has been thus produced I do not easily forget. And this is perhaps the best gift I have my Divine Maker to thank for." *

These hints and suggestions are necessarily bald and imperfect: necessarily, because the civilized world has but recently begun to study Inspiration, as a universal agency, in its connection either with the trance-faculty, or with the Spiritual hypothesis; and because, on that account, experience along either of these lines of research, is only beginning to accumulate. It has not yet become a common belief that one of the sources of man's noblest achievements, literary, artistic, spiritual, is in an ultramundane sphere. We puzzle over the anomalies of human character—its extremes of good and evil—repeating

> " How poor, how rich; how abject, how august;
> How complicate, how wonderful is man!"

But we do not work out one of the explanations. We have not practically realized how much the soul's bondage to the body tends to dull its perceptions and check its best aspirings: nor how it aspires more freely and discerns more clearly, when the severity of that bondage is relaxed. Nor have we practically realized how much man may learn and may improve in wisdom and in goodness, by being occasionally admitted to communion with a higher phase of being; nor how grievous a loser he may be, if debarred from such communion. We do not practically believe what Christ has told us of a Spirit of

* HOLMES: *Life of Mozart, including his Correspondence;* London, 1845: pp. 317, 318.

Truth, to come after him, who should "guide us into all truth."

Our researches in this matter have hitherto been prosecuted in far, misty clouds; not on the fair earth, illuminated from on high.

I think one reason for this is that the marvellous light which dawned upon the world eighteen hundred years ago has dazzled and blinded, even while it has informed and improved mankind. It was a spiritual phenomenon alike without example throughout all history and (to our remote ancestors) without apparent solution short of the miraculous: without example not solely, nor perhaps chiefly, on account of the wonderful works done by Christ; for the Jews, in their history, and even the Romans and Greeks in their mythology, could find more or less of precedent for many of these; but because the light of Christianity, alike in its moral and spiritual aspect and in its effects, is without parallel in man's previous experience. Not thus appearing, at first, except to a small band of followers; but gradually, as it rose upon the mind and soul of the world, has that light shone as might a sun, rising for the first time upon an earth of which the inhabitants, till then, had lived and labored under starlight.

Is such a simile to be rejected because it admits what seems at variance with all we see of the course of nature? Let us not hastily decide that there *is* such variance: Nature's action is multiform.

While God's works around us bear evidence that the principle of gradual progression pervades the entire economy of the universe, and that natural laws are invariable and persistent, still, under that economy and governed by these laws, there occur, at certain epochs, vast steps in human progress: even as, from time to time, political revolutions supervene which, while changing the wonted action of long-standing government, sometimes bring about in years an advance which ages had failed to effect.

History contains nothing more interesting than the record

of these gigantic steps; each, apparently, without precedent; each breaking in on the monotonous pace of the world. In cosmical history what incident stands by the side of the single discovery of Columbus, giving to the ancient world another half of our globe, about which to speculate, in which to live? The annals of literature record no victory to match, in practical result, the triumph of Faust, if to the goldsmith of Mentz be due the art of printing; that art which enables one man to converse with all his race. Even the world of Invention, where labor toils, has had its Titanic epoch, occurring little more than a century since; that epoch at which steam began to take the place of bone and sinew; at which the distaff and spinning-wheel, humble aids to human workers throughout three thousand years, were at last superseded by a Briarean system of manufacture that has multiplied five-hundred fold the productive labor-power of mankind.*

In the individual life of man, strictly progressive though it be, we find a still more remarkable phenomenon connected with an unprecedented advance. Infant, child, adult, patriarch—the boundaries which mark each successive state are imperceptible; but then comes the great epoch: the point of progress when our powers, perceptive, intellectual, spiritual, are suddenly increased we know not how much; when our means of communicating with our fellows are freed from bounds alike of time and space; when, like Columbus, we are borne into a new world.

So, again, in regard to the succession of animal life on earth, reaching back into prehistoric time. Geology informs us that there was a period of untold duration when this world, occupied by the lower races, was uninhabited by man. An eminent modern naturalist,† exploring that period and investigating the principle of vital progress, has brought prominently for-

* See preceding page 45.

† CHARLES DARWIN, A.M., F.R.S. *On the Origin of Species by Means of Natural Selection; or, the Preservation of Favored Races in the Struggle for Life:* London, 1859.

ward a great, general law governing gradual improvement of species by means of natural selection and the preservation of the best out of each—both animal and vegetable—in the struggle for existence. But he has adduced no facts attesting change of one species to another; nor disclosed to us any link connecting brute and man.* There remains, therefore, intact, the

* It has been surmised that intermediate forms between the higher quadrumana and the lowest variety of cave-dwelling humanity may some day be found; perhaps in large unexplored portions of interior Asia or Africa; but this is mere surmise, unsustained, as yet, by discovery.

The advocates of the Development theory admit the extreme difficulties which stand in the way of assigning to man predecessors from a lower race. "Admitting," says one of them, "man's structural modifications from the species that stand next under him, there still remains the fact that something new has been superadded—the organization fitted for higher functional performance, the intellect capable of improvement and progress. On no theory of mere transmission or heredity can these be accounted for. The predecessor did not possess them and could not bequeath them."—DAVID PAGE, LL.D.; F.R.S.E.; F.G.S.: *Man, Where, Whence, and Whither;* Edinburgh, 1867; pp. 152, 153.

Another writer on this subject—one of the earliest suggesters of the "natural selection" theory—makes quite recently the following admissions: "The capacity to form ideal conceptions of space and time, of eternity and infinity—the capacity for intense artistic feelings of pleasure, in form, color, and composition—and for those abstract notions of form and number which render geometry and arithmetic possible—how were all or any of these faculties first developed when they could have been of no possible use to man in his early stages of barbarism? How could "natural selection," or survival of the fittest in the struggle for existence, at all favor the development of mental powers . . . which even now, with our comparatively high civilization, are, in their farthest developments, in advance of the age, and appear to have relation rather to the future of the race than to its actual status?"—WALLACE: *Contributions to the Theory of Natural Selection*, London and New York, 1870; pp. 351, 352.

It is difficult to conceive a state of things in which there must not, in any event, have been some year, some month, some day, when there existed on earth no animal endowed with capacity for intellectual and

hypothesis—surely not an unreasonable one—that there inhered, in the law which regulated preadamite life, a condition according to which a creature endowed with reason and gifted with faculties and sentiments that enable him to conceive and desire a Hereafter, did, at a certain point of advancement, suddenly appear; a creature destined to subjugate earth and attain heaven. The vast induction, if one may so express it, failed at a certain stage of cosmical development; and the progressive ratio of the past series was no longer the progressive ratio of the succeeding. For, in virtue of a stride surpassingly great, there assumed place in the world a race—the only one *—which could transmit the experience of one generation to another, and which, after a time, learned to perpetuate that experience by artificial, enduring signs. Hence, as result of a single, unexampled step in advance, ethical, intellectual, spiritual progress.

And now, reverting from this digression to the subject immediately before us, we find the same analogy still holding out. The history of Ethics and of Religion, like that of Cosmogony

spiritual improvement from generation to generation; and then again, some next year, or next month, or next day, when such an animal—that is to say, when a man—came into existence. The question is of *capacity*, how undeveloped soever, however useless to palæozoic man: the highest quadrumane has it not; and even if in structural formation he approached much nearer to man than he does, the possession or non-possession of intellectual and spiritual *possibilities of development* still establishes a great gulf, which, if not, under God's economy, impassable is, at least, so far as human research has explored, unpassed.

But even if the Development theorist should succeed in tracing man to an anthropoid-ape-ancestry, or to an Ascidian origin, still a vast step in advance, however effected, is not the less a reality; a step which seems to have been made at once; at all events, a step without precedent in fact and without parallel in the immensity of its results.

* We have no warrant, so far as I know, for asserting that the beaver of to-day exhibits more ingenuity in constructing his dam than did the beaver of three thousand years ago: nor is it in evidence that the quadrumane of our own time is more intelligent than was the same animal in Homer's.

and Literature, and productive Science, has its epoch, whence dates a ratio of advancement till then unknown. In the earthly progress of Spiritualism, as in the succession of races and in the pilgrimage of human life, we have to note one eminent step upward, as from a lower to a higher sphere of being.

Unprecedented, unlike any other step: the progress which followed it incomparable with the march of any other revolution, political or religious.

The establishing of a kingdom *on* the world but not *of* it; called, sometimes the Kingdom of Heaven, yet coming not by observation,*—heralded by no earthly pomp, ushered through no opening in clouds of heaven—but founded lowly, peacefully, silently, in the heart of man. Christ's kingship is of the human soul.

If, to the sceptical, these claims seem overstrained, let them look, not to the assertions of theologians, nor yet to the uncertainties and obscurities of remote history, but to acknowledged facts, of grand outline, familiar to every educated man.

In what is usually called the civilized world millions will say, if asked as to their religion, that they are not Catholics, millions more that they are not Protestants; but, excepting the five or six million Jews, we shall not find there one man in a hundred who, if he has any religion at all, will say he is not a Christian.

If the Spiritual Teachings first heard in Galilee, eighteen hundred years ago (aside from alien creeds), be not the religion of Civilization, it has no other. What we may justly call the most enlightened portion of the world clings to these teachings, despite the deadening and retractive influence of alien creeds.

Is it strange that Christendom, before it began to recognize the universal reign of law, should have sought, in miraculous interference, the explanation of such a phenomenon as this? Is it strange even,—considering the presumption to which our

* Luke xvii. 20.

short-sighted race is prone—that Orthodoxy, knowing no natural solution of such an enigma, should take refuge in a conception—one scruples about plainly expressing its pretensions; for these not only involve the direct intervention and suspension of His laws by the Almighty Creator and Lawgiver of myriads of sun-systems and myriads on myriads of worlds; they virtually pre-suppose, also, His presence, in human form, throughout a generation of men, on this small planet of ours—all the world, indeed, to us, but a mere speck in immensity, to Him.

Yet if claims so transcendent were consonant with their day and generation, none the less they are now furnishing abundant food and occupation to Scepticism. There *is* impregnable ground; but Orthodoxy forsakes it, straying forth into the limitless regions of Dogmatism. It seeks miracles through the dim perspective of eighteen centuries; yet the miracle of miracles—if the marvellous constitute the miraculous—lies patent before us; is cognizable by our very senses.

Assume Scepticism's theory. Here it is: The son of a Jewish mechanic, living in an obscure village of Galilee, brought up in his father's house, with the most limited opportunities of culture, without access to the literature of Greece or Rome, without worldly experience to replace lack of learning, and also without spiritual aid—becomes, at the age of thirty, a Public Teacher; continues to teach during three years—three only; then, because of the latitude of his opinions, suffers death. His three-year sayings and doings, which he himself never committed to writing, are recorded, within half a century from his death by humble and comparatively unlettered followers. Yet, after more than fifty generations of men have passed away, there is found in that record—and in that record alone—a religion that cultivated men can indorse and civilized nations revere. Surely, the miracle of all miracles!—nay, as Scepticism has put it, a moral and intellectual impossibility.

The impossibility inheres in one of Scepticism's postulates. "Without spiritual aid." If such aid be essential to any high and noble achievement of man, is it conceivable that it should be lacking in connection with the highest and noblest of all?

But the difficulties attending this main feature in the sceptic's hypothesis do not end here. Unless the recording disciples have utterly belied their Master, it involves a direct charge of falsehood against him. For, though habitually calling himself "the Son of Man," * he also suffered himself to be called, and claimed to be, the MESSIAH, the CHRIST, ofttimes spoken of by the prophets of old, and long expected, as Deliverer, by the Jews. In other words—let those who doubt my rendering consult the lexicons, Hebrew and Greek—in other words, he claimed to be the ANOINTED of his Father † and our Father; a divinely-commissioned Messenger, Prophet, Spiritual King.

Shall we accord to him these titles? There is no sure warrant for so doing to be drawn from history. But his credentials are to be found in the Message itself, in the work that message has done, and in the recorded life of the Messenger.

All the great figures of antiquity pale, more or less, under the lights of modern civilization, save only that of Christ. The thinking world has, in a measure, outlived every phase of religious belief except Christianity. That was planted by its Author so far beyond the point of progress of the age in which its precepts were first heard, that the current of eighteen centuries, passing by all other systems, has failed to approach this. Christ's teachings, proleptic in character, are still in advance not of the modern world's purest practice only, but almost of its aspirations. Can we deny to their Author his own claim

* The term "Son of Man," as applied by Christ to himself, occurs some eighty times throughout the four gospel narratives.

† Jesus himself, at the very outset of his ministry, adopts this interpretation. In the synagogue at Nazareth, after publicly reading the words of Isaiah (lxi. 1), "The Spirit of the Lord God is upon me, because the Lord hath *anointed* me to preach good tidings unto the meek,"—words understood by the Jews of the Messiah—he applied them to himself: "This day is this Scripture fulfilled in your ears."—Luke iv. 18, 21.

that on Him, the Chosen One, had been poured the chrism of God?

That was the reply of Christ's most trusted Apostle, interrogated by his Master. "'But whom say ye that I am?' Peter answering said: 'The Christ of God.'" * It was the claim put forth by the same apostle in the first public address which he made to the Jews after the crucifixion: for in that he designated the Great Teacher whose disciple he was, as "Jesus of Nazareth, a man approved of God by miracles (dunamesin), and wonders and signs:" and, again, with slight variation of phrase, when discoursing before Cornelius and his Gentile friends in Cæsarea: there speaking of his Master as "Jesus of Nazareth whom God anointed with the Holy Ghost and with power, who went about doing good."

—Doing good His own nature—his character and his doings, as exhibited in the gospel biographies—are almost as marvellous as the system he gave to the world. They accord neither with his country nor with his time, nor—except as one illustrious example disclosing to us what Man may be—with that human race with which, on a hundred occasions, he expressly identified himself. It were difficult, in this connection, to improve on the words of an Anglican clergyman, whose early death was a misfortune to the Church he adorned: "Once in the roll of ages, out of innumerable failures, from the stock of human nature one bud developed into a faultless flower. One perfect specimen of humanity has God exhibited on earth. . . . As if the life-blood of every nation were in his veins, and that which is best and truest in every man, and that which is tenderest and gentlest and purest in every woman were in his character: he is emphatically the Son of *Man*." †

Not less eloquent on this subject is the author of a well-known modern work: "The story of Christ's life will always

* Luke ix. 20.

† *Sermons by the Rev. F. W. Robertson*, Incumbent of Trinity Chapel, Brighton; sermon xv.; pp. 365, 366 (of New York Ed., 1870). The word "man" is italicized by the author.

remain the one record in which the moral perfection of man stands revealed in its root and its unity, the hidden spring made manifest by which the whole machine is moved. . . . All lesser examples and lives will forever hold a subordinate place, and serve chiefly to reflect light on the central and original Example. In his wounds all human sorrows will hide themselves, and all human self-denials support themselves against his cross." *

Whence this preëminence? The germ of the Godlike lies, indeed, deep down in our common nature; but, ere it fructify, there must be divine breathings from a region purer than ours. Whether, in this supreme instance of Inspiration, these Holy Breathings † assumed an unwonted phase—executed an unwonted office—what mortal shall assume to decide?

Yet I think I should do wrong here to withhold the fact that I have received on this subject a communication—one only and that unsought for—which I believe to have had a spiritual source: it is one of the few such messages that have ever reached me, touching on any disputed point of doctrine. The reader has it below, ‡ for what he may deem its allegations

* *Ecce Homo*: a Survey of the Life and Work of Jesus Christ. London, 1866: pp. 188, 189. This work, published anonymously, is now known to have been written by Professor SEELEY, filling the chair of Modern History in the University of Cambridge.

† One scruples to write "Holy Breath," instead of "Holy Ghost" (from *gast*, Anglo-Saxon for *breath* or *spirit*); yet the terms are strictly synonymous. Peter, speaking of Jesus as a man "whom God anointed with the Holy Ghost and with power," certainly employed the term in some such sense. Christ himself, when he spoke of the Holy Ghost as the "Spirit of Truth," which "shall not speak of himself, but whatsoever he shall hear that shall he speak," as certainly did not intend thereby to designate one of the Persons of the Godhead.

‡ I copy literally from minutes of a sitting held January 26, 1862, during which I had but this single communication:

"Christ's birth was by inception, not by conception. Mary inherited a peculiar physical and spiritual organization from her ancestors of David's line. She was placed in a perfect trance, her bodily life sus

worth. These involve neither suspension nor violation of natural law, nor, I think, any improbability so violent that we must needs reject it straightway. The communication alleges

pended. The spiritual fructifying principle was received during the trance. Christ's mortal body was the result of Mary's perfect faith, ruling the organism—a faith of that transcendent kind which is the centre and circumference of all that is to be desired. It is a literal truth, and no figure, to say of such faith that it can remove mountains. It bears the same relation to the common faith of mankind which the crystallized diamond does to the charcoal.

"In Mary's case, it was the outgrowth of many centuries. It was a specific faith; the blossoming of that belief, preserved through ages, that a virgin should conceive and bear a son. No other possible conjunction could have produced a Christ. Yet there was no suspension of law. His birth was natural. The same conjunction of circumstances recurring, if we could suppose such a case, a similar birth might happen again.

"It was necessary for Christ to stand above the plane of mankind, in order to draw men up to him. He was devoid of appetite and passion to a degree that no man of human conception could have been. In a human and bodily sense, he was, on that account, a less complete man. Yet had it not been for the absence of these appetites and passions, the truth could not have come to us through him, pure as it did. There would have been obscurances and hindrances. Under their influence he could not have preserved his integrity as a Messenger. He would have been drawn sympathetically into the sphere of his day.

"Christ felt the trials and temptations that assail his brethren of mankind, even more acutely than they did themselves; but that was because of the strong *repellent* force within him; not by any attraction drawing him. These temptations did not attract, they only pained him. He had before him ever the eternal laws; seeing through the Present to the End."

The above was called forth by no question of mine, direct or indirect. I was not thinking of the subject, and of course expected nothing of the kind. It was not obtained from a professional medium. The lady through whose mediumship it came—a relative of mine, intellectual and cultivated—is a Unitarian; believing, in her normal state, that Jesus was born as other men. It purported to come from an intimate and highly-valued, long-deceased friend (see Book iv., chapter 3); and from the same alleged source there have come to me many valuable teachings on ethical and other cognate subjects.

that Christ's birth occurred under circumstances so peculiar that he grew to manhood devoid of appetite and passion to a degree—necessary to his pure integrity as Teacher—which no other person has ever shared. At this stage of our knowledge, I feel unqualified to avouch such a theory, and unwilling to gainsay it. Ungifted with spiritual clearsight—seeing here but as through a glass, darkly—why should I hasten to decide? I am content to wait—it can be a few years only, now—for better discernment and broader light.

The able author last quoted just touches on the subject of Christ's birth. Speaking of the spiritual enthusiasm which characterized Jesus, he asks: "How it was kindled in him who knows?" And his reply is: "'The abysmal depths of personality' hide this secret. It was the will of God to beget no second Son like him." *

Mr. Gladstone, the British premier, alluding, in a review of the work where they appear, to the above words, says: "They seem to deal with things that we know not of, and are ill able to touch." †

I agree with him.

Strange!—and sad as strange—that men in all ages have been called upon to touch, to deal with—ay! despite sense of incapacity, even despite counter convictions, compelled to decide—just such questions!

—Called upon by men like themselves, not by God. I am not more conscious of my own existence than I am that an all-wise and all-good Being will never remember it for judgment against me, nor against any of His creatures, that, after best diligence, we have been unable, as to many such arcana, to do more than confess, that we comprehend them not.

So far only I see: that Jesus was divinely favored and gifted to an eminent degree—but how and to what degree I have no means to determine. That there *were* limits, law-governed, his

* *Ecce Homo*, p. 321.

† *Ecce Homo* (reviewed), by the Right Honorable W. E. Gladstone; London, 1868: p. 190.

biographers inform us. In Christ's own country, where men asked one another "Is not this the carpenter, the son of Mary?" he "*could* do no mighty work, save that he laid his hands upon a few sick and healed them: and he marvelled because of their unbelief." * Again: all that he would have done for his hard hearted countrymen he himself tells us, in words breathing the very soul of sadness, that he could not do: "Oh Jerusalem, Jerusalem, thou that killest the prophets and stonest them which are sent unto thee, how often would I have gathered thy children together, even as a hen gathereth her chickens under her wings, and ye would not!" †

And again, who shall define the limits of his knowledge? As one reads, one feels, as the Jewish officers of justice felt: "Never man spake like this man." Yet, as the record now stands, ‡ we find many words and paragraphs which, if we are

* Mark vi. 3, 5, 6. Matthew, in the concordant passage, says that "he did not many mighty works there, because of their unbelief."

† Matthew xxiv. 37.

‡ Take an example. John gives a prayer, as offered up by Jesus, in presence of his apostles, immediately before he went forth into the garden where he was betrayed. There is no other example, in any of the gospels, of a public prayer by Christ. He retired into remote solitudes to pray (Mark vi. 46; Luke vi. 12). "When thou prayest," he had said, "enter into thy closet, and when thou hast shut thy door, pray to thy Father which is in secret." The three synoptical evangelists agree that, at the most solemn hour of his life—just before his betrayal—Christ's action corresponded to his precept, and that he did *not* pray in their presence. At Gethsemane, says Matthew, he said to his disciples: "'Sit ye here, while I go and pray yonder:' and he went a little farther and fell on his face and prayed, saying: 'Oh my Father, if it be possible let this cup pass from me; nevertheless not as I will but as Thou wilt.'"

Mark's relation is, almost word for word, the same as that of Matthew. Luke says he withdrew himself from them about a stone's cast and kneeled down and prayed: 'Father, if thou be willing, remove this cup from me; nevertheless not my will but thine be done.'"

I believe, with Matthew and Mark and Luke, that the communings of Jesus with his Father, ere he went to death, were in secret, unheard

to accept them, clearly show that Christ, like all other men, was liable to error. Examples will suggest themselves to the dispassionate student of the gospels.

Let timid souls who think all is imperilled if a single imperfection of doctrine, or inaccuracy of record,* be suggested, here be reminded that the spiritual system of Christ, with its world-wide influence on man, depends not at all on non-essential incidents like these. Its spirit and substance and efficacy remain intact. It profits, none the less, as rule for human conduct in the world which now is, and as guide, much needed, preparing us for that which is to come.

In this matter it is dangerous to repose confidence in incidentals, or in any warrant save the intrinsic excellence and inherent power of the Great Teachings themselves. Not on ancient fortresses of stone, how seemingly impregnable soever, may a nation, in her hour of peril, rely for defence: she must look to faithfulness and valor and affection, animating the hearts of her defenders. And so Christianity, when assailed by the legions of Doubt and of Materialism, must not put her trust in the old evidences of tradition or of remote history, though built up by learning and entrenched by the polemical labors of ages: if she is to become the Religion of Civilization,

by mortal ear; nor do I doubt that the brief words employed by the synoptical evangelists—sad, fervent, resigned—embody the spirit of Christ's secret prayer.

But as to John's narrative the internal evidence signally fails. Christ's love was of that eminent character which carries out of self, thinking not of glorification; and, above all, which embraces all humankind, unalloyed by trace of the exclusive. I believe that the prayer which the aged apostle, after half a century had intervened, spread over his seventeenth chapter was but what he himself erringly conceived to have been his Master's feelings ere he encountered his enemies; a document not more reliable than the long speeches which other old historians have imagined for their heroes on the eve of a battle. I am unable to accept it as Christ's, either in the spirit or in the letter. See further, as to this, foot-note on next page.

* Did Christ ever declare that he would be infallibly reported?

her kingdom must be protected by the loyal convictions and the bold candor and the enlightened love of free human souls.

Here let me be permitted to say a word with mere personal reference to myself. I could not more religiously venerate than I now venerate Christ's teachings and his person; I could not more deeply feel than I now feel the bounden duty to heed his sayings and to do what in me lies toward following his example—if theologians had succeeded in beating into my brain all the perplexities they have crowded into the Athanasian creed. If others find, through such subtilties, comfort in affliction, warmth for sinking faith, motive to stir flagging zeal, incentive to religious duty, it is well: let them profit by what they are able to accept. The Alexandrian Patriarch does not speak either to my heart or to my understanding. They who *can* receive his doctrine, let them receive it.

If, beyond a claim to be the promised Messiah—the Anointed Prophet of God, commissioned by Him to redeem the world from spiritual darkness—there be any reasonable ground for belief that Christ declared himself, or regarded himself, to be one of the Persons of the Godhead, I confess my inability to find it. * Very rarely, scarcely half a dozen times throughout

* There are sundry passages in John's Gospel which must be taken as asserting this dogma; but John wrote thirty or forty years later than the other evangelists, in his old age and at a period when speculative doctrine was already beginning to obscure the noble candor of Christ's words. How favorably does the simplicity of Luke's opening verses, inspiring confidence by their modesty, contrast with the mystical elaborateness of John's! Then we come upon such texts as viii. 23; x. 8; xvii. 9 (used by Calvin); xvii. 5; viii. 58; vi. 51, 54, etc. When one reads: "Ye are beneath, I am from above; all that ever came before me are thieves and robbers; before Abraham was, I am; glorify me, O Father, with the glory which I had with thee before the world was; I pray not for the world, but for them that thou hast given me," with other sayings of similar spirit—the internal evidence fails; we no longer recognize the Christ of the earlier gospels.

Yet, withal, though John is almost as unequal as Paul, we could as ill spare many portions of his Gospel as we could certain parts of Paul's

the three synoptical gospels, does Jesus speak of himself as the "Son of God:"* not nearly so often as he speaks of his

epistles. Like Paul, John is the Apostle of LOVE, in its purest and widest acceptation; and none of the gospels contain a narrative more eminently characteristic of the gentleness and mercy of Christ than John's story of the Fallen One, who was bid to go and sin no more. Its lesson is only beginning to make its way, now after nearly two thousand years, to the hearts of men.

* This expression, as applied by Christ to himself, scarcely occurs either in Matthew or Mark or Luke, except that, when interrogated before the High Priests and scribes as to whether he was the Son of God, he replied: "Ye say that I am;" to be interpreted as assent; but even during that very interrogatory, he still designates himself by his favorite expression, "The Son of Man." According to John, he speaks of himself several times as the Son of God (v. 25; ix. 35, 36; xi. 4; and on one or two other occasions more or less directly); besides assenting (xi. 27) to be so called by Martha. But, singularly enough, in the same gospel, x. 36) is given a remarkable conversation, which I can interpret but in one sense:

Christ asks the Jews: "For which of my good works do ye stone me?" They answer: "For a good work we stone thee not, but for blasphemy; and because that thou, being a man, makest thyself God."

Here, surely—in the sequel to the colloquy—if anywhere, we may seek the clue to Christ's exact meaning, when he calls himself God's Son. But what happens? Does he admit the truth of the Jews' accusation? On the contrary Jesus quotes to his accusers a text in which the author of one of the Psalms, speaking of men, called them gods; and his comment on that text is: "If he called them gods to whom the word of God came, and the Scripture cannot be broken, say ye of him whom the Father hath sanctified and sent into the world 'Thou blasphemest,' because I said, I am the Son of God?"

Did Christ here evade the question, seeking to deceive the Jews? We cannot for a moment entertain a thought so derogatory to his character? He claimed, indeed, to have been sanctified by the "Father;" he claimed to have been sent by God, as Peter and the rest of his disciples afterward claimed for him: but he *disclaimed* any pretension to godship; explaining to them, by a reference to their own Scripture, the sense in which he applied to himself the title of the Son of God. Had they listened to another discourse of his addressed to the Sadducees, and had they profited by it, they would not have needed this warning against the "letter which killeth;" for in that discourse (Luke

brethren of humankind as God's sons and daughters; bidding us in the only prayer he has left us, to address the Deity as "OUR FATHER." Then, too, as God's messenger, how preëminent *his* claims to the title he now and then assumes! If, as he himself teaches, the peacemakers are to be called the Children of God, is not he, the Prince of Peace—the Bearer of the Gospel which brings "peace on earth, good-will to men"—above all others most righteously to be spoken of as God's beloved Son, in whom He was well pleased?

Christ is the crowning exemplar of the INSPIRED: for he, while abiding among us, lived, more nearly than any other of God's creatures here, within sight and hearing of his future home. Therefore it is that his teachings are the noblest fruits of Inspiration.

In the highest phenomena of Spiritualism—in other words, in the best examples of the modern phase of powers and gifts connected with Inspiration—may be seen the fulfilling of Christ's promise to Christians, of works emulating his.* In the purest revealings of Spiritualism may be found the fulfilment of that other promise touching the imparting of truth and comfort through holy breathings from above.

Primitive Christianity, the greatest of all reformatory agencies, is best evidenced through modern Spiritualism; for the germ of modern Spiritualism is in primitive Christianity. In proportion as the epiphanies of Spiritualism are studied in a Christian spirit, will the attention of the world be withdrawn

xx. 36), speaking of those who are worthy to enter Heaven, he had said of them: "They are equal unto the angels and are the children of God."

Whither does literalism lead? To repeat, after Luther: "When Christ says 'Take, eat, this is my body,' every child must understand that he speaks of that which he gives to his disciples" (see preceding page 50); and so, to believe in the "real presence:" and again, interpreting according to the letter Matthew xvi. 18, 19, to accept, as Scriptural doctrine, the infallibility of the Pope.

* John xiv. 12.

from religious dogmatism and concentred in Christ's teachings, in their primitive form.

Can more powerful motive be adduced, to make proof of these signs and wonders?—rejecting whatever is alien and faithless, but holding fast to all that is loyal and good?

CHAPTER IV.

DIFFICULTIES AND PREJUDICES.

"A subject of study ought not to be abandoned because it is beset with difficulties, nor because, for the time being, it may elicit prejudice or encounter contempt."—BERZELIUS: *Jahresbericht*, 1846.

A VERY few words to the candid reader, ere I commence my narrative-illustrations.

Let not exception be taken to it if it appear that such researches have been chiefly prosecuted, at the outset, in a somewhat immethodical or rambling manner, and under the leading of volunteers untitled by learned societies. This may be for the best, even if, in one point of view, it is to be regretted. It may be for the best, even though it must be admitted that, among the names of note in the regular ranks of science, there are men who, of all others, are, in some respects, best fitted here to head the advance, and to obtain for us, if they would, reliable results.

—In some respects. For in alleging the peculiar fitness of distinguished scientific men to investigate a subject like that under consideration, the opinion is to be received with considerable allowance. Physical Science and Vital Science each disclose a great class of phenomena; the one distinct, even wide apart, from the other. Both, indeed, are subject to fixed and universal laws: the reality of both must be judged according to the same acknowledged canons of evidence. But the laws of physical science apply to obdurate matter, that has no nervous system to be soothed or excited; no consciousness to warm under kindness, or suffer from rude offence; no sense of wrong, to be outraged by unjust suspicion. The laws of vital science, on the contrary, govern animate agencies of delicate and sensitive and changeful organization. The materials for experiment are of two entirely different classes, and must be treated accordingly. Faraday *as* electrician, Herschel *as* astronomer, Liebig *as* chemist, have been studying laws under which the results to ensue or to be produced, at any given moment, on any given substance, can be rigidly controlled or predicted; laws which are the fit objects of mathematical calculation. The habits of rigorous investigation acquired by such men are invaluable; but yet, if they fail to bear in mind what an element of diversity and variableness vitality involves; and if they carry with them into investigations undertaken in the province of organic life the same purely materialistic and unconditional standard which they have been accustomed to apply within the domain of physics, they are liable to go far astray and to miss satisfactory results. Enlightened members of the medical faculty, taught by experience, know this well.*

Then, again, whatever the qualifications of the ablest leaders in science, they do not usually esteem it their vocation to lead the vanguard on an occasion like this. They abandon, to untrained experimentalists, an unpopular field. Or, if they speak, it is to give us prejudices only.† For if prejudice, as in

* Dr. Holland (*Chapters on Mental Physiology*, p. 2) has justly remarked: "Neither those accustomed to legal evidence only, nor such as have pursued science in its more simple forms, can rightly estimate the vast difference made by the introduction of the principle of life, or yet more of the states and condition of mind, in connection with bodily organization."

Bichat (*Recherches sur la Vie et la Mort*, *Art.* 7, § 1) has some excellent remarks on the same subject. He reminds us, that while physics, chemistry, and the like are sciences that approach each other, "an immense interval separates them from the science of organized bodies; and for that reason the latter should be treated in an entirely different manner."

† An exception is here to be admitted. An English periodical of repute, the *Popular Science Review*, edited by Mr. Crookes, an eminent chemist and Fellow of the Royal Society, has, in its number for last

etymological strictness it must, be construed to mean a judgment formed before examination, then must we regard as prejudices his opinions, however true, who has neglected to weigh them against their opposites, however false.

From students who devote themselves exclusively to physical research we must, as a general rule, expect this. They regard an ultramundane field as outside of their jurisdiction. The theory of intervention from another sphere of being—the idea of spiritual phenomena—is alien to their pursuits, and cannot win the scientific ear at once. The growth of any new-born hypothesis, so startling in character, resembles that of a human being. During its infancy its suggestions carry small weight. It is listened to with a light smile and set aside with little ceremony. Throughout its years of nonage it may be said to have no rights of property, no privilege of appropriation. Proofs in its favor may present themselves from time to time, but they are not deemed entitled to a judgment by the rules of evidence: they are listened to as fresh and amusing; but they have no legal virtue; they obtain no official record; they are not placed to

July, an article by its editor, giving a detailed account of experiments made on the (alleged) physical powers as a medium of Mr. Home, by himself (Mr. Crookes), Mr. Serjeant Cox, and Dr. Huggins, distinguished as astronomer and prominent member of the Royal Society. Mr. Cox and Mr. Crookes acknowledge that these experiments seem to prove the existence of a new force which they call "psychic": while Dr. Huggins, more non-committal, admits that they "show the importance of further investigation." The London *Spectator*, commenting on this, admits that there is *primâ-facie* evidence of the phenomena; and adds, as to the alleged "new force," that "it is most desirable that the scientific world should confirm, or explode, the hypothesis of its existence."—*Spectator* of July 8, 1871, p. 828.

The experiments included the playing on an accordion placed inside a copper-wire cage (purposely prepared by Mr. Crookes); the accordion floating without apparent support, and *not* played on by any visible agency. A comparatively unimportant phenomenon, but an excellent beginning, nevertheless—a beginning that may lead—one cannot tell how far.

the credit of the minor. An adolescent hypothesis is held to be outside the limits of human justice.

We ought not very strongly to complain of this. While we may condemn the manner in which the magnates of science are wont to treat spiritual researches, we may excuse it also. The best of us shrink before the world's laugh. Franklin, engaged in one of the most sublime experiments ever undertaken by man, sought, it is said, to escape the chance of ridicule by veiling his purpose. He took with him, as companion, a little boy; that the kite, destined to draw lightning from the thunder-cloud, might, in case of failure, pass as the plaything of a child.

But is nothing, therefore, to be done? Because men, with a hard-won scientific reputation at stake, will not peril it in such an inquiry, are others, more hardy if less well-trained for the task, to hold back?

I have put that question to myself and have answered it in the negative.

I proceed, then, to adduce, in support of various positions assumed in the preceding chapters, a few—my space admits but a few—of the many Spiritual phenomena, spontaneous and evoked, that have occurred under my observation, or come to me in authentic form, during the last fifteen years.

BOOK II.

SOME CHARACTERISTICS OF THE PHENOMENA.

"Facts like these, with which the world is filled, embarrass strong minds more than they are willing to acknowledge."—BAYLE.

CHAPTER I.

THEIR COMING USUALLY UNEXPECTED.

"Our eyes are holden that we cannot see things that stare us in the face, until the time arrives when the mind is ripened: then we behold them, and the time when we saw them not is like a dream."—EMERSON.

WHEN I recall what happened to me in March, 1856, I am reminded of Emerson's suggestive words.

Up to that time I had been living, as so many millions live, in vague unbelief that there are, in this world, any spiritual agencies cognizable by the senses. I had barely heard of the "Rochester Knockings," and had wondered what supreme absurdity would follow next.

I was then in Naples where, for two and a half preceding years, I had held the post of American Minister. The members of our diplomatic corps, living on pleasant and intimate terms, were in the habit of dropping informally into each other's apartments, for an hour or two in the evening. To this habit I am indebted for a strange experience which I shall entitle

THE MAID AND COOK.

On the twenty-fifth of March I passed the evening with the Russian Minister, Monsieur K——. Besides his family there were present the Chevalier de F——, Tuscan Minister, and his lady; together with several visitors from different parts of the world. During most of the evening we spoke English, the Tuscan Minister's wife being from England and another lady present from America.

Madame K——, a Parisian by birth and a lady of varied information, asked me, in the course of conversation, if I had ever heard of automatic writing. I confessed that I had not. Then she expressed her belief that some persons had the power of replying, in that way, to questions, the true answers to which were unknown to them.

"Pardon me," said Madame de F——; "I am very sure you would not say so unless you were quite convinced that you had proof sufficient: but I could not believe anything so wonderful, unless I witnessed it myself."

"Let us try, then," said Madame K——; and the proposal was eagerly assented to: each person sitting down, putting pencil to paper and awaiting the result. We were all unacquainted with Spiritualism and unbelievers in it.

Nothing, for some time: then one hand, that of a Mrs. M——, began to move, making irregular figures but no words or letters.

Then, at my suggestion that we should test the matter, Madame de F—— asked a question: "Who gave me these pins?"—pointing to three large gold-headed pins that fastened her dress, and adding: "If Mrs. M—— can answer that, I shall believe."

For several minutes that lady's pencil remained motionless; then, very slowly, it executed a few flourishes, finishing by writing out, in a cramped and not very legible hand, several words, *the last two written backward.**

* Let any one try to write even two such words backward, and he

Madame de F—— begged to look at the paper and gazed at it for some time, turning very pale.

"What is it?" some one asked eagerly.

"Magic, if there be such a thing," she replied. "It reads: '*The one that gives you a maid and cook.*'"

"How ridiculous!" exclaimed Mademoiselle K——: "it is no answer whatever to your question."

"You think not, Mademoiselle?" rejoined Madame de F——; "let me tell you the facts. These pins were given to me by my cousin Elizabeth, who lives in Florence. At my request she sent me, from that city, a lady's maid, who came into my service ten days since, and a cook who arrived day before yesterday."

The paper was passed from hand to hand, calling forth repeated expressions of astonishment, which were increased when some one suggested that the concluding portion of the flourishes which preceded the writing closely resembled a capital E; the initial letter of the donor's name.*

In myself this incident, trifling if it seem, excited far more than astonishment. During several hours of silent reflection, that evening at home, there came over me the indescribable emotion that is felt when one first awakes to the possibility that there may be experimental proof of another life. Ere I slept I had registered in my heart a vow—since kept—not to rest till I had proved this possibility to be a probability or a certainty—or a delusion.

Accordingly next day I called on Madame de F——, who had carried off the sheet of paper containing a reply which had at first seemed so enigmatical, but which proved to be so singularly appropriate; and, on stating to her that I desired to pre-

will discover the great difficulty of doing so. It should be added that Mrs. M—— was not only without experience in Spiritualism, but prejudiced against it.

* See next page.

serve it for record, she kindly ceded it to me.* In reply to an inquiry on my part, she stated, in emphatic terms, her conviction that the circumstances alluded to in the mysterious writing were not—indeed, could not be—known except to her own family. It was but a few weeks, she reminded me, since she herself arrived in Naples. Her cousin was unknown here, even by name; she herself had never mentioned her to any one in the city; much less alluded to the fact that the gold pins were her gift. But, in addition, she had never spoken to any one outside her family circle, about the servants who had recently arrived; or whence they came, or who sent them. And finally she stated that she had but just made the acquaintance of Mrs. M——, having only exchanged cards with her.

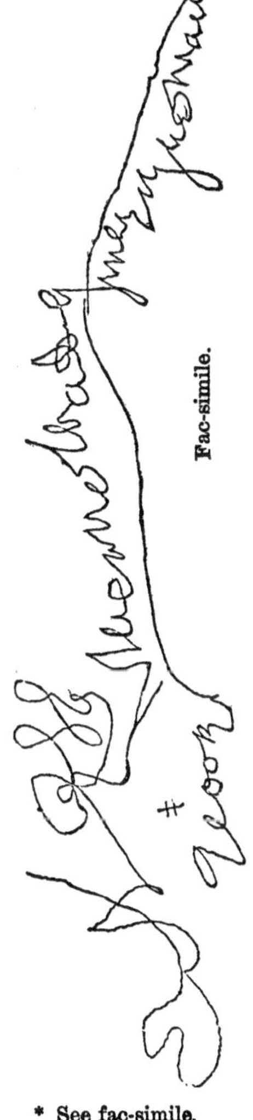

Fac-simile.

Intimately acquainted as I am with the circumstances of this case, to say nothing of the character and standing of the parties concerned, I am justified in asserting unqualifiedly that, whatever else the solution, collusion and deception are out of the question.

But, the facts accepted, how strange were the deductions! Restricting myself to commonly-received data, I found nothing that approached a satisfactory solution.

It was thus I reasoned the matter with myself. Had the reply to Madame de F——'s question been merely the

* See fac-simile.

name of her cousin, the donor of the pins (Elizabeth), it would have been equally relevant but much less surprising. We should probably have ascribed it to chance. Or, as Madame de F—— was doubtless, at that time, thinking of her cousin's name, we might have regarded it only as an example of a word thought of by one person, and unconsciously reflected (if that be the proper expression) from the mind of another; a phenomenon with which all vital magnetizers are familiar (even if they cannot explain it), and one of the reality of which Cuvier himself indicates the possibility.*

But the results I had obtained went much farther than this and were of a far more complicated character.

I inquired of Madame de F—— whether, at the time she put her question and was expecting a reply, she was thinking of the fact that her cousin had sent her two servants. She replied, that, very certainly, such a thought had not crossed her mind. Of course, if she had been asked who sent her the servants in question, she would readily have replied that her cousin had done so. But, in that case, the question would have called up the idea. As it was, the fact, though *within her knowledge*, was not *present to her mind.* If she herself had been required to answer her own question, she would doubtless have replied to it in a straightforward, simple manner, as: "My cousin Elizabeth;" or using some similar expression. We cannot imagine, that she would have gone out of her way to tell us that "it was the same person who had sent her a maid and a cook."

Then what thinking entity was it, which thus called up, out of the latent stores of Madame de F——'s memory, this dormant idea? What occult intelligence went out of its way to answer her question after this roundabout fashion? Who selected the unexpected form of reply?

* *Anatomie Comparée*, tome ii. p. 117. His admission is that, when two living beings are brought, under certain conditions, near each other, there exists sometimes "une communication quelconque qui s'établit entre leurs systèmes nerveux."

At first I scrupled about assuming that there was any external personality concerned. But a little reflection convinced me that if I dismissed that idea, I was shifting, not solving, the difficulty. For the question then recurred in another shape: What agency determined the special character of an answer thus indirect and far-fetched, yet strictly relevant and accurate?

And then (I went on to reflect) without assuming a personal entity, how are we to explain results that are never presented to us except as the mental operations of a sentient being; such as selection of appropriate facts from among many stored away in the memory, perception of the connection of these facts with a question which did not apparently refer to them, pertinent application of the selected facts to frame a truthful reply; nay, even an apparent intention, by giving to that reply an out-of-the-way and unlooked-for turn, to prove to us the presence of a reasoning and intelligent agent?

I was unable to answer these questions then; and, except on the spiritual hypothesis, I am unable, after fifteen years' experience, to offer any rational explanation to-day.

Probably most of those who assisted at the experiment I have recorded went away moved to simple wonder only; perplexed for the time, but ere a month had passed, forgetting, in the passing excitement of some fresh novelty, both wonder and perplexity; or at most, perhaps, relating now and then, to incredulous listeners of a winter evening, that very odd coincidence about three gold pins and a maid and a cook.

To me its lessons are still as fresh as on the day I received them. They preceded, and induced, a course of study that eventually changed the whole feelings and tenor of my life.

Within the last twenty-five years multitudes, in this and in all other civilized countries, have been overtaken, as unexpectedly as I was, with evidence of the reality of spiritual phenomena. And, to hundreds of thousands among these, conviction has come in the quiet of the domestic circle; has not been avowed to the world, and has not disturbed their relations with the churches they had been wont to frequent.

In illustration I here supply, out of many examples that have come to my knowledge, one which is the more noteworthy because it exhibits various phases of spiritual intervention. I entitle it

A DOMESTIC INVASION.

In the year 1853 there lived, in the town of R——, Massachusetts, a family of the utmost respectability and in easy circumstances, whose name, though known to me, I am not at liberty here to give. Let us call them Mr. and Mrs. L——.

Mrs. L—— appears to have been one of a class of which I have already spoken as resembling Reichenbach's "sensitives," if not identical with them: a class which has furnished what are called "mediums," and what might appropriately be called "spiritual sensitives." She shared many of the peculiarities of that class; peculiarities which, in her case as in many others, seem to have been hereditary.*

Her grandmother, one morning, preparing to go out walking and turning round to leave her bed-chamber, suddenly perceived, standing before her, the exact counterpart of herself. At first she imagined it to be an impression from some mirror; but, having ascertained that it was not so and seeing the appearance gradually vanish, she became very much alarmed; the popular idea occurring to her that to see one's *double*, or *wraith* as the Scotch term it, portended death. She immediately sent for the preacher whose church she frequented, the Rev. Mr. Eaton, and consulted him on the subject. He inquired whe-

* Out of 161 sensitives whose names are registered by Reichenbach, as among his odic subjects, 143 are from families marked by a similar peculiarity. Of these he found the faculty to have been inherited, in 28 cases from the father, in 50 from the mother, in 11 from both parents: and in 54 other cases it was shared by a brother or sister.—*Der Sensitive Mensch*, vol. ii. § 2662 to § 2666 (Stuttgart, 1854).

ther it was before or after mid-day that she had seen the apparition; and, learning that it was early in the forenoon, he assured her (whether from sincere conviction or merely to allay the extreme excitement in which he found her) that the augury was of long life, not of approaching dissolution. As it chanced, she lived after that to a good, old age.

Mrs. L——'s mother, Mrs. F——, was accompanied by knockings and other sounds in a house in Pearl street, Boston, at intervals as long as she resided there; namely, through a period of twelve years. Sometimes these sounds were audible to herself only; sometimes also to the other inmates of the house. Finally, they annoyed her husband so much, that he changed their residence.

Mrs. L—— herself, when about ten years of age (in the year 1830), had been witness to one of those phenomena that are never forgotten and produce a great influence on the opinions and feelings of a lifetime.

There was, at that time, residing in her mother's house, in the last stage of hopeless decline, a lady, named Mrs. Marshall, to whom Mrs. F——, from benevolent motives, had offered a temporary home.

Cecilia—that is Mrs. L——'s name—had been sitting up one evening a little later than usual, and, childlike, had lain down on the parlor sofa and dropped to sleep.

Awaking, after a time, she supposed it must be late; for the fire had burned low and the room was vacant. As she attempted to rise, she suddenly became aware that the figure of Mrs. Marshall, robed in white, was bending over her. "Oh, Mrs. Marshall," she exclaimed, "why did you come down for me? You will be sure to take cold." The figure smiled, made no reply, but, moving toward the door, signed to Cecilia to follow. She did so in considerable trepidation, which was increased when she perceived what she still believed to be the lady herself pass up the stairs backward, with a slow, gliding motion, to the door of her bedroom. The child followed; and, as she reached the landing of the stairs, she saw the figure, without turning the lock or opening the door, pass, as it were, through the material substance into the room and thus disappear from her sight.

Her screams brought her mother who, coming out of Mrs. Marshall's room, asked her what was the matter. "Oh, mamma, mamma," exclaimed the terrified child, "was that a ghost?"

The mother chid her at first, for nursing silly fancies; but when Cecilia related to her circumstantially what she had witnessed, Mrs. F—— shuddered. Well she might! Not half an hour before she had assisted at the death-bed of Mrs. Marshall!

It was remembered, too, that a few minutes before she expired, that lady, with whom Cecilia was a great favorite, had spoken in affectionate terms of the child and had expressed an earnest desire to see her. But Mrs. F——, fearing the effect of such a scene on one so young, had refrained from calling her daughter.

Did the earnest longing mature into action when the earth-clog was cast off? Was the dying wish gratified, notwithstanding the mother's precautions?

Later in her youth Cecilia, to her mother's great alarm, had from time to time walked in her sleep. This somnambulism was strictly spontaneous, no mesmeric experiments of any kind having ever been allowed in the family. It did not result in any accident; but, on several occasions, while unconscious and with her eyes closed, she had aided her mother, as expertly as if awake, in the household duties.

She had another peculiarity. In the early part of the night her sleep was usually profound; but occasionally, toward morning, in a state between sleeping and waking, she had visions of the night which, though they were undoubtedly but a phase of dreaming, she discovered, by repeated experience, to be often of a clairvoyant or prophetic character; sometimes informing her of death or illness. These intimations of the distant or the future so frequently corresponded to the truth that, when they prognosticated misfortune, Mrs. L—— hesitated, on awaking, to communicate them.

Such a dream, or vision, she had one night in the early part of the month of November, 1853. A sister, Esther, recently married, had gone out, with her husband, to California, some weeks before; and they had been expecting, ere long, news of her arrival. This sister seemed to approach the bedside, and said to her: "Cecilia, come with me to California." Mrs. L——, in her dream, objected that she could not leave her husband and children, to undertake a journey so long and tedious.

"We shall soon be there," said Esther, "and you shall return before morning."

In her dream the proposed excursion did not seem to her an impossibility: so she rose from bed, and, giving her hand to her sister, she thought they ascended together and floated over a vast space; then descended near a dwelling of humble and rude appearance, very different from any which she could have imagined her sister to occupy in the new country to which, in search of fortune, she and her husband had emigrated. The sisters entered, and Cecilia recognized her brother-in-law, sad and in mourning garb. Esther then led her into a room in the centre of which stood an open coffin, and pointed to the body it contained. It was Esther's own body, pale with the hue of death. Mrs. L—— gazed in mute astonishment, first at the corpse before her, then at the form, apparently bright with life and intelligence, which had conducted her thither. To her look of inquiry and wonder the living appearance replied, "Yes, sister, that body was mine; but disease assailed it. I was taken with cholera and I have passed to another world. I desired to show you this, that you might be prepared for the news that will soon reach you."

After a time Mrs. L—— seemed to herself to rise again into the air, again to traverse a great space, and finally to re-enter her bed-chamber. By and by she awoke, with this dream so vividly stamped on her mind, that it required some time to satisfy her that she had not made an actual journey.

"I have had *such* a dream!" she exclaimed to her husband. But his discouraging "What, Cecilia, at your foolish dreams again?" closed her lips, and she passed the matter off without further explanation, either to him or to any other member of the family.

It so happened that, the evening of the same day, Mrs. L—— sat down to a quiet family game of whist. Her husband and a younger sister, Anne, were of the party. In the course of the game Mrs. L—— handed the cards to her sister, whose turn it was to deal. Suddenly she saw Anne's arm assume a rapid rotary motion, and the cards flew in all directions. Turning to chide her for what she thought a foolish jest, she observed a peculiar expression spread over her face: the look was grave, earnest, thoughtful; and the eyes were fixed, as with affectionate anxiety, on Cecilia's face.

Very much alarmed, the latter cried out, "Oh, Anne, what *is* the matter? why do you look so?"

"Call me not Anne," was the reply; "I am Esther."

"Anne!"

"I tell you it is Esther who speaks to you, not Anne."

Mrs. L——, excessively terrified, turned to her husband, crying out, "Her mind is gone! she is mad! Oh that such a misfortune should ever have fallen on our family!"

"Your dream, Cecilia! Your dream of last night! Have you forgotten whither I took you and what you saw?" said Anne, solemnly.

The shock was too much for Mrs. L——. She fainted.

When, by the use of the usual restoratives, she had recovered, she found her sister still in the same trance-like state, and still impersonating Esther. This continued for nearly four hours At the end of that time Anne suddenly rubbed her eyes, stretched her limbs, as if awaking, and asked in her natural voice, "Have I been asleep? What is the matter? What has happened?"

Some four weeks afterward the California mail brought a letter from Esther's husband, informing the family of his wife's sudden death, by cholera, on the very day preceding the night of Mrs. L——'s dream.

When, about six months later, the brother-in-law, having returned to Massachusetts, heard from Mrs. L—— the description of the rude dwelling to which, in her dream, she had seemed to be conveyed, he admitted that it corresponded, accurately and minutely, to that of the house in which his wife actually died.

The above incidents were related to me by Mrs. L—— herself,* with permission to publish them, suppressing only the family name.

That lady also stated to me that, at the time referred to, the modern spiritual manifestations were unknown in the town of R——, except by some vague rumors of knockings said to have been heard in Rochester, and which Mrs. L——'s family had always treated as a matter too absurd to be seriously noticed. It need hardly be added that they had never sought or witnessed rapping or table-moving or trance-speaking or automatic writing, or any similar phenomena, now so common in this and other countries.

It was, therefore, with mingled feelings of grief and astonishment that they observed, in Anne, a repetition on several subsequent occasions of the same manifestation which had startled them during the rubber at whist.

* At the Fifth Avenue Hotel, New York, on October 15, 1860. The narrative, written out, was submitted by me to Mrs. L—— on the 17th of October; and she assented to its accuracy.

Had I not been the author of a work which had attracted the attention, and awakened the sympathies, of Mrs. L——, I should never have learned these particulars; for, during three years preceding 1860, that lady and her family had ceased to speak, outside of the domestic circle, on the subject of their spiritual visitations. The feeling which prompted this reticence sufficiently explains why the family name is withheld.

The next time that her sister's fixed gaze and changed manner indicated the recurrence of this abnormal condition, Mrs. L—— asked, "Is this Esther again?"

"Not so, my daughter," was the reply. "It is not your sister but another friend who desires to address you."

"What friend?"

"John Murray."

This was the name of an aged preacher under whom Mrs. L——'s mother had sat in the early part of her life, and who had died many years before, never personally known to Mrs. L——.

After this, the impersonation, by Anne, of the Rev. Mr. Murray was of frequent occurrence. On such occasions she usually addressed those present in the grave and measured tones that are wont to characterize a pulpit discourse. The subjects were always religious, and the spirit in which they were treated was elevated and often eloquent far beyond the natural powers of the speaker.

Nor was this all. Mrs. L—— herself, at first very much to her dissatisfaction, became influenced to write by impressional dictation. Long she resisted, additionally urged to opposition by the great repugnance of her husband and of her friends, who regarded, almost with horror, this sudden invasion of the household circle. "It must be some of these terrible spiritual extravagances that are going about," they used to say, in a tone very similar to that in which nervous people deplore the approach of a deadly epidemic.

After a time, however, when it was observed that these communications were pure and reverent in character, inculcating the highest principles of religion and morality, and that no further abnormalities succeeded, Mr. L—— and many of their friends became reconciled to the intrusion; and finally listened, with interest and pleasure, to the lessons, oral and written, which were thus mysteriously conveyed to them.

In the above remarkable narrative I invite attention to the evidence, therein incidentally presenting itself, of *identity.*

We may believe confidently in the spiritual origin of a message or of a lesson, and yet may be justified—we *are* sometimes fully justified—in doubting the identity of the spirit purporting to communicate.*

But what are we to make of Anne's exclamation: "Your dream, Cecilia! Your dream of last night! Have you forgotten whither I took you and what you saw?"

Not a single particular of that dream had been related by Mrs. L—— to Anne or to any one else. No wonder she fainted! No wonder she felt certain—as she told me she did—that it was Esther herself, and no other, who inspired the words. To what other credible source can we refer them? The hypothesis of chance coincidence is utterly untenable. As little can we suppose reflection by thought-reading: to say nothing of the incredibility of a simulated four-hour trance.

Of apparitions to relatives and dear friends at or near the time of death I have elsewhere † furnished authentic examples. This is more common than any other class of apparition. Numerous examples occur in German works, and the Germans have a special term (anzeigen) to designate such an appearance. ‡

But besides being commonly unexpected and often unwelcome, these phenomena have sometimes resulted in annoyance and loss to the parties who witnessed them; though usually

* Especially where celebrated names are given; and this may happen without intention to deceive. The name of Socrates or Aristotle or Confucius might be assumed by some spirit favoring the school of philosophy of the sage whose name he gives.

For myself, I have never received a communication purporting to come from any celebrity whom, in life, I had not known: and but rarely from any one except those with whom I had been connected by ties of consanguinity, or of affection.

† In *Footfalls on the Boundary of Another World*, at pp. 371–376, and throughout chapter 3, Book ii.

‡ "Er hat sich angezeigt" is the phrase usually employed.

without apparent intention to injure, on the part of the unseen agents.

An example is given in a London periodical,* attested by date, place, and name. It comes through an English clergyman. The Rev. S. E. Benbough, of Hadleigh, Rochford, Essex, writing in June, 1860, incloses a letter from a lady with whom he says he is "well acquainted and cannot doubt for a moment her trustworthiness." He goes on to say: "All well-authenticated facts connected, or apparently connected, with the supernatural are valuable as materials from which, in course of time, general laws may be deduced;" and adds an expression of regret that so many persons, in narrating such facts, withhold the guarantee of genuineness contained in a signature. The letter, which he incloses and which I have slightly abridged, tells the story. Let us call it

Why a Villa was sold at a Loss.

"Dear Sir: A few evenings since you expressed a wish to obtain, in writing, the circumstances which caused me to leave my former abode. Here are the facts.

"In January, 1860, I purchased a semi-detached villa, near Chiswick. The previous occupant was a lady who, sixteen years before, had built that and the adjoining villa. The latter had been sold to an elderly gentleman and his wife, who proved most respectable and quiet neighbors. My own family, as you know, consists of myself, my daughter, and a female servant.

"The front bedroom, eighteen feet by twenty-five, I selected for my own use. The very first night of my occupancy—there being a bright fire and a night-light burning—I heard a singular noise, commencing before midnight and continuing for some time; but I paid little attention to it. The same sound continued, with few interruptions, for many weeks, and grew

* *Spiritual Magazine* of July, 1860.

to a serious disturbance; regularly waking me from my first sleep at from half-past eleven to twelve o'clock, or occasionally at about twenty minutes past eleven. The sounds seemed to proceed from naked or thinly-slippered feet, walking to and fro, the length of the room, with heavy tread: so heavy that it caused a vibration of the crockery on the marble washstand, and of light articles on the toilet-glass.

"My first impression was that my next-door neighbors had restless nights; but, on making their acquaintance, I found that this was not the case. Next I sought to account for the strange sound in connection with a timepiece in my bed-chamber; and this I had moved from place to place, but unavailingly. The sound continued, and the ticking of the timepiece could be heard quite distinct from it.

"Another experiment was equally without result. I frequently placed myself so, as it were, that I might arrest the footsteps, but this caused no cessation or alteration of the sound.

"Sometimes I used to open the window and sit by it in the spring mornings. This made no difference: the sounds went on, all the same, until four or five o'clock.

"I discovered that to others the sounds conveyed the same impression as to myself. Three or four times I awoke my daughter; and to her as to me, they seemed to proceed from a heavy footfall. Again, on one occasion when a friend, who was visiting me, had been put in the room which my servant usually occupied, the girl slept on a sofa in my bedroom. Up to that time I had not mentioned it to her. Twice, when awoke in the night, she cried out, terrified: 'Oh, Ma'am, what is it? what is it?' and hid her head under the bed-clothes.

"At last this disturbance became not only annoying but so terrible to me that I resolved to leave the house. At a great loss I obtained a purchaser.

"When this was settled I heard, for the first time, from an old nurse who came to inquire after the former inhabitants of the house, that the lady who built it and who had died there, and from whose brother I bought it, suffered from painful and incurable disease, and that it was her sad fate, after a short sleep, to walk the room till four or five in the morning; then to sink on her bed, exhausted.

"On inquiry, an opposite neighbor confirmed this statement They had often seen the old lady walking to and fro, when sickness in their family caused them to be about in the early morning.

"This may be no solution of the singular affair. But I relate it in connection with the other events.

"I am, dear sir, yours respectfully,

"MARY PROPERT.

"*To the Rev. S. E. Benbough.*"

This will be recognized as one of a class of phenomena, often discredited, known as "house-hauntings." The remarkable point in the case is its business aspect. The lady from whom the story comes, and who seems to have been a dispassionate observer, found the disturbance so seriously real and so persistent that, at a great loss, she sold her house to escape it. I think it possible she might have been saved from this loss had she been willing—but no doubt the proposal would have shocked her—to enter into communication with her nocturnal visitant. In support of this opinion I here adduce an anecdote of

A REPENTANT HOUSEKEEPER.

There is a young lady, Miss V——, well and favorably known to me, frank and cultivated, a member of one of the old New York families. A few years since she was spending a week or two with her aunt, mistress of a spacious, handsome, and hospitable old mansion on the Hudson River. This mansion, like some of the ancient chateaux of Europe, has long had its haunted chamber. Little was said about this, but the room was not used except on pressing occasions. During Miss V——'s residence there, visitors accumulated to overflowing;

and the aunt, with an apology to her niece, asked her if she minded giving up her room for a day or two to the new-comers and running the risk of a visit from a ghost. Miss V—— replied that she was not afraid of visitors from another world: so the arrangement was made.

The young lady went to sleep quietly and without fear. Awaking about midnight, she saw, moving about her room, an elderly woman in neat, somewhat old-fashioned dress, apparently an upper-servant: but the face was unknown to her. At first she was not afraid, supposing it to be some one employed in the house who had come on some errand or other: but a moment's thought reminded her that she had locked the door before retiring. This startled her, and her alarm increased when the figure approached the bed, bent toward her and seemed to make an earnest but unavailing effort to speak. Greatly frightened she drew the bed-clothes over her face; and when, after a little, she looked up again, the figure had vanished. She sprang to the door of her room and found it still locked on the inside. "*Can* there be such things as ghosts?" she thought, as she returned to bed; "that *was* a reality, if sight could be trusted." In that conviction, after a restless hour or two, she fell asleep; but next morning in the bright light of day, it did not seem to her quite so certain; and after a few months it faded—as with young people such things will—to a dim belief.

Then, however, a circumstance occurred which renewed a faith, not again to be shaken, in the reality of her midnight visitor. Accepting the invitation of an intimate and highly valued friend to spend some days with her, she found that her hostess, in a quiet way, had been making experiments in Spiritualism and had obtained sundry communications. Miss V——, curious on a subject of which she had heard much and seen very little, joined her friend during several sittings.

On one of these occasions an (alleged) spirit announced itself as Sarah Clarke,* a name unknown to both ladies. The com-

* This is not the real name. I obtained this narrative from Miss V—— herself, in the winter of 1869–70; at first with permission to give names and exact dates. But afterward, on conferring with her aunt,

munication was to the effect that she had been, many years before, housekeeper in the family of Miss V——'s aunt; that she had endeavored, unsuccessfully, to communicate directly with Miss V—— when that young lady last visited the old mansion; that her object was to confess a criminal act of which she had been guilty and to ask her old mistress's pardon for it. A restless desire to do so (she added) had caused her to haunt the room she occupied when on earth. She then proceeded to say that she had been tempted to steal and hide away several small pieces of family plate, including a silver sugar-bowl and a few other articles which she enumerated; and that she would be very thankful if Miss V—— would tell her aunt this and express her (Sarah's) great sorrow for what she had done, and her hope for pardon.

The next time Miss V—— visited her aunt, she asked her if she had ever known a person named Sarah Clarke.

"Certainly," she replied, "she was housekeeper in our family some thirty or forty years since."

"What sort of person was she?"

"A good, careful, tidy woman."

"Did you lose any silver articles while she was with you, aunt?"

The lady reflected. "Yes, I believe we did; a sugar basin and a few other things disappeared in a mysterious way. Why do you ask?"

"Did you ever suspect Sarah of taking them?"

"No: of course she had access to them; but we considered her far too trustworthy to be guilty of theft."

Then Miss V—— related the message she and her friend had received; and, on comparing notes, it was found that the list of articles, as given by Sarah to the two ladies, corresponded with the things actually lost, so far as the aunt could recol-

she found the old lady unwilling to incur the notoriety consequent on doing so: and thus Miss V—— had to withdraw the permission to use any names in connection with her story.

lect. What that lady thought of her niece's story I know not all she said was that, if Sarah *had* taken the things, she most freely forgave it.

The remarkable point in this story remains to be told. From that time forth, *the haunted chamber was free from all disturbance.* Sarah Clarke never again appeared to any of its occupants.

Knowing the standing of the parties I am able to vouch for the truth of this story. Let us consider what it discloses as to the next world.

There is repentance there as here. There is restless regret and sorrow for grave sin committed while here. There is anxious desire for pardon from those whom the spirit wronged during earth-life. In other words the natural effects of evil doing follow us to our next phase of life; and, in that phase of life as in the present, we amend, and attain to better things, by virtue of repentance.

In this the mode of moral progression after death is similar to that which alone avails on earth. "Repent!" was Christ's first public exhortation. To the "spirits in prison" on the other side—spirits not yet released from earthly bondage and earthly remorse—the same exhortation, it would seem, is appropriate still.

Such indications as these induce Spiritualists to believe that the next world is more nearly like this than Orthodoxy imagines it to be.

Another corollary is, that when such spiritual phenomena present themselves, an endeavor to establish communication with the manifesting spirit may result in benefit alike to a denizen of the other world and to a disturbed inhabitant of this. In this way Mrs. Propert, getting rid of the midnight footfalls, might have been in quiet possession of her villa at this day.

I invite attention, also, to the strong proof of identity furnished by Miss V——'s story. The name of the housekeeper was unknown to both ladies when her (alleged) spirit gave the message. There was nothing to suggest such a name, or such a confession as was made. Yet, on inquiry, both name and confession were found to correspond with facts that had taken place thirty or forty years before: to say nothing of a new fact, tallying with all the rest: the cessation of the spiritual visits, as soon as the visitor had no longer any motive to show herself.

I pass now to another class of manifestations, in which, it will be remarked, the same element of unexpectedness is found.

CHAPTER II.

ANIMALS PERCEIVING SPIRITUAL PHENOMENA.

"The ass saw the angel of the Lord standing in the way."—NUMBERS xxii. 23.

THOSE who deem incredible certain details of the interruption which befell Balaam during his unwilling journey to meet the King of Moab, may find, in modern incidents, cause for belief that there might have been an important truth underlying the story.

I think it the more important to adduce some of these incidents because, if sufficiently authenticated, they set at rest the vague theories touching "expectant attention" and "dominant ideas," that have been propounded to explain away, as figments of the brain, all perceptions of spiritual appearances. First let us examine one which occurred in Holland.

WHAT BEFELL A SWISS OFFICER.

I take the following from a well-known English work on Sleep, by Dr. Binns. The author gives it on the authority of Lord Stanhope, who had it directly from the gentleman to whom the incident occurred, Mr. C. de Steiguer, a nephew of the celebrated Avoyer de Steiguer, of Berne. That gentleman, in relating it to Lord Stanhope, said: "I do not believe in apparitions, but there is something very extraordinary in the subject; and I would not relate what I am about to mention if many persons, some of whom are now alive, could not bear witness to its truth."

Lord Stanhope then proceeds to give "as nearly as possible

an exact translation of the expressions which he (Monsieur de Steiguer) used." Here it is:

"I was early in life in the Dutch service, and had occupied my lodgings, for some weeks, without hearing anything remarkable. My bedroom had, on one side of it, my sitting room; on the other, a room in which my servant slept; and it communicated with each of them by a door.

"One night, being in bed but not asleep, I heard a noise as if some person was walking, in slippers, up and down the room. The noise continued for some time.

"Next morning I asked my servant if he had heard anything. 'Nothing,' he replied, 'except that you walked up and down the room last night, when it was late.' I assured him that I had not done so; and, as he appeared incredulous, I told him that, if I should again hear the sounds I would let him know.

"On the following night I called him, desiring him to bring a candle and to take notice if he saw anything. He informed me that he did not; but that he heard a noise as if some person were approaching him, and then moving off in a contrary direction.

"I had three animals in my room; a dog, a cat, and a canary-bird; each of which was affected in a peculiar manner, whenever the noise was heard. The dog immediately jumped into my bed and lay close to me, trembling as if from fear. The cat followed the noise with her eyes, as if she saw, or attempted to see, what caused it. The canary bird, which was sleeping on its perch, instantly awoke, and fluttered about the cage, in great perturbation.

"Occasionally a noise was heard as if the keys of the piano in my sitting room were slightly touched, and as if the key of my desk was turned and the desk opened; but nothing moved. I mentioned these things to the officers of my regiment, all of whom slept by turns on the sofa in my sitting room, and heard the same sounds."

M. de Steiguer had the floor and skirting-board taken up, but could find not even a trace of rats or mice.

After a time he became unwell; and, his illness increasing, he sent for a physician who urgently advised him to change his lodgings, though he would give no reason for this advice. Finally M. de Steiguer had himself removed.

He stated further to Lord Stanhope that when he became convalescent and insisted on knowing why the doctor had so strongly urged him to leave his rooms, the latter informed him "that they had a bad reputation; that one man had hung himself in them, and that it was supposed another had been murdered." *

This narrative bears the stamp of authenticity. We cannot believe that Lord Stanhope would have allowed Dr. Binns to use his name and that of his Swiss friend, in attestation of such a story, without a deep conviction of its truth.

The witness appears to have been a cool-headed and dispassionate observer; but let us suppose him nervous and imaginative. Did his servant share his temperament? Were the senses of all the officers whom he called in, as additional witnesses, misled by the excitement of expectation? Let us concede these extreme improbabilities. Another difficulty remains. Was the dog, was the cat, was the canary-bird, nervously expectant? Were their senses deceived by "dominant ideas"?

As regards the most sagacious of domestic animals, what has been usually called popular superstition has assigned to it an occasional power beyond mere spiritual perceptions—a species of presentiment in certain cases of approaching death. I do not venture to affirm that dogs ever have such a power; yet I know of one strongly-attested case which goes to prove that sometimes they have an instinct which greatly resembles it.

* EDWARD BINNS, M.D., *Anatomy of Sleep;* second edition, London, 1845; pp. 479, 480.

What preceded a Child's unexpected Death.

For thirty years past I have been well acquainted with Mrs. D——, daughter of the late Rev. Mr. R——, long and favorably known in Indiana. Her grandparents, named Haas, were living in Woodstock, Virginia, when her mother, afterward Mrs. R——, was twenty years old and still unmarried. Miss Haas had a brother, two years old, and the child had a favorite dog, who was his constant companion and seemed to take special care of him. The circumstances connected with this child's sudden death, Mrs. L—— had often heard repeated by her mother.

It was about mid-day that this boy, running over the parlor floor, tripped his foot in the carpet and fell. His sister picked him up and soon succeeded in soothing him. At dinner, however, it was observed that he gave his left hand, not being able to stretch out his right. They rubbed the right arm with camphor and the child made no complaint.

While they were at dinner, the dog approached the child's chair and began whining in the most piteous way. They put him out, then he howled. They drove him off, but he returned and took his post under the window of the room in which the child was, continuing to howl from time to time; and there he remained during the night, in spite of all attempts to dislodge him. In the evening the child was taken seriously ill, and died about one o'clock in the morning. So long as it lived the dog's dismal lament was heard, at brief intervals; but as soon as the child died, the howling ceased, and was not renewed either then or afterward.

I have entire confidence in Mrs. D——'s truthfulness, and it was by her that the above story was related to me.*

This, however, is the only example of the kind that has come to me directly authenticated; and I refrain from build-

* On June 27, 1859. I took notes of it at the time.

ing on a single example. Animals may not have the gift of presentiment; but I think there is sufficient proof that they have spiritual perceptions. In a former work * I have, inci dentally, brought up some evidence of this; and I esteem my self fortunate in being able here to present, from an accredited medical source, one of the best-attested and most circumstantially related incidents in proof, that I ever remember to have seen. It is the more valuable because medical writers as a class—like other scientific men—are ever reluctant to admit anything that savors of the supernatural.

The story appeared, three years before the advent of Spiritualism in America, in one of the best-known Medical Journals of Scotland. It occurs in a review of a work on Sleep, then just published. The reviewer touches on the subject of apparitions and, after noticing several cases which he thinks of easy solution, thus proceeds:

"The following case, however, is one of those very rare ones, whose explanation baffles the philosophic inquirer. It is, indeed, almost the only authentic one to which we could refer; and, as it occurred to a particular friend and every circumstance was minutely inquired into at the time, the narrative is as authentic as such things can be. It may add to the interest of this case to state that it was communicated several years ago to Mr. Hibbert, after the publication of his work on apparitions, when he confessed that he could not explain it in the same philosophic way in which he had been able to account for all others, and that it appeared to him more nearly to approach the supernatural."

The story, thus strongly vouched for, is then given by the reviewer, as follows, the title only added by me:

THE DOG IN THE WOLFRIDGE WOOD.

"F. M. S—— was passing through the Wolfridge wood at Alverston, one night at twelve o'clock. He was accompanied

* *Footfalls*, pp. 217, 231, 398, 446, 448.

by his dog, of a breed between the Newfoundland and mastiff; a powerful animal, who feared neither man nor beast. He had a fowling-piece and a pair of pistols loaded, besides his sword; for he belonged to the Military School there and had been out for a day's shooting.

"The road ran centrally through the wood; and very nearly in the centre of the wood, at a part somewhat more open than the rest, there was a cross erected to point out the spot where a gamekeeper had been murdered. The place had the reputation of being haunted, and the ghost, it was said, had been repeatedly seen. S—— had frequently before passed this cross in the wood without seeing anything, and treated the story of the ghost so lightly that he had, on more occasions than one, for a bet, gone there at midnight and returned without meeting anything except an occasional gamekeeper or poacher.

"This night, when he approached the open space in the wood, he thought he perceived, at the other end of that space, the form of a man, more indistinct, however, than usual. He called his dog to his side (for previously it had been ranging about, barking furiously and giving chase to the game it started), patted it on the head to make it keep a sharp look-out, and cocked his gun. The dog, on this, was all impatience. S—— challenged the figure, but no answer was returned. Suspecting it was a poacher and prepared for an encounter, he directed the dog's attention to the appearance, and the animal answered by growling. He then kept his eyes steadily fixed on the figure; when, instantaneously it glided within arm's length of him. Still he looked steadily in its face while it kept its eyes on his. It had approached him without noise or rustling. The face was ill-defined, but distinctly visible. He could not turn his eyes from those of this apparition; they fascinated him, as it were, to the spot; he had no power in his frame. He felt no fear of bodily injury, only a certain indescribable sense of awe. So fascinated were his eyes by those of the figure, that he did not observe its dress, nor even its form. It looked calmly and with a mild aspect, for a space of time which he does not think exceeded half a minute; then suddenly became invisi ble. The form had flitted before him about five minutes altogether.

"The dog which before this was furious and growling, now stood crouched at his feet as if in a trance—his jaw fallen, his limbs quivering, and his whole frame agitated and covered with a cold sweat. After the form disappeared, S—— touched the animal, then spoke to it without its seeming to recognize him; and it was some time before it appeared to recover its senses. The whole way home, it never moved from his side but kept close to his feet; nor, on their way home, did it run after game, or take notice if game started near it.

"It was a fortnight before it recovered from the fright; and it was never afterward the same lively animal. No consideration could ever again induce that dog to enter the wood after nightfall, nor would it allow any of the family to enter it. When it was forced to pass by the open spot in daylight, it would only do so with its master, and it always exhibited signs of fear, trembling all the time and walking silently by his side.

"S—— has frequently since passed this spot in the wood at the midnight hour, but has never again seen the figure. Before this occurrence he had always treated with ridicule any stories about ghosts or spirits; now, he firmly believes in both."

The reviewer does not hesitate to express the opinion that the appearance witnessed by his friend was the result of supernatural agency.*

* *Edinburgh Medical and Surgical Journal* for 1845; vol. lxiv. pp. 186-7.

The reviewer's remarks are as follows:

"This is almost the only recorded case known to us where the evidence is so strong, as to leave no other impression on the mind but that it was the appearance of some supernatural agency, and, after having in vain endeavored to explain it on any other supposition, we found ourselves forced to conclude, with Hamlet, that 'there are more things in heaven and earth than are dreamed of in our philosophy.'"

This, published in a Medical Journal of old standing and established reputation, three years before the term Spiritualism in its modern acceptation had been heard of—is certainly a very remarkable admission.

The incident here related caused a complete revolution of opinion in the witness. From being an entire sceptic in apparitions and in spirits, he became, through the evidence of his senses, a believer in both. But to have faith in spirits and their appearance is to have faith in the reality of another life.

Could he, rationally, withhold belief? Is not one such incident, unmistakably evidenced, as complete proof of a future phase of existence as a hundred? And even if S—— had been willing, as some men have been, to give the lie to his own senses, rather than believe that the denizens of the next world sometimes return to this, was there not a dumb witness remaining to bear testimony, by his changed character and unconquerable terrors, against such stiff-necked and illogical unbelief?

CHAPTER III.

UNIVERSALITY OF SPIRITUAL MANIFESTATIONS.

'Miracles cease when men cease to believe and to expect them."— Lecky.*

This is what is usually called a rationalistic, but it is not a rational, view of miracles.

A portion of the alleged events which go currently under the name of miracles undoubtedly do not happen. But a larger portion do. Unfounded belief may cause us to imagine the former. The latter are not dependent upon our thought of them—be it credulous or incredulous † —for their appearance or non-appearance.

What the world has been wont to term miracles, cease to be regarded as such when they are critically examined: that is true.

But it is not true that phenomena similar to what theologians usually call the miracles of the New Testament cease, when we no longer have faith in them, or when we cease to look for their coming. It is not true, as to certain manifestations occurring through spiritual agency, and governed by intermundane laws, that these are the shadowy offspring of credulity, and that they disappear, like mist of the morning, when the Sun of Reason shines out.

* *European Morals*, vol. i. p. 373 : (Amer. Ed.)

† Hard-set unbelief may, now and then, by some law of mental science as yet imperfectly understood, arrest a certain class of spiritual phenomena, and so deprive a dogmatic sceptic of a chance to witness them: just as the contempt of Jesus' own countrymen diminished his spiritual power while among them (Mark vi. 5). But this is the exception only; as many of the narratives in this volume sufficiently show.

The great lesson taught in the few narratives I have already given, in many of those which follow and in a hundred others attested beyond reasonable denial,* is that genuine spiritual appearances show themselves in spite of distrust, unbelief, repugnance even—show themselves, when the sight of an angel from Heaven was as little expected as they—and, so far as the evidence goes, have always done so, though doubtless more frequently in some ages of the world than in others.

It is a popular notion that, about twenty-five years since, a superstitious epidemic, originating in Western New York, overtook millions of weak men and women, first in these United States, then in Europe and other parts of the world; creating in them a most unphilosophical belief: namely, that there had appeared among us a modern dispensation, under which there were occurring marvellous events without example in the past, and specially vouchsafed by God to this, his favored generation. The assumed theory is that this new faith was the mania prevailing for the time; soon to pass away, like a hundred other ephemeral delusions.

These short-cuts toward a solution of momentous difficulties are very convenient and very illogical. They save men trouble in investigating; but they cannot save them from errors of the gravest character.

Nothing more easy than to allege that if we go back even a few years before the time when the report of the "Rochester Knockings" disgusted the Church and scandalized the world of Science, we come upon an age barren of all miraculous inklings, save only within the suspicious precincts where Romish ecclesiasticism reigns.

—Easy to say, but at variance with notorious facts. The earliest date of the Rochester disturbances is March, 1848. Will it do to assert that, say ten or fifteen years before that time, one cannot find, in any sober, civilized nation, where science holds free and respected sway, trustworthy evidence that oc-

* See *Footfalls*, Books iii., iv., v.

currences as strange and as little capable of apneumatic explanation—spiritual manifestations in fact—were habitually showing themselves?

Let us see. Our own country is spoken of as young, impulsive, credulous, not given to thorough study. Let us, in this instance, pass her by, for another. The English are staid, practical, thoughtful; not easily moved from their equanimity; not specially tolerant of startling novelties; sufficiently sensitive to the sting of ridicule; sufficiently inclined to follow the old ruts of habit and custom, legally, materially, spiritually. In no country is Science more free; in none are scientific men harder students, more sceptical, or more active-minded.

The more valuable, because of these national traits, is the following narrative, or cluster of narratives, to which, through the kindness of a Scottish friend whom the world, alas! has recently lost,* my attention happened to be directed. He put into my hands a remarkable book, little known, written, thirty years since, by a gentleman of standing; an English officer and a Fellow of the Royal Society. †

The author of this work testifies to a disturbance of a very singular character which occurred at his country seat, near Woodbridge, Suffolk. It continued throughout nearly two months. The details are minutely given.

Fifty-three Days of Bell Ringing.

This disturbance commenced on the second of February, 1834, at the house of Great Bealings, inhabited by Major Edward Moor. On the afternoon of that day, being Sunday, during the absence of Major Moor at church and while only one man-servant and one maid-servant were at home, the dining-room

* Robert Chambers.

† *Bealings Bells.* An Account of the Mysterious Ringing of Bells, at Great Bealings, Suffolk, in 1834, and in other parts of England: with Relations of other unaccountable Occurrences in various places. By Major Edward Moor, F.R.S.; Woodbridge, 1841; pp. 142.

bell was rung, without visible cause, three times. The weather was calm; the barometer at 29°; the thermometer within its usual range. There were no remarkable atmospheric phenomena.

Next day the same bell sounded several times, equally without apparent cause. On the third day five out of the nine bells suspended in a row in the basement of the house, gave forth several loud peals, while nobody could detect any one meddling either with the pulls or the wires.

After this all the bells in the house, twelve in number, were (except one, the front-door bell) repeatedly rung in the same manner: five bells usually ringing at a time. The wires of these five *pealers* were visible in their whole course, from the pulls to the bells themselves, except where they passed through floors or walls by small openings.

This continued day after day throughout February and March. The bells usually rang after a clattering fashion, quite different from the usual ringing. "With no vigor of pull," says Major Moor, "could the violent ringing be effected." Pulling the horizontal wires with a hook, downward, produced only a gentle, tinkling sound. The Major further says: "The motion of the bells, and that of their spiral flexible support, when rung by hand, was comparatively slow and perceptible: not so, at the peals; it was then too rapid to be seen distinctly." *

Major Moor was naturally much surprised by these apparent prodigies; and he, his servants, and friends made many efforts to find some natural explanation, but wholly without success. Then he inserted a minute statement of particulars in the *Ipswich Journal*, † describing the situations of the bells and the arrangement of their wires, in hopes that some one would be able to suggest an explanation; but no explanation beyond surmises of trickery ever reached him: in reply to cer-

* *Bealings Bells*, p. 6.

† Of March 1, 1834. He states that during the very time he was writing his communication to this newspaper, the bells were repeatedly rung.

tain inquirers who probably thought they were suggesting adequate cause, he replied that his house was not infested with rats, and that he kept no monkey.

The last ringing was on March 27, 1834. It is abundantly evident, from Major Moor's book, that he spared no pains, throughout the seven and a half weeks during which the strange annoyance lasted, to detect fraudulent artifice, had artifice, under such circumstances, been possible. He avers: "The bells rang scores of times when no one was in the passage or back-building or house or grounds, unseen: I have waited in the kitchen for a repetition of the ringings, with all the servants present—when no one could be in concealment. But what matters? Neither I, nor the servants, nor any one, could, or can, work the wonderment that I and more than half a score of others saw." Finally, the Major declares: "I am thoroughly convinced that the ringing is by no human agency.*

Now, on the supposition that what have been called spiritual manifestations—doings which we can trace to no human agency—are the modern offspring of an epidemic commencing in 1848, what should we suppose might be the probable result of a newspaper article narrating the above occurrence, and published in an English paper in 1834? Simply that the foolhardy narrator would incur ridicule as a dupe, or encounter reproach as an impostor.

But what actually happens?

Disclosures through Bealings Bells.

From Major Moor's book we learn that his communication to the *Ipswich Journal* brought him letters containing *fourteen* different examples of mysterious bell-ringing, every one of them unexplained; all occurring in England, namely, in the Counties of Norfolk, Suffolk, Kent, Derby, Middlesex, and in or near the towns of Chelmsford, Cheltenham, Chesterfield,

* *Bealings Bells*, p. 5.

Cambridge, Bristol, Greenwich, Windsor, and London; all of comparatively recent date, and most of them attested by the signatures of those who witnessed them, with permission to give their names to the public. He received also three other communications disclosing further mysteries, to which I shall refer by and by.

The fourteen examples, be it remarked, are all of one particular phase of manifestation; a rare phase, so far as my observation goes: I have notes of but one such in the United States, namely, in a house in Pine street, Philadelphia; lasting during five days of the week between Christmas and New Year's Day, 1857.*

But even of this rare phase of manifestation, we cannot imagine that in the fourteen examples presented in *Bealings Bells*, we have more than a very small instalment of similar cases which might be found in England. The chances are that nine men or women of the world, out of every ten, would shrink from the notoriety, or shirk the trouble, attendant on the presentation of such narratives for publication.

Even in this small book, then, what a lifting of the veil on the thousand marvels that may have occurred in all ages, unrecorded or unexplained!

Unable for lack of space to notice Major Moor's fourteen relations, I here briefly condense the evidences in three of them.

An Eighteen-months' Disturbance.

In a house near Chesterfield, belonging to Mr. James Ashwell, "long and repeated bell-ringings," commencing in 1830 and continuing throughout eighteen months, occurred.

* In this case, there being a sick lady in the house, the attending nurse said the disturbance *must* be stopped, and she herself muffled the bells, wrapping the clappers with cloth and then tying them with twine. Three hours later they rang themselves loose of everything, pealing more violently than before. Finally they rang themselves loose from the wall itself, drawing out the staples, five inches long—*then the bells*

The details are given, partly by Mr. Ashwell himself, partly by Mr. W. Felkin, of Nottingham, a friend of his.

According to Mr. Felkin's statement, "all the bells in the house rang at one time or other; but never before five in the morning nor after eleven at night. The oscillation was like that of a pendulum, not a decreasing one. A bell was put up one Saturday evening, unattached to any wire, and rang in half an hour.* Another bell which had been taken down and laid on a closet shelf, lay there quiescent for some weeks; but being then fixed by means of the flexible bent iron to which it was attached between a wooden hat-peg batten and the wall against which the batten was nailed, it rang immediately. †

These bells were wont to ring continuously, with violent clatter and for a considerable time. Sometimes, during their greatest vibration, Mr. Ashwell would seize one of them between his hands, and compel cessation: but, as soon as he released it, it would resume its oscillation and ringing.

All the bells were hung out of reach. Bell-hangers, of course, were called to lend their aid; but nothing was found to indicate that bell or bell-wire had been tampered with. On a particular occasion, while a bell-hanger was engaged in re-attaching the wires, after a long silence, one of the bells began to ring before his face. Down dropped the man from the ladder; and, without waiting to gather up his tools, off he ran as fast as his legs could carry him, crying out that Satan was in the bells, and that he would have nothing more to do with them.

The house where all this happened was so substantial, its walls so thick, and its foundations so large that the highest winds were unfelt within it. "Every part of this extensive mansion," says Mr. Felkin, "was examined by me with the strictest care, and I could not divine the motive natural power adequate to the effect."

rang on the floor. The inmates of the house were not Spiritualists nor in any sense favorers of spiritual belief.

* *Bealings Bells*, p. 48.

† Page 56.

Mr. Felkin says of his friend, Mr. Ashwell, that "he is the reverse of superstitious; well-educated, philosophical, and indefatigable in research." Mr. Ashwell "tried various experiments with electrometers and other tests," and spoke on the subject with many men of science; but all without result. Mr. Felkin never heard Mr. Ashwell "hazard a guess as to the cause."

Again and again, indeed, attempts were made, as well by the family as by numerous visitors, to discover the occult agency, "both when the bells were connected with lines and when the wires had been cut for months: a circumstance which made no apparent difference in their sounding disposition." But "these events quite baffled the acutest inquirer."

Ringings so persistent caused great excitement, not only in the house, but, being noised abroad, in the neighborhood. The servants were greatly alarmed, and some left their places. The children, too, were frightened, but were pacified by being told that "the bells were ill."

A public footpath passed near Mr. Ashwell's front door; and "many passengers made a circuit rather than pass close to it."

Another observation is mentioned in connection with this case which is intelligible enough to us, but was, no doubt, a puzzle to Major Moor, writing at a time when "sensitives" and "mediums" had not yet been heard of. It was this: The gossips of the vicinity remarked, as to a young lady who resided in Mr. Ashwell's family, that the occurrences were nearly coincident with her stay in the house, and ceased about the time she left it. But (it is added) it does not appear that the slightest voluntary agency on her part was suspected by the family, who had the best means of detecting it.*

The next narrative comes from a Londoner

* This narrative extends from page 45 to page 56 of *Bealings Bells*.

A Lady's Account of Bell Ringings.

Among the numerous letters received by Major Moor was one from a Mrs. Milnes, dated No. 19 St. Paul's Terrace, Islington, May 17, 1834. .

The writer says: "In the early part of February, 1825, returning home from a walk (to our then residence, No. 9 Earl street, Westminster), about half-past four in the afternoon, I was astonished to find the family much disturbed at the ringing of bells in the house, without visible cause. The first bell rung was in the nursery, the pull of which was at the bottom of the house, quite unconnected with any others. This bell rang several times before the rest began; then that of the dining-room; next that of the drawing-room, and so on, through the house: sometimes altogether, as if they were trying to entice each other in uproar; at others one at a time, but always violently.

"By this time I was much alarmed and sent for Mr. Milnes who, thinking to find out what ailed them, had the cases taken down that concealed the wires. Finding this of no use, he next placed a person with a light in each room, while he himself held a candle under the row of bells below; but we could not then ascertain the slightest reason for this strange ringing, which lasted two hours and a half: nor have we ever since been able to discover more of it than we did then."

Here again, as in the preceding example, we have an incident probably intimating through whose unconscious mediumship these phenomena occurred. Mr. Milnes adds: "It had a surprising effect upon one of our servant girls, a mulatto. She, from the first, had been more terrified than any one else in the house; and, at the last peal, fell into strong convulsions; so strong as to require several men to hold her down. These convulsions continued sixteen hours and were succeeded by insensibility, and a stupor that lasted nearly a week: every means being used to restore her, but without effect. It is singular that the moment she was seized with these fits the bells ceased to ring." *

Bells in Greenwich Hospital.

The details in this case come, as in the preceding examples, from a witness present, namely, from Lieutenant Rivers, R. N., a comrade of Nelson, who had lost a leg in the service. They are given in a letter from that officer to Major Moor, dated April 26, 1841.

The bells began to ring September 30, 1834, in Lieutenant Rivers' apartments situated in the hospital; and they continued four days.

The ringing was at intervals of five to ten minutes; four bells sometimes sounding at once. "In the evening," says the Lieutenant, "about eight o'clock, I tied up the clappers: while so doing the bells were much agitated and shook violently. In the morning when I loosed them, they began to ring."

"The clerk of the works, his assistant and Mr. Thame, the bell-hanger, came and had another examination, without discovery of the cause. They requested that the family and servants would leave the apartments to them. We did so, dining at a neighbor's opposite; and while at dinner we heard the bells ring a peal. Mr. Thame and the assistant remained till eleven o'clock; the one watching the cranks, the other the bells below, in perfect astonishment."

He adds: "Several scientific men tried to discover the cause. The front-door bell, detached from the others, did not ring. I secured the door-pull to prevent its being used, leaving the bell to have full play. About three o'clock in the afternoon I went home and found many persons satisfying their curiosity. When explaining to them that I thought it extraordinary that the front-door did not join in the performance,

* *Bealings Bells*, pp. 60–62.

it immediately set up a good ring. * The cause of all this remains still mysterious."

Another observation made in this case is worth noting. "What appeared most extraordinary was the movement of the cranks which, the bell-hanger said, could not cause the bells to ring without being pulled downward: and this they did of themselves, in every room; working like pump-handles."

Lieutenant Rivers adds that similar phenomena occurred in another officer's apartments in the hospital, continuing for a week. †

To multiply examples from Major Moor's book would but involve tedious repetition; seeing that the narratives all resemble each other: the same violent ringings or pealings, sometimes for a few hours only, sometimes for months; the same care to detect trickery: the same anxiety to discover the cause; and, in every case, the same result: inability to trace the phenomena to any human agency.

There is another phase of manifestations, analogous to the above; sometimes, like them, of a mere material character, sometimes indicating intelligence; and which, because it has been popularly ascribed to restless spirits, revisiting their former homes, is commonly termed haunting. ‡

Of this, again, there are two varieties; one characterized by knockings and other unexplained noises; the other, often attaching itself to ancient family residences in England and other countries, marked by the phenomenon of apparition. A large proportion of the old, well-known English names of rank have their family legend, referring to peculiar disturbances or appearances, usually persistent through generations, and generally confined to some ancestral mansion.

Especially when the haunting assumes the form of a "family

* Yet, as this bell was so situated that the wire could readily be reached by the hand, the incident, taken by itself, is not conclusive.

† *Bealings Bells.* pp. 81–83.

‡ For numerous examples, see *Footfalls*, Book iii. chap. 2.

ghost" is the story, outside of the family itself, wont to be pooh-poohed as a nursery tale. No doubt such narratives often involve exaggeration, mystification, illusion. As little doubt, however—if we but sift the genuine from the spurious—that many of them have foundation in truth. We have testimony in proof from eye-witnesses of such standing that we have not the right to impugn their intelligence or their veracity.

Take an example, from a recent publication. Florence Marryat, daughter of the celebrated novelist, gave, less than a year ago, in an American periodical,* three stories of apparitions, which she attests as "strictly true and well autheticated." Of these the last was witnessed by her father, Captain Marryat, and is related as she heard it from his own lips. I condense portions of it, giving the main facts in the author's own language.

In one of the northern counties of England stands a country house, Burnham Green, inherited by the present occupants, Sir Harry and Lady Bell.† Their house had its ghost; but, "like most sensible people, they laughed at the report:" surrounding themselves with every luxury and not heeding the legend.

Their numerous friends, cordially invited, flocked to Burnham Green, thought the place and its host and hostess charming; yet, after a while, made paltry excuses to curtail their visits and were shy of being lured there again. It came out that they had heard of the ghost, some declared they had seen it, and the rest could not be persuaded to remain under a haunted roof.

"Sir Harry and Lady Bell were thoroughly vexed and did all they could to dissipate the superstition. They disinterred the

* *Harper's Weekly*, issue of December 24, 1870; pages 846 and 847.

† These are not the real names. The writer says: "While I preserve all details of these stories, I carefully hide the names of persons and places, lest by negligence in this respect I should wound the feelings of survivors." She says also that the stories which she has related are selected from a number of similar anecdotes which rise in her memory as she writes.

history of the ghost who went by the name of 'The Lady of Burnham Green,' and found that it was supposed to be the spirit of one of their ancestresses who had lived in the time of Elizabeth, and had been suspected of poisoning her husband. Her picture hung in one of the unused bedrooms."

Lady Bell caused this bedroom to be renovated and cheerfully fitted up; and she had the picture of the Lady cleaned and new-framed. In vain! "No one could be found to sleep in that room. The servants gave warning, if it was simply proposed to them, and visitors invariably requested to have their room changed after the second or third night. Guest after guest took flight, to return no more."

In this dilemma Sir Harry applied to Captain Marryat, an old friend of his, for advice. The Captain, utterly disbelieving the story, offered to occupy the haunted chamber: an offer which was eagerly accepted.

With a brace of loaded pistols under his pillow, he was undisturbed for several nights, and was beginning to think of returning home: but he was not to escape so easily.

After a week had passed, one evening when Captain Marryat was about to retire for the night, Mr. Lascelles, one of the guests, tapped at his door and asked him to cross to his room and inspect a newly-invented fowling-piece, the merits of which they had just before been discussing in the smoking room. The Captain, who had already divested himself of coat and waistcoat, picked up a pistol—"in case we meet the ghost" he said jestingly—passed along the corridor to Mr. Lascelles' room, and, after chatting for a few minutes, over the virtues of the new gun, turned to go. Mr. Lascelles returned with him "just to protect you from the ghost," he said laughingly, in imitation of the former allusion. The corridor was long and dark, the lights having been extinguished at midnight; but as they entered it they saw a dim light advancing from the farther end—a light held by a female figure. The children of several of the families were lodged on the floor above, and Lascelles suggested that this was probably some lady going to visit the nurseries. The Captain, remembering that he was in shirt and trousers and unwilling to face a lady in that guise, drew his companion aside. The conclusion shall be told in the narrator's own words.

The Lady of Burnham Green.

"The rooms in the corridor were placed opposite each other, and were approached by double doors, the first of which, on being opened, disclosed a small entry and the second door, which led to the bedchamber itself. Many persons, on entering their rooms, only closed this second door, leaving the other standing open; and thus, when Mr. Lascelles and my father stepped into one of these recesses, they were enabled to shelter themselves behind the half-closed portal.

"There, in the gloom, they crouched together, very much inclined to laugh, I have no doubt, at the situation in which they found themselves, but terribly afraid lest by a betrayal of their illegal presence they should alarm the occupant of the bedroom before which they stood, or the lady who was advancing to the place of their concealment.

"Very slowly she advanced, or so it seemed to them; but they could watch the glimmer of her lamp through the crack of the door; and presently my father, who had pertinaciously kept his eye there, gave the half-smothered exclamation, 'Lascelles! By Jove!—*the Lady!*'

"He had studied the picture of the supposed apparition carefully, was intimate with every detail of her dress and appearance, and felt that he could not be mistaken in the red satin sacque, white stomacher and petticoat, high-standing frill, and cushioned hair of the figure now advancing toward them.

"'A splendid "make-up,"' he said, beneath his breath; 'but whoever has done it shall find I know a trick worth two of his.'

"But Mr. Lascelles said nothing. Imposition or not, he did not like the looks of the Lady of Burnham Green.

"On she came, quiet and dignified, looking neither to the right nor to the left, while my father cocked his pistol, and stood ready for her. He expected she would pass their place of hiding, and intended to pursue and make her speak to him; but instead of that, the dim light gained the door, and then stood still.

"Lascelles shuddered. He was a brave man, but sensitive. Even my father's iron nerves prompted him to be quiescent.

"In another moment the lamp moved on again, came closer, closer; and round the half-closed door, gazing inquisitively at them, as though really curious to see who was there, peered the pale face and cruel eyes of the Lady of Burnham Green.

"Simultaneously my father pushed open the door and confronted her. She stood before him in the corridor just as she stood in the picture in his bedroom, but with a smile of malicious triumph on her face; and goaded on by her expression, hardly knowing what he did, he raised his pistol and fired full at her. The ball penetrated the door of the room opposite to where they stood; and, with the same smile upon her face, she passed through the panels and disappeared."

Of course there was no explanation except what the appearance and disappearance of the apparition afforded. If spirits *cannot* appear, what was it that these two gentleman saw and one of them fired at?

No narrative resembling the above was communicated to Major Moor; but he had sent to him, and has recorded in his book, three cases of hauntings.

They have this in common that the witnesses all testify to violent knockings, sometimes accompanied by other strange, disturbing noises; but they differ in this respect: one case seems to have been of a personal character, that is, dependent on the presence of some individual—*sensitive* or *medium*, as the modern phrase is; the two others, it would appear, were independent of personal attributes—were local and permanent, continuing through several generations: or, as we might express it, were endemical.

Such is the following contained in a letter written by an English clergyman in reply to an inquiry which had been made by Major Moor.

The House of Mystery.

Sydersterne Parsonage, near Fakenham, Norfolk, *May* 11, 1841.

Sir: You have, indeed, sent your letter, received yesterday, to the House of Mystery. In the broad lands of England you cannot, perhaps, find such another. But I regret to add that I can afford you no assistance in the "Bell" line.

"Our noises, in this parsonage, are of a graver character; smart successions of tappings, groanings, cryings, sobbings, disgusting scratchings, heavy trampings and thundering knocks, in all the rooms and passages, have distressed us here for a period of nearly nine years, during my occupancy of this Cure. They still continue, to the annoyance of my family, the alarm of my servants, and the occasional flight of some of them.

"I am enabled clearly to trace their existence in this parsonage *to a period of sixty years past;* and I have little doubt that, were not all the residents anterior to that time now passed away, I could be able to carry my successful scrutiny on and on.

"In 1833 and 1834 we kept almost open house to enable respectable people who were personally known, or had been introduced to us, to satisfy their curiosity. But our kindness was abused, our motives misinterpreted, and even our characters maligned. Therefore we closed our doors.

"In 1834 I had prepared my diary for publication. My work was to be published by Mr. Rodd, the eminent bookseller of Newport street, London; but as the end had not ar rived I postponed my intention from day to day and year to year, in hope of such consummation." * . . .

"(Signed) JOHN STEWART.

"*To Major Edward Moor.*"

Here we have an example how the knowledge and the memory of such occurrences slip away. I cannot learn that the Rev. Mr. Stewart's diary has ever appeared. The dislike of notoriety as a visionary, or worse, has caused the suppression of a hundred similar expositions.

The next case, one of knockings and other unexplained noises, apparently caused by the presence of a medium, I pass by; having, in a previous work, adduced many similar examples.

The last example I shall adduce from Major Moor's book is evidently one of

ENDEMICAL DISTURBANCES.

They occurred, says Major Moor, "in a respectable old manor-house, in the north-eastern part of ——shire, which was, in very early times, the seat of a family of distinction in the county."

For eighteen years past this house had been occupied by a clergyman, known to Major Moor, who vouches for him as "a gentleman of most unimpeachable veracity and of deservedly high estimation." The account is sent to the Major by this clergyman himself, under date June 28, 1841.

It is also confirmed, from personal observation, by a nephew of Major Moor, Captain Frazer, of the Royal Artillery, in a letter dated July 19, 1841.

About the year 1680 the chief part of the ancient mansion was pulled down and the present house erected on the spot. The remaining portion of the old house was allowed to stand,

* Given on pages 93 to 95 of *Bealings Bells.*

and, separated only by a party-wall, it became thenceforth a farm-house, occupied by the tenant of the adjoining lands.

The estate came into the possession of the present owner's father in 1818; and, at that time the house had the reputation of being haunted; many tales of strange sights and sounds circulating through the neighborhood. The popular belief ascribed these to the unblest spirit of a former owner, dead more than a hundred years ago.

In 1823 the clergyman who is the narrator came to reside there. Noises were often heard, but the family referred them, at first, to the occupants of the back portion of the mansion, the farm-house.

In 1826, however, this old part of the building was pulled down, and still the sounds continued, the same which the family had heard for years, and which have been heard, *almost nightly*, ever since.

These disturbances are thus described in the clergyman's letter: "In the dead of night, usually between the hours of twelve and two, when every member of the family is in bed and there is no imaginable cause to be assigned, a succession of heavy and distinct blows are heard, as of some weighty instrument upon a hollow wall or floor. They are sometimes so loud as to awaken one from sleep, sometimes scarcely audible."

On one occasion they burst forth with such violence that the clergyman, accustomed as he was to hear and disregard them, sprang out of bed and rushed to the head of the stairs under a conviction that the outer door of the house had been violently burst in. Another night, when going to bed, the thumpings, as violent, were continued so long that he had time to go to the back-door of the house and sally forth, in quest.

On yet another occasion, the sounds having long continued as if coming from the brew-house or the cellar, which adjoined each other, the clergyman and two of his brothers sat up and went to watch, two in the brew-house and one in the cellar. Then it ceased there, but was heard, by those in the brew-house, as if sounding from underneath the lawn, fifty yards distant.

Great pains were taken, the clergyman says, to discover some cause for these noises, but quite unavailingly. A large old drain running underneath the house might, it was thought, be connected with the sounds. It was thoroughly examined, a man being sent through it, from one end to the other; but the noise proceeded as before.

"After above twenty years," says the reverend writer, "we are entirely in the dark as ever. The length of time it has been heard; the fact of every domestic in the house having been often changed during that time; and the pains that have been taken to investigate the matter, while every member of the house except the watcher was in bed—have *put the possibility of any trick out of the question;* and have convinced all the inmates that it cannot be accounted for on any of the usual suppositions of "horses in the stable kicking," or "dogs rapping with their tails," or "rats jumping in the tanks or drains." Horses stamp and dogs rap and rats gallop; but they do not make such sounds as that one startling and peculiar noise with which our ears are so familiar." *

Another phase of the phenomenon, mentioned both by the clergyman and by Captain Frazer, was of a singular character. When the former was a young man, returning home for the holidays, he was awoke, one night, by a loud noise, as if a cart, heavily laden with iron bars, was passing slowly along the path, under his windows. He threw open the shutters and window; it was bright moonlight, but he could see nothing, though the noise continued for some time. When he mentioned this the next morning, he was laughed at, for his pains. This incident had almost faded from his memory when, eleven years afterward, it was very strangely recalled. An uncle of his, visiting the family, was put to sleep in the same room. The next morning, at breakfast, this gentleman related that he had been awakened in the night by the clatter of a cart, as if laden with iron, drawn over the gravel walk beneath the windows of his

* *Bealings Bells*, p. 115.

room. He, too, having risen, opened the window to investi gate, but nothing could he see. He retired to bed, thinking it might possibly have been a dream and lay awake for half an hour. At the end of that time he heard, a second time, with unmistakable distinctness, the same sounds of a loaded cart, again as if passing before the house.

"Now," thought he, "I'll make sure of it." And, certain that he could discover the cause, he instantly sprang to the window and opened it—again to be thoroughly mystified and disappointed. Nothing whatever to be seen!

This incident is certified to by the gentleman in question in a separate certificate.* Therein he states that it occurred during the month of September, 1840, about three o'clock in the morning.

Three young ladies, residents of the house, certify to the reality of the sounds. †

Captain Frazer, having sat up one night with his host, to witness these nightly visitations, thus describes the noises he heard:

"It was as if some one was striking the walls with a hammer or mallet, muffled in flannel. It began at first slowly, with a

* Work quoted, p. 123. This may appear too whimsical for credence. It would probably so seem to me had I not sufficient proof of analogous occurrences. A young lady, intelligent and truthful, member of one of the best-known families in New York (but I am not authorized to give the name), told me recently that while on a visit of a few weeks to her aunt's country house, an old mansion situated in the eastern portion of that State, she had, more than once, while sitting in the drawing-room in broad daylight, heard the sound of a carriage and horses on the gravel-drive, as if approaching the main entrance. On going to the front window, with one or other of her cousins and seeing nothing there, they would say: "Oh, it's only the ghost-carriage:" and so, return quietly to their seats. It was, they told her, a common sound. A similar phenomenon will be found related as occurring in an English park; the fact certified as well by the lady of the house as by her lady's maid and by her butler, in SPICER'S *Facts and Fantasies*, London, 1853: p. 90; and again pp. 93, 94, 95.

† *Bealings Bells*, pp. 123–125.

distinct interval between each blow; then became more rapid; afterward followed no rule, but was slow or rapid as if caprice dictated. The noise did not appear always to come from the same part of the house. Sometimes it was heard faintly, as at a distance; then startlingly near. It was much louder than I expected: I think if I had been outside of the house I should have heard it.

"I spent three days at ——— House; and heard the same noise two nights out of the three. . . . It seemed as if *moving* about the house, and coming, sometimes, so near that I expected to see the door open and some one come in. . . . The noise generally continued, at intervals, for about two hours. I think there was a slight interval between every five blows. But there was not any regularity in the striking of these five blows, and it was only at first that there was any regularity in the interval between them. . . . This noise usually seemed to me to become loud or faint, not so much from any intensity of the blows, as from a change of distance or position. And the opinion of the other witnesses bears me out in this remark. . . . I tried, in vain, to form even a probable conjecture as to the cause." *

The reverend gentleman who occupied the house (designated by Captain Frazer as L——) related to him the result of inquiries made by the family in regard to the antecedents of the house, as follows:

"It appeared from some of the oldest inhabitants of the parish, that —— House had formerly been occupied by an eccentric and dubious character, Squire ——. This gentleman had, in his younger days, travelled much on the Continent, had visited Italy and brought home an Italian valet—also a character. The two lived in seclusion; and after a time many reports and suspicions got abroad respecting them and the doings at the Hall; though nothing definite was brought against the squire except that he was a great miser. At last

* *Bealings Bells*, p. 129.

he died or disappeared (I forget which L. said), and shortly afterward noises began to be heard in the house. The common legend was that he had been *bricked up* by his Italian servant, between the walls in some room or vault, and so left to perish.*

This disturbance was known familiarly in the family as "the ghost." The inconvenience of its reputation, the clergyman said to Captain Frazer, had been great; at times they had difficulty in getting servants to stay in the house. All allusion to the subject in general conversation was dropped by common consent. †

Here let me beg, of any earnest reader of mine, a brief hearing. I ask him:

Upon what rational plea can you set aside such evidence as this of ultramundane agency? I say nothing of the legend, and aver nothing as to the identity of any restless spirit causing disturbance. But the simple *facts!* under what tenable theory can you explain them away?

The clergyman did not give his name: are you surprised at that? Are you sure you would have given it yourself, under similar circumstances, thirty years ago? Another clergyman, ‡ who gave his name, opened, about that time, the "House of Mystery," in which he lived, to respectable investigators. His reward was to find his motives misinterpreted and his character maligned: that was not encouraging.

Major Moor vouches for the unnamed clergyman as a gentleman highly and deservedly esteemed and of unimpeachable veracity; and the Major's nephew, Captain Frazer, during a visit of three days to the haunted mansion, finds all the statements made to be fully borne out by what he witnessed.

If you reject as monstrous—and I think you will—the supposition that these three gentlemen, all of professional standing

* Work cited, p. 129.

† The story is given in detail in *Bealings Bells*, pp. 112–133.

‡ The Rev. John Stewart. See proceding page 325.

and one of them Fellow of an eminent Society, should have combined to palm on the public, without conceivable motive, a tissue of lies, then what theory of mundane agency, as cause, have you left?

That it was a trick?—that they were imposed upon? That is the explanation usually set up to explain such phenomena; and, on the material hypothesis, there seems to be no other.

—A trick? You will find, if you look closely at the matter, that this supposition is more monstrous than the first. "Almost nightly," were the clergyman's words, and for twenty years. "Two nights out of three" Captain Frazer witnessed them; and their duration was about two hours at a time. Two nights out of three for twenty years is nearly five thousand nights. So some one, prompted by mischief—or by malignity if you will—is to prowl about the house, hours at a time, for the purpose of disturbing the family, four or five days a week throughout half a life time. And so ponderous are the blows he strikes that they may be heard outside the house! And he is to move about the house, thus pounding, without being discovered for twenty years together. A servant to do this? No, they had all been often changed during the time. A member of the family? What! annoy themselves and frighten away their domestics, and raise every kind of unpleasant rumor throughout the neighborhood! An outsider? But why multiply absurdities?

Yet here is but one instalment of the difficulties. Twenty years is the clergyman's time of residence only. Go twenty years farther back; and, according to the united testimony of aged residents, the same disturbances still! And the dwellers of that day had it from their ancestors that the haunting began a hundred years ago. Are there centenarious nightly-disturbers of the peace of private families?

I pray you, earnest reader, to reflect on these things, and to ask yourself whether the theory of intermundane agency is so incredible that one ought to resort to unheard-of vagaries in order to escape it.

At this stage of our book-voyage together, some reader may think that an observation should be taken, so as to determine what progress, up to this point, we have made. He may grant, perhaps, that we have sufficient proof of the occasional occurrence, through the medium of bells and otherwise, of noises which we cannot rationally ascribe except to an extramundane or spiritual cause; and yet he may ask what is gained by such proof? He may suggest further that evidence of a Hereafter—spiritual revealings—should be intrinsically solemn and reverent; not, like tinklings of bells and rappings on walls, of trifling or whimsical character.

I might reply, in a general way, that nothing in all the works of Nature around us, how little soever appreciated by man, is trifling in the sight of Him who

> "Sees, with equal eye, as God of all,
> A hero perish or a sparrow fall:
> Atoms, or systems, into ruin hurled,
> And now a bubble burst, and now a world."

But, aside from this great truth, is there anything very solemn or reverent, to the common mind, in the fall, from its parent tree, of an apple? An infant sees it and claps its tiny hands; an uncultured peasant notes it as evidence that his orchard-crop is ripening; but to a Newton it suggests the law which holds planets to their course and governs half the natural phenomena that occur throughout the world.

As to what may be gained by proving such incidents as this chapter records, Southey, speaking, in his *Life of Wesley*, of analogous disturbances in Samuel Wesley's parsonage,* and of the good end such things may be supposed to answer, wisely suggests that it would be end sufficient if sometimes one of those unhappy sceptics who see nothing beyond the narrow sphere of mortal existence should, "from the well-established truth of one such story, trifling and objectless as it might otherwise appear," be led to believe in immortality.

* *Footfalls*, pp. 224–239.

Let us go a step farther. There is not habitual intercourse between the world which now is and that which is to come: it is only now and then that the denizens of the one perceive those of the other. We seem, probably, something like apparitions to the immortals, as they, when they revisit earth, to us. But no one who ever truly loved and who believes in another life, can doubt that, for a time, the better class of those who have left friends and kindred here still cling to and sympathize with them. We have abundant evidence, even in these pages, that they often earnestly desire to convince us, past possible denial, of their continued existence, of their well-being, and of their undying love. That evidence goes to show that they often diligently seek communion, sometimes from affection, sometimes from other motives, and that they have difficulties in reaching us: difficulties wisely interposed, no doubt; for if spiritual intercourse were as common as worldly communion, who would be willing to labor and to wait in this dim and checkered world of ours?

They seek, from time to time, to visit us. But, coming from their world of spirits, invisible to ordinary sight, inaudible by ordinary speech, how are they to make their presence known? How are they to attract our attention?

In what manner does a traveller, arriving under cloud of night, before a fast-closed mansion, seek to reach the indwellers —seek to announce *his* presence? Is it not BY KNOCKING OR RINGING?

Are we sure that Scripture texts are not read in the next world, and do not find their application there? Are we sure that, to the earth-longings of love immortal, the words of Jesus never suggest themselves: "Seek, and ye shall find; knock, and it shall be opened unto you."

The inhabitants of a mansion at which admission is sought, seeing no one in the darkness, may at first not heed the knock or the ring; and the pilgrim, for the time, may turn away, disappointed. So it has been, probably, in thousands of cases, before any one ventured to interrogate the sounds. Men either doubted whether these came from a living intelligence; or they feared to question that intelligence; or they despaired of any answer, having been taught that though there had been spirit-communion in ages past, it was impossible, or forbidden, to-day.

So it may have been in the cases related in this chapter. In many, possibly in all the cases cited, some spirit may have desired to communicate with earth, as did that of the "Repentant Housekeeper," whose story I have told on a preceding page.* But if so, they were doomed to disappointment. In early days the witnesses of spiritual appeals were as that multitude on the Galilean shore to whom Jesus spoke, from the ship, in parables; and of whom he said, "Hearing they hear not, neither do they understand." The field was not yet white to harvest. The time had not come.

I have a few more words to say, in the next chapter, touching the apparent triviality of some spiritual manifestations.

* See preceding page 297.

CHAPTER IV.

Spiritual Phenomena sometimes result in seeming Trifles.

"Nec deus intersit, nisi dignus vindice nodus
Inciderit." HORACE.

HORACE, in his advice to writers of plays, assumes that it is not fitting a god should intervene, unless the case is worthy of divine interference. If God ever *did* directly intervene—in other words, if there *were* miracles—the poet would be in the right. But what have been interpreted as miracles do frequently manifest themselves, as the rainbow does, with little or no apparent use or benefit, except it be, like the bow in the clouds, to inspire hope into the heart of man: a sufficient proof that they are not, any more than the rainbow, interferences of God.

This is true even of the highest class of spiritual phenomena; for example, of apparitions. Witness the story of

The Earl of Buchan's Butler.

Thomas, Lord Erskine, though he entered the legal profession comparatively late in life, was, at the commencement of the present century, one of its brightest ornaments. Elevated to the peerage for his abilities, and Lord Chancellor under the Grenville administration, his character, both as regards uprightness and sagacity, has every element of trustworthiness. He died in 1823.

In the year 1811 and on the Saturday first succeeding the appointment of the Prince of Wales (afterward George IV.) as Regent, Lord Erskine and the Duchess of Gordon called on Lady Morgan, the well-known literary celebrity.

"The Duchess," says Lady Morgan, "related a very curious

and romantic tale of second-sight in her own family, which amused, if it did not convert me; while the affecting manner in which it was told left no doubt of the sincerity of the narrator." Lady Morgan then continues thus:

"I also," said Lord Erskine, "believe in second-sight, because I have been its subject. When I was a very young man I had been, for some time, absent from Scotland. On the morning of my arrival in Edinburgh, as I was descending the steps of a close on coming out from a bookseller's shop, I met our old family butler. He looked greatly changed, pale, wan, and shadowy as a ghost. 'Eh! old boy,' said I, 'what brings you here?' He replied: 'To meet your honor, and solicit your interference with my Lord,* to recover a sum due to me, which the steward, at the last settlement, did not pay.'

"Struck by his looks and manner, I bade him follow me to the bookseller's, into whose shop I stepped back; but when I turned round to speak to him, he had vanished.

"I remembered that his wife carried on some little trade in the Old Town. I remembered even the house and flat she occupied, which I had often visited in my boyhood. Having made it out, I found the old woman in widow's mourning. Her husband had been dead for some months, and had told her, on his death-bed, that my father's steward had wronged him of some money, and that when Master Tom returned, he would see her righted.

"This I promised to do, and shortly after I fulfilled my promise. The impression was indelible; and I am extremely cautious how I deny the possibility of such supernatural visitings as your Grace has just instanced in your own family." †

The manner in which the talented lady who relates to us this story sees fit to receive and to interpret it, should be, to candid inquirers, a warning lesson.

Lady Morgan, following the dictates of that persistent scep-

* Lord Erskine was a younger son of the tenth Earl of Buchan.

† *The Book of the Boudoir*, by Lady MORGAN, London, 1829: vol i pp. 123–125.

ticism which men and women having a reputation in society are wont to adopt, or to assume; and having settled it, probably, in her own mind, that it behooves all who would be deemed enlightened to think, or at least to speak, of a belief in apparitions as a superstition—is content to set down Lord Erskine's narrative as due—these are the exact words she uses—as due only to the "dog-ears and folds of early impression, which the strongest minds retain." To the narrator, however, she ascribes sincerity. She says, "Either Lord Erskine did, or did not, believe this strange story: if he did, what a strange aberration of intellect!—if he did not, what a stranger aberration from truth! My opinion is that he *did* believe it."

What sort of mode to deal with alleged facts is this? A gentleman distinguished in a profession of which the eminent members are the best judges of evidence in the world—a gentleman whom the hearer believes to be truthful—relates what, on a certain day, and in a certain place, both specified, he saw and heard. What he saw was the appearance of one, in life well-known to him, who had been some months dead. What he heard from the same source was a statement in regard to matters of which previously he had known nothing whatever, which statement, on after inquiry, he learns to be strictly true; a statement, too, which had occupied and interested the mind of the deceased just before his decease. The natural inference from these facts, if they are admitted, is that, under certain circumstances which as yet we may be unable to define, those over whom the death-change has passed, still interested in the concerns of earth, may, for a time at least, retain the power of occasional interference in these concerns; for example in an effort to right an injustice done.

But rather than admit such an inference—rather than accept disinterested evidence coming from a witness acknowledged to be sincere, and known to the world as eminently capable—a lady of the world assumes to explain it away by summarily referring the whole to the "dog-ears and folds of early impression"! What human testimony cannot be set aside on the same vague and idle assumption?

It is time we should learn that the hypothesis of spiritual intervention is entitled to a fair trial; and that, in conducting that trial, we have no right to disregard the ordinary rules of evidence.

Either Lord Erskine, one morning in Edinburgh, issuing from a bookseller's shop, met what wore the appearance of an old family servant who had been some months dead—or else Lord Erskine lied. Either Lord Erskine heard words spoken as if that appearance had spoken them, which words contained a certain allegation touching business which that servant, dying, had left unsettled—or else Lord Erskine lied. Either Lord Erskine ascertained, by immediate personal interrogation of the widow, that her husband, on his death-bed, had made the self same allegation to her which the apparition made to Lord Erskine—or else Lord Erskine lied. Finally either, as the result of this appearance and its speech, a debt found due to the person whose counterpart it was, was actually paid to his widow—or else Lord Erskine lied.

But Lady Morgan expresses her conviction that Lord Erskine did not lie.

In itself that was a trifle. Thousands on thousands of such cases of petty injustice occur and pass away unnoticed and unredressed. To the widow it was, undoubtedly, of serious moment; but I think no sensible man will imagine it a matter to justify the direct interference of God. If so, and if Lord Erskine spoke truth, an apparition is a natural phenomenon.

There are cases, however, where the triviality of result from phenomena that are clearly of a spiritual character is even more apparent than in the preceding example. Here is one:

Prediction in regard to a mere Trifle.

In the spring of the year 1853, a young gentleman, well-known to me, whom I shall designate as Mr. X——, who is not a Spiritualist, and has never given any attention to spiritual phenomena, had a remarkable dream. He was then engaged in a retail store in Second street, Philadelphia; and his dream was to the effect that, the next day at twelve o'clock, he would sell a hundred and fifty dollars' worth of a particular kind of goods, namely, drap d'été (summer cloth), to a customer; the particular person, however, not being designated.

Going down to the store next morning, he related his dream, between eight and nine o'clock, to a young clerk employed in the establishment. "Nonsense!" was the reply; "the thing is impossible. You know very well that we don't sell so large a lot of drap d'été to one customer in ten years."

Mr. X—— assented to the truth of this; and, in addition, he called to mind that, according to his dream, it was he himself who was to sell it. But it so happened that it was not he who attended at the counter where the article was sold, but another: in whose absence, however, should he be accidentally called off, Mr. X—— was wont to take that place.

So deep was the impression produced by the dream that, as the time approached, Mr. X—— became very nervous; and his agitation increased when, some little time before mid-day, the salesman referred to *was* called off, and Mr. X—— had to supply his place.

Almost exactly at twelve a customer entered, approached the counter and asked for drap d'été. Mr. X—— felt himself turn pale, and had hardly presence of mind enough left to reach down the package. It turned out that the article was required for clothing in a public institution; and the amount purchased amounted either to a hundred and forty-eight dollars or a hundred and fifty-two dollars; Mr. X—— does not now recollect which.

The above was related to me* by Mr. X——, now in business for himself in Philadelphia; and I know sufficient of that gentleman's character to warrant me in saying that the particulars

* In Philadelphia, July 13, 1859.

here given may be confidently relied on; and that Mr. X——'s word may be unhesitatingly taken when he assured me, as he did after completing the story, that there had occurred no antecedent circumstance whatever which could give him the slightest reason to imagine that any one would apply for drap d'été; or that there was the most remote chance of his effecting the sale in question.

In this case the minute particulars of time, place, and attendant circumstances—the unforeseen absence of the usual salesman, the specific article demanded, the unusual quantity so closely approaching the amount actually sold—are such that we are compelled to reject the idea of chance coincidence.

In the Erskine case one can comprehend the motive that recalled the departed spirit; the same which operates in the majority of such cases—attraction through the affections: here displayed in humble fashion, indeed—in anxiety that the "auld gude-wife," as a Scotch domestic of those days would be likely to phrase it, should, in her poverty and widowhood, have her own—yet none the less a phase of the longings of true love.

But in the Philadelphia case one can imagine no attracting motive whatever: seeing that the predicted sale, to a particular amount and at a particular hour and day, was of no consequence to any human being, except only as proof that, when Paul enumerated among the gifts common in the early Christian Church, the gift of prophecy, he was speaking of a phenomenon which actually exists and which is not miraculous.

BOOK III.

PHYSICAL MANIFESTATIONS.

CHAPTER I.

THE SPIRIT-RAP.

It is not a difficult thing, if one has time and patience and an honest love of truth, to satisfy one's self, past all possible peradventure, that what is called the spirit-rap is, like the electric spark, a genuine phenomenon, with momentous sequences. And these strange echoes may be as surely referred to agencies from another sphere as the spark from the Leyden jar may be identified with the lightning from the thunder-cloud. They occur, like that mysterious spark, under certain conditions; but they cannot, as it can, be called forth with certainty at any moment; for, being spiritual in their origin, they are not at the beck and call of man.

The conditions under which they present themselves are sometimes of a personal, sometimes of an endemical character. They occur more frequently and more persistently in certain localities than in others, and they are heard much more frequently in the presence of some persons, called mediums or sensitives, than of others. They are usually most loud and powerful where the two conditions, personal and local, are found combined.

I have heard them as delicate, tiny tickings, and as thundering poundings. I have heard them not only throughout our own land, but in foreign countries; as in England, France, Italy. I have heard them in broad daylight and in darkened rooms; usually most violent in the latter. I have heard them in my own house and in a hundred others; out of doors; at sea and on land; in steamer and in sail-boat; in the forest and on the rocks of the sea-shore.

But in no circumstances have I witnessed this wonderful phenomenon under such varied conditions, and with such satisfactory results, as in the presence of two members of that family, in whose dwelling in Western New York, it originally showed itself—namely, the eldest and the youngest daughters of Mrs. Fox.* The faculty of mediumship, or as it might otherwise be expressed, the gift of spiritual sensitiveness, was hereditary in the family. † In Leah Fox (Mrs. Underhill) and in Kate Fox I have found the manifestations of this power, or gift, in connection with the spirit-rap, more marked and more readily to be obtained, than in any other persons with whom I am acquainted, either here or in Europe.

And it is due to these ladies and to Mr. Underhill to say that they have kindly afforded me at all times every facility I could desire to test these and other spiritual phenomena under the strictest precautions against deception: well knowing that I took these for the sake of others rather than to remove doubts of my own. Nor, in all my intercourse with them, have I ever seen the slightest cause for believing that they were actuated by other motive than a frank wish that the truth should be ascertained and acknowledged.

In the autumn of the same year in which I published "Footfalls," I accepted from Mr. Underhill ‡ an invitation to spend a week or two at his house: thus obtaining ample opportunity to investigate this and cognate manifestations.

* For particulars of the disturbances in the Fox family, especially on March 31, 1848, and succeeding days, see *Footfalls*, pp. 287–298.

† *Footfalls*, pp. 284, 285.

‡ Daniel Underhill, President of an old-established Insurance Company in Wall street, New York.

One of my first experiments was to pray Mrs. Underhill to accompany me over the house, in quest of rappings. Beginning in the lower parlors, I asked if we could have raps on the floor, then from the walls, then from the ceiling, then on various articles of furniture. In each case the response was prompt, and the raps loud enough to be heard in the next room. Then I asked for them on the steel grate and on the marble mantle-piece. Thence they sounded quite distinctly, but less sharply—with a duller sound—than before. Then, setting open one of the doors into the passage, placing myself so that I could see both sides of it and putting my hand on one of its panels, I begged Mrs. Underhill to stand a few feet from it and, reaching out one of her arms, to touch it with the tips of her fingers. Within two or three seconds after she had done so, there were raps on the door as loud as if some one had knocked on it sharply with his knuckles; and the wood vibrated quite sensibly under my touch, as if struck by a pretty strong blow.*

When we passed out into the corridor and up the stairway, it was no longer necessary to request rappings. They sounded under our feet as we went; on the steps and then from the hand-rail, as we ascended; from various parts of a sitting-room and of other apartments on the second floor: then, again, on the stairs leading to the third story and in every chamber there. It was evident that, in Mrs. Underhill's presence, they could be had from any spot in the house. I found, too, that if I requested to have any particular number of raps, they were given with unfailing precision.

The sounds were peculiar. I could not imitate them with the hammer, nor with the knuckle on wood, nor in any other way. They seemed more or less muffled.

I have repeated similar experiments several times with Mrs.

* Some time afterward I repeated the same experiment at the house of Mrs. C——, sister of one of the best known among the New York editors, where I accidentally met Mr. and Mrs. Underhill, and where conversation happened to turn on the raps.

Underhill and with her sister Kate, in various places, and always with the same result. With other mediums the responses were more or less prompt; and sometimes they were confined to the table at which we were sitting.

Passing by, for the moment, the hundreds of proofs which teach that an occult intelligence governs the spirit-rap and speaks through it, I keep to the physical aspect of the phenomenon.

On the Water and in the Living Wood.

On the tenth of July, 1861, I joined a few friends in an excursion from the city of New York, by steamboat, to the Highlands of Neversink; Mr. and Mrs. Underhill being of the party.

It occurred to me, while sitting on deck by Mrs. Underhill, to ask if we could have the raps there. Instantly they were distinctly heard first, from the deck; then I heard them, and quite plainly *felt them*, on the wooden stool on which I sat.

In the afternoon our party went out in a sailing-boat, fifteen or twenty feet long. There, again at my suggestion, we had them, sounding from under the floor of the boat. It had a centre-board, or sliding keel, and we had raps from within the long, narrow box that inclosed it. At any part of this box where we called for the raps, we obtained them.

In the evening we ascended a hill, back of the hotel, to the light-house. In returning and passing through a wood on the hill-side, I proposed to try if we could have raps from the ground: and immediately I plainly heard them from beneath the ground on which we trod: it was a dull sound, as of blows struck on the earth. Then I asked Mrs. Underhill to touch one of the trees with the tips of her fingers, and, applying my ear to the tree, I heard the raps from beneath the bark. Other persons of our party verified this, as I had done.

In returning, next morning, on another steamer, we had raps on the hand-rail of the upper promenade deck, and also

15*

from within a small metal boat that was turned upside down, on the deck below. *

The next experiment was one which I imagine that no one but myself ever thought of trying.

Moving a Ledge of Rock on the Sea-shore.

On the twenty-fourth of August, 1861, I accepted an invitation from Mr. S—— U——, of New Rochelle, a sea-side village on the western shore of Long Island Sound, to spend the next day with him, in company with Mr. and Mrs. Underhill.

On the afternoon of August 25, Mr. U—— drove us out in his carriage, through the picturesque country adjoining the village; the party consisting of Mr. U—— and his wife, Mrs. Underhill, and myself.

In the course of the drive, coming near the shore of the Sound, at a point where there were long ledges of rock slanting down into the water, it suddenly suggested itself to me that here was an excellent opportunity for a crucial test. I inquired of Mrs. Underhill if she had ever tried to obtain raps on the sea-shore. No, she said; she never had.

"Do you think we can get them here?" I asked.

"I have never found any place where they could not be had," she replied; "so I dare say we can."

Thereupon there were three raps—the conventional sign of assent—from the bottom of the carriage.

So we drove down to the beach, and got out to test the matter.

The portion of rock whither we repaired was not an isolated block, detached from the rest, but part of a large, flat mass of rock, covering at least half an acre and running back into a bluff bank that rose beyond it: there were also several under-

* Notes of these experiments were taken, immediately on my return to New York.

lying ledges. We were about thirty feet from the sea and, as there was a moderate breeze, the surf broke on the rocks below us.

But yet, standing on the ledge beside Mrs. Underhill, and asking for the raps, I heard them quite distinctly above the noise produced by the surf. This was several times repeated, with the same result.

Then Mrs. Underhill and Mrs. S——U—— sat down, and I, stepping on a lower ledge, laid my ear on the ledge on which the ladies were sitting and repeated my request. In a few seconds the raps were heard by me from within the substance of the rock and immediately beneath my ear.

I then sought to verify the matter by the sense of touch. Placing my hand on the same ledge, a few feet from Mrs. Underhill, and asking for the raps, when these came audibly, I felt, simultaneously with each rap, a slight but *unmistakably distinct vibration or concussion of the rock.* It was sufficiently marked to indicate to me a rap, once or twice, when a louder roll of the surge for a moment drowned the sound.

Without making any remark as to what I had felt, I asked Mr. U—— to put his hand on the ledge. "Why!" he suddenly exclaimed, "the whole rock vibrates!"

During all this time Mrs. Underhill sat, as far as I could judge, in complete repose.

It will be observed that it was at my suggestion this experiment on a plateau of rock was tried. From that day forth I did not consider it necessary further to test the spirit-rap.*

It is true, however, that there were, to dispel my scepticism, other proofs (one obtained more than a year before this), and to which I have not yet alluded. In the above there was appeal to two senses—of hearing and of touch. The previous proofs to which I allude were evidenced by a third sense, usually considered the most trustworthy of all.

* Written out from notes taken the same day.

Seeing the Raps.

It was during an evening session at Mr. Underhill's, February 22, 1860. Besides Mr. and Mrs. Underhill, Kate Fox, and myself, there were present Mr. Underhill's aged father and mother; venerable examples of the plain, primitive Quaker, both of whom took the deepest interest in the proceedings.

By request, through the raps, the gas was extinguished and we joined hands.

Very soon lights were seen floating about the room, apparently phosphorescent. At first they were small, just visible; but gradually they became larger, attaining the size and general outline of hands: but I could not distinguish any fingers. These lights usually showed themselves first behind and between Leah and Kate, near the floor. Then they rose; sometimes remaining near Leah's head, sometimes near her sister's. One of them was nearly as large as a human head. None of these touched me, though one approached within a few inches. Another made circles in the air, just above our heads. After floating about for a brief space, they usually seemed to return either to Leah or to Kate.

While the hands of the circle remained joined, I looked under the table and saw lights, as many as ten or twelve times, on or near the floor, and moving about. Once while I was looking intently at such a light, about as large as a small fist, it rose and fell, as a hammer would, with which one was striking against the floor. At each stroke a loud rap was heard, in connection. It was exactly as if *an invisible hand held an illuminated hammer and pounded with it.*

Then, desiring conscious proof that what I saw was not by human agency, I asked *mentally:* * "Will the spirit strike

* I have found it necessary, in making a mental request, or asking a mental question, to concentrate my thoughts, by an effort, on what I wish to obtain or to inquire.

with that light three times?" which was done forthwith: and then, after an interval, repeated.

When, a second time, the light was seen and I was noticing the corresponding sounds, some one said: "Can you make it softer?" Almost instantly I saw the light diminish and strike the ground, at intervals, with a soft and muffled sound, just distinguishable.*

On another occasion, during the summer of the next year, I obtained still more remarkable manifestations.

Touched by the Agency that Causes the Spirit-rap.

On the evening of the twelfth of June, 1861, having two days before arrived in New York as Commissioner to purchase arms for the State of Indiana, I called, unexpectedly to the family, on Mr. Underhill and proposed that we should have a spiritual session. Mr. and Mrs. Underhill, who knew that I had already begun to collect materials for this volume, readily assented.†

For greater quiet we ascended to a parlor on the second floor; the party consisting of Mr. and Mrs. Underhill, Mr. Gilbert, an aged gentleman and old friend of the family who happened to call in the course of the evening, and myself.

Soon after we sat down there was spelled out, by raps on the floor: "Go in back room." This back room was Mr. and Mrs. Underhill's bed-chamber. Adjourning to it we sat down to a small rectangular table (one of a *nest* of tables), Mr. and Mrs. Underhill on my left and Mr. Gilbert on my right. The small size of the table brought us close together.

* From notes taken next morning, February 23.

† To those who know Mr. Underhill's family, I need hardly say that they never accept any remuneration, directly or indirectly, on such occasions. Nor has Kate Fox, knowing the work I was engaged in, ever been willing to take payment from me for any sitting with her. "You have a better chance to get the highest manifestations 'without money and without price,'" she said to me one day.

To this bedroom there were three doors; one opening into a bath-room, a second on the second-floor corridor, and a third on a passage leading into the parlor, which we had first selected to sit in. In this passage were several closets and presses.

At Mr. Underhill's suggestion, before sitting down I thoroughly examined these closets and presses, as well as the bedroom itself and the parlor to which the passage led. I also locked the outer door of that parlor and the doors of the bedroom leading into the bath-room and the corridor. The door between the parlor and bedroom did not lock; but by the preceding precautions no one from without, even if provided with a key, could enter either of the rooms.

Soon after we sat down there was spelled out, "Darken." We extinguished the gas. Then was spelled, "Sing." While Mrs. Underhill sang, the raps, from different parts of the floor, kept time. After a brief interval they shifted from the floor to a lower bar of the chair on which I sat, still keeping time to the measure. The chair was sensibly jarred—a vibration to each rap.

After sitting about six or seven minutes, there appeared, floating above our heads, a light which seemed phosphorescent. It was rectangular in shape, and about three or four inches long. After a time it rose to the ceiling, floating backward and forward from one part of the room to another. At times it descended till only a foot or two above our heads; moving slowly from side to side, over our circle.

As I was looking intently at it, there was spelled out, by delicate raps on the floor: "I was near you in early life, dear Robert, and am still nearer to you now."

Mrs. Underhill. "Is it Mr. Owen's mother?"

Answer (by the raps). "No."

Myself. "Does the first name begin with C?"

Answer. "Yes."

Mrs. Underhill. "How many letters in the name?"

Answer. "Seven."

Mrs. Underhill. "Caroline, is it?"

Myself. "Caroline has eight letters. Is it another name, under which I have had many communications?"

By the raps. "Yes, yes."

Then the light floated toward me and remained stationary, back of my left shoulder. I turned and looked fixedly at it. It appeared to be about the size of a small human hand, and as if covered with a shining veil. I could not, however, distinguish a defined outline.

Presently it approached my left shoulder, then receded from it, five or six times. Each time I felt a light touch, as of fingers on my shoulder; each touch exactly contemporaneous with the motion of the light.

Then it floated away, rising just above the table at which we were sitting, nearly to the ceiling. I asked that it would pass to the door leading into the corridor and rap there, if it could. Thereupon we saw it pass to the upper part of the door in question, and perceived its motion, and heard the corresponding rap, as it struck it, eight or ten times in succession. It was evident, too, that it was not we alone who heard the sounds; for a lap-dog, outside in the corridor, barked, as if alarmed. Again, as on the former occasion, the idea that suggested itself to me was that of a luminous hammer.

Then the light floated down to Mr. Underhill, increasing in brightness, and seeming to touch him. He said it did touch him, as if with some fine, soft, woven stuff.

I asked that it would touch my hand. It moved slowly across the table, rested for a brief space above my hand, then dropped and touched my wrist. The feeling was like that from the gentle touch of a finger.

Mr. Gilbert (to me). Are you not tempted to grasp it, so as to feel what it is like?

Myself. I have reason to believe that one is not justified in doing so; and for that reason I refrain.

By the raps. Thank you.*

* Two highly-intelligent friends of mine, now deceased, Dr. A. D. Wilson and Professor James Mapes, both formerly of New York, each

Then the light passed to Mrs. Underhill, touching, as she stated, her head and neck.

I asked that it would touch my head also. It floated from her to me, passing behind me; and I felt as if a soft and fine piece of gauze, gathered up loosely in the hand, were pressed gently against the back of my head and neck. Also, now and then, it seemed as if some more solid substance—part of a hand holding the gauze, was the impression I got—touched me lightly. The action was as if by a person standing directly behind me; yet, had I not seen it, a few minutes before, cross the table and touch my wrist before my very eyes? Besides, as the touchings on my head and neck continued for some time, I several times spoke of them during their continuance and all present joined in the conversation. Thus I am *certain* that they were still seated at their places.

Then the light rose again into the air. Looking closely at it, as it floated near the ceiling, I observed that there moved across the luminous body, back and forth, dark lines, or rods, as thick as a finger. I could not, however, make out the form of fingers. Mr. Underhill said he saw fingers distinctly.

While the light was floating above us there proceeded from it occasionally a slight crepitation.

There was not, throughout this sitting, the slightest indication, by footfall, rustle of dress, or otherwise, of any one rising or moving about the room. When the luminous body I have been describing came near either of the assistants I could

on one occasion, firmly grasped what seemed a luminous hand, appearing as above. In both cases the result was the same. What was laid hold of melted entirely away—so each told me—in his grasp. I have had communications to the effect that the spirit thus manifesting its presence suffers when this is done, and that a spirit would have great reluctance in appearing, in bodily form, to any one whom it could not trust to refrain from interference with the phenomena, except by its express permission. In my experiments I have always governed myself accordingly; and I ascribe my success in part to this continence.

dimly perceive, by its light, the outline of the person it approached. *

Sometimes when spirits that have exhibited, while on earth, a violent character, seek to communicate, the raps are of corresponding violence.

Heavy Poundings by a Homicide.

At an evening session, August 17, 1861, at Mr. Underhill's † (by bright gas-light), we heard, after a time, not the usual moderate raps, but instead loud thumpings or poundings, such as might be produced by blows dealt on the floor by a ten-pound mallet. By these we had spelling, on calling the alphabet. Inquiring the pounder's name, there was spelled out, "Jackson."

I inquired if the spirit had formerly lived in Indiana, where I had known a man of that name. Answer, by a single thump, "No!"

Then we asked if it was a person known to any of us. Answer: "The man you do not admire."

Thereupon it occurred to me that it might possibly be Jackson, the innkeeper of Alexandria, at whose hands, some two months before, Colonel Ellsworth, having taken down the Confederate flag from the roof of Jackson's inn, had met his death. As soon as I suggested this, there was an affirmative reply, by three sonorous poundings.

We spoke of Ellsworth and, by the poundings, was spelled out: "His manner tantalized me."

Mrs. Underhill said: "I pitied that man; no doubt he did what he thought right." Reply, by the poundings: "I defended the flag."

* I took notes of the phenomena as they presented themselves; writing with pencil in the dark.

† Mr. and Mrs. Underhill and myself were the only sitters; and I took notes of this sitting at the time.

He then said, further, that he had once visited one of Mrs. Underhill's circles; and that there were in the Southern States many believers in spiritual phenomena.

I found, by experiment, that when these poundings occurred on the second floor, I could hear them, as distinctly as if a mechanic were at work, both on the first floor, below, and on the third floor, above. They caused the floor to vibrate; and it was scarcely possible to resist the conviction that there actually was a ponderous mallet at work under the table; yet, though I looked several times to satisfy myself, there was nothing there.

Occasionally, it would seem, the character of the raps may depend, in a measure, on the medium: yet, of this I have not sufficient evidence to speak with certainty.

Blows of startling Violence.

During an evening sitting, on October 25, 1860, in the front parlor of Mrs. Fox's residence, in the city of New York, there were present Kate Fox, her sister Margaret,* and myself.

From this parlor were two doors, one opening on the passage, the other on a back parlor. Both were locked before we sat down.

Raps spelled out, "Darken." We did so; then, after the appearance of a few luminous phenomena, there came suddenly a tremendous blow on the centre of the table; a blow so violent that we all instinctively started back. By the sound it was such a stroke, apparently dealt by a strong man with a heavy bludgeon, as would have killed any one, and such a blow as would have broken in pieces a table, if not very stout, and would have left severe marks upon any table, no matter how

* The only time, I believe, at which she joined our circle. Having become a Catholic, she had scruples about sitting.

hard the wood. The same blow, apparently with the same force, was repeated five or six times. It was impossible to witness such violent demonstrations without a certain feeling of alarm; for it was evident that there was power sufficient to produce fatal results; yet I myself felt no serious apprehensions of injury, knowing of no case on record in which any one had thus been seriously hurt.

When, after a time, we relit the gas, the most careful examination of the table, above and below, convinced me that there was not a scratch, nor the slightest indentation, either on the polished top or on the under surface.

I consider it a *physical impossibility* that, by any human agency, blows indicating such formidable power should have been dealt without leaving severe marks on the table which received them.

Mrs. Underhill afterward informed me that she had several times, in presence of her sister Margaret, been greatly alarmed by blows as tremendously violent as those I have described. I never heard any so apt to terrify weak nerves, either before or since. But, several years afterward, I witnessed a demonstration of occult power, more quiet indeed—not calculated to alarm—but, to judge by the sound, of nearly equal force.

Knockings that shook the House.

On this occasion, March 10, 1864, Mr. and Mrs. Underhill and myself only were present, in the second-story front parlor of their house; and the session was in the evening, by bright gas-light.

In a few minutes after we sat down there came sounds of a very peculiar character. Each stroke—if that term be applicable—sounded exactly like the dropping on the floor, from the height perhaps of two feet, of a medium-sized cannon ball. At each sound the entire floor of the room shook quite distinctly. We felt the concussion beneath our feet; and it was communicated through the shaken table to our hands.

Occasionally it sounded exactly as if the cannon ball rebounded, dropping a second time with diminished force.

By these cannon-ball-droppings there was a call for the alphabet (five strokes), and sentences were spelled out to the effect that the operating spirit was no stranger to me; that the book for which I was then collecting materials would be acceptable, as supplying a great public need; and that I should "witness some startling things from time to time." Then was added:

"I am little changed. My knowledge of the spirit-world is not so great as you would suppose. I am sure of the things I once hoped for. I have found my beloved friends in Heaven, and I know I live in immortality. A. D. Wilson."

Not much, if one will; not much, as a superficial mind may receive it: only a brief, homely message. Yet, if it be true, how immeasurable its importance! How infinitely consoling the simple truths it unveils!

Dr. Wilson, well-known to me and an intimate friend of the Underhills, was an earnest spiritualist and an excellent man. He was a New York physician of large practice and had died less than a year before.

The sounds by which the sentence (coming, as alleged, from this deceased friend) had been spelled out, letter by letter, seemed to be so unmistakably those of a ponderous metallic globe dropped on the floor, that Mrs. Underhill said: "I can scarcely persuade myself that there is not a heavy ball there." Upon which there was spelled out by these same mysterious poundings:

"Well, then, look!"

We removed the table and carefully examined the floor. Nothing whatever to be seen.

As on a previous occasion, I went downstairs; and, on the floor below, I heard the poundings just as distinctly as when in the upper room. It was the same when I ascended to the floor above. Mrs. Underhill expressed a fear that the sounds would disturb the neighbors in the adjoining houses; and I think they must have heard them.

With a single additional example I close this branch of the subject.

Effects when Local and Personal Influences combine.

A Haunted House.

On the twenty-second of October, 1860, I paid a visit, along with Mr. and Mrs. Underhill, Kate Fox, and another lady and gentleman, to Quaker friends of theirs, Mr. and Mrs. Archer, then living within five-minutes drive of Dobbs' Ferry on the Hudson, in a large, old house, surrounded with magnificent trees, and in which, at one time, Washington had his head-quarters.

This house has been, for a long term of years, reputed haunted. The person still supposed to haunt it is a former owner, Peter Livingston, who, on account of lameness, was wont to use a small, invalid's carriage; and the report was that, at the dead of night, the sound of that carriage was heard in the corridors and especially in one of the rooms of the house.

We sat, late in the evening, first in this room; a lower bed-chamber, having two doors of exit. Both were locked before the session began, the keys being left in the doors. Besides our own party, there were present only Mr. and Mrs. Archer. By direction of the raps we extinguished the lights and joined hands.

Within a single minute afterward, such a clatter began, apparently within three or four feet of where I sat that (as we afterward learned) it was heard and commented on, by some visitors in a room separated from that in which we sat by two doors and a long passage. It seemed as if heavy substances of iron, such as ponderous dumb-bells or weights, were rolled over the floor. Then there were poundings, as if with some heavy mallet; then sharp, loud knockings, as if with the end of a thick staff. Then was heard a sound precisely resembling the rolling of a small carriage on a plank floor. At first this sound seemed close to us, then it gradually lessened, as if the carriage were wheeled to a great distance, until it became, at last, inaudible. Then we asked to have it again, as if coming near; and forthwith it commenced with the faintest sound, approaching by degrees till the carriage might be supposed almost to touch the backs of our chairs. Occasionally there was a pounding on the floor, so heavy as to cause a sensible vibration.

When we relit the lamp and searched the room, the doors were found still locked, with the keys in them; and there was not an article to be found with which such noises could, by human agency, have been made.

Then, at my suggestion, we transferred the experiment to a large parlor opposite, that had been used, I believe, by Livingstone as a dining-room. Again we locked the doors, and, obeying a communication from the raps, put out the lights and joined hands. And again, in less than two minutes, the disturbance began as before. At times the racket was so overpowering that we could scarcely hear one another speak. The sound, as of heavy metallic bodies rolled over the floor was very distinct. Also some weighty substance seemed to be dragged, as by a rope, backward and forward, as much as fifteen or twenty feet each way.

All this time we kept a candle on the table, with a box of matches beside it; and, several times, when the clatter was at its height, we struck a light, to see what the effect would be. In every instance the sounds almost immediately died away, and the search we made in the room for some explanation of the strange disturbance was quite unavailing. The sudden transition, without apparent cause, from such a babel of noises to a dead silence, was an experience such as few have had, in this world. Till the experiment was repeated, again and again, always with the same result, there was temptation to imagine that our senses had been playing us false.

The impression on myself and the other assistants with whom I conversed was such, as to produce a feeling that it was a physical impossibility such sounds could be produced, except by employing ponderous bodies.*

After a time the centre-table at which we sat was pounded on the top, and then from beneath, as with the end of a heavy bludgeon; and that (to judge by the sound) with such violence that we felt serious apprehensions that it would be broken to pieces.

When the noises ceased and we relit the lamps, I and others examined the table minutely; but no indentations or other marks of injury were to be found; nor was there an article to be seen in the room with which any one could have dealt such blows; nor anything there except the usual furniture of a parlor.

Both these rooms were in a portion of the house known to have been built and occupied by Peter Livingstone.

I feel confident that the sounds could have been heard a hundred yards off.†

It is seldom that any one, going in search of phenomena of this class, comes upon anything so remarkable as the foregoing. The conditions are rare: a locality where, for several generations, ultramundane interventions have spontaneously appeared; and the presence, in that locality, of two among the most powerful mediums for physical manifestations to be found in this, or it may be in any other country.

I cannot reasonably doubt that, before the present decade closes, the intelligent portion of society will be as thoroughly convinced of the reality of the spirit-rap as enlightened inquirers already are that the size and form of the brain have

* See, for similar phenomena, *Footfalls*, p. 231.

† See *Footfalls*, pp. 217, 252, 275, for similar noises. I wrote out this account on the morning after the incidents occurred. We sat till midnight.

something to do with intellect, and that magnetic influences may produce hypnotic effects.

When we have admitted the intermundane character of these wonderful echoes, the first short step in experimental Spiritualism is taken: but only the first. The rap may be ultramundane; and yet that single fact is insufficient to prove that deceased friends can communicate with us. We must seek, in the rap-spelled communications themselves, for conclusive evidence that intercourse from beyond the bourne is not forbidden to man.

If I have devoted more space than seems needed to the proof, in a physical sense, of so simple a phenomenon, I beg to remind the reader of the persistent nonsense that has been spoken and written about spirit-rapping, and of the prejudices that have grown up under the ridicule which has thus attached itself to the term.

CHAPTER II.

MOVING PONDERABLE BODIES BY OCCULT AGENCY.

"When they came to Jordan, they cut down wood. But as one was felling a beam, the axehead fell into the water: and he cried, and said [to Elisha], 'Alas, master!' for it was borrowed. And the man of God said, 'Where fell it?' And he shewed him the place. And he cut down a stick, and cast it in thither; and the iron did swim."—2 KINGS vi. 4–6.

THE raising from the ground of weighty substances, or the moving of these from place to place, is one of the most common, and most easily verified, of physical manifestations. I have elsewhere given many examples of it.* Here I shall add but two or three out of the numerous cases that have come under my eye during spiritual sessions.

A most satisfactory test of the power, by occult agency, to raise ponderable substances was suggested to me by that practical thinker, the late Robert Chambers, the well-known author and publisher, during his visit to the United States, in the autumn of 1860; and we carried it out on the thirteenth of October of that year.

On the evening of that day we had a sitting in Mr. Underhill's dining-room; there being present Mr. and Mrs. Underhill, Kate Fox, Mr. Chambers, and myself. In this room, we found an extension dinner-table of solid mahogany, capable of seating fourteen persons. This we contracted to the form of a centre-table, and, having procured a large steelyard, we found that it weighed, in that form, a hundred and twenty-one pounds.

We suspended this table by the steelyard, in exact equipoise

* *Footfalls*, pp. 110, 112, 113 (note), 252, 256, 276, 279 to 282, and many others.

and about eight inches from the floor. Then we sat down by it; and while our experiment proceeded, Mrs. Underhill sat with the points of both feet touching one of mine; and Kate in the same relation to Mr. Chambers. This was done, at their suggestion, so as to afford us proof that they had no physical agency in the matter. Their hands were over the table, near the top, but not touching it. There was bright gas-light. Thus we were enabled to obtain

A Crucial Test.

The table remaining suspended, with the constant weight at the figure 121, we asked that it might be made lighter. In a few seconds the long arm ascended. We moved the weight to the figure 100: it still ascended; then to 80; then to 60. Even at this last figure the smaller arm of the steelyard was somewhat depressed, showing that the table, for the moment, weighed less than sixty pounds. It had *lost more than half its weight*, namely, upward of sixty-one pounds: in other words, there was a power equal to sixty-one pounds sustaining it. Then we asked that it might be made heavier; and it was so: first as the figures indicated, to 130, and finally to a hundred and forty four pounds.

The change of weight continued, in each instance, from three to eight seconds, as we ascertained by our watches: and during the whole time the ladies maintained the same position of feet and hands; Mr. Underhill not approaching the table.

We had given Mr. Underhill no notice of our intention to ask for this experiment. The steelyard was borrowed for the occasion from a wholesale grocer, living in the neighborhood.

How much a Jewish axehead commonly weighed, in the days of Elisha, I know not; it could be but a few pounds. Our miracle (*dunamis*) exceeded that of the prophet, as far as regards the weight of the body that was made lighter: but the Hebrew seer was at a greater distance from the object raised than were our mediums.

On the evening just preceding that on which we tried the above experiment I had a sitting at Mr. Underhill's, with very satisfactory result.

A HEAVY DINNER-TABLE SUSPENDED IN THE AIR, WITHOUT CONTACT.

Our session was on the evening of October 12, 1860, lasting from half-past nine till eleven.* It was held in the same room and at the same table mentioned above, and by gas-light. Present Mr. and Mrs. Underhill, Kate Fox, Mr. Harrison Gray Dyar, of New York, and myself.

We had very loud rappings, from various parts of the room and on the chairs.

Then, while our hands were on the table, it began to move, sometimes with a rotary motion, sometimes rising up on one side, until finally it rose from the ground all but one leg.

Then we sought to induce it to rise entirely from the floor. After (what seemed) strenous efforts, almost successful, to rise, we aided it by each putting a single finger under it; and, with this slight assistance, it rose into the air and remained suspended during six or seven seconds.

After a time we asked whether, if we removed our fingers from the table-top, while it was in the air, it could still remain suspended; and the reply (by rapping) being in the affirmative, after aiding it to rise as before, we withdrew our fingers entirely, raising them above it. The table then remained, nearly level, suspended without any human support whatever, during the space of five or six seconds; and then gradually settled down, without jar or sudden dropping, to the floor.

Then, anxious to advance a step farther, we asked if the table could not be raised from the floor without any aid or contact whatever. The reply being in the affirmative, we stood up and placed all our hands over it, at the distance of three or four inches

* We found, by repeated trials, that our experiments succeeded better when we sat at a late hour, after the servants had gone to bed, when the house and the streets were quiet.

from the table-top: when it rose of itself, following our hands as we gradually raised them, till it hung in the air about the same distance from the ground as before. There it remained six or seven seconds, preserving its horizontal, and almost as steady as when it rested on the ground: then it slowly descended, still preserving the horizontal, until the feet reached the carpet. As before, there was no jar or sudden dropping.*

The same experiment was repeated, next evening in the presence of Robert Chambers, after we had completed our tests with the steelyard; and with exactly the same results. At first, as before, we raised it on our fingers; then, withdrawing them, it remained in the air six or seven seconds. On the second trial it rose entirely without contact, remaining suspended for about the same space.

It should here be remarked that we were in the habit, during these experiments, of moving the table to different parts of the room, and of looking under it from time to time.

Upon the whole I consider this moving of physical objects —*les apports*, as the French spiritualists term it—to be as conclusively established, in its ultramundane aspect, as the spirit-rap. A hundred-and-twenty-pound dinner-table is no trifle to lift. The conditions exclude the possibility of concealed machinery. And by what conceivable bodily effort, undetectable by watchful bystanders, can two or three assistants heave from the ground, maintain in the air, and then drop slowly to the floor, so ponderous a weight, with their hands, the while, in full view, under broad gas-light? No one, in his senses and believing in his senses, can witness what I have witnessed, and yet remain a sceptic in this matter.

It makes not, under the circumstances, at all against it, that Mrs. Underhill and her sister were, at one period of their lives,

* The accounts of this and of the sitting of October 13, were both written out the next morning. To prevent repetition I here remark that notes of all the sittings recorded in this volume were taken either at the time, or next day or (in a few cases) a day or two later.

in the habit of sitting as professional mediums. But even if it did, still, in the seclusion of a private family and in the absence of every one who had ever, till a few months before, been suspected of possessing spiritual powers—I have witnessed occurrences even more marvellous than those above related. Thus it happened:

A Table, flung into the Air, rotates.

In the spring of 1870 I was visiting a friend of mine, Mr. B——, whose charming residence on Staten Island commands a magnificent view over the Bay of New York, with the distant city on one hand and the Narrows, opening into the ocean, on the other.

The family had no knowledge of Spiritualism and scant faith in any of its phenomena, until a month or two before my visit, when one of the sons, a young man whom I shall call Charles, suddenly found himself, as much to his surprise as to that of his relatives, gifted with rare spiritual powers.

Passing by, for the present, the most remarkable of these, I here reproduce, from minutes taken next day and submitted for correction to the assistants, part of a record of what I witnessed at two sessions, both held on the second of April, 1870.

The first was in the afternoon. We had been sitting previously in a back parlor; but, on my proposal, we adjourned to the drawing-room, on the front of the house, where, until then, we had not sat. There were present, besides Charles and myself, two other relatives of the family, Mr. N—— and Mr. L——. The room was darkened with heavy curtains which we drew close; but sufficient light came through to enable us to see the outlines of objects.

We sat at a heavy deal-table, made, expressly for the purpose, very thick and strong; the legs more than two inches square; size two feet seven inches by one foot eight inches, and weighing twenty-five pounds.

At first there was a trembling motion, then a tilting from

side to side, gradually becoming more powerful, and at last so violent that it was snatched from our hands. Then, at our request, the table was made so heavy that I found it scarcely possible, with all my strength, to move it even half an inch from the floor; the apparent weight some two hundred pounds. Then, again at our request, it was made so light that we could lift one end of it with a single finger; its weight seeming ten or twelve pounds only. Then it was laid down on its side; and, no one touching it, I was unable to raise it. Then it was tilted on two legs and all my strength was insufficient to press it down.

Finally, after being jerked with such sudden violence that we all drew back, fearing injury, and merely reached our fingers on the edge of its top, it was projected into the air so high that when we rose from our chairs we could barely place our fingers on it; and there it swung about, during six or seven seconds. Besides touching it, we could see its motion by the dim light.

We sat again in the evening at ten o'clock, in the same room, darkened: only three at the table, N——, Charles, and myself.

Then—probably intensified by the darkness—commenced a demonstration exhibiting more physical force than I had ever before witnessed. I do not believe that the strongest man living could, without a handle fixed to pull by, have jerked the table with anything like the violence with which it was now, as it seemed, *driven* from side to side. We all felt it to be a power, a single stroke from which would have killed any one of us on the spot. Then the table was, as it were, flung upward into the air, again so high that, when we stood up, we could just touch it, and shaken backward and forward for some time ere it was set down. Again it was raised, even more violently than before and swung backward and forward, as far as by the touch we could judge, in an arc of seven or eight feet, some five or six times. A third time it was hurled into the air, sometimes out of our reach, but we felt it *turn over and over, like a revolving wheel, eight or ten times.* As nearly as we could judge without reference to our watches, it was some *twelve or fourteen seconds* in the air, before it descended. Sometimes we were able to touch it, sometimes not.

Then I asked whether, some time hereafter, we might not be able to obtain objective apparitions. The answer was given by raising the table three times from the floor, each time slamming it down with such force that the noise was distinctly heard in the story above; and, when a candle was lighted, we found the top (of inch board), split entirely across and wrenched from the legs; the long nails with which it had been secured to prevent such accident being drawn out.

While these manifestations were in progress, it occurred to me, as very strong evidence of the humane care of the operating spirits, that when such tremendous power was exerted close to us, no serious accident happened; and that I had never heard of any such, on similar occasion. Once N——'s wrist was sprained, and twice his knees and also Charles' were struck; but though this pained them a good deal at the moment, the pain ceased in a few minutes—through spiritual influence, as they supposed. I certainly would not trust myself within reach of any similar demonstrations, if produced by human hands.

I expressed my thankfulness and gratification at having been allowed to witness such manifestations. The answer, by impression through Charles' hand, was: "Don't you know that we are as much gratified to give them as you to receive them?"

Then they informed us that "their powers were a little shattered for to-night;" and, at midnight, we adjourned.

I beg that my readers will here note the attendant circumstances. The locality, selected by myself, the drawing-room in a gentleman's house; no professional medium present; the assistants, the son of the gentleman in whose house we were sitting and two other gentlemen, his near relations; the motion out of our reach, so that it was a sheer impossibility that those present could have produced it. The shattered table remained, a tangible proof of the strong force employed.

How thoroughly out of place here the suspicion of deception or imposture! How utterly untenable the hypothesis of illusion or hallucination! Thomas, touching, would have believed. It would need a disciple of Berkeley to witness these phenomena, and still remain a sceptic in the reality of such manifestations.

CHAPTER III.

Direct Spirit-writing.

"In the same hour came forth fingers of a man's hand, and wrote over against the candlestick upon the plaster of the wall of the king's palace: and the king saw the part of the hand that wrote."—Daniel v. 5.

A traveller, bound on some mission of passing importance, may now and then, amid the prosaic details he encounters from stage to stage in his journey, lose sight of the great object to which it leads: yet, in proportion as he nears the goal, his thoughts concentre, more and more, on the ultimate issue. So, in the journey through these pages, may it happen to the reader. He is travelling in search of proofs, cognizable by human senses, of another life. As he proceeds, the phenomena, homely at first, gain in living interest; for they go to establish, ever more and more conclusively, the existence of an agency not occult, not ultramundane only, but intelligent, but spiritual: the agency of beings like ourselves, though they be no longer denizens of earth.

There was published, in Paris in the year 1857, by a young Russian nobleman, a book* which did not attract the attention it deserved. Its author, whose acquaintance I had the pleasure of making in Paris, a year after his book appeared, had devoted his life, almost exclusively, to the study of what he deemed the Supernatural and of the relations between the

* *La Réalité des Esprits et le Phénomène merveilleux de leur Ecriture directe demontrées*, par le Baron de Guldenstubbé, Paris, 1857.

For particulars regarding the Guldenstubbé family and their residence, see *Footfalls*, pp. 262 and 260 (note).

visible world and that which we have yet to see: the object of his studies being to obtain positive demonstration of the soul's immortal existence. His work is that of a classical scholar, and contains curious and interesting researches touching the Spiritualism of antiquity. It exhibits much sagacity, with the drawback that the Baron believes not only in influences from the next world but also in direct, miraculous intervention of God; as the arresting, by Him, of the earth and the moon in their orbits for the space of a day.* The book is chiefly occupied, as its title implies, with proofs of direct writing by spirits.

In the ten months from August, 1856, when M. de Guldenstubbé first observed this phenomenon, to June, 1857, he obtained more than *five hundred* specimens; out of which he gives us lithographs of sixty-seven. These experiences were witnessed by more than fifty persons; of whom he names thirteen.† These witnesses furnished the paper that was used in the experiments.

These experiments were chiefly made, and were most successful, in old cathedrals or in other ancient places of worship, or in historic residences. But before I reached Paris, in the autumn of 1858, there had been an order issued, either by the government or the clergy, prohibiting such experiments in churches and other public buildings. It was vigorously enforced, as we found when Baron de Guldenstubbé, his sister and myself visited the Abbey of St. Denis, on the twenty-ninth of September, and placed a paper in one of the side chapels. I had determined, however, to persevere in my endeavor to

* Work cited, p. 44. Joshua x. 12–14.

† Namely: Prince Léonide Galitzin, of Moscow; Prince S. Metschersky; General the Baron de Bréwern; Baron de Voigts-Rhetz; Baron Borys d'Uexkull; Count de Szapary; Count d'Ourches; Colonel Toutcheff; Colonel de Kollmann; Doctor Georgii, now of London; Doctor Bowron, of Paris; M. Kiorboë, a distinguished artist, and M. Ravené, proprietor of a gallery of paintings at Berlin.—*Introduction*, p. xv.

verify this important phenomenon then and there; but was prevented from doing so by a telegram from England, informing me of the dangerous illness of my father, Robert Owen, with whom I remained till his death, six weeks afterward.*

Baron de Guldenstubbé impressed me very favorably as a man of great earnestness and perfect good faith; one who pursued his researches in a most reverent spirit. Enthusiastic he certainly was; and, for that reason, a less dispassionate observer; yet the multitude of his experiences, obtained under every variety of circumstance, and the number of respectable witnesses who permit their names to appear in attestation of the results, leave little room to doubt their genuine character.

I reproduce three out of the many specimens this author has given.

The first, in French, was obtained August 16, 1856, in the presence of Count d'Ourches, under these circumstances: The Count, a believer in spiritual phenomena but leaning a little toward demonology, prepared two papers; the one was blank, on the other he had written the well-known text, "Hereby know ye the spirit of God: Every spirit that confesseth that Jesus Christ is come in the flesh is of God." † These he placed side by side, on a table, within view. After ten minutes he found written on the blank leaf: "*I confess Jesus in the flesh.*"—*A. v. G.* The signature was known to the Baron as the initials of a deceased friend. ‡ Here is a fac-simile of the writing:

* I find the following entry in my journal, written just after his death: "During the last seven or eight years of my father's life he was an unwavering believer in Spiritualism; though I doubt whether the same amount of evidence which convinced him would have satisfied me. To the last he spoke of a future life with the same undoubting certainty as of any earthly event, which he expected soon to occur. His death was the most peaceful I ever witnessed.

† 1 John iv. 2.

‡ *Réalité des Esprits*, p. 69.

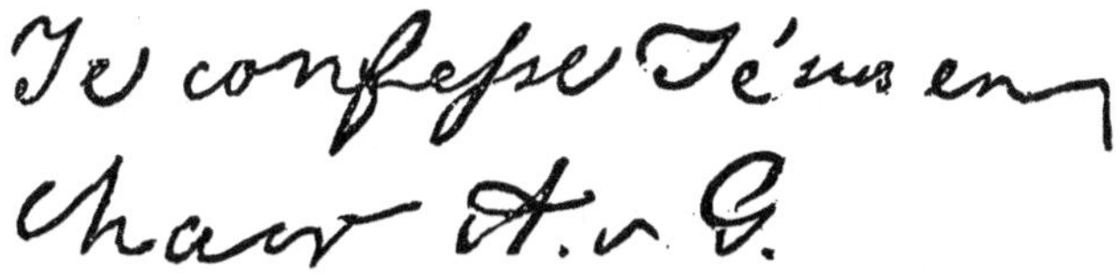

The second, in English, was written, also in the presence of the Count d'Ourches, September 9, 1856, near the column of Francis II. Under two crosses, as the fac-simile here given shows, is written: "*I am the life;*" and the initials, in monogram, are those of the unfortunate Mary Queen of Scots. *

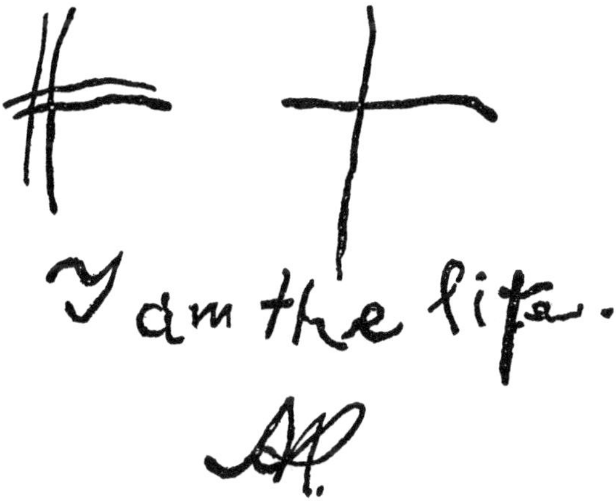

A reminder may here be acceptable to the reader: "In the north transept of the church of St. Denis, on one side of the door, is a composite column of white marble, erected by Mary Stuart to the memory of her husband, Francis II., who died in 1561." †

* Count d'Ourches personally confirmed to me the authenticity of these two examples of spirit-writing, when I called on him October 1, 1858. See *Footfalls*, p. 112 (note).

† *Paris and its Environs*, London, 1859; p. 323.

The last of the examples selected, is also of historic interest It is the conventual signature of the frail and repentant Duchesse de la Vallière (*Sœur Louise de la Miséricorde*), obtained by M. de Guldenstubbé, December 29, 1856, in the church of Val-de-Grâce: Colonel de Kollmann being the witness present. Here it is:

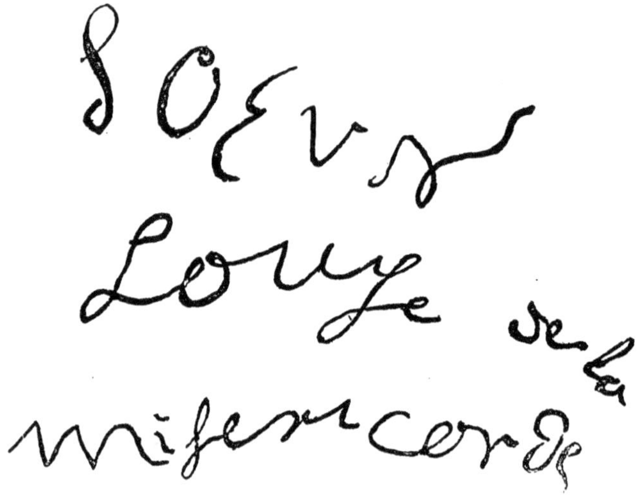

If the reader ask why especially in the chapel of Val-de-Grâce, and why not the family name, the following may be worth recalling:

" A small confessional, with a strong iron railing, opens into the church of Val-de Grâce, from one of the passages behind. This was the confessional used by Mademoiselle de la Vallière, previous to her taking the vows; and from the windows of the above-named passage is seen the building she occupied at that period." *

" The Carmelite convent in which the celebrated Mademoi

* *Paris and its Environs*, p. 174.

selle de la Vallière took the veil in 1675, as 'Sœur Louise de la Miséricorde,' is in the Rue d'Enfer, behind St. Jacques du Haut Pas." *

How strangely suggestive all this! We search pyramid and cathedral and vaulted catacomb in quest of hieroglyphics and sepulchral sculpture and lapidary epitaphs: little thinking what relics of the departed, far more precious than all inanimate memorials, might there be obtained, attesting the continued existence and memory of those, more alive than we, whom we are wont to think of only as dead celebrities of the Past.

Though I was prevented, by business, from revisiting Paris after my father's death and there verifying M. de Guldenstubbé's observations, I have since been fortunate enough to procure, in the United States, personal evidence, in corroboration. And, in some cases, this evidence was obtained under conditions so strict that I think any candid and intelligent person, witnessing what I have witnessed, must cease to doubt that which millions will deem incredible; namely, that, here upon earth, we may receive communications dictated by other intelligence, written by other hand, than the hand and the intelligence of any among earth's inhabitants. It avails nothing to allege that this is impossible, if it shall appear that it is true.

I obtained examples of spirit-writing, during a sitting with Kate Fox, as early as February 27, 1860, and on one or two subsequent occasions. But it was during sittings in darkened rooms; and, on carefully looking over the minutes of these experiments, I perceive that, until the autumn of the next year, I had not taken *all* the precautions which might, in the dark, be taken; nor ever seen any hand while it was writing. Therefore, and because space is precious, I pass over these

* Same work, p. 191.

earlier examples and shall here record the results of two sittings only, both of remarkable character. One carefully authenticated case is better than twenty, loosely attested.

During the first of these sittings, held August 8, 1861, in Mrs. Fox's house, in West Forty-sixth street, New York, I had an experience, such, probably, as few persons have ever enjoyed.

Seeing a Luminous Hand write.

I sought an evening session with Kate Fox, hoping to obtain an apparition, which had been promised me by rappings—but without setting the time—a few evenings before. Kate proposed that we should sit in the lower parlor; but, as I knew there was a front parlor on the second floor and wished to avoid interruption, I proposed that we should hold our sitting there, to which she readily assented.

It was a small room, very simply furnished with sofa, chairs, and a table, about two and a half feet by three. There were no closets nor presses in this room, and but two doors; one on the upper passage, the other communicating with an adjoining apartment. The table stood in the corner; we moved it to the centre of the room.

I locked both the doors, and took the additional precaution of *sealing* them. This I did with short strips of paper connecting the door with the door-sill, attaching the upper part of each strip with wax to the door, and the lower part to the sill; and impressing both seals with my engraved signet-ring. I told Kate (and I know she believed me) that I did so for the sake of those who might hereafter read the record of this sitting, not to quiet any suspicions of my own.

As we were sitting down, she said laughingly: "You ought to look under the sofa, Mr. Owen." I thanked her for the reminder, rolled the sofa out from the wall, turned it over and examined it thoroughly, before replacing it. Then I minutely inspected every part of the room.

On the table was an ink-stand and a steel-pen with wooden

holder; nothing else. In case of a dark sitting, I had brought with me a small package consisting of eight or ten slips of writing paper, cut from foolscap sheets and about four inches in depth: to be used, successively, in case I took notes in the dark. They were blank, except that I had put, on one corner of each, a private mark.

This package, with a pencil, I laid on the table on my left hand, within reach; Kate sitting beside me, on my right: and then we awaited instructions.

These soon came, by raps; spelling out "Darken." We effectually excluded light through two front windows on the street by outside shutters and window-blinds: after which we extinguished the gas and resumed our seats.

Then came the additional instructions. "Rest your hands on the table. Join hands." I caused Kate to rest her hands on the table, clasped; and I placed my right hand on both hers, reserving my left hand free.

Then was spelled: "Put your hand under table." I placed my left hand under the table, on my knee.

Then, by the raps: "Cover left hand and hold writing-paper and pencil in it." I had to remove my right hand from Kate's for a few moments, so as to cover my left hand with a handkerchief and place the package of paper-slips and the pencil in it. But I had hardly done this, when it spelled: "Join hands." I replaced my right hand on both of Kate's.

Then I felt the paper drawn from my hand, but the pencil was left. About a minute afterward the pencil was taken and my hand was tapped with it, quite distinctly, three times; after which it was carried off. There was no sound of its falling, but, after an interval, there was a distinct rustling of paper on the floor. This alternated with the sound of a pen scratching on paper; and continued, at intervals, for a considerable space, during all which I kept my hand on both of Kate's.

After a time, attracted by a rustling on her right, Kate looked on the floor and, with an expression of surprise, called my attention to what she saw. Rising and leaning over the table, but without releasing Kate's hands, I could distinctly perceive, on the carpet close by Kate on the right, a luminous appearance, of rectangular form, very clearly defined, and, as nearly as I could judge, the size and shape of one of the slips of writing-paper that had been taken from my hand.

Then, by the raps: "Do not look at present." Whereupon I reseated myself.

Kate then asked: "Cannot the spirit raise that illuminated paper and put it on the table before us?"

Reply, by the raps: "First let me show you the pencil."

After a little, Kate informed me that she again saw the luminous appearance, even more brightly than at first. Then, leaning over as before and watching it for some time, I distinctly saw, above what seemed to be the illuminated slip of paper, the outline, in shadow, of a small hand holding a pencil and moving slowing over the paper. I could not, however, distinguish the writing.

Kate exclaimed, in tones of delight: "Do you see the hand? —and the pencil, too?—do you see it write?" So that she evidently saw it, just as I did.

All this time both Kate's hands were on the table; for I bethought me of this, even at that moment.

Then was spelled: "Don't look!" and I withdrew a second time.

Shortly after, by the raps: "Put hand under table." I placed my left hand on my knee. Thereupon a slip of paper was gently placed in my hand, and the tips of my fingers were distinctly touched, as by human fingers. I brought up the paper, laid it on the table before me, and replaced my hand. Very soon something was put into it, which, by the touch, I knew to be a wooden pen-holder; and that also I laid on the table.

Some time after this, as we could distinguish nothing but the rustling of paper, Kate again asked if an illuminated sheet could not be laid on the table. In a short time what seemed such was raised a little above the height of the table; then it gradually sank down again, out of sight.

After a considerable interval my left hand was again touched by a piece of paper; but it dropped before I could lay hold of it.

Another interval, and we had, by the raps: "Light the gas." Only then I released Kate's hands. We lit the gas, and I immediately examined the doors of the room. The seals were intact and the strips, connecting them with the door-sills, unbroken. I looked round. Everything remained just as when we sat down, except that several slips of paper lay scattered on the floor, with my pencil among them; while, on the table, there lay the single slip and the pen-holder which had been handed to me.

My first thought was that I was now qualified to swear in a court of justice, had that been necessary, that, during this sitting, Kate and I had been the sole occupants of the room.

Then I examined the papers. One, that on the table, was written in ink; three others, on the floor, in pencil; two or three short lines on each. The first had these words:

"The night is not favorable for appearing. I will soon overcome difficulties. You shall see me, believe me."

This, though legible, was evidently written by a very bad pen, which *sputtered*, as we sometimes say. Witness these two words:

for appearing.

Here is a fac-simile of the writing on one of the other slips; originally in pencil, but the pencilling carefully inked over by me, to preserve it:

Be not discouraged

You shall see me face to face

On one of the other slips an allusion was made to the state of the atmosphere, as being unfavorable to an appearance in bodily form. It was, in effect, a murky evening, with drizzling rain. Such weather, as I had repeatedly verified, is unfavorable for spiritual experiments.

On a fourth slip there was expressed, in strong terms, the earnest anxiety of the writer to gratify my desire for an appearance, so that I could recognize her features. *

My feelings, when I had carefully examined these results, are such as seldom fall to the lot of a human being.

I took up the slip that was written in ink. Some one—an intelligent agent, a denizen of this world or of another—had taken up the pen-holder that lay on the table before me, had dipped the pen in ink, and had written these lines. The same pen-holder had been handed to me under the table by some invisible agency. And all this had happened during the time when the only two hands in the room except my own were under my grasp. Then, too, I had *heard* the writing.

I took up the steel-pen and tried to write out a few notes of our session. It was nearly worn out. It sputtered in my hands, as it had done in those of the mysterious writer. After managing to write a few lines, I relinquished the wretched pen, as she had done, for my pencil.

It was a gold one. I remarked to Kate what a heavy pencil and what a miserable pen they had been obliged to employ: thus writing under great disadvantage.

Were these spiritual autographs? What else? Had I not *seen* one of them written? Had I not seen one of these slips, illuminated, rise higher than the table and then sink back again? Had I not felt Kate's two hands under mine at the very time when that hand wrote and that paper rose and fell? Did Kate

* Of the writer whose name was appended to each of these communications I shall speak at large, in the chapter entitled: *A beautifu. Spirit manifesting herself;* Book iv., chap. 3.

write eight or ten lines with both her hands clasped? Did I write them with my left hand, without knowing it? Or had Kate brought the slips, ready written? I picked them up and examined them critically, one by one. My private mark, on one corner of each—namely, letters of the German alphabet, written in German character—still there!

What way out?

Are the senses of seeing and hearing and touch, in sane, healthy persons, unworthy to be trusted? Then of what value the evidence taken in a criminal court, or the experiments made in a chemist's laboratory?

For me, common sense bars that way out. I believe in a phase of life, succeeding the death change. I see nothing unlikely—not to say incredible—in the theory that God may vouchsafe to man sensible proof of his immortality. And thus I accept the evidence of my senses when they inform me that human beings who have passed to another phase of existence, are sometimes permitted to communicate, from beyond the earthly bourn, with those they have left behind.

For others, to whom spiritual intercourse seems an absurdity —for those, more especially, to whom the hypothesis of another life wears the aspect of a baseless dream—let them select their own path out of the difficulty. I think that, on any path they may take, they will have to accept theories infinitely less tenable than those they decide to reject.

I remark, in regard to the foregoing experiment, that the room in which it was made had been selected by me, after another had been proposed; also that I expected one sort of manifestation and obtained something quite different. The chief objection, by sceptics, will be that the phenomena occurred in a darkened room. But, in a preceding example,* it has been shown that when a light was sprung upon spiritual phenomena of the most startling character, the only effect was

* See chapter 1 of Book iii., preceding page.

to arrest them, without disclosing any earthly cause for their occurrence.

Yet I need not rest the case here. It is but rarely, and under very favorable circumstances, that direct writing can be had in the light. Yet it can sometimes be obtained. Witness the following:

Direct Spirit-writing by Gas-light.

At Mr. Underhill's on the evening of September 3, 1861, in the back room, second story. Present, Dr. A. D. Wilson,* Mr. and Mrs. Underhill and myself. Precautions in regard to locking doors and the like, as usual. The room was brightly lighted during the entire sitting. We sat at a rectangular table, thirty-three inches by fifty-three, which had no drawers, and from which we had removed the table-cover. The gas lit the space under the table, so that we could inspect it at any time. I sat on one side of this table, Mrs. Underhill opposite; Mr. Underhill at one end, on my right, and Dr. Wilson at the other, on my left.

A few minutes after sitting down we heard, very distinctly, the jingling of an iron chain; then a sudden stroke, as if by the point of a blunt dagger, against the under side of the table-top, so strongly dealt as to shake the whole table; then a metallic sound, as if two steel rods clashed against each other; then a jingling, as of steel rings.

During all this time, as I particularly remarked, the hands of all the assistants were on the table; and below the table there was nothing to be seen, for I looked more than once.

Then, after witnessing several other phenomena, we asked if we could have direct writing in the light; to which the reply, by raps, was in the affirmative. Then came a call for paper

* He then lived in East Eleventh street, near Broadway.

He was one of the most careful and dispassionate observers I have met with, and he expressed, in the strongest terms, his conviction of the conclusive character of this experiment.

and pencil. I myself selected a sheet from the middle of a quire of foolscap and examined it carefully under the gas burner: it was entirely blank. I held it and a pencil on my knee, looking under the table as I did so. Scarcely had I looked up again, to be assured that all the hands of the assistants still remained on the table, when paper and pencil were taken from me, a finger distinctly touching mine, as they were taken. Then, for *six or eight seconds* we heard a sound resembling that of a pencil writing rapidly on paper; and instantly, before I had time to look again, the raps spelled: "Take it up." I did so, and found written upon it in pencil, in a bold, rude, dashing hand, the words: "*The North will conquer.*" *

The *t* in the word "North" is crossed with a sweeping dash. "Conquer" is written *conq*, then the *u* is written partly over the *q*, and the final *e* and *r* run into one another; but the word is still legible enough. †

I do not think that more than twenty, or at most twenty-five, seconds elapsed from the moment I put the paper under the table till I took it up, written as above.

The foregoing may suffice as far as regards my own experience in this matter. I add here, in corroboration, the results obtained by two friends of mine, both of whom have been, in some respects, even more highly favored than myself, in the character of evidence establishing the reality of spirit-writing.

The first, obtained by artificial light, is an experience of Mr. Livermore, of New York, ‡ during an evening session with Kate Fox, on the eighteenth of August, 1861. No one present but the medium and himself. The doors locked and bolted;

* The reader need hardly be reminded that this was but six weeks after the disaster at Bull Run; at one of the darkest epochs of the Great Contest, when the hopes of the South were triumphant, and the North was just beginning to take heart, after so severe a check.

† See fac-simile on plate I.

‡ Of this gentleman and of the wonderful experiences he has had, touching the phenomenon of objective apparitions, I have spoken at length, in Book v., chap. 4; which see.

Plate I.

the windows secured, and the room thoroughly examined. Then the lights extinguished. Soon an oblong light, about the size and shape of a melon, rested on the table, remaining there a considerable time without moving. Mr. Livermore asked if it could rise; whereupon it rose into the air, flashing out occasionally, and floating about the room. Finally it returned to the table, shining with increased brilliancy.

Mr. Livermore had brought with him two very large, blank cards, each with a private mark, hoping to obtain direct writing. These he now deposited, together with a small silver pencil, on the table, near the light; at the same time securing both hands of the medium. They were soon taken from the table and carried near to the floor, remaining apparently suspended, however, some three or four inches above it; and the light was so moved that its rays fell directly upon the cards. What Mr. Livermore then saw I give in his own words, copied from the record he himself made at the time: "The cards became the centre of a circle of light a foot in diameter. Carefully watching this phenomenon, I saw a hand holding my pencil over one of the cards. This hand moved quietly across from left to right, and when one line was finished, moved back to commence another. At first it was a perfectly-shaped hand, afterward it became a dark substance, smaller than the human hand, but still apparently holding the pencil, the writing going on at intervals, and the whole remaining *visible for nearly an hour.* I can conceive of no better evidence for the reality of spirit writing. Every possible precaution against deception had been taken. I held both hands of the medium throughout the whole time. I have the cards still, minutely written on both sides; the sentiments there expressed being of the most elevated character, pure and spiritual."

The italics are from the original record. Nearly an hour, it will be observed, the phenomenon continued to present itself, and under a bright light, even if one not kindled by human hand.

But the next example occurred in broad daylight. It was

communicated to me by one of the witnesses present, at first verbally, afterward by letter, in which the writer kindly permits me to use her name; a name which cannot fail to secure, for the narration, respect and consideration. The lady is the sister of Bancroft, the historian, and the widow of John Davis, formerly governor of Massachusetts, and best remembered in New England under the honorable cognomen of "honest John Davis."

The circumstance occurred in Mrs. Davis's dining-room, in Worcester, Massachusetts, the medium present being Mr. Willis, formerly a student of Harvard University, and who had some difficulty there, because of an honest avowal of his belief in the epiphanies of Spiritualism. "The room," says Mrs. Davis in her note to me, "had four windows facing east, south, and west; the hour between eleven and twelve, A.M.; so that we had the full light of a summer sun, shut off only by green blinds. We were at a table on which I had put paper and pencil; but we had no intention of forming what is called a circle: we merely sat chatting of some wonderful manifestations we had witnessed the evening before."

While they were so engaged, the pencil rose from the table, stood at the usual angle, as if guided by a human hand, though no hand was to be seen, and began to write. The amazement of Mrs. Davis may be imagined. The motion of the pencil was regular, and a slight scratching sound was heard as it moved. Both Mrs. Davis and Mr. Willis saw and heard this alike. It wrote a brief message of affection from a dear friend of Mrs. Davis, deceased some years before: then dropped on the paper.

The evidence in this case, it will be observed, is more direct than in any of the Baron de Guldenstubbé's experiments, for he did not see the writing done; and it has a certain advantage also over Mr. Livermore's experience and mine; seeing that, in both our cases, the light was artificial and might by some be thought less trustworthy than that of day.

What element of authenticity is lacking here? The writing was done in the seeing and hearing of both, and in broad daylight. For anything which we have not witnessed ourselves, how seldom is more conclusive testimony to be had!

Commending these various experiments to the critical consideration of the candid reader, I proceed to give a few examples of another species of writing, often discredited, yet of which I have had proofs which I find it impossible to set aside.

Writing on the human Hand and Arm.

Mr. Robert Chambers and myself were well acquainted with a gentleman whom I shall call Mr. M——, not being at liberty to give the real name. He is one among the most successful and best-known business men of our country; *not* a resident of New York.

At the time I am speaking of, however, he was on a visit to that city; and Mr. Chambers and I induced him to call, with us, on Mr. Charles Foster, one of the very best test-mediums I have ever known. Mr. M—— was an unbeliever in spiritual phenomena, unacquainted with Mr. Foster, and agreed to visit him merely to gratify Mr. Chambers' wish and mine. We had given Mr. Foster no notice of our visit, and we did not make Mr. M——'s name known to him. We sat down to an ordinary-sized centre-table.

After several remarkable phenomena which I omit, Mr. M—— expressed a wish for a test of the reality of spirit-intercourse. Thereupon Mr. Foster requested him to think of a deceased friend. Then he bade him write, on one slip of paper, a number of *first* names, among them the first name of his friend; and on another slip a number of *family* names, among them the family name of his friend, keeping the writing concealed. Mr. M—— wrote out both lists accordingly; the total number of names being twenty-three. At Mr. Foster's request he then tore the names asunder, made up each separately in a pellet, and held these pellets under the table, in his hand, the palm open. Then Mr. Foster, who was sitting opposite to

Mr. M——, taking up my hat, held it by one hand under the table and said: "Spirit, will you please select the two pellets that have your name and surname, from that gentleman's hand, and put them in Mr. Owen's hat?" In somewhat less than a minute raps came, Mr. Foster brought up the hat, and handed two pellets which it contained, unopened, to Mr. M——. The latter undid them, without showing them to any of us, and merely said: "These *are* the two pellets with the name and family name of my friend." Then Mr. Foster, suddenly exclaiming "Here is his first name on my arm," bared his arm and we saw, written on it, in large pink letters, the word *Seth*. After a minute or two, as we were looking at the writing, it faded out and Mr. Foster asked: "Will the spirit write the first letter of his family name on the back of my hand?" holding it out. We watched it closely: there was not the least mark on it. But, after the lapse of a short time, pink marks began to appear, gradually growing more plain, until we all saw, and read, very distinctly written near the centre of the back of Mr. Foster's hand, the capital letter C. Then, for the first time, Mr. M—— showed us the two pellets. The name *was* Seth C. . . .

Mr. Foster then inquired of Mr. M—— if the spirit was a relative of his; and when the other replied that it was, Mr. Foster sat, as if musing, for a minute or two; then turned to Mr. M——, saying: "Ah! it comes to me: it is your father-in-law."

Mr. C. . . . *was* Mr. M——'s father-in-law, as that gentleman then informed us; but until that moment the fact was not known either to Mr. Chambers or to myself.*

Several times during this session, Mr. M—— became extremely pale, and more than once, exclaimed in surprise. I did not share his astonishment, because, the day before (Sep-

* A record of this sitting was made the same day and submitted by me, for revision, to Mr. Chambers. That gentleman was then on a visit to this country. He took the deepest interest in such experiments.

tember 28), I had had a private sitting with Foster where I obtained a test, perhaps even more satisfactory than the above, seeing that it came at my own request. I begged Foster to bare his arm and I said: "Can I have the first letter of the family name of a deceased friend of whom I am thinking written there?" I kept my eyes steadily fixed on the arm, after a time the letter W gradually appeared, then, as gradually, faded out again. That *was* the first letter of the name I had thought of.

Two marvels here: an answer to a mental question, and writing upon a human arm before my eyes and in reply to an unexpected request.

More than a year after this I had, also through Mr. Foster, a similar test; and as my notes, taken on that occasion, describe the appearance minutely, I add the record here, at the risk of being tedious.

The Letter F.

A circle of eight persons had assembled, on the evening of November 15, 1861, to meet Mr. Foster. It was at a well-known house in East Twentieth Street, New York; the dwelling of two ladies, both earnest spiritualists, and of whom our country has recently had to mourn the loss, Alice and Phœbe Cary.

We had all been invited, early in the evening, to write one or more names, of deceased friends, each on a small bit of paper; and to fold these up tightly and mix them in the centre of the table. There were some twenty or thirty of these in all, thus promiscuously placed together.

From time to time Mr. Foster addressed some message to one or other of our party, and, at the close of each message, he selected one of the bits of paper and handed it unopened, to the party addressed. In every case, the message was appropriate and the name was given to the right person. In six different cases the name of the deceased friend was written in full, on Mr. Foster's arm; but the arm was not bared beforehand, the writing appeared when he drew up his sleeve.

When some eight or ten bits of paper only remained, I said to Mr. Foster: "There is a name written by me among those you have not yet distributed. Do you think you could get the first letter of it on your arm?" I was going to add "and I should like you to bare your arm before it is written;" but I refrained, lest Mr. Foster should think that I entertained a suspicion which I did not feel.

Mr. Foster sat silent for a minute or two, both his hands resting passively on the table the while; then he said to me: "You are to look at my wrist:" at the same time extending toward me the left arm with the hand downward and the fist clenched, and drawing back his sleeve so as to expose three or four inches of the wrist. I observed that it was free from all mark whatever, and it remained so for about one minute. Then a faint pink stroke appeared across it which, in about half a minute more, having gradually increased in distinctness, became a capital F. It extended almost across the wrist, near to where it joins the hand; and the top of the F, being the last part of the letter which appeared, crossed into the back of the hand. The letter was formed by pink lines, about as thick as the down-strokes in ordinary text-hand. It was the written, not the printed character; and though it appeared as if written hastily or carelessly, it was unmistakably distinct and legible; so that each member of the circle, when it was shown to them, recognized it at once. It remained visible for as much as two or three minutes; and then faded away, while we were looking at it, as gradually as it had appeared.

Then Mr. Foster picked up the folded bits of paper, one after another, until, as he touched one, there were three raps. That one he handed to me. It was the one on which I had written "Florence," the name of a daughter of mine whom I had lost in infancy twenty years before. Neither Mr. Foster, nor any member of the circle, knew that I had lost a daughter, nor had the name ever before come up, at any of our sittings.

Was the particular character of this test—stricter than that of any other obtained during the evening—determined by my unexpressed wish to see the writing while in progress of formation? The important thing is correctly to state the circumstances: let the reader make his own deductions.

The feeling, as the letter grew under my gaze, was somewhat like that I remember to have had when, for the first time, under the microscope, I witnessed the sudden coming into existence of crystals.

Space fails me to say more touching spirit-writing. In the way of recital can stronger proof be given? Let those who still doubt test the matter for themselves.

CHAPTER IV.

Spirit Touches.

In the spring of the year 1858, then living at Naples, I had four sittings with a medium of world-wide reputation, D. Dunglas Home; and, in his presence, I witnessed a phenomenon which no earnest thinker can witness, believing it to be genuine, without a strange feeling that he is brought near to the next world.

The sessions were held in the parlor of my apartments on the Chiaja: present, besides my family and the medium, the Count d'Aquila; or, as we usually called him, Prince Luigi, third brother of the King of Naples. They were evening sessions, the room brightly lighted. We sat at a centre-table, three feet nine inches in diameter, and weighing, with the lamp on it, ninety pounds.

During the second session we were all touched in succession; and this was preceded by a singular manifestation. At various points all round the table, the table-cover was pushed outward, and occasionally upward at the edge of the table-top, as by a hand underneath. Mrs. Owen touched it and felt, through the cover, what seemed a small human hand, doubled up. By the raps it was alleged that it was our eldest daughter, Florence, whom we had lost when an infant.

Then Mrs. Owen's dress was pulled, on the side farthest from Mr. Home, as often as eight or ten times, and so strongly that Mrs. Owen says had she been asleep it would certainly have awoke her: and, as it was, it instantly arrested her attention. She *saw* her dress move each time it was pulled.

Then she asked that it might touch me three times, which it did instantly and quite distinctly. Then I put on my knee my hand covered with a handkerchief; and, at my request, it immediately touched my hand through the handkerchief. Then Mrs. Owen invited it to touch her hand which she placed, uncovered, under the table: upon which it went under one of the flounces of her dress and touched her hand through the silk; but did not touch the bare hand.

When under the table-cover, on the opposite side from Mr. Home, it tapped three times on Mrs. Owen's hand, when she put it against the cover.

All this time Mr. Home's hands were resting on the table, and immediately afterward the table rose entirely off the floor some four or five inches, and was carried about twelve inches toward where Mrs. Owen sat, and there set down again, Mrs. Owen rising: then raised a second time and carried about six inches farther in the same direction. This time the foot of the table rested on Mrs. Owen's dress; and had to be removed to extricate it.

Then a large arm-chair, weighing forty-eight pounds,* and standing empty behind Mr. Home and about four feet and a half from the arm-chair in which he sat, moved suddenly and very swiftly close up to the table between Mr. Home and Mrs. Owen. Sitting opposite to them, I happened to be looking in that direction at the moment, and saw it start. It moved so suddenly and rapidly, that I expected it to strike with force against the table; but it stopped, as suddenly, within an inch or two of it, and without touching. It is proper to add that it moved on castors. Mr. Home was, at that moment, sitting close to the table, with both hands lightly resting on it, and without the slightest appearance of any muscular effort.

During the next session, April 6, the touchings were repeated; † and still more distinctly, during the fourth sitting on

* I had chair, table, and lamp carefully weighed, and recorded the weight at the time.

† A phenomenon which occurred during this sitting is well worth recording. All our chairs were shaken, as distinctly as during an earthquake (we had a violent one, while I was in Naples, so that I speak here by the book); yet the table, the while, remained motionless. Then the

April 12; on which occasion the hand touched was uncovered. Here is the record: "Mrs. Owen's hand, placed on her knee under the cloth, was touched with what exactly resembled to the touch a human hand, soft, moderately warm, and a little moist. The touch was on Mrs. Owen's bare hand, and was so distinct that there was no possibility of mistaking it. Mrs. Owen, having on two previous evenings, witnessed the same phenomenon, was quite self-possessed, and she stated to me that she felt not the least nervousness or alarm.

"Prince Luigi was touched repeatedly, as we were; and he afterward expressed to me, in unqualified terms, his conviction that the phenomena we had witnessed were genuine. He had had previous experience of his own." *

Soon after my return to this country, I had evidence confirmatory of this phenomenon.

chairs ceased their motion, and the table was similarly agitated. Then, at request, the table ceased its motion, and that of the chairs recommenced: and so on, several times; the change from one motion to the other being instantaneous. I know of no human force that could imitate this. Machinery there was none, for it was in my own parlor. It was evidently not the floor that was shaken, or that communicated motion either to the table or to the chairs.

* Here is an item from his experience. He told me that he had sometimes (as on after reflection he concluded) pressed with unwarrantable eagerness for answers; and, for a time, could obtain nothing more. On one occasion, when he had done so, there was spelled out:

"Tu es un vrai diable."

The Prince.—"De qui parle tu?"

Answer.—"De toi, Louis de Bourbon."

French and English magnetizers agree in stating that somnambules are wont to use the familiar *tu* and *du* to persons whom in their waking state they always addressed either by their titles, or else using the formal *vous* and *Sie*. See, for an example: *Histoire de la Guérison d'une jeune personne par le Magnétisme Animal, produit par la Nature elle-même;* by the Baron F. C. De Strombeck: Paris, 1814, p. 38. "Jamais elle ne m'avoit tutoyé."

In the spiritual realm, it would seem, there is no respect of persons. —Acts x. 34.

SPIRIT TOUCHES BY BRIGHT GAS-LIGHT.

Session of October 23, 1860, held in Mr. Underhill's dining-room in the evening. Present Mr. and Mrs. Underhill, Mr. Underhill's father (Levi Underhill), Mrs. Price, of Westchester, and myself. The usual precautions taken as to locking doors, etc.

Spelled out by raps: "Look under the table." I did so very carefully. There was nothing there.

After a time it spelled, "Put handkerchief over hand." I asked: "Is that addressed to me?" Answer: "Yes." I put my right hand, covered, under the table.

Then it spelled: "Lower." I reached down as far as I could.

At this moment all the assistants had their hands on the table, in sight. Mrs. Underhill suggested that we join hands. We did so: but as my right hand was underneath the table, Mrs. Price, who sat next to me, put her hand on my shoulder, to complete the circle.

In about two minutes after this circle was thus formed, my hand was laid hold of and pressed by the fingers of a hand, as I felt with unmistakable certainty. Then I asked to have the hand touch me once more. It did so; and, this time, it was the points of the fingers that were pressed against my hand: I felt the sharp impression of the nails.

During the whole of this time the gas was burning brightly, and the circle of joined hands was maintained. During the whole time the hands of all the assistants were in sight, and I kept my eye on them.

But for the reminder, by the raps, to look under the table before the experiment began, I might have omitted to take that precaution.

A year later I had a similar experience, also in the light.

It was during the session, already noticed, of September 3, 1861, when we obtained direct writing by gas-light:* Dr. Wil-

* See preceding page.

son and Mr. and Mrs. Underhill present. The table thirty-three inches by fifty-three; without drawers and without cloth.

It spelled: "Put down hand." I put my left hand under the table. My foot was touched and pressed and my leg was seized, as by the firm grasp of a strong hand; but my hand was not touched.

Then it spelled: "Handkerchief." As soon as I covered my hand it was touched, through the handkerchief, as by a large finger. Then my fingers were grasped firmly, as by two fingers and a thumb. Then, a third time, my fingers were grasped and tightly pressed as by three fingers and a thumb of a large, strong hand.

After a time, fingers apparently of a small hand were laid lightly on mine: and, by delicate raps, it was spelled: "Violet touched you last."

This experiment was made in a room brightly lighted, without any cloth on the table, and with the hands of every assistant full in sight.

Some readers, theorizing only, may persuade themselves that a single sense, especially that of touch, is insufficient evidence in cases like the foregoing. Let them try the experiment. Let them try, when they find themselves laid hold of by a hand, vigorous and real, as firmly as by the grasp of a cordial friend, to set it down as pure imagination and to rest in the conviction that they have not been touched at all. Short of Pyrrhonism, they will not succeed. When through the avenues of actual sensation the testimony comes, they will find out, like Thomas, what are the difficulties of disbelief.

I here close my record of manifestations such as are usually called physical; and proceed to consider a problem of more intricate character: that which relates to the identity of spirits.

BOOK IV.

IDENTITY OF SPIRITS.

CHAPTER I.

STUBBORN FACTS CONNECTING TWO WORLDS.

THERE is, among spiritual phenomena, a class, rare of occurrence, but wonderfully convincing when we happen to meet with them. They teach us much more than the reality of the next world, invaluable as that truth is. They give us glimpses into that world, dissipating many preconceptions touching its character and its inhabitants. We learn from them that our friends there may still have earthly thoughts and human sympathies; may still recognize us; may still, for a time, interest themselves even in petty matters that are going on in the world they have left. They do not, by any means, prove to us that every ultramundane communication is truly from the spirit who professes to communicate; but they do prove to us that this is sometimes the case. In doing so, they establish, in certain cases, the identity of spirits. They give us satisfactory assurance that we shall recognize our friends in the next world, and that we shall find them there much less changed than theological fancy has painted them.

Such proofs are the more valuable when they come unsought, unexpected, at first unwelcome even, in the privacy of home: where we cannot imagine motive for deception, nor chance of juggler's trick.

I am fortunate in being able to supply such an example,

furnished to me by friends in whose good faith and sagacity I have entire confidence. I know the names of all the parties whose initials are given in the following narrative; and if I am not permitted to publish them, in attestation, the world has itself to blame. When society, learning to treat uprightness with respect, ceases to denounce or to ridicule such testimony as this, it will be time enough for it to condemn the reticence of those who meanwhile seek refuge from such injustice under an anonymous veil.

A Spirit arranging its Worldly Affairs.

Mrs. G——, wife of a captain in the regular army of the United States, was residing, in 1861, with her husband, in Cincinnati. Before that time she had, of course, often heard of spiritual experiences; but she had avoided all opportunities to examine the reality of these, regarding the seeking of communications from another world as a sin. She had never seen what is called a professional medium.

It so happened that, in the above year, a lady of her acquaintance, Mrs. C——, found that she (Mrs. C——) had the power to obtain messages through raps; and she occasionally sat, for that purpose, with some of her intimate friends; among the rest with Mrs. G——. These sessions, continued throughout the years 1861 and 1862, in a measure overcame Mrs. G——'s aversion to the subject; awakening her curiosity but failing to bring full conviction.

In December, 1863, her husband's brother Jack (as he was familiarly called) died suddenly.

In March, 1864, Mrs. G——, then in the quiet of a country residence near Cincinnati, received a visit from a friend, Miss L—— B——. This lady having power as a medium, Mrs. G—— and she had a session one day. After a time the young lady rose and Mrs. G—— remained alone. Thereupon, with her hands only lightly touching the table, it moved across the room in which they had been sitting, and, through an open door, into a room adjoining. Later it moved, in Mrs. G——'s presence, without being touched. Thus, for the first time, she discovered her own powers.

Sitting down again with Miss B——, the name of "Jack" was unexpectedly spelled out.

Mrs. G—— asked: "Is there anything you wish done, brother?" The reply was: "Give Anna that ring."

Now Anna M—— was the name of a young lady to whom, at the time of his death, the brother was betrothed. Mrs. G—— did not know what ring was meant; but she remembered that when Jack died, a plain gold ring—the only one he wore—had been presented by her husband to a friend of his brother, a Mr. G——. She asked if that was the ring, and the reply was in the affirmative.

Some days after this Jack's mother paid them a visit. Nothing was said to her of the above communication. In the course of conversation she told them that Miss Anna M—— had called upon her; had stated that she had given to Jack, at the time of their betrothal, a plain gold ring and that she wished to have it again. Mrs. G—— and her husband were both ignorant that the ring in question had been Miss B——'s; Jack never having said anything to them on the subject. Measures were taken to have the ring returned.

Some time after Jack's death three persons, G——, C——, and S——, came, severally, to Captain G—— and told him that his brother had died indebted to them. He requested them to send in their bills in writing.

Meanwhile, not knowing anything of debts due by his brother to these individuals, Captain G—— asked Mrs. G—— to have a session, hoping to obtain some information on the subject. The following was the result.

Jack announced himself and his brother asked:

"Did you owe G—— at the time of your death?"

"Yes."

"How much?"

"Thirty-five dollars."

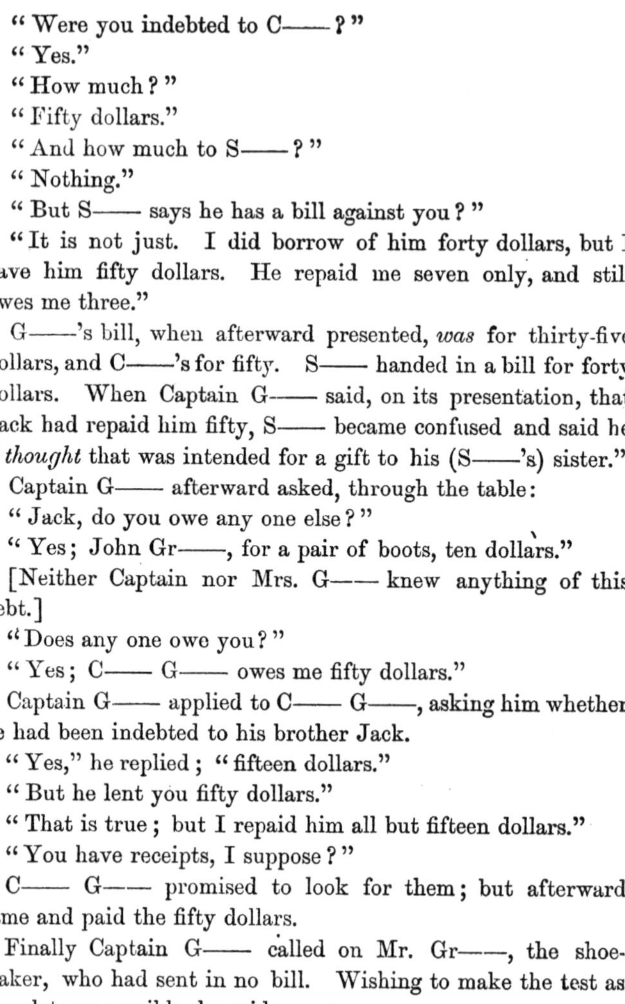

"Were you indebted to C——?"

"Yes."

"How much?"

"Fifty dollars."

"And how much to S——?"

"Nothing."

"But S—— says he has a bill against you?"

"It is not just. I did borrow of him forty dollars, but I gave him fifty dollars. He repaid me seven only, and still owes me three."

G——'s bill, when afterward presented, *was* for thirty-five dollars, and C——'s for fifty. S—— handed in a bill for forty dollars. When Captain G—— said, on its presentation, that Jack had repaid him fifty, S—— became confused and said he "*thought* that was intended for a gift to his (S——'s) sister."

Captain G—— afterward asked, through the table:

"Jack, do you owe any one else?"

"Yes; John Gr——, for a pair of boots, ten dollars."

[Neither Captain nor Mrs. G—— knew anything of this debt.]

"Does any one owe you?"

"Yes; C—— G—— owes me fifty dollars."

Captain G—— applied to C—— G——, asking him whether he had been indebted to his brother Jack.

"Yes," he replied; "fifteen dollars."

"But he lent you fifty dollars."

"That is true; but I repaid him all but fifteen dollars."

"You have receipts, I suppose?"

C—— G—— promised to look for them; but afterward came and paid the fifty dollars.

Finally Captain G—— called on Mr. Gr——, the shoemaker, who had sent in no bill. Wishing to make the test as complete as possible, he said:

"Do I owe you a bill, Mr. Gr——?"

"No, sir. You have paid for all you had of me."

Captain G—— turned, as if to go; whereupon the shoemaker added:

"But your brother, Mr. Jack, who died, left a small account unpaid."

"What was it for?"

"A pair of boots."

"And your charge for them?"

"Ten dollars."

"Mr. Gr——, there is your money."

The above was related to me by Captain and Mrs. G—— during a visit I made to them at their country residence.*

If, by way of explaining the above, we imagine deliberate, circumstantial, motiveless falsehood in persons of the utmost respectability, of earnest character and of unblemished reputation, we violate all received rules of evidence. But if we admit the facts, what theory which does not admit the reality of spirit-communication will suffice to account for the above? How explain away these stubborn links, actual, tangible, thus unmistakably connecting the spiritual with the material—the world yet concealed from our view with that other world, not more real, which lies around us, palpable to the senses?

And what stronger proof could well be given of the identity of a communicating spirit than these simple, homely details supply?

If it seem to us inconsistent with the dignity of our spiritual abode that its denizens should still be able to recall trifling details of their earthly life, let us bear in mind that, without such memory of past incidents, the natural consequences of well-doing and evil-doing would not follow us to the next world. We cannot repent of sin if we cannot call to mind its commission: and even Heaven would be a curse if there we

* April 9, 1865. I took notes, the same day, from which I wrote out the above narrative. I afterward submitted it to Captain G——, for correction and approval. He had kept a record of these various communications and of the attendant circumstances, at the time; and so was able to give me every particular with exactitude.

remembered our evil deeds only. On the other hand we may reasonably conclude that, as children when they advance in years put away childish things, so will it be with spirits, as they go up higher. Petty interests will fade from our thoughts, to be replaced by the momentous concerns of a better life. And this will doubtless happen at an earlier or at a later period, in proportion as the actor in these new scenes had been spiritually-minded, or the reverse, during his sojourn upon earth.

I add here another incident which has its peculiar interest aside from the proof of identity which it supplies. It furnishes an example of the gift called by St. Paul the "discerning of spirits;" or of what, in modern parlance, is called a subjective apparition, visible to the seer but invisible to other spectators: together with evidence that such appearances are not, because of such subjective character, to be classed among hallucinations.

SISTER ELIZABETH.

One Sunday evening, during the summer of 1855, a New York physician, Dr. H——, attended morning service in the Rev. Dr. Bellows' church.

During the sermon and while his attention was engrossed by the argument of the preacher, it was suddenly diverted, in a most unexpected manner; namely, by the apparition of three female figures. They first became visible on the left of the church and they glided slowly across the vacant space in front of the pulpit. As they passed, Dr. H—— recognized two of them, both deceased relatives; one his wife, the other his mother. The third figure, appearing between the other two and with an arm round the mother, was that of a beautiful young girl. The attitude and gesture suggested the relationship of daughter; but the features were unknown to Dr. H——; not at all resembling (he thought) those of the only sister he had lost by death: Anne, who had died, in childhood, thirty-nine years before.

This group of figures paused as they reached the extreme right of the church; two of them, the wife and the young girl, gradually fading away. The mother, remaining still, turned toward her son and gazed at him, with a look of affection, for several minutes; then vanished like the others. Dr. H—— had full time to note every well-remembered item of dress: the plain Quaker cap, the snow-white muslin kerchief pinned across the breast, the gray silk gown: all just as the good old lady, a strict member of the Society of Friends, had worn them up to the day of her death.

It was the first time in his life that Dr. H—— had seen an apparition. Nor, up to that time, had anything seemed to indicate that he had any spiritual powers, except that, on one occasion, a table from which he had just taken a book had moved, without apparent cause, a few inches toward him. The effect produced on him by a phenomenon so new and unlooked-for as the appearance of these figures was proportionately great.

Deeply pondering the matter and inclining to believe that the third figure must have been his deceased sister Anne, he called, on the evening of the next day, on a medium (one of the Fox sisters), hoping to have his doubts resolved.

At her suggestion he wrote out a number of female names, in secret; and as he pointed to these in succession, the name Anne was passed by, and the raps indicated *Elizabeth*. Dr. H—— taxed his memory in vain in search of any relative of that name whom he had lost by death. But when, on another sheet, he had written out as many various relationships as he could think of, all were passed by till he came to the word *Sister*, at which the raps came very distinctly.

"That's a mistake," said Dr. H——. "I never had a sister called Elizabeth. I did lose a sister by death, but her name was Anne." Then, as appealing to the occult intelligence; he asked: "Do you mean to say that the figure I saw with its arm round my mother was my sister?"

Answer by raps.—"Yes."

"And that her name was Elizabeth?"

By louder raps.—"Yes."

"Well, it isn't so: that's all I can say."

Three still louder raps reaffirmed the assertion.

Very much mystified, and somewhat staggered by this persistence, it occurred to Dr. H—— that the family Bible which he had not inspected since he was a child, was in the possession of his step-mother, living seventy miles off, in the country. Happening sometime afterward to be in the neighborhood, he paid her a visit and had an opportunity of examining the family record of births and deaths. There, to his amazement, he found registered, in the year 1826, the birth of a daughter, Elizabeth, together with the record of her death a few weeks afterward.

This event occurred during a five-years absence from his father's house: and though letters were interchanged far more rarely in those days than now, Dr. H—— thinks it likely that the circumstance may have been incidentally mentioned in one of his father's infrequent bulletins from home. He has not the slightest recollection, however, that he ever received any such intelligence, or that he ever heard the birth or death of this infant alluded to in the family. A life so very brief usually passes away without leaving a trace, except in the secret depths of a mother's memory.

Dr. H—— has been well known to me for years, as an intelligent man and a dispassionate observer. I confide in his truth and accuracy. I had the narration from himself, wrote it out next morning, submitted the manuscript the same day* to the narrator who, after making a single correction, assented to its accuracy.

In this case, it will be observed, the fact indicated by the apparition and confirmed by the medium was not only not known to the observer but was contrary to his convictions; and he remained incredulous until enlightened by incontrovertible evidence.

With a single additional narrative connecting, like the fore-

* January 2, 1870.

going, a spiritual appearance with the realities of earthly life, I close this chapter.

The Grandmother's Promise.

In the month of March and in the year 1846, three ladies, a mother and two daughters, were sitting in the dining-room of a dwelling in C—— street, West Philadelphia. It was between one and two o'clock in the day. The house was a double one, with a central entrance-hall: a parlor on the left as one entered, and the dining-room on the right; the windows of both rooms looking on the street.

The mother, Mrs. R——, wife of Dr. R——, was sitting close to a front window and to the wall dividing the room from the entrance-hall. Between her and the door opening into the hall was a sofa, set against the dividing wall; and thereon sat her eldest daughter, then unmarried and about nineteen years of age, now the wife of the Rev. Mr. T——, an Episcopal clergyman. Both these ladies were sitting with their faces turned from the window, so that they could see the door entering from the hall, and could observe what happened in the room. Facing the mother and seated on a low stool between her and the elder daughter, was a younger daughter, A——, then aged seventeen. All three ladies were engaged in needlework and were quietly conversing on ordinary topics.

The door leading into the entrance-hall was ten or twelve feet from the front wall. At the time I am speaking of it happened to be ajar, open some three or four inches only.

Of a sudden, and at the same moment, the mother and eldest daughter perceived, advancing silently from this door, a female figure. It appeared in a black Turk-satin dress and over it a white book-muslin handkerchief crossed on the breast; and it wore a white bonnet. In its hand the ladies distinguished a white silk bag, such as is often carried by Quaker ladies, the string of the bag wrapped several times round the wrist, and the bag gathered up in the hand. The younger sister, observing after a time the looks of the other two ladies, turned round and saw the appearance also; but not as long not as distinctly as they did.

The figure advanced slowly into the room, till it came within two or three feet of the front wall. There it stopped opposite a portrait of Dr. R——, which hung between the two front windows, and gazed at it, for the space perhaps of half a minute; then it turned and moved slowly to the door where it had first been seen. The door did not open; but the figure, coming close up to it, there suddenly disappeared. The ladies were looking at it, at the moment of its disappearance. In moving through the parlor and returning, it passed so close to the elder daughter that its dress seemed almost to touch her's. Yet there was no echo of a footstep, nor the least rustle of the dress, nor any other sound whatever, while the figure moved. This circumstance and the disappearance of the apparition without opening of the door to permit natural exit, alone caused the appearance to seem other than an ordinary and material one. To the sight it was as distinct and palpable as any human visitor; and though the ladies afterward recollected that its motion seemed more like gliding than walking, yet this was an after thought only. Not a word was spoken, during the scene here described.

"Who was it?" was Mrs. R——'s exclamation, addressed to the elder daughter, as soon as their first mute astonishment had a little subsided.

"It was grandmamma!" she replied.

Thereupon the mother, without another word, left the room. The house was searched, from garret to cellar, but not a trace was found of any one except its usual inmates.

In addition to this negative evidence there was the positive proof furnished by a slight, recent fall of snow. The path to the door-steps (the house standing back from the street line), and the steps themselves, showed no trace of human foot. Add to this that two children who were playing, at the time, on the front veranda, saw no one enter or depart.

On subsequently comparing notes, the ladies ascertained that the impressions left on each of them by this extraordinary appearance were the self-same. I had the particulars, first from the elder daughter, Mrs. Y——, and afterward confirmed by the mother. To both the figure seemed a real person. Both recollected the precise dress, and their recollections exactly corresponded. To the eyes of both the figure had crossed the room, approached the front wall, lingered there to look at the portrait, recrossed to the door and there vanished. Neither heard any sound. It should be added that they had not been talking or thinking of the lady whose image thus suddenly appeared before them.

Mrs. R——, as well as her daughter, had instantly recognized the figure as that of Mrs. R——'s mother, who had died about ten years before. Not only the face and form, but every minute particular of the dress, as above described, were the counterpart of that lady and of her usual walking attire, when in life. Originally she had belonged to the Society of Friends, and she had, in a measure, retained the style and peculiarities of their apparel.

The ladies related this incident, on the evening of the same day, to the Rev. Mr. Y——, from whom I first obtained it: his recollection of what they told him, only a few hours after the event, tallying exactly with their account to me of what they had seen. He informed me that he had never seen old Mrs. R——; but, the next morning, meeting three elderly ladies, sisters, who had been intimately acquainted with her, he asked them (without mentioning what had been related to himself) to give him a description of her personal appearance and ordinary walking-dress. It agreed, point for point, with that of the apparition, as it had been described to him.

Some other particulars which add greatly to the value of this narrative remain to be stated. Shortly before her death Dr. R——'s mother had strongly advised her son to buy a house in the neighborhood in which he ultimately purchased. She had also, about the same time, stated to a friend of hers, Mrs. C——, that if her son (he was an only son) did well, she would, if permitted, return from the other world, to witness his prosperity. This was afterward mentioned by Mrs. C—— to the Rev. Mr. Y——, and by that gentleman to me.

But it so happened that, on the very day, and as nearly as could be ascertained at the very hour, when his wife and daughters witnessed the apparition of his mother, the deeds by which Dr. R—— became the legal proprietor of the house in which she appeared were delivered to him by its former possessor. Though he had spoken to his wife and family of his intention to purchase, they had no reason to suppose that the bargain would be closed on that day. When, on his return in the evening, he threw the deeds on the table, it was an unexpected surprise. Is it to be wondered at that, after the first feeling of gratification, the next thought, both of mother and daughter, should be of her who had so earnestly wished for this acquisition, and who had appeared to them, in her son's house, at or near the very time at which that house passed, by legal conveyance, into his hands? Is it surprising that Mrs. C—— should call to mind her old friend's promise, thus, to all outward seeming, strangely and punctually fulfilled?

It may, perhaps, occur to the reader as singular that the spirit of the mother should not, at the time of the purchase, have appeared to her son, rather than to her daughter-in-law. But it is not certain that this was possible. It would seem that, as a general rule, apparitions, like other spiritual phenomena, can present themselves only under favorable circumstances, and that these circumstances are often connected with the personal attributes, or peculiarities of organization, of the spectators, or some one of them.

But Mrs. R——, the daughter-in-law, evidently possessed some such peculiarities. For, at various periods of her life, she had had dreams of a prophetic character. To these I shall advert when I come to speak of the gift of prophecy.

In connection with the above incident it behooves us to bear in mind:

That it occurred two years before modern Spiritualism had made its appearance in the United States, when the suggestion of "epidemic excitement," even if that plea be ever good, was out of the question.

That the apparition, as far as one can judge, was objective; seen by three persons at once, who coincide in their report of it; in broad daylight and at a moment when the thoughts of the witnesses were occupied by every-day matters.

That these witnesses were disinterested and their social position such as to forbid the supposition of wilful deception.

That the coincidence between the conditional promise and its fulfilment at the moment the condition was accomplished, is too striking to be rationally referred to chance.

Whether, under these circumstances, the identity of the grandmother is made out with reasonable certainty, it is for the reader to determine.

CHAPTER II.

A CASE OF IDENTITY THREE HUNDRED YEARS OLD.

THAT branch of Pneumatology which relates to intermundane phenomena has come into notice so recently, and has been, till now, the subject of so little careful study, that one ought to speak very cautiously of its laws, especially those which govern the conditions under which spirits may, or may not, communicate with earth. It is hazardous to generalize in view of a comparatively small array of facts.

Nevertheless I think we may assume it to be probable that a very large proportion of all the spirits who manifest themselves here, do so for a limited time only after they reach their new homes. Their destiny is upward and onward; and we may suppose the better class among them to be more occupied by the scenes of beauty and excellence that are opening before them, than by any recallings of the dim and checkered sojourn they have left.

With one drawback, however: drawn down sometimes to that lower sphere by a power that is greater in Heaven than on earth—by an attraction that rules most surely in natures that are noblest and best.

The most powerful of all the heart's agencies—human love which so often bridges over a thousand difficulties here—that same emotion it is, triumphing over the death-change, which would seem the most commonly to overcome the gulf fixed between earthly life and spiritual existence. And thus, sometimes, for a few years—ten, thirty, fifty, perhaps—so long as the loved ones still linger behind—that deathless emotion appears to rule a divided heart.

—Divided between Heaven and earth; unable, yet, while its mourners are on the other side, fully to realize that peace which passeth all understanding; unable cordially to rejoice with them who do rejoice, till these mourners—now removed, as if *they* were the dead—become alive again, at its side; eager, meanwhile, to make known its undying affection, to evince its constant care; anxious to aid, to comfort, to encourage.

But these earth-bound labors of love are transient only in that higher sphere. Death is an Angel of Mercy there. He is Heaven's Herald of joy, for whose messages yearning souls wait. Through him, the Comforter, comes re-union in the many mansions that had been lonely, even amid celestial surroundings, till he brought the earthly wanderers home. Then satisfied hearts stray no longer from heavenly abodes.

It is true that what on earth we call philanthropy, and what in the next world seems chiefly to take the form of earnest desire to bring immortality to light in this darkling world, may cause benevolent spirits to seek us here even when their own circle of love is complete. And this doubtless happens: Franklin (Book v., chap. 4) seems an example. Yet I think it is the exception rather than the rule. In a general way it would seem that it is not the higher class of spirits which continue, generation after generation, more especially century after century, to revisit earth: not such men as Confucius or Socrates or Solon; nor yet such as Milton or Shakspeare or Newton.

Yet I give this as my individual opinion only. I have found no proof of identity in the case of any spirit, once celebrated either for goodness or talent, returning, after centuries, to enlighten or reform mankind. My idea is that they have completed their earthly task, and that their duties, now, are of another sphere. I think that we are left to work out, in the main, our worldly progress. The help we receive from above is not to supersede our exertions here below. Only so far we are to be directly helped—to an ardent, living conviction, instead of a cold, barren belief, of that truth of truths—immortality. That once secured to our race, we are to trust, it seems, to our own industry and courage for the rest; with this consoling reflection, however, that though spirits, long since departed, descend not to do our work, yet other spirit-friends—though it be unconsciously to us—often secretly aid the faithful worker to do his own.

But other motives than our benefit appear sometimes to urge mundane return. Guilty spirits seem the most frequently to be earth-bound, as in the case of the lady of Burnham Green,* and hundreds of other house-haunters. But a purely worldly spirit, unstained by crime, yet to whom trifles were wont to take the place of momentous things—who never, while here, bestowed a thought on regions beyond—may, long after it passes away, be recalled hither by the levities that made up its empty earth-life.† Of this I have succeeded in finding a noteworthy example.

How a French King's favorite Musician manifested himself.

In those days, not long past, when Paris still thought herself the centre of civilization, and while she had many claims to be called the gayest and the most brilliant among the capitals of the world—in the year 1865—there lived in that city a worthy old gentleman, inheriting, from musical ancestors, the family gift. I believe he is still alive.

Monsieur N. G. Bach, then sixty-seven years of age, was the great-grandson of the celebrated Sebastian Bach,‡ who flourished during the first half of the eighteenth century. Though in somewhat delicate health, this gentleman was, at the time, in full enjoyment of his mental faculties, a busy composer, and

* See preceding page 322.

† See *Footfalls*, p. 427.

‡ John Sebastian Bach, one of the most eminent of German composers, was born at Eisenach in 1685, and died at Leipsic in 1754. He held several high musical offices, was an inimitable performer on the organ, and left many compositions of great merit. The family is said to have produced, in the space of two hundred years, fifty celebrated musicians.—BOUILLET: *Dictionnaire de Biographie.*

highly esteemed by his brother artists, alike because of his professional talents and as a thoroughly upright and amiable man.*

On the fourth of May, 1865, M. Bach's son, Léon Bach, a gentleman of antiquarian tastes, found, among the curiosities of a bric-a-brac shop in Paris, a *spinet*, evidently very old, but of remarkable beauty and finish, and unusually well-preserved. It was of oak, ornamented with delicate carving in tasteful gilded Arabesque, encrusted with turquoises and intermingled with gilt fleur-de-lis. It had evidently belonged to some person of wealth or distinction; but all the dealer knew about it was that it had quite recently been brought from Italy by the person from whom he bought it.

Thinking that it would please his father, the young man purchased it. Nor was he disappointed. M. Bach, who shares his son's taste for stray waifs of the past, was delighted with his new acquisition, and spent most of the day in admiring it, in trying its tones and inspecting its mechanism. It was about five feet long by two wide; it had no legs; but was packed away, like a violin, in a wooden case for protection. When about to be used, it was set on a table or stand. Though richly decorated, it was but a small, weak beginning of what has culminated in the elaborate Steinways and Chickerings of our day, with their wonderful power and superb tones. In general arrangement, however, as may be seen from the plate here given,† it resembles them; its small keys being arranged in the same order: but these keys, when touched, move a set of

* The Paris "Grand Journal" (No. 62) speaks of him as "élève de Zimmerman, premier prix de Piano du Conservatoire au concour de 1819, un de nos professeurs de piano les plus estimés et les plus honorés."

The Paris correspondent of the New York "Nation" (June 12, 1866) speaks in the highest terms of his acknowledged reputation for uprightness and honesty.

† See Plate II. M. Bach kindly entrusted the spinet to a Parisian friend of mine, who had it photographed for me.

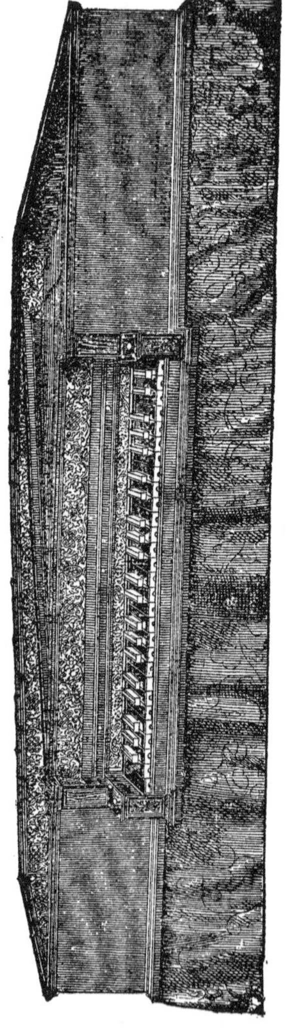

SPINET

GIVEN BY KING HENRY III. TO HIS FAVORITE MUSICIAN.

PLATE II.

wooden sticks as thick as a lady's finger, each furnished with a point which strikes the corresponding wire. The quality of the tone may be readily imagined.

Before the day closed, however, M. Bach had made a discovery which atoned for all imperfections. On a narrow bar of wood which supported the sounding-board he thought he could distinguish writing. Fitted in above this bar were two small blocks, interposed between it and the sounding-board. They entirely concealed part of the writing: but by turning up the instrument and letting in a powerful light, he could read the rest of it. Of this he has sent me a copy. It contains the words, "*In Roma Antonius Nobilis;*" then a blank caused by the intervention of one of the blocks; then the words "*Brena Medislani Patriæ;*" then, after another blank similarly caused, the date "*Die xiy Aprillis* 1564."* Of course these words were written before the instrument was framed.

Thus M. Bach learned that his spinet was more than three hundred years old; having been made in Rome, in the year 1564, by a certain Antonius Nobilis, apparently from the neighborhood of Milan; and probably finished on the fourteenth of April of that year. M. Bach's specimen was located and labelled. And, as in all cases in the eyes of the paleontologist, so in this case in those of the antiquarian, this greatly added to the value of a curious relic of the past.

Much pleased, the old gentleman retired to rest; and naturally enough, he dreamed of his son's gift. His dream, however, was peculiar. There appeared to him a handsome young stranger, wearing a carefully-trimmed beard, and elegantly dressed in the ancient costume of the French court—rich doublet with ample lace collar and close-fitting sleeves that were slashed in the upper part; large, slashed trunk-hose, long stockings and low shoes with rosettes. Doffing a high-pointed, broad-brimmed, and white-plumed hat, this young man ad-

* There are also several imperfect words cut off by the blanks; an O; the letters *soné* and *A per*, and, after the last blank, the word *reducit.*

vanced, bowing and smiling, toward M. Bach's bed, and thus addressed the wondering sleeper:

"The spinet you have belonged to me. I often played on it to amuse my master, King Henry. In his youth he composed an air with words which he was fond of singing while I accompanied him. Both words and air were written in memory of a lady whom he greatly loved. He was separated from her, which caused him much grief. She died, and in his sad moments he used to hum this air."

After a time this strange visitor added: "I will play it to you, and I shall take means to recall it to your recollection, for I know you have a poor memory." Thereupon he sat down to the spinet, accompanying himself as he sang the words. The old man awoke in tears, touched by the pathos of the song.

Lighting a taper he found it was two o'clock. So, after musing on his dream, and with the plaintive melody he had heard still sounding in his ears, he speedily composed himself to sleep.

Nothing remarkable in all this.

If anything happened to M. Bach before he awoke next morning, it was while he remained in a completely-unconscious state. He had not the faintest remembrance of anything until, as he opened his eyes in broad daylight, he saw, to his unbounded amazement, a sheet of paper lying on his bed and headed, in these formal old characters:

Air et paroles du Roy henry III

His astonishment increased when he examined the sheet more closely. It was a rare archæological specimen:* the notes minute; the clefs those used in former times; the writing careful and old-fashioned, with here and there the Gothic tails to be found attached to certain letters in the manuscripts of the sixteenth and seventeenth centuries; the orthography, too, that of two or three hundred years ago.

* See Plate III. for fac-simile of the first two lines of the song, reproduced from the original.

PLATE III.

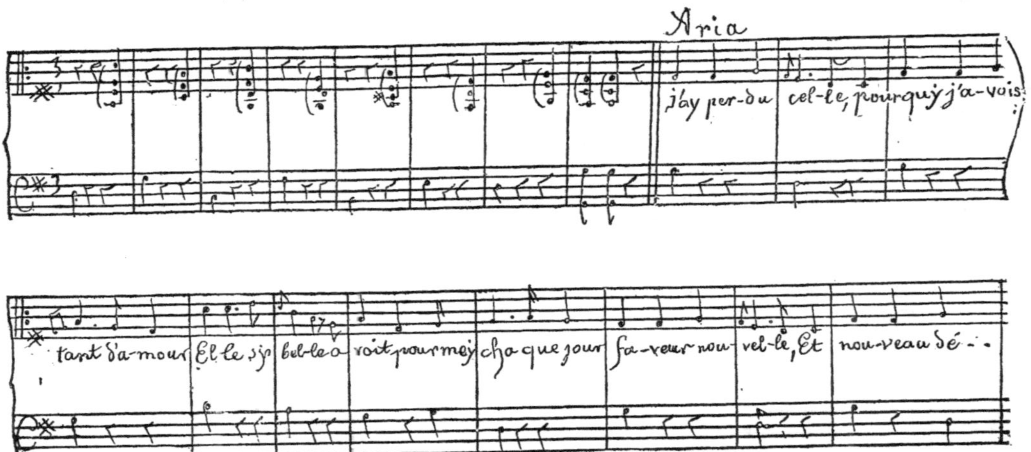

FAC-SIMILE OF MUSIC, FOUND BY M. BACH, ON HIS BED, MAY 5, 1865.

This song, with English words—a translation, by the author, of King Henry's original ballad—is published and copyrighted by J. SHUBERTH & CO., New York and Leipsic.

His eye glanced over the first notes. Was it the song of his dream? And the words—yes, he remembered them! He hastened to his piano, and soon convinced himself, beyond possible doubt, that here were, in truth, reproduced the very air, and the very verses, which his dream-brought visitor had sung and played!

The first feeling was one of perplexity and trouble—even alarm. What could it all mean? To the dream itself, though very vivid and remarkable, he had, when he awoke in the night, attached no importance. But what was this? Absently turning over the mysterious missive, he observed that it was a four-page sheet of music-paper, two pages of which contained a composition of his own which he had sketched the day before, leaving the sheet in his escritoire. It must have been taken thence during the night. Who had taken it, and filled the two blank pages with this mysterious music from a bygone age? Somebody must have been there!

Or had it been himself? But he was no somnambulist—had never, that he knew, walked or written in his sleep. Nor had he any knowledge or faith in modern Spiritualism: so that the possibility of an actual spirit-message did not suggest itself. He was mystified, bewildered: the more so, when he remarked the coincidence of names and dates. The man of the vision had spoken of "his master, King Henry;" the song itself purported to have been written by Henry III.: but the spinet was made in 1564, when Henry (then Duke d'Anjou) was fourteen years old. What more likely than that so handsome an instrument should have found its way, after a few years, from Rome to the court of France, and been bought there by a young prince, himself (as history tells us) a musical composer of some little merit?

M. Bach spoke of these marvels to his friends, who repeated the story to others; and soon a host of the curious—literary men, artists, antiquarians and others—thronged the apartments of the well-known musician, to hear, from his own lips, the strange narrative, and to see, with their own eyes, the wonderful spinet. Among these visitors came some earnest spiritualists; and then, for the first time, M. Bach heard of writing mediums, and listened to the suggestion that his hand might have been guided to write while he slept.

All this, though too new and strange to enlist his belief, set him to thinking; and, one day, three or four weeks after his dream, feeling a headache and nervous trembling of the arm, the idea struck him that perhaps some spirit wished to write through him and thus to furnish an explanation of the mystery he had been unable to penetrate. No sooner had he put pencil to paper than he lost consciousness, and, while in that state, his hand wrote—in French, of course—"King Henry, my master, who gave me the spinet you now possess, had written a four-line stanza on a piece of parchment, which he caused to be nailed on the case (étui), when, one morning, he sent me the instrument. Some years afterward, having to travel and take the spinet with me, fearing that the parchment might be torn off and lost, I took it off, and for safe-keeping put it in a small niche, on the left of the key-board, where it still is."

This communication was signed Baldazzarini, and then followed the stanza alluded to above, which, literally translated, is as follows:

> "The King Henry gives this large spinet
> To Baldazzarini, an excellent musician;
> If it is not good, or not stylish enough,
> At least, for my sake, let him preserve it carefully." *

Here, at last, was a chance to obtain tangible evidence in connection with these mysteries. Here was a test furnished, whereby to determine whether this Baldazzarini, as he called

* Here is the original, as written by M. Bach's hand:

> "Le roy Henry donne cette grande espinette
> A Baldazzarini, très-bon musicien.
> Si elle n'est bonne ou pas assez coquette,
> Pour souvenir, du moins, qu'il la conserve bien."

himself, was a myth or a real person, capable of disclosing un known facts.

To gratify public curiosity the spinet had been deposited, for a few days, in the Retrospective Museum of the Palace of Industry; and it was still there when the above communication was written. Of course it was sent for, at once.

One can imagine with what nervous eagerness father and son awaited its arrival, and then set themselves to ascertain whether this story about a parchment, said to contain a stanza written by the hand of a French king, and still to be found within the spinet, was pure romance or sober fact.

During an hour or two, M. Bach says, they explored every nook and corner of the old instrument—in vain! At last, when hope had almost deserted them, Léon Bach, looking over what his father's hand had written, proposed to take the instrument to pieces, so far as they could do so without injuring it. When they had raised the key-board and removed some of the hammers, they detected, underneath, on the left, a narrow slit in the wood containing what proved to be a bit of parchment eleven and a half inches long and two and three-quarter inches wide, on which was written, in a bold, dashing hand, four lines, similar to those which M. Bach's hand had traced. And there was a signature—yes, Henry's sign manual!

They cleansed it as well as they could, and here is what they read:

> "Moy le Roy Henry trois octroys cette espinette
> A Baltasarini mon gay musicien
> Mais s'il dit mal soñe, ou bien [ma] moult simplette
> Lors pour mon souvenir dans l'estuy garde bien.
> HENRY." *

The stanza, literally translated, reads as follows:

> "I, the King Henry III., present this spinet
> To Baltasarini, my gay musician:
> But if he finds it poor-toned, or else very simple,
> Still, for my sake, in its case let him preserve it."

* See, on next page, fac-simile taken from a photograph of the original parchment, which I obtained through the kindness of M. Bach.

It is difficult, in this prosaic world, to realize the feelings of these excited searchers when at last, from its secret hiding-place, they drew forth—stained by time and covered with the dust and cobwebs of centuries—this mute witness—of what? The father, as he looked at it, was conscious that the announcement which led to this discovery was written by no agency of his, unless a pen is to be called an agent. When he awoke from the trance during which his hand had written, he had read the lines as he would have read anything else penned by a stranger and then first presented to him for perusal. And yet it was substantially true; and here, under his eyes, lay evidence, not to be gainsayed, of its truth.

PARCHMENT, WITH AUTOGRAPH OF HENRY III., FOUND IN SPINET.

—Substantially, not literally true. "*The King Henry*" in the announcement, "*I, the King Henry III.*" in the original; the word large, applied to the spinet, omitted in the original; a variation in the spelling of the recipient's name, and "*excellent*" written "*gay*"* in the original; also "*not good*" replaced by "*poor-toned*," and "*not stylish enough*" by "*very simple*" finally, in the last line, the original refers to the

* See, as to this word *gay* and as to the spelling of the musician's name, a remark made a few pages farther on.

case (*l'estuy*, as *l'étui* was then written), while in the stanza, as announced, there is no such reference.

Amazed they must have been! Yet I doubt whether it occurred either to father or son, as it occurs to me, that the evidence thus brought to light is vastly stronger on account of its peculiar character—is much more convincing because, while absolutely substantial in its coincidence with the promised stanza, it bears no stamp of literalism.

The interpolated *ma* in the discovered stanza greatly puzzled them at first, but was subsequently explained. When exhibiting the original parchment to the friend through whom I obtained this narrative, M. Bach said: "No one could imagine the meaning of the word *ma*, surrounded by lines, as you see. But one day my hand was again moved involuntarily, and there was written: '*Amico mio*: the King joked about my Italian accent in the verse he sent with the spinet. I always said *ma* instead of *mais*.'"

Ma, Italian for *but*, corresponds to the French *mais*; and I have observed that Italians, in speaking French, frequently make this mistake. Thus "ma moult simplette," in Baltazarini's patois, would mean "but very simple."

The original parchment (blackened by age, as the plate shows) was taken by M. Bach to the "Bibliothèque Impériale" (if that be still the title of France's great national library) and there compared with original manuscripts. In these last Henry's hand was found to vary, as in that age handwritings often did: but with some of the acknowledged originals the writing on M. Bach's parchment—verse as well as signature—was found most strictly to correspond. "L'identité était absolue," M. Bach said. It was also submitted, for verification, to experienced antiquarians, and by them, after critical comparison, pronounced to be a genuine autograph of Henry, whencesoever obtained.

The minute holes visible along the upper edge of the parchment (see fac-simile), indicating that it had originally been tacked to some wooden surface, sustain the allegation that Henry had caused it "to be nailed to the case." On the lower edge it seems to have been cut off inside of the nail-holes; but the marks of four larger holes, one at each corner of the parchment, are distinctly visible. The rough cross above the quatrain is an additional voucher of authenticity; for a similar token of easy piety heads almost every specimen of Henry the Third's writing that has come down to us.

These marvellous incidents, more or less correctly related, could not fail to find their way into the newspapers. They appeared in several Parisian journals, and were thence copied far and wide. For a week or two M. Bach's spinet, with its supernatural accessories, was the great sensation of the novelty-seeking French metropolis. The whole was usually set down as incomprehensible; they stated the facts, with some such comment as—"Mystère que nous n'osons pas approfondir:" and though there were general suggestions that some natural explanation must exist, yet—so firmly established was M. Bach's reputation for integrity—these never took the shape of doubts that he had acted in entire good faith. After a time, of course, the excitement was replaced by that of some other engrossing rumor, but without leading to any solution or explanation whatever.

The song was published. As no treble accompaniment, but only the air with bass, was given in the original (see fac-simile of music on preceding page), M. Bach had to supply the accompaniment for the right hand, which he did with taste and judgment. The words are pretty and suit well with the sentiment of the romance.* They contain two special allusions; one to the royal author having met the object of his passion at a distant hunt ("chasse lointaine"); and the other to the lady having sadly passed her last days in a cloister. ("Triste et cloistrée," now written *cloitrée*—are the words).

* Here they are, with the original orthography:

REFRAIN.

J'ay perdu celle pour quy j'avois tant d'amour.
Elle, si belle, avoit pour moy, chaque jour,
Faveur nouvelle et nouveau désir:
Oh ouy! sans elle, il me faut mourir.

It need hardly be said that the publication of the incidents above related and of the mysterious song caused various researches into the annals of the sixteenth century, to determine how far the historical record of the times bore out M. Bach's story. It was soon discovered that, according to the best biographies, the "grande passion" of Henry's life was for the Princess Marie de Clèves; and that, according to a diary kept of those times, that princess appears to have died in an abbey.

Also a passage was brought to light, occurring in one of the works of that laborious chronicler, the Abbé Lenglet-Dufresnoy, and reading thus: "In 1579, Balthazzarini, a celebrated Italian musician, came into France, to the court of Henry III." *

1r. VERS.

Un jour, pendant une chasse lointaine,
  Je l'aperçus pour la première fois;
Je croyais voir un ange dans la plaine,
  Lors, je devins le plus heureux des Roys! . . . mais!

2nd. VERS.

Je donnerois certes tout mon royaume
  Pour la revoir encor un seul instant,
Près d'elle assis dessous un humble chaume,
  Pour sentir mon cœur battre en l'admirant . . . mais!

3me. VERS.

Triste et cloistrée, oh! ma pauvre belle
  Fut loin de moi pendant ses derniers jours.
Elle ne sens plus sa peine cruelle,
  Ici bas, hélas! . . je souffre toujours! . . . ah! . . .

In singing, the *refrain* is repeated after each verse.

The word *si*, in the second line of the refrain, seems at first to be written *sy*; and it was so printed in the song: whereupon a critic wrote to M. Bach, calling his attention to the fact that the French have *never* written the word *si* with a *y*. On examining the supposed *y*, however, with a magnifier, M. Bach and his friends came to the opinion that it was but the long Italian *i*, often used when *i* was a final letter, in those days. It is evidently unlike any other *y* in the original, as may be seen by examining the two lines in fac-simile (page 416).

* *Tablettes Chronologiques de l'Histoire Universelle*, vol. ii. p. 704. (Ed. of 1778.)

But I determined to obtain, if possible, further testimony, and have succeeded in procuring some other important particulars.

Henry, the Last of the Valois.

This favorite son of Catherine de Médicis is best known by the one great crime of his life; his assent to that massacre of St. Bartholomew, which took place, at the instigation of his mother and by the authority of his elder brother, Charles IX., in August, 1572.

But Henry was not without redeeming qualities. When but nineteen years old, he won, for his brother, the battles of Jarnac and Montcontour; thus achieving a military reputation which, three years later, procured his election as King of Poland.

One among the most discriminating of modern historians says of him: "Henry wished to lead a palace life, divided between pious exercises, the pleasures of the city, retirement and the reverence due to the sovereign magistrate. He was little inclined to cultivate the society of old generals, politicians, and men of learning, who might have informed and instructed him: preferring young and gay people of handsome exterior, who emulated him in the faultlessness of their costumes and the brilliancy of their ornaments." *

But this was one side only of his character. "His nature," says Ranke, "was like that of Sardanapalus which, in seasons of prosperity, abandoned itself to enervating luxury, but in adversity became courageous and manful. . . . His failings were obvious to every one. His deficient morality, his eagerness for enjoyment, and his dependence upon a few favorites gave general and well-founded offence. Occasionally, however, he rose to the full height of his vocation; showing an intellectual capacity corresponding with his exalted position, and,

* Ranke: *Civil Wars and Monarchy in France;* p. 307. (New York Ed. 1854.)

though subject to many vacillations, great susceptibility of mind and goodness of disposition." *

Such was the monarch who, according to the allegation made in M. Bach's dream, composed the elegiac song. The name of the lady whom it mourns was not mentioned; but—the genuineness of the song being conceded—there cannot be a doubt as to the person intended. The name of Beatrice is not more inseparably connected with the memory of Dante, nor Laura with Petrarch, than is the name of Marie de Clèves with that of Henry III. Not a detailed history of the time, not a biography of Henry, but alludes to it.

He met her, while still Duke d'Anjou, and sought her in marriage; but she was a Protestant and he a Catholic of Medicean blood. The difference of religion, insuperable of course in the eyes of the Queen Mother, seems to have been the sole cause that prevented their marriage. † She was married, in July, 1572, to the Prince of Condé, one of the chief Protestant leaders; and, the next year, 1573, Henry left France to assume the throne of Poland, carrying with him, according to Chateaubriand, remorse for the massacres of St. Bartholomew, but—in still stronger measure—regret for his disappointment in love. "He wrote with his blood," says that historian, "to Marie de Clèves, first wife of Henry, Prince of Condé." ‡

* Ranke: work cited, pp. 314, 394.

† "La difference de religion, suivant quelques mémoires, fut la seule cause qui l'empecha de l'épouser."—*Biographie Générale*, tome x. p. 854. The same assertion is made, in more positive terms, in the *Biographie Universelle*, vol. ix. p. 95.

‡ "Le Duc d'Anjou (depuis Henry III.) alla prendre la couronne de Pologne, et raconter, dans les forêts de la Lithuanie, à son medecin Miron, les meurtres dont la pensée l'empêchait de dormir: 'Je vous ai fait venir ici, pour vous faire part de mes inquiétudes et agitations de cette nuict, qui ont troublé mon repos, en repensant a l'execution de la Saint-Barthelemy.' En quittant la France, le duc d'Anjou avait été moins poursuivi du souvenir de ses crimes que de celui de ses amours; il écrivait avec son sang à Marie de Clèves, première femme de Henri, Prince de Condé."—*Analyse raisonnee de l'Histoire de France*, par Cha-

Charles IX. died in 1574, and Henry speedily returned from Poland to Paris, as heir to the throne of France. A month after his return Marie died: and so deeply, according to his biographers, did Henry take her death to heart, that he remained several days shut up without food, in an apartment hung with black; and when he reappeared in public, it was in garments of deep mourning, with deaths'-heads worked all over them. *

The poets of that day allude to Henry's bitter grief. In the works of Pasquier, a contemporary of Henry, is to be found a

TEAUBRIAND, Paris, 1853, p. 315. I think Henry's remorse for the St. Bartholomew massacres may have been more sincere than Chateaubriand regards it. There is a curious incident, related by Ranke, in this connection:

"Charles IX., about eight days after the massacre, caused his brother-in-law, Henry, to be summoned to him in the night. He found him as he had sprang from his bed, filled with dread at a wild tumult of confused voices, which prevented him from sleeping. Henry himself imagined he heard these sounds; they appeared like distinct shrieks and howlings, mingled with the indistinguishable raging of a furious multitude, and with groans and curses as on the day of the massacre. Messengers were sent into the city to ascertain whether any new tumult had broken out, but the answer returned was that all was quiet in the city, and that the commotion was in the air. Henry could never recall this incident without a horror that made his hair stand on end."—RANKE, work cited, p. 278.

Henry III. probably witnessed this startling phenomenon; at all events, he must assuredly have known of it, at the time: and it was an occurrence likely to leave a life-long impression on a mind like his.

A historian, to avoid the charge of superstition, has to say, as Ranke does, that Henry *imagined* he heard the same sounds. But how about the messengers who brought answer back that "*the commotion was in the air*"?

* Marie mourut en couches en 1574. Henri III. qui venait de succéder à Charles IX., et étoit depuis un mois de retour de Pologne, en fut saisi d'une si vive douleur, qu'il resta enfermé plusieurs jours sans manger, et ne reparut ensuite en public que couvert de vêtements de deuil, parsemés de têtes de mort."—*Biographie Générale*, tome x. pp. 854, 855.

monody on the death of Marie de Clèves, which the poet puts in the mouth of the king.*

With all this tallies closely what history tells us regarding the lady herself.

Marie de Clèves.

This princess seems to have been almost as noted for grace and beauty as her more celebrated namesake, Mary of Scotland.

She had been the admiration of the court of Charles IX., by her loveliness and her virtues.† The poets of that day celebrate her as the "Beautiful Mary;" ‡ and so great was the fascination her charms exerted over Henry that the credulity of the times was fain to ascribe it to the influence of sorcery. §

We have additional testimony both as to the character of this lady, and as to the profound sorrow felt by Henry for her loss, in the following extract from a manuscript Diary kept, throughout the reigns of Henry III. and Henry IV., by Pierre de l'Estoile, Sieur de Gland, a gentleman of an honorable and well-known family, occupying important posts in the magistracy and Parliament of Paris : ‖

* "On trouve dans les Œuvres de Pasquier une complainte sur la mort de Marie de Clèves, ou le poète fait parler le roi lui-même."—*Biographie Universelle*, tome ix. p. 96.

† "Cette princesse, qui avait fait l'admiration de la cour de Charles IX., par sa beauté et ses vertus, mourut en couches, etc."—*Biographie Universelle* (Paris, 1813), tome ix. p. 96.

‡ "Les poëtes du temps la celèbrent sous le nom de la *Belle Marie.*"—*Biographie Générale*, tome x. p. 854.

§ "Selon l'usage de ces temps de crédulité, on crut que la princesse avait employé quelque charme pour enflammer Henri."—*Biographie Universelle*, tome ix. p. 96.

‖ Pierre de l'Estoile, conseiller du Roi, et grand audiencier en la chancellerie de France, étoit issu d'une famille parlementaire. Sa position sociale lui permettait de bien connaitre les hommes et les choses de son temps. Il parait qu'il se donna, pour principale occupation de sa vie, le soin de recuiller très attentivement, et de consigner dans des registres

"On Saturday, October 30, 1574, died at Paris, in the flower of her age, leaving a daughter as heir, Dame Marie de Clèves, Marchioness d'Isle, wife of Messire Henry de Bourbon, Prince of Condé. She was endowed with singular goodness and beauty, by reason of which the King loved her devotedly (éperdûment); so dearly, indeed, that the Cardinal de Bourbon, her uncle,* when about to entertain the King, caused her to be removed from his Abbey of Saint-Germain-des-Près: declaring to His Majesty that he (the King) could not enter so long as the body of the princess remained there. She said, on her deathbed, that she had wedded the most generous, but also the most jealous, prince in France; to whom, however, she felt conscious that she had never given the slightest cause for jealousy." †

I have found no positive evidence that Marie passed her last days in the Abbey in which she was buried; but it is, in the highest degree, probable. We know that she died in Paris, and that her husband, the Prince of Condé, fearing that the Queen

ou des tablettes, les événements marquants qui se passait autour de lui."—*Notice of the Life and Manuscripts of Pierre de l'Estoile*, prefixed to the Paris reprint of his "Memoires," Didier, 1854.

Speaking of D'Estoile's diary, Bouillon says, in his *Dictionnaire de Biographie Universelle:*

"This collection comprised in five folio volumes, and which was never intended for publication, is a most valuable source of information as to events occurring in the reigns of Henry III. and Henry IV."—*Art.* "Etoile."

* He was her uncle by marriage only.

† PIERRE DE L'ESTOILE: *Memoires pour servir à l'Histoire de France.* Edition by Didier, 1854.

The wording, in the original, is somewhat obscure: "le roy l'aimoit si fort qu'il falust que le Cardinal de Bourbon, son oncle, pour festoier le Roy, la fist oster de son Abbaye de Saint-Germain-des-Près: disant Sa Majesté qu'il n'estoit possible qu'elle y entrast tant que son corps y seroit." But the meaning evidently is that the Cardinal, knowing the violence of the King's grief, thinking that he might insist on seeing the body of the princess, and fearing the effect on his mind, took the precaution to have the corpse removed from the Abbey, previous to the King's visit.

Mother designed his death, had, some months before, taken refuge in Germany, where he remained till late in the year 1575; * that is, until a year after Marie's death. Marie's father had died several years before. † The prince, in leaving his wife behind, doubtless entrusted her to the care of his uncle, the Cardinal de Bourbon. But the cardinal evidently resided in his Abbey, since it was there, according to Etoile, that he proposed to entertain the King. Under these circumstances, we can scarcely doubt that the forsaken and fatherless niece lived with her uncle in his Abbey. Sad must her life there have been, uncertain as she was of her husband's fate! All this strikingly coincides with the "triste et cloistrée" of the song.

I pass on to say a few words of the musician, to whom, as alleged, the spinet belonged.

BALTAZARINI.

His name does not occur either in the *Biographie Générale*, or the *Biographie Universelle;* and, after long search, I had begun to despair of finding any biographical notice of such a personage, when I was fortunate enough to discover in the Athenæum Library of Boston, a French Dictionary of Musicians, in some eight or nine volumes. There Henry's favorite has a place.

"BALTAZARINI: an Italian musician, known in France under the name of *Beaujoyeux*, was the first violinist of his day. The Maréchal de Brissac brought him from Piedmont, in 1577, to the court of Queen Catherine de Medicis, who appointed him her Director of Music, and first *valet de chambre.* Henry III. entrusted to him the management of the court fêtes; and

* RANKE: "Civil Wars and Monarchies in France," p. 292.

† Marie was the daughter of Francis I., Duke of Nevers. I do not know the exact year in which he died, but it was before 1565: for Louis de Gonzaque, having in that year married the heiress of Francis, then succeeded to the Dukedom of Nevers.—BOUILLON: *Dictionnaire de Biographie Universelle*, art. "Nevers."

he long discharged the duties of that post with credit. It was he who first conceived the idea of a dramatic spectacle, combined with music and dancing." *

Baltazarini was, then, at Henry's court, surnamed *Beaujoyeux*—" the handsome and the joyous." Compare, with this, the second line of the stanza, as it appears on the discovered parchment:

" A Baltazarini, mon *gay* musicien "—

gai being the synonyme of *joyeux.*

But in the stanza, as M. Bach's hand predicted it would be found, the same line reads:

" A Baldazzarini, *tres bon* musicien."

A trifling coincidence, this; yet a most significant one, because inconsistent with any arranged scheme of deception. There can be no stronger proof of authenticity, than just such incidental trifles as these.

What shall we say of M. Bach's story? The documents from which I have compiled it were procured for me by an English friend in Paris, to whom I cannot sufficiently express my obligations for disinterested and untiring kindness, and whom I wish that I were at liberty here to thank by name. That friend, having made M. Bach's acquaintance, obtained personally from him all the particulars, with corrections of the newspaper statements and answers to various queries of mine, suggested by the documents as I first obtained them: also, through M. Bach's courtesy, the various photographs I possess, together with the following certificate, in M. Bach's hand-

* *Biographie Universelle des Musiciens*, vol. i. p. 232.

From the last sentence in the above it would appear that to Baltazarini—or *Balthazzarini*, as Lenglet-Dufresnoy spelled it, or *Baldazzarini*, as it was written by M. Bach's hand—the modern world owes its favorite amusement, the opera.

The uncertainty, in these old times, as to the spelling of proper names, especially in the case of persons of little note, is notorious.

writing, appended to that fac-simile of the original music, of which I have given two lines on page 416:

"This is a correct fac-simile from the sheet of music paper which I found on my bed, the morning of the fifth of May, 1865. The air and the words are truly those which I heard in my dream.

"N. G. BACH."

In addition, M. Bach (in reply to a suggestion of mine which some men would have deemed importunate) did me the favor to send me a letter, dated March 23, 1867, in which he says: "I attest the existence of the parchment, still in my possession, containing the verses composed by the king and addressed to the celebrated musician, Baldazarini; and that it was found in a secret compartment of the spinet which the king had given him; and also that the communication announcing the existence of the parchment, and stating that it had been placed there, is, in every point, the exact truth. I add that the photographs of the spinet and of the parchment, and the reproduction of the autograph of the music and words, are well executed and perfectly exact."

Such is the case in all important details. It is for the reader to decide whether, under the circumstances, the supposition of imposture is tenable.

What motive? Nothing whatever to gain, in a worldly sense. Much to risk and something to lose. To risk misconception, suspicion, perhaps the allegation of monomania; perhaps the charge of conspiracy to palm off on the world a series of deliberate, elaborate forgeries; forgeries involving a sacrilegious deception, seeing that there is question of sacred things connected not with this world only, but with that which is to come. Thus, to risk the loss of a character earned by the consistent integrity of a long and honored life. More certainly still, to attract importunate visitors, perhaps impertinent questioners, and thus to break up that domestic quiet so dear to a cultivated and studious sexagenarian.

But if character and all imaginable motive did not give the lie to any such suspicion, the circumstances are such that the theory of fraud is beset with extreme difficulties. The friend to whom I owe my documents showed the original of the song to Monsieur D——, one of the greatest harmonists of the day and quite a thesaurus of musical lore. This gentleman examined it critically, and declared to my friend that it was so exactly in the style of the epoch that it would require not only a great musical genius, but the special studies of a lifetime, to produce such an imitation. Monsieur D——, lacking faith in spirit intercourse, did not pretend to explain the mystery, but simply said that, though M. Bach was a meritorious musician, he regarded it as *absolutely impossible* that he should have composed the song.

Again, if composed by him, it must have been suddenly, in a single night, without chance of reference to old authorities. Whence, then, the coincidences between the words of the song * and the incidents in the life of Henry III. and of Marie de Clèves?

Every allusion has been verified, except that to the distant hunt (chasse lointaine): and—let Sadducism smile at my easy faith in the unseen—I confess my belief that if I had opportunity to consult the library of the British Museum, or, better yet, the *Bibliothèque Impériale*, I could verify that also.

Add to all this the minor peculiarities to which I have already adverted. Would any one, concerting a plan of forgery and similated prediction, be likely to contrive the variations between the predicted stanza and the original? or the inclosed ⌊ma], with its explanation? or the *si*, apparently a blunder, yet proving correct? or even the variations in spelling the musician's name?—most natural, if we consider the uncertain orthography of that day, but how unlikely to be planned? Again, it is only by inference and after long search that I con-

* My Paris informant tells me that M. Bach never wrote a verse of poetry in his life.

clude the words "triste et cloistrés" to be in exact accordance with the facts: how remote the chance, then, that M. Bach, during that mysterious night, should have acted upon a similar conclusion?

Yet again: if the communication indicating the hiding-place of the parchment be a forgery, then M. Bach must have found the parchment, without any directions as to its whereabouts, before the spinet was sent to the Retrospective Museum. Is it within the bounds of probability that the surprising discovery of such an interesting document should have been studiously kept concealed from every one, the spinet sent off under false pretences to the Museum, and then the communication concocted as an excuse to send for the instrument again and institute a pretended search?

I do not think that dispassionate readers will accept such violent improbabilities. But if not, what interesting suggestions touching spirit-intercourse and spirit-identity connect themselves with this simple narrative of M. Bach's spinet!

CHAPTER III.

A BEAUTIFUL SPIRIT MANIFESTING HERSELF.

More than forty years ago there died a young English lady, whom I knew intimately. She had enjoyed all the advantages of the most finished education that her country affords; spoke French and Italian fluently, had travelled over Europe, there meeting many distinguished persons of the day. And she had been favored by nature as much as by fortune. She was as amiable as accomplished, gifted with strong affections, great simplicity, and a temperament eminently spiritual and refined. I shall call her Violet.*

When, twenty-five years after her death, I first instituted researches in Spiritualism, the thought crossed my mind that if those who once took an interest in us during earth-life, were permitted still to commune with us when they had passed to another phase of being, Violet's spirit, of all others, might announce itself to me. But I have never, on any occasion, evoked spirits; deeming it wisest and best to await their good pleasure. And when month after month passed away and no sign came, I had quite ceased to expect it, or to dwell upon such a possibility.

I can scarcely express to the reader my surprise and emotion when, during a sitting held October 13, 1856, at Naples (Mrs. Owen and one other lady, not a professional medium, being present), the following incidents occurred.

The Promise kept.

The name of Violet was suddenly spelled out. After my

* Her true baptismal name (a somewhat uncommon one), which I dc not feel justified in giving, is, like that with which I have replaced it, typical of a favorite flower.

astonishment had somewhat subsided, I asked *mentally*, with what intent a name so well-remembered had been announced.

Answer.—" Gave pro—"

There the spelling stopped. Repeated invitations to proceed were unavailing: not another letter could we obtain. At last it occurred to me to ask: " Are the letters *p*, *r*, *o*, correct?"

Answer.—" No."

Question.—" Is the word 'gave' correct?"

Answer.—" Yes."

Then I said: " Please begin the word after 'gave' over again:" whereupon it spelled out, now and then correcting a letter, the sentence:

" Gave a written promise to remember you, even after death."

I think that no human being except such as have been unexpectedly brought, as I was then, almost within speech of the next world and its denizens, can realize the feeling which came over me, as these words slowly connected themselves. If there was one recollection of my youth that stood out, beyond all others, it was the reception, from Violet, of a letter written in prospect of death and containing, to the very words, the promise which now, after half a lifetime, came back to me from beyond the bourn. Such evidence as it was to me it can be to no one else. I have the letter still; but its existence was unknown except to me: it has never been seen by any one. How little could I foresee, when I first read it, that, after a quarter of a century, in a far, foreign land, the writer would be enabled to tell me that she had kept her word!

A few days afterward, namely during a session held on October 18, the same spirit having announced herself, I obtained, to various mental questions, replies characterized by the same pertinency and exactitude as are above evinced; the subjects of my questions being of a private character and the true replies being known to me alone. There was not a single failure; and, in the course of these replies, allusions were made to circumstances with which, so far as I know or believe, no one living in this world is acquainted except myself.

It is within my knowledge that many results similar to the above have been obtained by others. Yet very few of these reach the public at all; and when they do, they are usually couched in the most general and unsatisfactory terms. It needs, in such cases, as prompting motive to overcome a natural reluctance, the earnest wish, by such disclosure, to serve truth, and supply important testimony on a subject of vital importance to humankind. Let us examine that which is here supplied.

The results obtained were not due, in any sense, to what has sometimes been assumed as a cause of similar phenomena, under the name of "expectant attention." We were, at the time, in search of various physical tests which we had heard that others alleged they had witnessed; as motion without contact, writing by occult means, the exhibition of hands and the like. What came was utterly unforeseen, by me the person chiefly concerned as certainly as by the other assistants. When long-slumbering associations were called up by the sudden appearance of a name, it was assuredly in response to no thought or will or hope of mine, if consciousness be a guide to the existence of thought or feeling. And if not traceable to me, far less can it be imagined to have originated in either of the other assistants. They knew nothing of the letter, not even that it existed. They knew nothing of my question, for it had been mentally propounded. This narrows down the question of mundane influence to myself alone.

But there is additional proof that my expectations had no agency in this case. When, at the first attempt to reply to my question, the unlooked-for sentence had been partly spelled out—"Gave pro"—it did occur to me that the unfinished word might be "promise:" and it did suggest itself that the reference might be to the solemn pledge made to me, so many years before, by Violet. But what happened? The letters *p*, *r*, *o*, were declared to be incorrect; and I still remember my surprise and disappointment, as I erased them. But how much was that surprise increased when I found that the correction had been insisted on, only to make room for a fuller and more definite wording!—so definite, indeed, that if the document in question had been set forth in full, it could not have been more certainly designated. Under the circumstances, it is not even conceivable that *my* mind, or any intent of mine, had anything whatever to do in working out results. If a spirit-hand had visibly appeared, had erased the three letters, had inserted the omitted word "written" and then finished the sentence, it would have been more wonderful, certainly; but would the evidence have been more perfect that some occult will—some intention other than mine—was at work to bring about all this? And if to no earthly origin, to what other source than to the world of spirits can this occult agency rationally be traced?

Yet this was but the commencement of the numerous proofs, recurring throughout many years, that have assured me of the continued existence, and the identity, of a dear spirit-friend. These came to me chiefly after my return in 1859, from Naples to the United States.

Proof from a Stranger, Five Hundred Miles distant.

Five or six weeks after the publication of a work already referred to,* in February, 1860, my publisher introduced to me a gentleman who had just returned from Ohio, and who informed me that my book had attracted much attention in that State; adding that I might add to its circulation by sending a copy to Mrs. B——, then residing in Cleveland, proprietor of a book-store and one of the editors of a paper there. "She takes a deep interest in such subjects," he said, "and is, I believe, herself a medium."

* *Footfalls on the Boundary of Another World*; published January 1 1860.

I had never heard of the lady before, but I sent a copy of the book, with a brief note asking her acceptance of it, and soon had a reply, dated February 14.

In this letter, after some business details, the writer expressed to me the great satisfaction with which she had read the chapter in "Footfalls" entitled "The Change at Death," and added: "I am what is called a 'seeing medium.' While reading that chapter a female spirit that I had never seen before stood by me, as if listening, and said: 'I guided him in writing that; I helped to convince him of an immortal life.'" Then she subjoined a personal description of the appearance—including color of hair and eyes, complexion, etc.—which exactly corresponded to that of Violet. She added that a Cleveland merchant, who came in at the time and who is an impressional medium (though not known, nor desiring to be known, as such), said: "You have a new spirit to visit you to-day—a lady. She says she knew a Mrs. D——, naming an English lady not then living; known to Mrs. B—— (*not* to the merchant), by literary reputation, but never having been known to either of them personally.

Now Mrs. D—— was Violet's sister. But in my reply, which was partly on business, I neither alluded to the personal description that had been sent to me, nor to what had been said of Mrs. D——. In order to make the test as complete as possible I refrained from any expression which might lead Mrs. B—— to suppose that I recognized the person who had appeared to her. I merely added, to the business part of my letter, a few words to the effect that if she could obtain the spirit's name, or any further particulars tending to identify her, she would confer an obligation on me by informing me of it.

In reply I received two letters; one dated February 27, the other April 5. In these were stated: first, the baptismal name; second, that the spirit said that Mrs. D—— was her sister; third, one or two further particulars as to Violet: all this, accurately according to the facts. Mrs. B—— went on to say that some other details were added; but these seemed to refer to matters of so private and confidential a character that she thought it might be best to state them personally if, in returning to the West, I could pass through Cleveland. Being, however, obliged to start for Europe on business in two weeks, I asked, in reply, that she would put these on paper, which she did in a fourth letter, dated April 20. The particulars which she gave me had been obtained partly by herself, partly through the mediumship of the merchant to whom I have above referred.

When I said that the evidence in this case could never be to others what it was to me, I but faintly shadowed forth the truth. A portion of the wonders that opened upon me the reader can, indeed, appreciate. I had written a brief and purely business letter to a complete stranger, five hundred miles away, in a town which Violet had never seen, where I myself (so far as I can remember) had never been. Anything like suggestion or thought-reading or magnetic rapport was, under the circumstances, out of the question. Equally so was any knowledge, by a Cleveland editor or a Cleveland merchant, of a lady unknown to fame, who had died thousands of miles away, in another hemisphere. Yet from these distant strangers comes to me, unasked and as unexpected as a visit from Heaven, first a personal description agreeing with that of Violet and the mention of a name which strongly indicated that she was the person who had been communicating with them; then her own name; then her relationship with Mrs. D——: all, without the slightest clue afforded by myself.

These things my readers may appreciate, and they supply wonderful proofs of identity; but when, as in Mrs. B——'s last letter, various minute particulars connected with Violet's early life and mine—particulars unknown to any living creature on this side the Great Boundary—particulars indicated only, so that the writer herself could but very partially understand their import—particulars buried away not in the past alone but in hearts of which they were the most sacred remembrances—when these things came forth to light under the eyes of the survivor, they were, to him, internal evidence of the continued existence, beyond the death-change, of human memories, thoughts, affections—evidence such as cannot be transferred to any second person: such evidence as, from its very nature, can be received directly alone.

Here it may occur to the reader that, as all things, spiritual as well as material, are subject to law, there must have been *some* attraction or cause of election, determining Mrs. B—— as the medium, or Cleveland as the place, whence such a communication should come to me.

No doubt. And one can see how this may have been. Mrs. B—— has the olden gift,* by St. Paul called the "discerning of spirits;" and, at the time the spirit appeared, she was reading—with approval, it seems—a chapter on the "Change at Death," into which I had thrown some of the strongest and deepest of my religious convictions. † This seems to have been the attraction; for it was during the perusal of that portion of my book that Violet, for the first time, showed herself to Mrs. B——.

Is this explanation far-fetched? Is it irrational to ascribe, to so slight a cause, the spirit's unexpected visit? Yet there had come to my knowledge, a year before, a similar case, perfectly authenticated.

The Apparition of the Betrothed.

In October of the year 1854, my father called on Miss A——, a young lady of his acquaintance, residing near London. Her powers as a medium, though known only to a private circle of friends, are of the highest order. She has habitually discerned spirits from her earliest age, years before the modern phase of Spiritualism had come up. Various other

* 1 Corinthians xii. 10.

† *Footfalls on the Boundary of Another World*, Book vi. chap. 1; pp. 476–503.

manifestations, also, of a striking kind, occur in her presence.

My father found her somewhat indisposed, reclining on a sofa, engaged in reading. She laid aside her book, as he entered, and was about to rise; but he begged her to remain, adding that, as he had come hoping for opportunity of examining spiritual phenomena, he would sit down alone at a table not far from the sofa, to ascertain if he could obtain rappings. He did so; and after a time raps were heard, though Miss A—— did not touch the table.

"Can you perceive," my father asked, "the presence of any spirits?"

"Yes," she replied; "I see one, that of a young lady."

"Can you tell her name?"

"No; she has never given it to me, though I have several times seen her, as I sat reading this book"—and she pointed to the volume beside her—"but perhaps we can get the name by rapping."

And, in effect, there was immediately spelled out, "Grace Fletcher."

"What!" said my father; "my old friend, Grace Fletcher?"

"Who is Grace Fletcher?" the young lady asked: "I never heard the name before."

"You could not have known her, for she died thirty or forty years ago. I knew her intimately; and a more beautiful character, moral and intellectual, I never met."

"It is singular," said the young lady, "that I almost always see her spirit when I sit down to study this book; and only then."

"Pray what work is it you have been studying?" my father asked.

"Dr. Thomas Brown's Mental Philosophy;" and she handed my father the volume.

He took it, exclaiming: "How strange! What a wonderful coincidence!"

"What is there wonderful in it?"

My father then explained that, as he had always understood, Dr. Brown and Miss Fletcher were deeply attached to each other, and that their intimacy was expected to ripen into marriage. "But she died at nineteen," he added, "and I do not think poor Brown ever got over it; for he survived her three or four years only."

Grace Fletcher who, from all I have heard of her, well deserved my father's encomium, was the daughter of a talented mother, long noted in the literary circles of Edinburgh and who died some thirteen or fourteen years since, at a very advanced age. I have ascertained through a lady who was well acquainted with the family that between Dr. Brown and Miss Fletcher there was well known to exist, probably not a positive engagement, but certainly so strong a mutual attachment, that their friends felt confident it would be a match. She died about the year 1816; and he, in 1820.*

I had the above from the young lady herself;† and I know that its accuracy may be strictly depended on. One of the recollections of my childhood is my father's sorrow when the unexpected news of Grace Fletcher's death reached him.

The point in this case which gives it value is, that the young seeress had never heard Miss Fletcher's name, nor had she the least idea, till my father informed her, of the connection there had existed in life between the lady whose spirit the raps announced, and the author of the book during the perusal of which that spirit was wont to appear. As a chance coinci-

* In the prime of life, aged forty-two. He was Professor of Moral Philosophy in the University of Edinburgh. His well-known *Lectures on the Philosophy of the Human Mind*, above referred to, reached the eighth edition in 1834.

† In 1859, I met her in London at Lady B——'s, where she was always a welcome guest. All her friends speak of her in the highest terms, and my own acquaintance with her, through several months, confirmed my opinion of her intelligence and integrity.

dence we cannot reasonably regard it. Standing alone it is insufficient foundation for a theory. But the appearance of Violet to Mrs. B——, an utter stranger alike to her and to me, during the perusal of a book of mine, is an incident of the same class; and if such should be found to accumulate, they will furnish proof that a spirit may occasionally—though it be rarely—look back from its next phase of life to this, drawn down by the desire to note the effect which efforts, made on earth, by a dear friend, to enlighten mankind, may, from time to time, be producing. It is a reasonable belief that benevolent spirits, in their world, continue to take interest in the improvement of ours.

I know not that, in this case, I can adduce stronger proof of identity than the above, but I have had additional tests, some of which may tend to fortify the faith of my readers.

Typical and Literal Tests.

Some two weeks after the receipt of Mrs. B——'s second letter, namely, on the thirteenth of March, 1860, in the forenoon, I called on Mr. Charles Foster, to whose mediumship I have already referred. A lady well and favorably known to the literary world, and whom I shall call Miss P——, accompanied me. The visit was at her request, as she had never witnessed any spiritual phenomena whatever; but had heard much about them, and desired to judge for herself. She had never seen Mr. Foster.

I mentioned to Mr. Foster, in a general way, that I had recently received, from a stranger at a distance, an alleged communication from a spirit, which had passed away many years before; but I studiously withheld the name and all clue to personal identity, adding, however, that I should be glad if, through him, any further test could be given.

During the first part of the session Mr. Foster addressed himself entirely to Miss P——. The incredulous look with which that lady sat down soon changed to one of seriousness, then of deepest feeling. The test she received that day led to researches which made her a spiritualist for life.*

Then he turned suddenly to me: "Mr. Owen, I see a spirit —a lady—standing beside you, perhaps the same of whom you spoke to me. She holds in her hands a basket of flowers. Ah! that is peculiar; they are all violets."

I.—"Does she communicate her name?"

Mr. Foster paused. After a time, "No," he said, "but she has taken one of the flowers—a single violet—and laid it before you. Has all this any meaning for you?"

"Yes."

"But we ought to get the name. I usually do."

And, at his request, I wrote down seven female baptismal names, including that of Violet, taking care not to pause more at one than at the other.

Mr. Foster took the paper, and, with a single glance at it, tore off each name separately; rolled them up into small pellets and threw these down on a pile of pellets (some twelve or fourteen) which he had previously made, some of them being blank. There were thus about twenty pellets in all. He bade me take them up and hold them, in my open hand, under the table. I

* I am at liberty to give an outline only of the test here referred to, and have substituted another name (Medway) for the true one.

Mr. Foster said he saw the appearance of a young man standing beside Miss P——; and he described his appearance. "Above his head," he went on, "I see the words: 'Fidelity even beyond the grave!'" Miss P——'s face betrayed much emotion, mingled, however, I plainly saw, with doubt. Then Foster suddenly added: "Ah! here is a name—Medway." Upon which the lady sank her face on the table, without a word. Nor, throughout the rest of the session, did she allude to what had passed.

I afterward mentioned the name to a sister of Miss P——, asking if he had ever been among their acquaintances.

"How did you hear of him?" she asked me, astonished.

I told her.

"It is all true," she said in reply. "Many years ago we were intimately acquainted with him. My sister was engaged to him; but he died a short time before the day appointed for their marriage."

did so. After a time he said to me: "The spirits desire to have your hat under the table." Accordingly he put it there, but immediately replaced both his hands on the table, saying: "Spirit, when you have selected the pellet, will you let us know by rapping?" About a minute passed when the raps sounded.

Mr. Foster.—"Shall I take up the hat?"

Answer.—"No."

I.—"Shall I?"

Answer.—"No."

Miss P.—"Shall I?"

Answer.—"Yes."

Thereupon the table, with a sudden and somewhat violent movement, tilted up on Miss P——'s side, so that, without moving from her seat, she could reach the hat from the floor. Therein, lying between two gloves, was the pellet. She handed it to me and I was about to open it, when Mr. Foster said:

"Please do not open it yet. Let me try if I can get the same name written under the table."

He tore off a small piece of thin paper, took that and a pencil in one hand, and held both for twelve or fifteen seconds beneath the table. Then, withdrawing his hand, after a glance at the paper and the remark, "I believe there is a name on it," he handed it to me. The name was in pencil, but I could not make out a single letter. At Mr. Foster's suggestion I held the paper, reversed, against the window-pane. Then I read distinctly through the paper from the unwritten side, in minute characters, the name Violet.

Then only I first opened the pellet. The same name there.*

I did not suffer Mr. Foster to see either. After a few seconds his arm seemed slightly convulsed, as by a feeble electric shock; and he said: "The name is on my arm;" where-

* I have preserved the bit of thin paper, and also the pellet. I need scarcely here remind the reader, that, as already stated, Violet is an assumed name. Of course it was the true name, and the flower typical of that name, which were actually given.

upon he bared his left arm to the elbow, and I read thereon distinctly the name VIOLET. I did not, however, pronounce it, but left him to spell it out, letter by letter. The letters looked as if they had been traced by a painter's brush, with pink color. They were about an inch and a quarter in height; printed characters, as if somewhat carelessly done, but perfectly legible; the strokes being about an eighth of an inch in thickness. The first letter was near the elbow joint, and the rest were traced along the inside of the arm; the last letter being on part of the palm next to the wrist, just below the root of the thumb. Miss P—— read the name, deciphering it without any difficulty.

During all the time of these experiments except at the moment when he placed my hat on the ground, and during the few seconds when he put the paper under the table to have the name written on it, Mr. Foster sat quietly *with both hands on the table.*

The room was well lighted by two windows.

Miss P—— had never heard Violet's name; nor, as I have already stated, had Mr. Foster.

Here were four tests: not presenting themselves spontaneously, indeed, as did those which came to me through Mrs. B——; on the contrary obtained by aid of a professional medium whom I had visited, hoping for something of the kind: but yet to be judged fairly, by their internal evidence, notwithstanding.

1. The appearance to Mr. Foster of the basket of flowers, and the single flower laid down before me, when I asked for Violet's name.

2. The pellet, selected out of twenty, taken from my hand and placed in my hat.

3. The writing, under the table, of the name so that it read on the reverse side.

And 4. The name written on the arm.

The peculiarity of the basket containing a single species only of flower, and the name of that species corresponding to the name of the alleged spirit, together with the selection of a single flower when I asked for the name, cannot rationally be ascribed to chance.

As to the pellet, since Mr. Foster had his hands on the table, full in view, it was a physical impossibility that he should have taken it, even if he had known which, out of the twenty, to select.

As to the writing under the table, though it may be alleged that practice might enable a person to write so that it should read on the reverse side, and that this might have been done with one hand on the knee, yet the writing itself (now before me) seems to refute this. I have just carefully examined it. The paper is nearly as thin as tracing paper; the name is written in a current lady's hand, as if the pencil-point had just lightly touched the surface, the pencil not having sank at all into the paper; and there is no indication of the writing on the reverse. I do not think it possible for any one, holding a pencil and paper, in one hand, for fifteen seconds, under a table, to have produced a word thus written. But, in addition to this, Foster had no clue whatever to the name.

The same is true of the name on the arm, with this added difficulty: the arm having been covered, up to the moment when the medium bared it and showed the name, and his hands up to that time, having been seen by us resting quietly on the table, by what possible expedient could he have produced the pink lettering?

During the decade from 1860 to 1870 I have had, through various mediums, numerous communications from Violet: none, however, of any length; the longest being that relative to the birth of Christ. * They were usually only brief, cordial messages of affection, or short suggestions on ethical, philosophical, or spiritual subjects. On two occasions, at intervals of years, instead of the name, there was only allusion made to the flower. One of these came through a Boston medium, the

* See Book i. chapter 3, where it is given in full.

other through a lady (not a professional medium) in Washington city: both being strangers to each other and to Violet's name or history.

Finally I obtained, by accident as we usually say, a remarkable test, differing in character from any of the above.

The Portrait with Emblem.

In the spring of 1867, being then in New York, I made the acquaintance of a Mr. Anderson, who, without previous instruction and by spirit influence, as he alleged, had produced likenesses of deceased persons, many of which were recognized by their friends. He stated to me that a clergyman of his acquaintance desired to meet me; and I met him, by appointment, at Mr. Anderson's rooms, on the afternoon of the twenty-first of March.

While we were conversing, Mr. Anderson brought me a large sheet of drawing-paper, requesting me to observe that it was blank on both sides, and asking me to tear a small piece from one corner of the sheet, so as to be able to identify it. I tore irregular pieces from *two* corners. He then requested me to note the hour, and retired to an inner room.

I supposed that I should have a portrait; and, as my father was a well-known man, of whom many engraved likenesses exist, I thought it would probably be one of him, and felt that, under the circumstances, even if it resembled, it would be an insufficient test.

But in exactly twenty-eight minutes, Mr. Anderson, returning, pinned against the wall a portrait, in pencil, not of my father, but a female head and bust, life-size, which, from its general outline and expression, I recognized at once as Violet's. On looking again, however, the features seemed to me more regular than her's and the whole face idealized. The *pose* was graceful: my eye ran over the lines, but was suddenly arrested —could it be? Hardly trusting my senses, I went closer to examine. It was unmistakable. There—as ornament at the lower point of the opening of the dress in front—was the *typical flower!*

I need not say that I had never made the least allusion to Violet in Mr. Anderson's presence; and that I am convinced he spoke truth when he declared to me that he had never heard of her.*

I carefully adjusted the torn fragments of paper to the corners whence I had taken them, and found the proof thus afforded that it was the same sheet I had marked twenty-eight minutes before it reappeared, absolutely perfect.

I showed the portrait, some days afterward, to my friend Mr. Carpenter, the artist,† without telling him how I obtained it.

He examined it carefully. "A little out of drawing," he said, "but clever and graceful: peculiar, too. A young artist?"

"One without much experience, I believe. How long would a good artist take to make such a portrait?"

"That depends upon whether he hit off the likeness at once. If he did and worked hard, he might finish it in a day. But, in a general way, it would take two days, perhaps more."

"How if the artist had begun and finished it within half an hour?"

"There is no man living who could do so."

That was my opinion also, supposing the artist left to his own resources: but I was glad to have it confirmed by so competent a judge.‡

Upon me these cumulative proofs of identity have produced

* Mr. Anderson appeared to me a quiet, frank, simple man: speaking modestly of what he deemed a spiritual gift, and blaming himself for his own wavering faith in its continuance. He would accept of no remuneration from me: it having been, as he reminded me, a volunteered effort.

† Best known as the author of that most truthful and valuable historical painting: *The Emancipation Proclamation before the Cabinet.*

‡ I shall be glad to show to any artist or other sincere inquirer, the original portrait, with the attesting fragments, exactly as I obtained it, at the end of the twenty-eight minutes.

a profound conviction that Violet has manifested herself; keeping a sacred promise after long years, and sending to me, from another sphere, missives of friendship and words of instruction. I cannot judge what degree of belief this recital of these proofs may create in others.

BOOK V.

THE CROWNING PROOF OF IMMORTALITY.

"And when they heard of the resurrection of the dead, some mocked: and others said, 'We will hear thee again of this matter.'"—ACTS xvii. 32.

CHAPTER I.

THE GREAT FAITH-ARTICLE OF THE FIRST CENTURY.

"If the dead rise not, then is not Christ raised: and if Christ be not raised, your faith is vain."—1 CORINTHIANS xv. 16, 17.

ACCORDING to the best authorities, the Book of Acts was written about thirty years after the crucifixion. It is one of the most interesting and instructive of historical episodes, if we read it, as but few of us do, unblinded by the glamour of stereotyped preconceptions.

There was, of course, no New Testament in those days. During the first half of these thirty years there was not even a biography of Christ; and but one, that of Matthew, until near the close of that period: nor have we any proof that even Matthew's narrative was then known, or read, in the Christian congregations. All the apostolic letters of Paul, with the single exception of Thessalonians,* were written but a few years before the Acts were penned. The same is true of the other epistles; with the exception of that of James, which last was written about the middle of these thirty years.

Thus the faith of the disciples during this period was based

* Written about the year 53, or twenty years after Christ's death.

only on personal recollections, and on oral traditions of recent date. It was much strengthened, no doubt, by the appearance among them of those spiritual gifts * which Christ promised to such as trusted in him. † But it was founded chiefly on one great phenomenon: the appearance of Christ, after death, to a number of witnesses, of whom many yet survived. To this, on every great occasion, the apostles were wont to appeal. ‡ It was, indeed, the rock-foundation of their creed, failing which they admitted that the entire superstructure must fall. "If the dead rise not, then is not Christ raised; and if Christ be not raised, your faith is vain."

The triumph of their faith, then, was, that immortality had been brought to light: not set forth as a probability by analogical argument, not recommended to belief by glosses and quiddities of the schools; but brought into the light of day, where the senses can perceive it, where the highest of all human evidences can assure its reality. And the test-proof of immortality among these early disciples of Christ was *that the dead could return;* § it was that they themselves, to use the modern term, had seen the apparition of their Master.

Sceptics deny that they saw him. Strauss, assuming that an apparition would be a miracle, and holding miracles to be impossible, discredits the narrative. Yet he candidly states his conviction that the disciples, self-deceived through the excited state of their minds, firmly believed that Christ had appeared to them. He says:

* 1 Corinthians xii. 8–11.

† John xiv. 12.

‡ Acts ii. 32; iii. 15; iv. 33; x. 40, 41; xiii. 30, 31; and others.

§ It was not Christ alone whom (as we are told) they had seen: if we may trust the record "the graves were opened; and many bodies of the saints which slept arose, and came out of the graves after his resurrection, and appeared unto many."—Matthew xxvii. 52, 53.

The decayed body does not come out of the grave; that is not the mode in which an apparition is formed: but that was the popular conception of the phenomenon in Matthew's day. How often are genuine phenomena incorrectly explained!

"From the epistles of Paul and the Acts, it is certain that the apostles themselves had the persuasion that they had seen the Arisen. . . . For the rest, the passage from the first Epistle to the Corinthians is not hereby weakened which, undoubtedly genuine, was written about the year 59 after Christ, therefore not thirty years after his resurrection. Upon this information we must admit that many members of the first community, still living at the composition of that epistle, particularly the apostles, were persuaded that they had witnessed the appearance of the risen Christ." *

The text to which Strauss here refers is St. Paul's assertion that he has taught what he himself had received, namely, that, after Christ was risen "he was seen of Cephas [that is, Peter], then of the twelve: after that, he was seen of above five hundred brethren at once; of whom the greater part remain until this present, but some are fallen asleep. After that, he was seen of James; then of all the apostles." †

—Seen, not by Peter and James alone, not by the apostles alone, but by *five hundred* brethren at once. And the belief of these men in the reality of what they saw was such that they endured bonds and scourgings and persecutions even unto death, under that sustaining faith. The record of all this, too, was made within thirty years of the time it happened; and is admitted, by a critic so learned and critical as Strauss, to be "undoubtedly genuine."

For any natural event such testimony would be overwhelming. Strauss, having made up his mind that an apparition is an impossibility, disbelieves the story. I, having, like the disciples, witnessed an apparition, ‡ know, as they did, that it is not impossible; and believe as they did, that Christ showed himself to them. I can thoroughly understand, though I might not have imitated, that constancy of faith which braved sufferings and death.

* *Leben Jesu*, pp. 629, 652.

† 1 *Corinthians* xv. 5, 6, 7.

‡ See Book v. chapter 3.

If the religious world is ever to attain the vantage ground that was occupied by the Christians of the apostolic age, it must convince itself that an apparition is a natural phenomenon, of occasional occurrence. Till then, a large fraction of the intelligent portion of society—its scientific leaders especially—will continue to deny, like Strauss—will stand out, like Thomas, saying: "I must see before I believe."

Therefore the question "Is it important to study the subject of apparitions?" resolves itself into another: "Is it important to have assured proof of immortal life?"

I make, to the reader, no apology for the space I occupy in illustrating this and cognate phenomena. The world owes to itself an apology for its apathy on the subject.

CHAPTER II.

APPARITIONS SHOWING THEMSELVES SPONTANEOUSLY.

"To a mind not influenced by popular prejudice, it will be scarcely possible to believe that apparitions would have been vouched for in all countries, had they never been seen in any."—REV. GEORGE STRAHAN, D.D.*

ONE of the most remarkable phases of scepticism is that which denies, what all ages have admitted, the occasional reappearance of what we call the dead. The fantastic accessories of current ghost stories—hideous spectres, naked skeletons clanking chains, odors of brimstone, lights burning blue—have mainly contributed to this modern Sadducism. False ideas and morbid feelings touching death have unsettled our judgment, even our perceptions. Those whom we loved in this world we have learned to fear, as soon as they passed to another. We think, with terror, of their reappearance; we faint, perhaps, if they suddenly present themselves: for terror blinds; it is the parent of superstition.

In the nursery, or by the home fireside, our children hear horrible ghost-stories, shuddering as they listen. This is spiritual poison, fatal alike to equanimity and to simple religious truth. If we speak to children of ghosts at all, we ought to tell them, just as we relate any natural event, that we shall all be ghosts by and by; that only part of our life is spent here; the rest of it in another world which we cannot see, but which is better and more beautiful than this. We ought to add that perhaps we shall be able to come back from that world and show ourselves to some of our old friends; and that, may be,

* In the Preface to his *Prayers and Meditations of Dr. Samuel Johnson*, London, 1785.

they themselves will be so fortunate, before they go, as to see some person who has gone before—or what people call a ghost. *

Possibly their nerves might be somewhat tried, in case this should happen; just as a person, hearing thunder for the first time, often trembles at the sound. But, if well-trained, they would soon witness, without undue excitement, either phenomenon. Whenever men, in the mass, attain to this frame of mind, apparitions will probably become more common. Spirits, reading our thoughts, doubtless often refrain from showing themselves when they perceive that they will only be objects of terror.

Short of space and having already treated the subject of spontaneous apparitions at considerable length, † I here confine myself to a single example; a narrative which I am able to fortify with name, place, and date. It is one of a numerous class, an appearance of a dear friend soon after death. ‡

A Father, dying in Europe, appears to his Son in America.

In the year 1862, Mr. Bradhurst Schieffelin, of the well-known firm of Schieffelin & Co., New York, kindly furnished me with this narrative, sent with the following note:

"New York, *June* 11, 1862.

"Dear Sir: Herewith inclosed I have the pleasure to hand

* I taught my children after that fashion. The result, even in early childhood, was some such expression as this: "I *do* wish I could see a ghost: could not you show us one, Papa?"

† In *Footfalls on the Boundary of Another World*, Book iv. chapter 3, pp. 358–430.

‡ One of the members of a society formed in 1851 by distinguished graduates in the English University of Cambridge, for the purpose of investigating spiritual phenomena, told me that their researches had resulted in a conviction, shared, he believed, by all the members, that there *is* sufficient testimony for the appearance, about the time of death, or after it, of deceased persons.—See *Footfalls*, note, pp. 33, 34; and, for the printed circular of the society, see Appendix to that work, Note A., p. 513.

vou a letter from the Rev. Frederick Steins, relating the apparition of his father. Mr. Steins, a German gentleman of the utmost respectability, is pastor of the Madison Street Presbyterian Church in this city, having a large German congregration.

"This letter, which you may preserve as evidence, I have obtained for publication, and I shall be glad if it prove of service to you.

"Yours truly,

"BRADHURST SCHIEFFELIN.

"To the Honorable
ROBERT DALE OWEN."

The inclosure is as follows:

"NEW YORK, *June* 10, 1862.

"In compliance with the request in your note, I here give the special facts connected with the apparition of my father.

"It was on the thirteenth of December, 1847, as I was walking, with my two eldest sons, in Grand street, New York. It was in the forenoon, before twelve o'clock, and the sidewalk was full of people. There the whole figure of my father suddenly appeared to me. He was in his usual dress, his well-remembered cap on his head, his pipe in his hand, and he gazed on me with an earnest look; then, as suddenly, disappeared.

"I was very much terrified, and immediately wrote home, relating what had happened. Some time afterward I received a letter from one of my brothers, written from Neukirchen, Rhenish Prussia, the family residence, informing me that on the morning of the thirteenth of December, our father had died there. At breakfast on that day he was in his usual health, and had been speaking of me with great anxiety. After breakfast he passed out into the yard; and, in returning, he dropped dead, overtaken by a sudden fit of apoplexy.

"I learned afterward that, at the moment of death, he wore

the very dress in which I had seen him; the same cap on his head; his pipe, as usual, in his hand.

"Yours,

"FR. STEINS.

"To BRADHURST SCHIEFFELIN, ESQ."

The anxious interest which the father expressed in his ab sent son, immediately before death, is a noteworthy incident in this case.*

Narratives of cases similar to the above could be multiplied indefinitely. A very remarkable one—a family reminiscence—furnished to me by my friend, William Howitt, will be found in the work to which I have referred.†

* Compare with this a similar expression of affection by the dying Mrs. Marshall toward the child Cecilia; to whom, immediately after death, she appeared. See preceding Book ii. chapter 1.

† *Footfalls*, p. 371.

CHAPTER III.

MY OWN EXPERIENCE TOUCHING APPARITIONS.

"Segnius irritant animos demissa per aurem,
Quam quæ sunt oculis subjecta fidelibus."

HORACE—A. P.

I HAVE no mediumistic powers—none of the spiritual gifts enumerated by Paul and considered by him as desirable. I can see nothing, hear nothing, except what others, with quick eyes and ears, can see and hear. As to the reality of subjective apparitions I have to trust to the testimony of the seer or seeress; fortified, sometimes, by information touching worldly affairs that has been furnished by these invisible forms, and afterward ascertained to be true.* Perhaps, at this stage of spiritual progress, I am, because myself an outsider, more likely to gain the ear, and the confidence, of the outside world.

If, some day, there should appear a man, endowed alike with the highest spiritual gifts and with the most eminent moral and intellectual powers, his influence on civilized society might be immense. Meanwhile a mere spectator may obtain a degree of credit for dispassionate judgment which would be refused to an actor.

I regret, however, that it has never been my good fortune to witness an objective apparition, spontaneously presenting itself. I had to seek before I found. But if my readers will follow me in the relation of what I did find, I think they will admit that I have taken what reasonable precautions I could, alike against self-delusion and imposture. That I was in search of what I found is, in itself, no proper bar to my testi-

* A remarkable example will be found in *Footfalls*, Book iv. chapter 3; story of the *Old Kent Manor House*, pp. 414–427.

mony. If I were about to make a study of earthquakes and volcanic phenomena, I should be likely to visit the western coast of South America, the southern portion of the Italian peninsula; perhaps the islands of Sumatra, Java, Iceland. It is no disparagement to results that they have been obtained by expressly placing one's self in the way of obtaining them.

My experience in this field, though not so varied as that of some others, has been a remarkable one. If my life were extended to the term ascribed to the antediluvian patriarchs, I should remember, to my dying day, the first time I was visited by an appearance which all the attendant circumstances concurred in proving to have been a visitor from another phase of being. It occurred, eleven years ago, at the house of Mr. Daniel Underhill, in New York.

An eventful Hour with Leah Fox.

It was on the evening of Sunday, the twenty-first of October, 1860. The sitting was held in Mr. Underhill's dining-room, lasting from ten till eleven o'clock P.M.

The room was lighted by gas. There were two windows fronting the street; three doors; one opening on a corridor whence a staircase ascended to the next floor; another opening on a short passage leading to the kitchen; the third, the door of a pantry in which were crockery and various other articles, including a barrel of loaf-sugar in one corner.

Before we had any demonstrations the raps requested us to wait until the domestics had retired. There were two servant girls in the kitchen, whom Mrs. Underhill sent upstairs to bed, so that everything was profoundly still on that floor of the house. Then we fastened the inside blinds of both windows, so as to exclude all light from the street.

Before commencing the session, at Mr. Underhill's request, I shut and locked the three doors above referred to, leaving the keys in the doors; so that no one, even if furnished with keys, could open them from without. I satisfied myself, by careful personal inspection of the furniture, and otherwise, that there was no one in the pantry, nor any one in the dining-room except the three persons who, along with myself, assisted at the sitting.

These persons were Mr. Daniel Underhill, Mrs. Underhill (Leah Fox), and her nephew, Charles, twelve years old. We sat down to a centre-table, three feet eleven inches in diameter, of black walnut, and without table-cover. (I had previously looked under it; nothing to be seen there.) The gas-burner was immediately over it. I sat on the east side of the table, Mr. Underhill opposite to me, Mrs. Underhill on my left hand, and Charles on the right. There was no fire in the room.

The rappings commenced, gradually increasing in number and force. After a short interval they spelled: "Put out the gas." It was accordingly extinguished and the room remained in total darkness. Then, "Join hands." Shortly after doing so I felt, several times, a cool breeze blowing on my cheek.* Then was spelled: "Do not break the circle." We obeyed; and, except for a second or two at a time, it remained, on my part, unbroken throughout the rest of the sitting.

After a few minutes I perceived a light, apparently of a phosphorescent character, on my left, near the floor. It was, at first, of a rectangular form, with the edges rounded. I judged it to be about four inches long and two and a half inches wide. It seemed like an open palm illuminated; but though the light which emanated from it showed quite distinctly its entire surface, I could distinguish no fingers. For a time it moved about, near the floor; then it rose into the air and floated about the room, sometimes over our heads.

* See an article entitled *The Child's Bones Found;* "Footfalls," Book iv. chapter 3. It relates to the Seeress of Prevorst. After stating that her mother and sister did not see an apparition which showed itself to her, it is added: "But both, at the times when the spirit appeared to the seeress, frequently felt the sensation as of a breeze blowing upon them:" p. 399.

Such a sensation, as I know from personal experience, frequently precedes, or accompanies, spiritual phenomena.

After a time it changed its appearance and increased in brightness. It then resembled an opaque oval substance, about the size of a child's head, muffled up in the folds of some very white and shining material, like fine linen, only brighter. As it moved about, I began to hear, at first imperfectly, afterward somewhat more distinctly, the rustling as of a silk dress, or of other light article of female apparel; giving the impression that one or more persons were moving silently about the room. Then the light passed behind Mrs. Underhill; then I saw it close to Mr. Underhill and just opposite to me. Mr. Underhill said: "Can you not go to Mr. Owen; do try." Thereupon it moved slowly around to my left side. This time the folds appeared to have dropped; and what seemed a face (still covered, however, with a luminous veil,) came bending down within five or six inches of my own face, as I turned toward it. As it approached, I plainly distinguished the semi-luminous outline of an entire figure of the usual female stature. I saw, very distinctly, the arms moving. At the lower extremity of its right arm, as if on the palm of the hand, the figure bore what seemed a rectangular substance, about four inches by two, as nearly as I could estimate. This substance was more brightly illuminated than the rest of the figure. It may have been only the illuminated palm, but I do not think it was; it seemed more like a transparent box with phosphorescent light within it. Whatever it was, the figure raised it above its head and then passed it slowly down close to what seemed the face and then over the upper part of the body, as one might pass a lantern over any object, with intent to make it visible. This action it repeated several times. By aid of the illumination thus afforded I saw, more distinctly than before, the general form of the face and figure; but both appeared covered with a half-transparent veil, and I could distinguish no features: nor were the outlines of the body, nor of the limbs, sharply defined. The motion of the right arm, with the light, was the most marked and frequent.

While this was taking place I held Mrs. Underhill's hand

and Charles's. As the various phases of the phenomena succeeded each other, I remarked on what I saw; and Mr. Underhill, from the opposite side of the table, responded to my remarks; so that I am quite certain he was seated there.

I expressed a wish that the figure would touch me: and Mr. Underhill said, from his place: "We are very anxious that the spirit should touch Mr. Owen, if it can."

Thereupon I felt what seemed a human hand laid on my head. And, as I looked steadily at the figure, which stood on my left side, I saw its head bend toward my left shoulder. A moment afterward I *felt*, and simultaneously *heard*, just behind the point of that shoulder, a kiss imprinted.

I could not, for any physical fact, obtain the evidence of three senses—sight, touch, and hearing—more distinctly than in this case I did.

Immediately afterward, I saw this luminous body pass behind me; what seemed, by the touch, to be hands gently laid hold of both my shoulders and turned me round to the right. I looked on that side and the figure now stood by my right shoulder.

After pausing there for a few seconds, it moved toward the window farthest from me, and we heard the sounds as if some one were attempting to open the window blind. Mr. Underhill, from his place, remarked that it would probably be able to effect this; for it had done so on a previous occasion. The blind was in four compartments, each of which could be opened or closed by raising or lowering a wire attached to movable slats. The figure opened the upper, left-hand quarter of the blind, so that a faint light shone in from the street lamps. I was looking at the window when this occurred.

Up to this time the appearance, gradually becoming more luminous, had been in sight, moving about the room, fully five minutes. There was not the slightest footfall when it moved. My hearing is very acute; I listened for every sound; and as, in the intervals of conversation, the silence was unbroken, I could have detected the fall of the lightest footstep.

From this time the light which illuminated the figure gradually faded; and soon I could no longer distinguish any form. The slight, rustling sound, unaccompanied by footsteps, still, however, continued.

Suddenly we heard a noise as of the door opposite to me being unlocked; then of its being hastily opened and shut; then the rustling sound approached me on the left, and a key was laid on my left hand. Then a second door was heard to be unlocked in the same way, and I heard another key laid on the table just before me. Then a third door (that of the cupboard, by the sound,) was heard to be unlocked and opened, and a key, as if pitched over our heads, was heard to drop, with a clatter, on the table.

While this was going on, I commented, from time to time, on each occurrence, and received answers from Mr. Underhill, from his place at the table opposite to me.

While we were conversing, there was a rattling of the crockery in the cupboard. Mrs. Underhill expressed her apprehensions as to some favorite china, but Mr. Underhill replied: "I will trust the spirits;" and then added: "Cannot the spirit bring something to Mr. Owen?" Almost immediately there was set down on the table, close to my left hand, some object which I touched, and it proved to be a cut-glass goblet. In setting it down, what seemed a human hand touched mine, and immediately afterward was laid, several times, on my shoulder. I expressed a desire that it would distinctly grasp my hand, to which Mr. Underhill responded. Instantly a small hand, or what in touch perfectly resembled one, took hold of my hand and grasped it. Then it clasped my bare wrist, gently but with a firm grasp; then my lower arm, then my upper arm; each time with a distinct grasp. I could not have distinguished the touch from that of a human hand. It was a little cooler than mine, but not disagreeably so. There was nothing chilly or clammy or otherwise unpleasant about it. There was, after this, throughout the sitting, no sound whatever of opening or closing doors.

While it was touching me thus, Mr. Underhill said: "Can you fill the goblet you brought to Mr. Owen with water?" There was a rustling but no footstep; a slight noise in the pantry, and then the sound of something dropped into the goblet; but, putting my hand in, I felt no water. In so doing I broke the circle only for a moment.

Then, just behind me, I heard a sound as if the glass of the clock on the mantle-piece were touched and shaken.

All this time there was no word spoken except by those at the table; but, once or twice, there was a whistling sound in the air.

When, soon after, we were bidden, by the raps, to relight the gas, I found three door-keys on the table, the goblet also and, within it, a lump of loaf-sugar. Both the room-doors were closed, but, on trying them, I found that neither was locked. Two of the keys on the table fitted them. The door of the pantry, which the third key fitted, stood open, and the cover of the barrel of sugar was pushed partly off. The left-hand upper portion of the blind at which we had seen and heard the figure, was open.

These are facts, all briefly noted down the same evening on which they happened, and written out in full the next morning.

The allegations, by the raps, were that the spirit present was that of a daughter of Mrs. Fox who had died young, and that other spirits were present (among them an Indian spirit), aiding her to show herself to our circle. Emily—that was the girl's name—had been Mrs. Underhill's favorite sister, long mourned over, and had lain, during the last hour of her life and at the moment of death, in Mrs. Underhill's arms. Mr. Underhill stated to me that he had seen the same spirit, as distinctly, several times before; and that he had been able to distinguish the features. He appeared, also, on this occasion, to have perceived the whole figure, and especially the features, more distinctly than I did, though my natural sight has always been keen, and, except within ordinary reading distance, is still nearly as strong as it was thirty years ago. With these exceptions, all present, so far as I could judge by comparing notes with them during and after the sitting, seemed to have seen and heard the succession of phenomena here described just as I myself had done.

Up to this time, never having witnessed any such phenomena as these, I had often doubted within myself how I should be affected by witnessing an apparition, or what I had reason to consider such. It *seemed* to me that I should experience no alarm; but of this, in advance of actual experience, I could not be assured. Now I know just how far I can trust my self-possession. Awe I undoubtedly felt—awe and intense interest; but, in looking back on my feelings throughout that wonder-bringing hour, I feel certain that a physician might have placed his finger on my wrist, even at the moment when that dimly-illuminated Presence first bent over me, with scarcely six inches intervening between its veiled face and mine—its hands placed on my head, its lips touching my shoulder—and not have found the beatings of my pulse unduly accelerated: or if he had detected acceleration, it could not, I am very sure, have been justly ascribed to any tremor or fear, but solely to the natural effect of solemn and riveted expectation. If a man, under such circumstances, may trust to his own recollections not twenty-four hours old, I can aver, on my honor, that I was not, at any time while these events were in progress, under other excitement (though it may be, greater in degree) than a chemist might be supposed to experience while watching the issue of a long-projected and decisive experiment, or an astronomer when the culminating point of some important observation is about to be reached.

I beg it may not be supposed that I mention this as boasting of courage. There was, in truth, nothing of which to boast. The preceding and attendant circumstances were such as to preclude alarm. I was not alone, nor taken by surprise. I was expecting some phenomena and hoping that they would be of a phosphorescent nature. And though I had not any expectation of seeing an actual form, yet, as the allegation was that a deceased sister, beloved by one of the assistants, was present, and as all the demonstrations were gentle and seemingly arranged, by friendly agencies, to satisfy my desire for the strongest evidence in proof of spiritual appearance, I was under very different circumstances to those which have often shaken the nerves even of the boldest, while encountering, for the first time, what is usually called a ghost.

I state the fact of my equanimity, then, merely as one of the attendant circumstances which may be fairly taken into account in judging the testimony here supplied in proof of the appearance, in visible and tangible form, of an alleged spirit of a deceased person. It is often assumed that a man who believes he sees an apparition is (to use a common phrase) frightened out of his senses; and so, is not entitled to credit as witness.

If it be objected that, before the sitting closed, the doors were unlocked, I reply first that all the most remarkable and interesting portion of the phenomena *occurred before this happened;* and, secondly, that, as the keys of the locked doors were left in them, they could only be opened from the inside. If, in reply to this last, it be still urged that Mr. Underhill, deserting his post for a few seconds, might have opened one of the doors, I reply that I happened to be conversing with him at the moment we first heard the key turned. I add that during the next sitting, when still more wonderful phenomena occurred, I took a precaution (as will be seen), which made it impossible that either Mr. Underhill or any of the assistants should leave their seats, even for a moment, without my knowledge.

Five days after this I had the session here referred to, in the same room, with the same assistants; during which similar phenomena were repeated, but with one highly noteworthy addition.

A Ghost Speaks.

The date was the twenty-sixth of October, 1860; and it was an evening session; from half-past ten till midnight. The same precautions which I had taken before the commencement of the former sitting as to locking all the doors, looking under the table, examining the room and furniture, etc., I carefully adopted on this occasion also. As before, we waited until the servants had retired and all was still.

After a time there was spelled "Darken;" then "Join hands." We obeyed; but on this occasion I took an additional precaution. Grasping Mrs. Underhill's right hand and Charles' left, I brought my own hands to the centre of the table; and Mr. Underhill, across the table, laid his hands on mine. This we continued throughout the entire sitting. I am able, therefore, to assert that, from the beginning of this sitting till the end, the circle remained unbroken.

After a few minutes, there appeared a luminous body of an irregularly circular form, about four inches in diameter, floating between us and the door which was back of Mrs. Underhill. It was somewhat brighter than when it first appeared on the previous occasion; that is, on the twenty-first of October.

Then, after an interval, the light, rustling sound seemed to indicate the approach of some one. The figure was not so distinct as on the previous occasion, the lower portion losing itself in a grayish cloud. The highest light seemed to be on the spot corresponding to the forehead. But I saw no features; nor did I see the arms moving. Very soon I was gently touched on the head, then on the shoulders, then laid hold of, as with both hands of some one standing behind me.

Then the figure seemed, by the sound, to move away, toward Mr. Underhill. He stated that the figure was approaching him. He asked it if, as a test, it could take something out of his pocket; but there was no reply, by raps or otherwise. Immediately I heard a sound as if some one were moving the key about in the door opposite to me.

Soon after Mr. Underhill said the figure had again approached him. I saw the illuminated circular substance close to his head, but could not distinguish any figure. Mr. Underhill said that he could dimly discern the figure.

After a time it moved round to the lad Charles, who exhibited much alarm; crying out "Oh, go away! Pray don't!" when it approached, as I saw it do, close to his head, which he had bent down on the table. It was now very bright, so that, by the light, I could see the outline of the boy's head. Charles afterward stated that he saw it distinctly, and that a hand touched him repeatedly. While it was close to Charles, it appeared to me as if a white handkerchief or some article of the like texture were thrown over a hand or some similar support. I saw no figure. When it rose behind Charles, as if to leave him when he cried out, I could perceive what resembled a hand grasping some illuminated substance, the outline of the hand appearing as a shadow across the illuminated ground.

Then it moved, as I could see, to Mr. Underhill, and after a time crossed over to me, and touched me gently on the shoulder. Of a sudden it occurred to me that one other evidence was lacking. I expressed a desire that, if it could, it would speak. It seemed to make several efforts to do so, as indicated by a slight, guttural sound; then I heard a sound resembling the syllable *es*, twice repeated.

Then, by the raps was spelled out: "Sing." Mrs. Underhill complied. The figure which had seemed to move away and return, again touched me from behind, drawing me slightly toward it. Then, in a brief interval of the singing, I heard, in a low voice, just behind me, the words: "God bless you." As additional assurance that it was no momentary illusion, I asked that it would speak again; and again, in an interval of the music, I heard, in distinct tones, the same words, "God bless you." They seemed to be pronounced close to my ear. The voice was low—apparently a woman's voice—just louder than a whisper, and the words seemed to be pronounced with an effort; in subdued tones, as a person faint from sickness might speak. I particularly noticed, also, that each word was pronounced separately, with a perceptible interval between; and there was not the usual accent on *bless*, followed by the shortened *you;* but each word was equally accented. In other respects the sounds resembled the human voice, when low and gentle.

Mrs. Underhill afterward stated to me that she distinguished the word *you*, but not the others. Mr. Underhill said he had heard articulate sounds, but could not make out any of the words: he only knew that something had been said to me.

After a time I saw the figure pass behind Mrs. Underhill and remain, for a few minutes, near her husband; then it returned to me, appearing on my left side. I saw the outline of a head and face, but still, as before, covered with a veil which concealed the features. I perceived, however, what I had not observed before, what seemed tresses of dark hair dropping over the face; and the dim outline of an arm raised one of these tresses, and then dropped it again, several times, as if to attract my attention. Behind was the vague outline of a figure, but less distinct than during the previous sitting.

Then the figure passed behind me. I was leaning over the table, so that Mr. Underhill might not have so far to stretch, in order to reach my hands. I felt a kiss on my shoulder, then there was the feeling of two hands laid each on one shoulder and I was drawn very gently back till my shoulders, above the chair back, were pressed against what seemed a material form. Almost at the same moment my hand was kissed.

Mr. Underhill cried out, "Ah, you were drawn back;" and Mrs. Underhill said, a little impatiently: "Every one is touched but me. Can't you come to me?"

The words were hardly pronounced when she screamed out, as in alarm: she had been suddenly and unexpectedly kissed on the forehead.

From that very moment the manifestations entirely ceased. No luminous object to be seen, not another touch, not a rustle, not a sound of any kind, in the room. I listened attentively, and am certain that no door opened or shut. And scarcely a minute or two elapsed ere it was spelled out: "Light the gas."

When we had done so we found everything as before, with a single exception. I ascertained by looking under the table and in the pantry that there was no one in the room but ourselves: I found all the three doors locked; but the key belonging to the door opposite to me was missing. We asked where it was; the raps replied: "Look." We could not see it anywhere. Then we examined our pockets; and, from one of his coat-pockets, Mr. Underhill produced a key, which was found to fit the door.

Mrs. Underhill asked if her alarmed exclamation had injured the spirit?

Answer, by the raps—"Not much."

Mrs. U.—"I'm so *much* afraid I hurt her!"

Answer.—"It frightened her."

Question (by me).—"Did Mrs. Underhill's cry of alarm cause the manifestations to cease?"

Answer.—"Yes."

As to the door-key, I remark—

That Mr. Underhill asked, as a test, to have something taken from his pocket; but it was a better test, since he could not move from his place, to take the key from the door and deposite it in his pocket. Who *but* a spirit could take it, our circle remaining unbroken? Is the taking by spirit agency incredible? But the hands that pressed my shoulders, that grasped my hand, that clasped my wrist, were surely material enough to extract a key from a door-lock and drop it in a coat-pocket.

Then all the doors, this time, were left locked; so that no one could enter from without: to say nothing of the absurd supposition that a spirit should open a door in order to admit human assistants.

Though I had every reason to be satisfied with my success I resolved to prosecute these researches, hoping for an apparition by gas-light or daylight. But I was unable at that time to do so. My duties as military agent of the State of Indiana called me from New York; and, in the rush of events during these stirring times, my time and thoughts were otherwise engrossed. In the spring of 1862 Judge Holt and myself were appointed a Government Commission on Ordnance and Ordnance stores,* requiring a residence in Washington; and a year later I became chairman of another Government Commission, charged with the duty of reporting on the condition of the recently emancipated freedmen of the United States. Thus it was not till the close of the war that I could sufficiently withdraw my attention from public duties to follow out, in any regular or consecutive manner, spiritual studies. Perhaps this mingling of mundane work and ultramundane contemplations is of wholesome character; tending to infuse broader views and a more practical tone into speculative researches.

My experience of 1860 led me to the opinion that an objective apparition must be the workmanship of spirits, possible under rare circumstances. Sometimes these appear to be wholly independent of human agency or intention; sometimes we can, in a measure, promote them, and even anticipate, with more or less uncertainty, however, the result. In this latter case, we seem to obtain something corresponding, in a measure, to a production of human art; and, specifically, of the art of sculpture; but of sculpture in spiritual phase; evanescent, only partially material, and liable, at any moment, to dissolve or disappear.

What I particularly desired was to have an opportunity, in the light, of witnessing the formation of such an apparition;

* Judge Holt was a member of President Buchanan's Cabinet and afterward Judge Advocate General. We reported on accounts amounting to more than forty-nine millions of dollars, reducing the liabilities of the General Government, by our decisions, nearly seventeen millions: and our report was sustained.

Some men imagine that profound convictions touching Spiritualism and Spiritual phenomena incapacitate for business duties; but that is a mistake.

its actions, its movements from place to place, and its disappearance. But it was not until the year 1867 that I obtained any further satisfaction. During the spring of that year I heard of Miss B——, of Boston, an elderly lady long known and esteemed in that city as a successful teacher of music and dancing. It was said that she, in a private circle, had obtained numerous objective apparitions, in a partially lighted room. This was afterward confirmed to me by a most estimable lady, who had herself been present at many of these sittings; Mrs. John Davis, widow of the well-known ex-Governor of Massachusetts, and of whom I have already spoken. *

Mrs. Davis expressed to me her conviction that Miss B—— was entirely sincere and disinterested; and that the phenomena which she (Mrs. Davis,) had witnessed in Miss B——'s apartments were genuine.

Miss B——, it seems, had several friends, married ladies in the middle rank of life, who had more or less power as mediums, especially in connection with spiritual appearances of an objective character. On several occasions, sometimes in one of their houses, sometimes in another, Miss B—— had herself seen an apparition.

None of these ladies were professional mediums; but it occurred to them that, if they met occasionally, they might, by their united powers, obtain very interesting results. Miss B—— offered the use of her spacious apartments; and during a series of experiments which were conducted there, phenomena of a marvellous character were observed: a great variety of spirits appearing, chiefly strangers to any of the assistants, in various costumes.

This was noised abroad, and brought requests, from the curious, for admission to witness such wonders. These were usually granted, but uniformly as a favor and without charge. Opinions were various: some visitors were convinced; others went away in doubt whether it was not an exhibition got up to mystify the credulous, or gratify a longing for notoriety.

* See Book iii. chap. 3.

This, of course, was very unpleasant to the ladies concerned; and when I called on Miss B——, in May, 1867, I found that, for several months, they had almost ceased to meet. When, however, I expressed to Miss B—— my earnest desire to investigate the matter, intending, some day, to publish the results, she acceded to my wishes with the utmost alacrity. "I am so glad," she said, "to have some one, who will be listened to, test these phenomena. When one has no other interest or desire than to get at important truth, it seems hard to be subjected to groundless suspicion."

At the first two or three sittings a portion only of the ladies could attend; and Miss B—— was of opinion that the discontinuance of their regular sittings had, for the time, weakened their power. We had only rapping and phosphorescent phenomena, but of a remarkable character. Bright stars appeared on the person of one medium, a line of light along the forehead of another, the word "Hope," on the back of the hand of a third. These appearances were brilliant and could be seen, twenty feet off, across a dimly-lighted room. At other times the raps were so violent as to shake the sofa on which we sat.

But until the session of June 4, there was no apparition. On that occasion we had one under very satisfactory circumstances; but I did not consider the test complete; for I did not witness either the formation of the figure or its disappearance.

It was not until the twenty-fifth of June that we were able to bring together all the ladies who had composed the original circle. I consider that day, like the twenty-first of October, 1860, an era in my spiritual experience.

An Apparition in Shining Raiment.

Miss B——'s rooms, which occupied the entire third floor of a corner house in Washington street, Boston, consisted of a large apartment, thirty feet front by thirty-five feet deep; opening, by folding doors, into a parlor back of it, which was twenty-five feet by twenty. From each room there was one door of exit only, on a passage or stair-landing, thus:

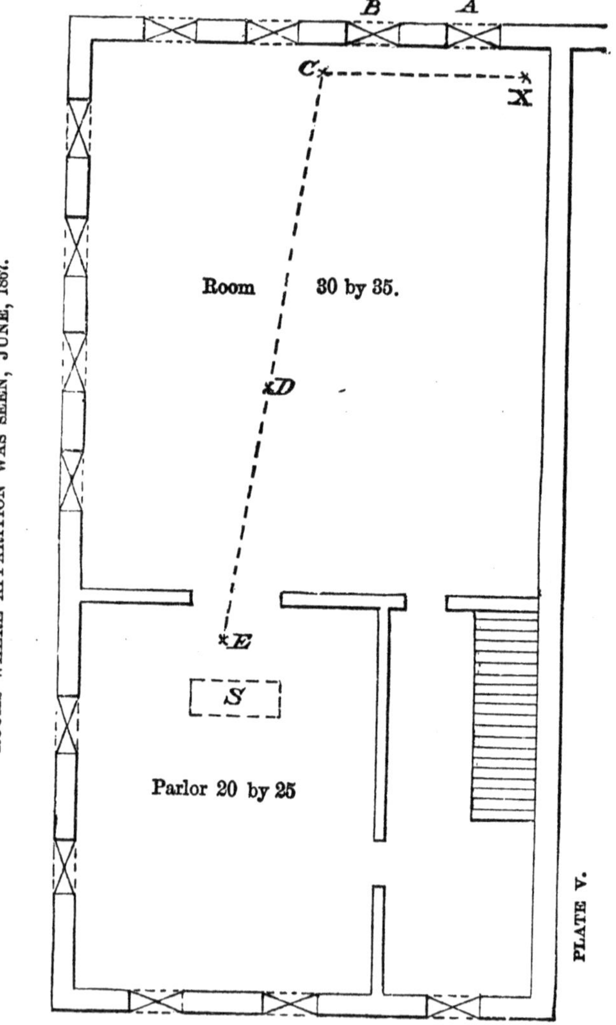

ROOMS WHERE APPARITION WAS SEEN, JUNE, 1867.

PLATE V.

The front room was lighted by eight windows, four on Washington street, and four on a gas-lit court-yard. As there were no curtains drawn nor shutters closed during the sitting, which was held after lamp-lighting, this room was so far lit from without that, by any one seated in the back parlor, a few feet from the folding-doors, the dress and general appearance of persons in the front room could be readily observed and every motion they made distinctly seen. I took notice, however, that there was not light enough to recognize features, except close at hand. In this room, employed for dancing lessons, the floor was uncarpeted and waxed. All footsteps of persons walking across it could be very distinctly heard.

Except myself there was but one visitor present, Mrs. John Davis. The amateur mediums who assisted at the sitting were six in number: Mrs. S. J. D——, Mrs. George N. B——, Mrs. Sarah A. K——, Mrs. Fanny C. P——, Mrs. William H. C——, and Mrs. Mary Anne C——: all ladies, apparently, from thirty to forty years of age.

Before the sitting began, Mrs. Davis and myself passed around the room and examined carefully every part of it. The furniture consisted of a sofa, a piano, and numerous chairs set against the walls. There was no pantry, or press, or recess of any kind. We locked the sole door of exit, and Mrs. Davis kept the key in her pocket during the sitting. Then we locked the door of the back parlor, retaining the key.

We sat down in that parlor directly before the folding-doors. The sofa (marked s. on ground-plan), on which Mrs. Davis, Miss B—— and myself were seated, was about four or five feet within the parlor. I sat at the left-hand corner of this sofa: the entrance through the folding-doors was draped by curtains, which were looped back; so that, from where I sat, I could see three of the four front windows looking out on Washington street and the corner of the room to the right of them. The six mediums sat three on each side of us.

All was quiet during the early part of the sitting, which

commenced a little after eight P.M. Scarcely any rapping. A few phosphorescent lights.

About a quarter past nine, all the mediums being seated by us, I saw dimly, near the right-hand corner of the front line of the large room (at X), at first a grayish, slightly-luminous vapor; after a time, a figure draped in white. At first it was stationary; then it moved very slowly past the two right-hand windows (A and B) to the centre of the front line of the room (at C), between two windows. There it remained one or two minutes, still but indistinctly visible. Then, very slowly and without sound of footstep, it advanced down the room, coming directly toward the centre of the folding doors. It stopped (at D) about twelve or fourteen feet from where I was sitting. Thereupon, of a sudden, a brilliant light, coming from the right, striking directly on the figure and only on it—not directly illuminating the rest of the room—enabled me to see the appearance as perfectly as if the entire room had been lit with gas.

It was a female figure, of medium height, veiled and draped, from head to foot, in white. The drapery did not resemble, in material, anything I have ever seen worn. It gave me, as on a previous occasion,* the exact feeling of the Scriptural expression, "shining raiment." Its brilliancy was a good deal like that of new-fallen snow, in the sunshine; recalling the text which declares the garments of Christ, during his transfiguration, to have been "exceeding white as snow;" or, again, it was not unlike the finest and freshest Parian marble with a bright light on it, only more brilliant. It had not at all the glitter of spangles or any shining ornament; the tone being as uniform as that of a newly-sculptured statue. It stood upright, in a graceful attitude, motionless. Had I suddenly seen it elsewhere, and without having witnessed its previous movements, I might have imagined it a beautiful piece of sculpture, of singularly-pure material, and marvellously lighted up. The drapery fell around the figure closely, as usual in a statue; not

* June 4; already alluded to.

at all according to the modern fashion of amplitude. I think it was shown to us, under the bright light, as long as fifteen or twenty seconds.

Mrs. K—— stepped out to meet it, going close up to it, and then returning to us. The figure followed her; and, as Mrs. K——, when she passed the folding-doors, had stepped aside to the right, the apparition advanced, with a gliding motion, into the parlor, till, as nearly as I could judge, it was within two or three feet of me. There it stopped (at E).

As it remained immovable I raised my left arm, hoping that I should be touched. As I stretched it out, the figure extended its right arm, covered with drapery, toward me; and dropped into my hand what proved to be a white rose; but its hand did not touch mine.

Thereupon the appearance, still keeping its face to us, slowly retired with the same silent, gliding motion which had marked its advance; not the slightest sound of footstep, on the waxed floor, being audible.

A second time it stopped, again about twelve or fifteen feet from me; and, a second time, an instantaneous light, coming from the right and falling upon it, gave it to be seen with the utmost distinctness. I was enabled to verify my former observations in regard to its appearance, and the unique, rich, resplendent character of the drapery.

Then it slowly receded, still facing us, to the centre of the opposite wall (at C), gradually diminishing in brightness; and finally it vanished before my eyes.

Mrs. K—— had followed it and remained, a few seconds, near the spot where it vanished. Then I saw her cross the window to the right on her return to us. She was dressed in black.

I am *quite certain* that one figure only—that of Mrs. K—— as she returned to us—left the spot. From the time the figure in white reached that spot, I kept my eyes intently fixed there, *without taking them off for a single moment;* and the light from the street was such that it was impossible for any object, black or white, to pass one of the windows without my seeing it.

When a minute or two had elapsed after the disappearance of the figure, and while my eyes were still fixed on the spot, the thought rushed vividly upon me: "Is it possible that there can be nothing there?" This thought, *to which I did not give utterance*, had hardly crossed my mind when, as if in reply to it, the same sort of mysterious light which had previously illuminated the figure suddenly flashed over the space of wall between the two windows where the figure had disappeared, completely lighting it up, *while the windows and wall on either side were not illuminated.* The light remained long enough to show me that there was nothing whatever there, except two chairs set against the wall, as I had seen them before the sitting began.

Then, with my eyes still fixed on the place of disappearance, I rose and passed entirely around the room: nor did I, for a moment, take my eyes off the spot that had been illuminated till I reached it. Everything in the room was exactly as it had been before the sitting, so far as I could recollect. The outer door was still locked.

It is proper to add that two of the mediums, Mrs. K—— and Mrs. D——, informed me, after the sitting was over, that they did not remember seeing anything of the figure; both having awoke, as from a trance, at the close of the sitting. This, Miss B—— informed me, was usual with them.

I do not think that any of the assistants perceived the formation of the apparition as soon as I did; but while the figure was advancing and retreating, the whispered remarks of the ladies near me—"There it is!"—"Now it stops!"—"Did you see that light?" etc.—made me aware that they saw it just as I did. This was confirmed to me, on after inquiry, by all the ladies except Mrs. K—— and Mrs. D——. All the others observed the sudden illumination of the spot where the figure disappeared.

As on a former occasion, it is proper I should state here that, throughout the sitting, though the impression produced was profound, solemn beyond expression, never to be forgotten, yet it did not partake at all of the emotion of fear. The predomi nant feeling was a deep anxiety that there might be no interruption, and that the sitting might not terminate until I had obtained incontrovertible evidence of the fact that the appearance was of a spiritual character, yet as real as any earthly phenomenon.

The allegation, by raps, at the close of the sitting, was that the apparition was that of Violet. Seven years before, during a sitting with Kate Fox, I had had a promise, purporting to come from her, that, some day when the conditions were favorable, she would appear to me. The veil quite concealed the features; but the height, the form and carriage of the figure, so strictly corresponded to hers that, when it approached me, I ceased to doubt that she had kept her promise.

My faith in the reality of this appearance is not at all shaken by reflecting that a Signor Blitz, or a Robert-Houdin, having a theatre at command, arranged with ready entrances and exits, with practical trap-doors, with dark lanterns in the wings, with the means of producing dissolving views—could probably reproduce all I witnessed.

But here were a few ladies, in private life and in moderate circumstances, quietly meeting in two apartments which were daily used as school-rooms by one of their number; on the third story of a private house,* containing not even a recess where a chair could be hidden away. They meet to satisfy a laudable curiosity; admitting visitors, now and then, by courtesy only. No remuneration is demanded; nor, very surely, would any have been accepted. They meet, on this occasion, at my request, after having discontinued their researches for months, vexed with unjust suspicions. They allow us to lock every exit, after a close examination of the rooms. Here is

* The floor below was daily used for mercantile purposes.

neither motive, nor opportunity—to say nothing of qualification—for deception. The coin of the realm may be counterfeited, but the coiners must have professional skill, an appropriate location, and expensive machinery. Nor do counterfeiters ply their unholy calling except with the prospect of large gains.

Certain it is, that I beheld the gradual formation of the figure; that I witnessed its movements; that I received from its hand an actual flower;* that I saw the figure disappear. Add to this that the place of its disappearance was illuminated by invisible agency, in answer to an unexpressed thought of mine. If Robert-Houdin can read thoughts, he has a spiritual gift.

If the reader still withholds belief, deeming two or three examples insufficient to prove so strange a phenomenon as the formation, by spiritual agency, and the subsequent disappearance, of a form sufficiently material to grasp a substantial object and hand it to a human being—let him read the next chapter.

* I asked Miss B—— if there had been any white rose in the room. She replied that there were several nosegays there that had been presented to her by her pupils, and, very probably, there might have been such a rose among them. The flower which was given to me is still in my possession.

CHAPTER IV.

A NEAR RELATIVE SHOWS HERSELF, THROUGHOUT FIVE YEARS, TO A SURVIVING FRIEND.

A JUDICIOUS man of science, experimenting in his laboratory, seeks, before giving to the world the result of an important experiment, to repeat that experiment more than once. Inasmuch as the governing law endures, any result obtained under that law must be capable of being reproduced: and its reproduction, time after time, will usually be deemed necessary to give assurance of its genuine character; seeing that a fallible observer may readily mistake or misinterpret, when his observation is limited to a single example.

Some physical phenomena, however, are spontaneous and cannot be produced at will. We cannot evoke an aurora borealis, or call down aërolites from the sky. Apparitions have usually been thought to be of that character, if believed in at all: and, to a certain extent, they are. Among the superstitious a belief has sometimes prevailed that the dead may be recalled by mystic and unlawful rites, as Saul by the so-called "Witch" of En-dor. But such a superstition finds few believers in modern times. All that there is of truth underlying it consists in this, that, under favorable conditions, of rare and difficult combination, we may occasionally obtain apparitions; and may even be favored so as to witness these again and again: not during weeks or months only, but throughout years.

I am fortunate enough to be able to lay before the reader one of the most remarkable—perhaps *the* most remarkable—example of this that has ever occurred; or, at least, that is to be found on record: with permission, from the witness, to give his name in attestation. It is a name well known in the commercial and social circles of New York,—Mr. Livermore.

This gentleman, eleven years ago, lost a near and dear relative: let us call her Estelle. On her death-bed, perceiving the poignant grief that overwhelmed her relative at the prospect of his approaching loss, she earnestly expressed the desire that it might be possible for her, after death, still to assure him of her continued existence.

He attached little importance to this except as evidence of her affection; having himself, up to that time, found no proof satisfactory to his reason touching a Hereafter. Neither he nor Estelle had any faith whatever in spiritual phenomena; and both had been wont to regard the whole subject with repugnance.

When Mr. Livermore found himself alone, his extreme grief was terribly embittered by the thought that it was a separation forever. Expressing this in strong terms to his friend, Dr. John F. Gray, who had been Estelle's physician from childhood, that gentleman (one of the earliest believers in intermundane phenomena) suggested that there *was* a remedy capable of alleviating his grief, if he (Mr. L.) saw fit to resort to it. The reply was a contemptuous fling at Spiritualism and its delusions: and the sufferer went his way, hopeless and desolate.

After a time, however, came the sober second-thought that there *might* be something in a doctrine which so earnest and thoughtful a man as Dr. Gray implicitly accepted. Accordingly, at his friend's suggestion, he resolved to seek sittings with Miss Kate Fox.

The sittings were held sometimes in Mrs. Fox's parlor, sometimes in Mr. Livermore's. * In all cases the necessary precautions were taken to give assurance that no one entered the room, or left it, during the sitting: the room itself being thor-

* Both Mrs. Fox and Mr. Livermore changed residences during the time these sittings were held; so that the phenomena were obtained in *four* different dwellings.

oughly examined, and doors and windows effectually secured. At several of the first sittings three or four visitors were admitted as additional witnesses. But it soon became apparent that the best results could be obtained with a single sitter only: and accordingly, as a general rule, Mr. Livermore only was present.

During the first sitting, which was held January 23, 1861, he, Mr. L., for the first time, heard the mysterious echoes —the "raps," as they are usually called. Then, throughout the first ten or twelve sittings, followed the usual phenomena; spirit-touches, spirit-communications, moving of ponderable bodies, etc.: finally spirit-writing. During the twelfth sitting came a message, purporting to be from Estelle, to the effect that if her friend persevered, her spirit could be made visible to him. Then, throughout a dozen sessions more, came phosphorescent lights, disappearing and reappearing at intervals; at last, on the twenty-fourth sitting (March 14th), the dim outline of a figure, moving about. Three days afterward there came this message: "I know that I can make myself visible to you. Meet to-morrow night. Secure the doors and windows, for I wish the test to be beyond all doubt, for your good and the good of others."

The next evening the session was at Mrs. Fox's residence, but the family were absent, so that the medium and the sitter alone occupied the house. Mr. L. sealed the windows, sealed and locked the doors, and placed heavy furniture against them; then searched the room thoroughly and extinguished the gas. Soon came the words: "I am here in form." Then a globular light appeared, with crackling sounds. After a time it became a head, veiled: then, but for a single instant only, Mr. L. recognized the features of Estelle. Then a figure was seen: all this being visible by phosphorescent or electrical lights in various parts of the room. During all this time Mr. L. held both of the medium's hands. Then the mode of producing raps was shown: an orange-shaped luminous ball, with blunt point attached, bounding up and down on the table, and the sound of each rap coinciding with the approach of the ball to the table-top.

It was somewhat later, however, that

THE CRUCIAL TEST

was first obtained. I copy from Mr. L.'s record:

"*No.* 43. *April* 18, 1861. Wind south-west. Weather fair. Having absolutely secured doors and windows, we sat in perfect quiet for half an hour, my faith becoming weak. Then we were startled by a tremendous rap on the heavy mahogany centre-table which, at the same time, rose and fell. The door was violently shaken, the windows opened and shut: in fact, everything movable in the room seemed in motion. Questions were answered by loud knocks on the doors, on the glass of the windows, on the ceiling—everywhere.

"Then an illuminated substance like gauze rose from the floor behind us, moved about the room and finally came in front of us. Vigorous electrical sounds were heard. The gauze-like substance assumed the form of a human head covered, the covering drawn close around the neck. It touched me; then receded and again approached. I recognized an oblong substance, concave on the side that was presented to us, and in this cavity the light was brilliant. Into this I looked intently for a face, but none appeared. Again it receded and again approached: this time I perceived an eye. A third time it moved backward, accompanied by electrical sounds, and when, a third time, it came close to me the light had brightened, the gauze had changed in form; a female hand grasped it, concealing the lower part of a face; but the upper part was revealed: it was that of Estelle—eyes, forehead, and expression in perfection. The moment the emotion of recognition passed into my mind, it was acknowledged by a succession of quick raps from all parts of the room, as though an unseen audience expressed its applause.

"The figure reappeared several times, the recognition becoming each time more nearly perfect. Afterward her head was laid upon mine, the hair falling over my face.

"Miss Fox (whose hands I had secured during all this time) and I sat about ten feet from the wall of the room which faced us. The light moved to a point about midway between us and the wall; the electrical cracklings increased; the wall was illuminated and brought out an entire female figure facing that side of the room, the light apparently in one of her hands. The form remained in sight *fully half an hour* and each movement was distinctly visible. Then came the message:

"'Now see me rise:'

"And immediately, in full brightness, the figure rose to the ceiling, remained there a few moments suspended; then gently descending, disappeared.

"Afterward she showed herself between us and a mirror. *The reflection of the figure in the glass was distinctly visible,* the light being so bright as to show the veins in a marble slab beneath.

"Here a heavy shower of rain fell, and there was spelled out: 'The atmosphere has changed. I cannot remain in form:' whereupon both light and figure finally disappeared."

At a sitting held two days later, the following communication was received: *

* I here remark that all communications obtained through Kate Fox were either—

Spelled out, letter after letter, by the raps:

Or else written, sometimes by Kate's right hand, sometimes by the left; but the writing *always executed inversely;* so that it could only be read by holding it against a mirror.

Occasionally she writes two communications at once; both hands moving at the same time, each on a separate sheet. And I have myself witnessed the following: While her hand was writing, there was, by raps, a call for the alphabet; whereupon Kate called over the letters and took down the message, letter by letter, *without for a moment discontinuing her writing.* Mr. L. has often witnessed all the above phases of communication.

In addition to this, the internal evidence of many of the messages is, especially to those who know Miss Fox well, conclusive evidence that these originate entirely outside of her will and of her intelligence.

"My heart is full of joy. We cannot be grateful enough to the Giver of this great boon. I have seen your heart—the shadows that rested upon it, the lights that now glorify it. Be happy and fear not. Peace be with you alway.

"ESTELLE."

So far, the upper part of the face only had been seen; but on the evening after the above message was received (namely, April 21), the complete test was obtained. After giving the details of various manifestations apparently of a phosphorescent character, Mr. Livermore says: "At last a luminous globe which had remained stationary some six feet to my left floated in front, and came within two feet of me. It was violently agitated, crackling sounds were heard, and a figure became visible by its light. Then there was revealed the full head and face of Estelle, every feature and lineament in perfection, spiritualized in shadowy beauty, such as no imagination can conceive or pen describe. In her hair, above the left temple, was a single white rose; the hair being apparently arranged with great care. The entire head and face faded and then became visible again, at least twenty times; the perfection of recognition, in each case, being in proportion to the brilliancy of the light."

But, at this session, he, Mr. L., obtained other proof than that of sight to confirm the reality of the appearance. The head of the appearing figure rested for a time upon his, the luxuriant hair dropping over his face and into his hand. He says: "I laid hold of the hair, which seemed, to the touch, at first identical with human hair; but, after a brief space, *it melted away, leaving nothing in my grasp.*"

I select, at hap-hazard from numerous subsequent descriptions, the following:

"*No.* 66. *June* 2, 1861: 8.30 P.M. There came a reminder, by raps: 'Examine the room and take the keys of the doors;' which I did.

"We had scarcely seated ourselves when there were violent

movements, succeeded at first by raps from various parts of the room, then by terrific, crashing reports on the table-top, like miniature thunderbolts, or loud discharges of electricity.

"A rustling succeeded; and a form stood beside me; its sphere permeating every fibre of my organization. Then there was rapping on the back of my chair, afterward on my shoulders; and the figure, bending forward, placed a hand on my head. A bright light sprang up behind us; it rose, attended by electrical sounds. Then I was kissed on the head and a light but distinctly-felt substance passed over me. Thereupon I raised my eyes and beheld the face of Estelle, plainly visible in front of the light, which now vibrated rapidly, throwing its fitful gleams upon such beauty as, in beings of this world, it is not given us to witness. She looked at me with an expression radiant with blessedness.

"At this point Miss Fox became so excited that her irrepressible exclamations of wonder and delight seemed momentarily to disturb the appearance; for it receded, not appearing again until she became calm; and this occurred several times. Simultaneously lights appeared, floating about in different parts of the room.

"A card with which I had provided myself was then taken from my hand and, after a time, *visibly returned to me.* On it I found a communication beautifully written in pure, idiomatic French; not a word of which was understood by Miss Fox: she has no knowledge whatever of the language."

Passing over several intervening appearances on separate evenings, I find this, under date June 4:

"*No.* 81. Weather cool and pleasant. Wind north-west." After detailing sundry less important phenomena, Mr. L. proceeds:

"There were very distinct rustlings, and there rose, several feet above the table, a light so vivid as to illuminate all surrounding objects. As it approached me, a dark substance was suddenly interposed. This descended from the light and remained stationary about two feet from my eyes. Gradually it opened, disclosing a glimpse of Heaven and of an angel as bright as imagination can picture. The figure of Estelle stood there, the same pure, white rose in her tresses: features and expression absolutely perfect under a full blaze of light.

"Six or seven times in succession, this form instinct with life and beauty vanished and then reappeared, before my eyes. When perhaps a quarter of an hour had elapsed, figure and light both disappeared; but in a short time the light again showed itself; this time in a corner of the apartment, where it shone out so brightly that every article of furniture in that part of the room was distinctly visible. And there, just as plainly visible, stood a female figure, in full proportions, the back toward us, and a veil, apparently of shining gauze, covering the head, and dropping, in front, to the knees.

"I asked if she would raise her arm. She did so—the attitude inexpressibly graceful. No pen can describe the exquisite, transcendant beauty of what was this night revealed."

I do not see how we can reject, or explain away, such evidence as the above, even if the record were arrested here. But what will the reader say when he is informed that more than THREE HUNDRED additional sittings were still to be held; all confirmatory of the above experiences.

It is impossible, within the limits of this volume, to follow Mr. Livermore throughout his voluminous record. I can but pick out, here and there, a few of the more salient and irrefutable results.

Corroboration throughout Several Years.

Here is an item touching on the resemblances between this world and the next:

"*No.* 93. *July* 17, 1861. Each succeeding appearance seems more nearly perfect. This evening the figure of Estelle was surrounded by floating drapery of shining, white gauze. In her hand, held under her chin, was a bunch of flowers; and neck and bosom were completely covered with roses and violets.

"I asked: 'Where do you obtain these flowers?' The answer was: 'This world is a counterpart of yours. We have all that you have—gardens and spiritual flowers in abundance.'"

Next month came this, among many others:

"*No.* 116. *August* 29. The figure of Estelle appeared soon after we entered the room. She stood quietly while a light floated close to face, head, and neck: as if to show each part more distinctly. While we were looking on, her hair fell over her face, and she put it back several times with her hand. Her hair was dressed with roses and violets, beautifully arranged. This was the most perfect of her efforts: she appeared almost as distinctly as in life.

"By her side stood a form, dressed, as we clearly saw, in coat of what seemed dark cloth. Miss Fox became greatly alarmed and very nervous. Because of this, or for some other reason, the face of this second form was not visible and it soon disappeared." [More of this figure hereafter.] The form of Estelle, however, remained.

Then we have an incident going to prove that an apparition may handle earthly objects. The weather being warm, Mr. Livermore had brought with him, and laid on the table before him, a fan. This was taken and held by her, in various positions, sometimes concealing a portion of her face. He (Mr. L.) adds:

"The figure must have been visible to us, during this sitting, *for an hour and a half.*"

It appears that the robes with which it was invested, though they dissolved in the hand, had a certain materiality.

"*No.* 137. *October* 4. The figure of Estelle came in great vividness and with extraordinary power. A light floated about the room and she followed it, gliding through the air; at one time her long, white robes sweeping over the table, and *brushing from it pencils, paper, and other light objects,* which fell to the floor."

Doctor Franklin.

By the raps it was announced that the dark-robed figure which had once or twice appeared was that of Dr. Franklin; but no further proof of his identity was obtained until the sitting *No.* 162, of *November* 11. Then his face was first seen, by a light which seemed to be held by another figure. "If any judgment can be formed from original portraits of the man," Mr. L. says, "there would seem to be no mistake about his identity. He was dressed in brown coat of the olden style, with white cravat: his head very large, with whitish or gray hair behind the ears; the whole face radiant with intelligence, benevolence, and spirituality."

The next evening he came again. Here is the record: "The raps requested that a chair be placed for Dr. Franklin on the side of the table opposite to where we sat. But the idea of such a vis-à-vis made Miss Fox so nervous that I did not insist. After a time she became quiet, and we heard the chair moved to the desired spot.

"At this time the lights were dim; but I perceived a dark figure standing near me. Very soon it moved round the table, a rustling was heard, the lights brightened, and we saw what seemed the old philosopher himself seated in the chair; his entire form and dress in perfection. So vivid was the light, and so palpable (as it would seem) the form before us, *that its shadow was thrown upon the wall*, precisely as if it had been a mortal seated there. The position was easy and dignified, one arm and hand on the table. Once he bent forward, as if bowing to us, and I observed that his gray locks swayed with the movement. He sat opposite to us *more than an hour*. Finally I asked him if he would draw nearer: whereupon figure and chair moved toward us, and our silent neighbor was in close proximity. Before he disappeared he rose from his chair; both face and form distinctly visible."

This was at Mrs. Fox's; but the sitting of November 30th

was held in Mr. Livermore's own house. He tells us what he then and there saw:

"*No.* 175. Doors locked and sealed. Heavy concussions and electrical sounds; a chair opposite moved into position; then a request for matches. These were taken from my hand, as I held them at arm's-length.

"After a time, the sound of friction, as in drawing a match, was heard; and, after several apparent efforts, a match ignited. By its light we saw that it was held by the figure, supposed that of Franklin, which appeared in perfection, dressed as before, only that the color of his coat showed more perfectly. But as soon as the match went out the figure disappeared.

"Afterward he reappeared (by match-light) ten or twelve times. The third time my hat was on his head, worn as by a living person; and then it was removed from his head to mine. The last time he appeared, the figure of Estelle showed itself, leaning on his shoulder: but Miss Fox became nervous, and her exclamations (apparently) caused the final disappearance of both figures. Then there came the following:

"'This is what we have long labored to accomplish. You can now say that you have seen me by the light of earth. I will come again, in further proof.

"'B. F.'"

This promise was kept on December 12; again, in Mr. Livermore's house. His record is:

"*No.* 179. At my own house. I had procured a dark lantern, covered with a cloth casing and provided with a valve so that I could throw a circle of light two feet in diameter on a wall ten feet distant.

"I placed this lantern, lighted, on the table and held the medium's hands. Soon it rose into the air and we were requested to follow. A form, carrying the lantern, preceded us. The outline of this spirit-form was distinct, its white robes dropping to the floor. The lantern was placed on a bureau; and we stood facing a window which was between that bureau and a large mirror.

"Then the lantern again rose, remaining suspended about five feet from the floor between the bureau and the mirror; and, by its light, we discerned the figure of Franklin seated in my arm-chair by the window, in front of a dark curtain. For fully ten minutes at a time, the light from the suspended lantern rested on his face and figure, so that we had ample time to examine both. At first the face seemed as if of actual flesh, the hair real, the eyes bright and so distinct that I clearly saw the whites. But I noticed that gradually the whole appearance, including the eyes, was deadened by the earthly light and ceased to wear the aspect of life with which the forms I had seen by spiritual light were replete.

"Several times I was requested to adjust the valve, so as to allow more or less light; and this I did while the lantern remained suspended, or held by invisible power.

"At the close of this sitting we found written on a card:

"'My son: it is for the benefit of the world. I have worked for this.'

B. F."

Other strange items come up, incidentally, in this record. Here is one:

Spirit-flowers.

"*No.* 218. *February* 7, 1862. Sky clear; atmosphere cold. Doors and windows secured with sealing-wax.

"A card which I had brought with me was taken from my pocket; a bright light rose from the table, and by it there was shown to us the card, to the centre of which there had been fixed what seemed a small bunch of flowers. The light faded and we were requested to light the gas. The flowers were a red rose, with green leaves and forget-me-nots; very beautiful, and apparently real.

"I inspected them for several minutes, at intervals; turning off the gas and relighting five or six times. The flowers still remained. Above them was written:

"'*Flowers from our home in Heaven.*'

"Finally the flowers began to fade, and we were requested

to extinguish the gas. When we did so, it was replaced by a spirit-light under which the flowers were again distinctly visible. Then, by the raps: 'Do not take your eyes off the flowers: watch them closely.'

"We did so. They gradually diminished in size, as we gazed, till they became mere specks; and *then they disappeared before our eyes.* When I lighted the gas, I found no trace of them on the card.

"Then I carefully examined the seals on the doors and windows, and found them intact."

Here is another item from the record of sitting 283, November 3, 1862.

"The hair of the figure (Estelle's) hung loosely over her face. I lifted it, so as to see her more perfectly. Then she *rose into the air and passed over my head,* her robe sweeping across my head and face."

And here is another of an incident that occurred during sitting 335, of December 31, 1862:

"I turned down the gas partially only. By its light I distinguished a hand, with white sleeve encircling the wrist. It held a flower which, with its stem, was about three inches long. I reached my hand to take it; but at the moment my fingers touched it, there was a sharp snap, as from a powerful electric spark. Then I turned on the full gas. The hand, floating about, still held the flower; and after a time, placed it on a sheet of paper which lay on the table. It proved to be a pink rose-bud with green leaves: to the touch it was cold, damp, and glutinous. Then a peculiar white flower, resembling a daisy, was presented. After a time they all melted away. *While this occurred the room was as light as day.*"

Under date October 21, 1863 (session 365), Mr. Livermore says: "I brought with me, this evening, the dark lantern already described; and, as soon as the figure of Estelle appeared, I threw its light full on her. She quailed a little, but stood her ground, for some time, while I directed the light to her face and eyes, afterward to different parts of her dress. Then she disappeared and I had the communication: 'It was with the greatest difficulty that I could hold myself in form without disappearing.'"

Through all of the above experiences it will be observed that Mr. Livermore himself and the medium were the only witnesses; and it will suggest itself that the proof would have been more complete had others been admitted to the sittings. This did occur, during the latter years in which these experiments were made.

Two additional Witnesses.

It is well known to those who have experience in spiritual researches that the admission of an additional sitter into a circle always diminishes the power for a time; retarding and weakening the phenomena. Sometimes it arrests them altogether; but, in many cases, after a few sessions, the new-comer seems gradually to fall into magnetic relation with the circle, and the phenomena resume their vigor. This law became manifest when additional members were admitted to Mr. Livermore's circle. That gentleman has recorded *ten* sittings at which Dr. Gray was present, and *eight* at which his (Mr. L.'s) brother-in-law, Mr. Groute, assisted.

Dr. Gray is well known in the city of New York, as one among its most esteemed and successful medical men; * and I doubt if there be any one in the United States who has devoted more time and attention than he to the phenomena and the philosophy of Vital Magnetism and of Spiritualism.

The first opportunity he had of joining Mr. Livermore's circle was during sitting No. 256, of June 6, 1862. On that occasion the figure of Dr. Franklin appeared, but evidently with difficulty, and without the full expression which he had

* With the single drawback, as some men would esteem it—but I am not among that number—that his practice is homœopathic.

previously worn. The hair, however, and clothing were both nearly as usual, and were handled by Dr. Gray.

Eleven days later, Dr. Gray was present a second time. On this occasion the figure of Dr. Franklin showed itself several times; but the features, at first, were not recognizable, and, on another occasion, a portion of the face only was formed, presenting a deformed and disagreeable aspect. This had not occurred during any of Mr. Livermore's previous sittings. Estelle did not show herself on either of these occasions.

The third time (June 25) the figure of Franklin appeared in perfection, and was recognized by Dr. Gray.

During the fourth sitting, there was a message to the effect that a piece of the spirit's garment might be cut off with scissors and examined. Both Dr. Gray and Mr. Livermore availed themselves of this permission. For a time the texture was strong, so that it might be pulled without coming apart. They had both time to examine it critically before it melted away.

Other observations touching the partial, and the gradual, formation of apparitions, were made, during subsequent sessions by Dr. Gray, and will be adverted to in the next chapter.

During subsequent sittings the figure of Dr. Franklin appeared to Dr. Gray as perfectly, and under as bright light, as it had ever done to Mr. Livermore. But Estelle showed herself before the Doctor on a single occasion only; during sitting 384, of November 10, 1865. This was at Mr. Livermore's house. She appeared with a white gossamer covering over her head and a transparent veil; the lower portion of the dress loose and flowing.

Mr. Groute was present during sitting No. 346, of February 28, 1863; and he held the medium's hands. As soon as the gas was extinguished, Mr. L. was pulled, apparently by a large hand, to the sofa; above which Franklin's figure then appeared, the light rising from the floor. When Mr. Groute saw him and became convinced that it *was* the appearance of a human figure, he went instantly to the doors to assure himself that they were still locked. He then returned and handled the garments of the figure.

But he seems to have been of sceptical temperament; for, a week later, he came again, resolved to make all safe. He himself secured doors and windows: he "had no idea," he said, "of being deceived."

This time the figure of Franklin appeared much more vividly than before. It held, in its hand, a light, as if that it might be thoroughly examined, and the "unbelieving Thomas" be fully satisfied. Mr. Groute, who had been holding both Mr. Livermore's and Miss Fox's hands from the beginning of the sitting, approached the figure, saw and touched; and, like the apostle, frankly acknowledged his conviction.

During one sitting (No. 355, of May 1, 1863), both Dr. Gray and Mr. Groute were present: the form of Dr. Franklin was perfect and was fully recognized by both gentlemen. Next evening, Dr. Gray being the only visitor, the figure of Dr. Franklin appeared in the air, about two feet above Dr. Gray's head, as if stooping toward the doctor and looking down upon him. He was clothed in a dark mantle, and floated, for some time, about the room. Dr. Gray, familiar as he was with spiritual phenomena, declared this manifestation to be "stupendous."

The last time the figure of Estelle appeared, was during session No. 388, held April 2, 1866. From that day forth, though Mr. Livermore has received, even up to the time I write, frequent messages of sympathy and affection, he has seen the well-known form no more.

The first thing which will occur to any upright man, having the good of his race at heart, is that—supposing this narrative to be strictly true—the witness of such unexampled phenomena—selecting, of course, his own time, place, and manner—had no moral right to withhold from the world the experience which God had permitted him to enjoy. To whom much is given of him shall much be required. I know that Mr. Livermore testifies with that natural reluctance which men feel to expose themselves, even for the greatest truth's sake, to the imputation of being either deceivers or deceived. I know that he gives his testimony under the solemn conviction that the most trivial misstatement, the slightest exaggeration, the least attempt at false-coloring for the sake of effect, would be little less than blasphemy—would be treason to a sacred cause.

Deceived by anything resembling imposture it is impossible to imagine that he could have been. I have known Kate Fox for years: she is one of the most simple-minded and strictly impulsive young persons I have ever met: as incapable of framing, or carrying on, any deliberate scheme of imposition as a ten-year-old child is of administering a government. Dr. Gray, who has been intimate with her from her early infancy, writing to a friend in England in regard to Mr. Livermore's experiments, under date January, 1867, says: "Miss Fox, the medium, deported herself with patient integrity of conduct; evidently doing all in her power, at all times, to promote a fair trial and just decision of each phenomenon as it occurred." But if she had been the wiliest of impostors the attendant circumstances would have rendered her intentions powerless. The locality of the experiments was, in every instance, selected by Mr. Livermore; often in his own house. Doors and windows were secured with sealing-wax. The medium's hands were held during all the most important manifestations. Finally the experiences stretched over *six entire years*, and were observed throughout *three hundred and eighty-eight* recorded sittings, under every variety of circumstance. The theory of persistent imposture, in such a case, is a sheer absurdity.

There remains the hypothesis of hallucination, so often put forth as a last resort. But, in this instance, it is singularly out of place. Mr. Livermore is, in the strictest sense, a practical man of business. He has been engaged, during most of his life and up to the present day, in enterprises, financial and industrial, of an extensive, sometimes of a colossal character; and in these—this the world can appreciate—he has been uniformly successful. During the very time of his spiritual experiments he was conducting vast operations involving constant watchfulness and responsibility.

This, then, is no dreamer, secluded in his study; shut out from the world and feeding on his own thoughts: no theorizer, with a favorite system to uphold; and, though a man of decided convictions, not even an enthusiast. Dr. Gray, writing to an English periodical in 1861, says of him: "Besides his general character for veracity and probity Mr. Livermore is a competent witness to the important facts he narrates, because he is not in any degree subject to the illusions and hallucinations which may be supposed to attach to the trance or ecstatic condition. I have known him from his very early manhood, and am his medical adviser. He is less liable to be misled by errors of his organs of sense than almost any man of my large circle of patients and acquaintance."

Add to this that the evidence does not rest upon Mr. Livermore's testimony alone. There is the corroborative experience of Dr. Gray and of Mr. Groute. I have conversed quite recently (October, 1871) with both these gentlemen, and they have declared to me, in the strongest terms, their unqualified conviction touching the reality of the phenomena and the accuracy of the entire record.

Upon what theory with any claim to consideration is this mass of testimony to be set aside? Are we to imagine, on the part of these gentlemen, a base plot to palm upon the world, in support of the great doctrine of immortality, an impious falsehood? Did the sittings *not* take place? Or, if they did, was no figure seen, touched, examined, month after month, year after year? Is the story of its appearance and disappearance, hundreds of times, by spiritual light and by the light of earth—of its floating through the air, of its thousand actions, demonstrations, messages written by no human hand—is all this but baseless fable? Is the entire six-years' record a forgery?

Each reader must decide this question for himself. I will

not, however, withhold my opinion that any one, who should put forth such a hypothesis as ground sufficient for rejecting these proofs of man's continuous existence in another world and of his occasional power thence to communicate with earth, would be setting a precedent which, if consistently followed out, would go to subvert all reasonable confidence in human testimony.*

* This chapter has been read over by me to Mr. Livermore (October, 1871), and its accuracy assented to by him. I had previously received from him, with permission to publish it, this note:

FIFTH AVENUE, NEW YORK,
July 26, 1871.

MY ESTEEMED FRIEND:

I cannot refuse your request for particulars of some of those experiences which I have read to you from my Journal of 1861–66. In giving them I desire, by way of averting misconception, to make a few explanations.

I commenced these investigations an out-and-out sceptic. They were undertaken solely with a view to satisfy my own mind; and with no thought, motive, or desire for publicity.

After thorough and careful scrutiny I found, to my surprise, that the phenomena were real. After ten years of experience, with ample opportunities for observation (often with scientific men), I arrive at these conclusions:

First. That there exists, in presence of certain sensitives of high nervous organization, a mysterious force, capable of moving ponderable bodies, and which exhibits intelligence.

For example: A pencil without contact with human hand, or any visible agency, apparently of its own volition, writes intelligently, and answers questions pertinently.

Second. That temporary formations, material in structure and cognizable by the senses, are produced by the same influence; are animated by the same mysterious force, and pass off as incomprehensibly as they came.

For example: Hands which grasp with living power; flowers which emit perfume and can be handled; human forms, and parts of forms; recognizable faces; representations of clothing and the like.

Third. That this force and the resulting phenomena are developed in a greater or less degree, according to the physical and mental con-

I do not expect to see this ground taken. I fear, rather, the thoughtlessness with which a busy world—engrossed with a thousand cares, duties, pleasures of this life—passes by, like the Jews listening to Paul in the Athenian Areopagus, anything that relates to another. "And when they heard of the resurrection of the dead, some mocked, and others said: 'We will hear thee again of this matter.'"

Yet I know there are many, longing for full satisfaction, in whom the above narrative—even if it fail to work entire conviction as to spirit intercourse—will kindle an earnest desire, should opportunity offer, to examine for themselves whether such phenomena—inestimable if they can be substantiated—are a bright reality or a perilous delusion.

ditions of the sensitive; and, in a measure, by atmospherical conditions.

Fourth. That the intelligence which governs this force is (under pure conditions) independent of, and external to, the minds of the sensitive and investigator.

For example: Questions unknown to either, sometimes in language unknown to either, are duly answered.

The origin of these phenomena is an open question.

You may rely on these records as being free from exaggeration, in each and every particular.

Very sincerely your friend,

C. F. LIVERMORE.

The Honorable

ROBERT DALE OWEN.

CHAPTER V.

WHAT APPARITIONS ARE AND HOW FORMED.

"Handle me, and see; for a spirit hath not flesh and bones, as ye see me have."—LUKE xxiv. 39.

THESE words are ascribed by Luke to Jesus, as having been spoken to his affrighted disciples, when he appeared in the midst of them, on the third day after his crucifixion. They are not given by any other Evangelist; John, who touches on the subject, merely saying that Jesus "showed unto them his hands and his side."

It so happens that these words are quoted by Ignatius, * one of the oldest and most eminent of the Apostolic Fathers, the disciple and familiar friend of the Apostles. But, as he quotes them, there is a variance from the text in Luke, thus: "Handle me and see, for I am not a spirit without body:" (daimonion asomaton.)

I believe this to be the true reading. Facts appear to favor the opinion that man is composed—*First*, of an earthly or natural body, visible to us and which, subjected immediately after the death-change to the chemical laws which govern inanimate matter, rapidly decays: *Second*, as St. Paul alleges, of a spiritual body; and this, it would seem, pervades, during earth-life, the entire natural body, and issues from it at the moment of death: *Third*, of a soul, as to which we have no evidence that it ever appears or exists except in connection with the spiritual body. † According to this view, we must regard the

* He is usually believed to have been a disciple of St. Peter, and was Bishop of Antioch about the year 70. He suffered martyrdom under Trajan, at an advanced age, probably about A.D. 107.

† Throughout this work I have employed the word *spirit* to mean a soul invested in a spiritual body.

denizens of the next world as men disencumbered of the natural body: the soul and the spiritual body surviving the death-change.

It is an opinion fortified by all we hear on the subject through ultramundane sources, that the spiritual body exhibits a close resemblance, in form, to the natural body. There seems good reason why we should think of our departed friends not as impalpable shades, but as real, individual personages, whom we shall recognize, at sight, in another world, even as we recognized them, erewhile, in this: their forms, perhaps, gradually becoming more felicitous expressions of a gradually ennobled individuality.

This spiritual body is not usually visible to human sight. Those only can see it to whom, as Paul has expressed it, the power of "discerning of spirits" is given. Naturally-gifted seers undoubtedly see the Spirit; that is, the spiritual body animated by a living soul. Nor should this surprise us. "Men have no right," says John Stuart Mill, "to mistake the limit of their own faculties for an inherent limitation of the possible modes of existence in the universe."

But as this gift of spirit-discernment is rare, and as the proof it furnishes can bring direct conviction only to the seer himself, it is evident that if the outside world is to obtain similar conviction, there must be presented to our sight something more material than the celestial body which appertains to our next phase of being.

The evidence I have adduced goes to show that a spirit may —under certain conditions and aided, probably, by other spirits—fabricate an ephemeral *eidolon*, resembling the body it had while on earth; but evanescent, especially under earth-light; so that the poet's line,

> "It faded at the crowing of the cock,"

is in strict accordance with the character of the actual phenomenon.

Those who have been fortunate enough to witness this product of spiritual art under its various phases, allege that it may sometimes, under favorable conditions, be marvellously perfect and even transcendently beautiful. Dr. Gray, one of the most accurate and dispassionate of observers, told me that on one of the occasions, already referred to, when the image of Franklin presented itself, he looked steadily in the eyes of the figure and noticed their life-like and expressive character; even that their expression changed in accordance with what was passing at the time. "The living glance of these eyes," he said to me, "wrought in me a thorough conviction that it *was* the old philosopher himself, and no other, who sat in the opposite chair."

By what process this temporary induement (if it be correct to regard it as induement) is effected, we certainly do not know at this time; and perhaps we never shall, until we learn it, on the other side, from the spiritual artists themselves. All that one seems justified in surmising is that there are invisible exudations from the human organization—more or less from all persons, but especially from the bodies of spiritual sensitives *—

* Like Leah and Kate Fox, D. Dunglas Home and other favored "mediums;" in whose presence these formations occasionally appear. There are facts which seem to indicate that there exists in the physical systems of some so-called "mediums," a superfluity of phosphorus; and this may be one of the principal ingredients. Dr. Wilson, of New York, whom I have already mentioned, told me that he had been one of a committee of six persons who, during a carefully-conducted experiment where the strictest precautions against deception were taken, obtained from the tips of the fingers of a well-known medium, phosphorus, slightly varying from the phosphorus of commerce. He showed me a small quantity of this which he had preserved, as evidence of the result.

There appear to be exceptions, however, to the rule that apparitions and other spiritual phenomena can be manifested only when a "medium" is present. I have already stated that endemical, as well as personal, influences seem occasionally to make possible such phenomena, persistent through several generations, in certain localities; usually in old houses which thereby acquire the character of being haunted. It may be said, in a general way, that we know very little touching the precise conditions under which such occurrences take place.

which spirits can condense, or otherwise modify, so as to produce not only what to the senses of human beings is a visible and tangible form, but also substances resembling earthly clothing and other inanimate objects. It appears that they can thus produce also what we might call sculptured representations of portions of the human figure, as of hands and parts of hands, and the like. Let us bear in mind, however, that the fact of a phenomenon is independent of its explanation.

I have myself had one opportunity of witnessing the last-mentioned phenomenon.

What appeared as detached portions of a Human Figure distinctly seen.

On the evening of July 27, 1861, I was at Mr. Underhill's house. Mrs. Underhill proposed that, instead of sitting there, we should adjourn to her mother's residence, No. 66 West 46th street, where we should probably be able to add her sister Kate to the circle. We did so.

Preparations were made to sit in the lower parlor; but as I observed that there were no keys in the doors, I proposed to sit in the upper parlor, which was at once assented to; and we moved thither.

By the raps, I was requested to secure the doors, which I did, putting the keys in my pocket. I also carefully examined the whole room, which had no press or closet. Then we were bidden to put out the gas. Within a few minutes afterward there were three or four most violent raps, as by a heavy bludgeon, on the table; then a quiet interval of some fifteen minutes; after which there suddenly appeared, between Kate and Mrs. Underhill, the figure of an arm and shoulder. The hand was not distinct. The arm was well-shaped and seemed that of a woman of medium size; the elbow bent and the lower arm turned upward. Behind it was a light, but I could distinguish no central point whence this light emanated, as it might from a lamp or candle. The arm showed quite distinctly, from the wrist to the shoulder, against this light:—distinctly, but not in sharp outline; the outlines being softened off, as in a mezzotint engraving. There depended, from the arm, drapery, hanging down some five or six inches; it was gauze-like and semi-transparent. This arm and shoulder approached, moving just above the table and passing Mrs. Underhill in front, until it came within seven or eight inches of me; the drapery waving to and fro, with the motion of the arm.

There it remained for about a minute; then disappeared and reappeared, at intervals of some four or five minutes, three several times; so that I could deliberately observe it and make sure of my observations; for the light, whencesoever its origin, moved with the figure; appearing and disappearing coincidently with it. I saw no head or features above the arm: but adjoining it, dimly indicated, what seemed a small portion of a human form.

After a time a luminous appearance, more bright than the first, came over the table and stopped not more than four or five inches from my face. It resembled a cylinder, illuminated from within; its length being about five or six inches and its apparent calibre about one inch. Over it was something hanging in dark streaks. By the raps was spelled out "Hair." I asked that it might touch me: whereupon it was waved forward and touched my forehead with unmistakable distinctness: the touch resembling that of human hair. After a few minutes it disappeared.

The other sitters described these appearances as seen by them precisely as they were seen by me.

As soon as the sitting closed I examined both doors and found them locked. The room in which we sat, be it borne in mind, was selected by myself.

Some years after the above,* Dr. Gray, speaking of the sittings he had with Mr. Livermore, told me that, at one of

* May 5, 1868.

these, there was laid on the table before them a cylinder about the same size as that I saw: but, more fortunate than I, they had an opportunity of handling it. It seemed, Dr. Gray said, to be of rock crystal, or some similar hard, perfectly transparent material, and to be filled with some incandescent fluid, which was only faintly glowing when at rest; but when the cylinder was agitated the light shone out brightly. During the time they saw and examined it, there was no other light in the room except that which it emitted. By the raps it was stated that the cylinder was the light-vehicle employed by the attendant spirits to illuminate their ephemeral productions; being, itself, as ephemeral as the rest.

On the same occasion Dr. Gray stated to me that he saw a detached hand appear and disappear four or five times. At first it was of a dark-bronze color; but each time it became lighter in color, until, on its final exhibition, it was as fair as any Caucasian hand.

At another time his spectacles, which he had on at the time, were carried off and soon after brought back. He asked to be shown how this was done: whereupon there appeared two imperfect fingers, almost resembling talons, attached to a small strip of hand reaching into the darkness. These appeared to be animate, or at least obedient to some will: for, like living tongs, they picked up and bore away the spectacles; then, after a minute or two, replaced them. *

To a question asked by Dr. Gray why the whole hand was usually shown instead of two detached fingers, the reply, by raps, was that most persons would be alarmed or disgusted at sight of such an amorphous formation.

At another time a mass of what seemed flesh was laid on Dr. Gray's naked foot which he had exposed for the purpose. Left there, at his request, for some time, it became intolerably hot; and he supposes it would ultimately have burned him. This suggests that phosphorus may have been one of the ingre-

* Session 342. Mr. Livermore found the fingers solid to the touch.

dients employed: and perhaps it affords a clue to the stories of a spectre grasping the wrist or hand of some terrified wretch, and leaving thereon the marks of burning fingers.

Dr. Gray related to me a still more interesting observation. On one of the last occasions that the figure of Franklin presented itself, the face appeared, at first, imperfectly formed: showing one eye only: for, in place of the other eye and part of the cheek, there was a dark cavity which looked hideous enough. Kate Fox caught sight of it and screamed out in mortal terror, causing the temporary extinguishment of the light under which the figure appeared.

"Silly child," exclaimed the Doctor, seizing her hands; "don't you see you are interrupting one of the most interesting experiments in the world—the gradual formation of an apparition?"

This philosophical view of the case quieted, by degrees, Kate's excited nerves and dispelled her superstitious terrors: so that when, after less than five minutes' interval, the face of the sage again appeared, every feature perfect and the expression that of bright, calm benignity, she herself was the first to exclaim: "How beautiful!"

This was during one of the last sittings at which Dr. Gray assisted. On several of the earliest occasions, as the Doctor informed me, the face, though distinctly marked, seemed sometimes shrivelled and as if made of dough, at other times it resembled the face of a corpse.

Other details* and minor incidents I omit; seeing that all we yet know furnishes no sufficient basis on which to found

* Both Dr. Gray and Mr. Livermore informed me that, on several occasions when apparitions presented themselves—especially when Estelle appeared—the room was suddenly pervaded by a delicious perfume. This seemed to be emitted from the person of the appearing figure.

When the Church of Rome speaks of some of its saints "dying in the odor of sanctity," the expression may possibly refer to an actual phenomenon.

any distinct theory touching the precise character and formation-process of apparitions.

I do not doubt that, even in this world, we shall, some day, know much more about the matter.* These eidola appear to be gradually becoming more common; and it may enter into God's purpose that, in the future of our world, such a phenomenon shall be the foundation of a universal belief in immortality.

I consider this the more probable because it is apparent that moral and spiritual progress has not, in modern times, kept pace with intellectual and material. But ability, mental or physical, is a doubtful good, if there lack an ethical and religious element to give beneficent direction to it.

Nor do I see how such a civilizing element can manifest itself in full power—can prevail against error and vice, can dominate our race—without the aid—not of a vague belief adopted from written creeds—but of a living, abiding, fervent conviction (such as sense-evidence brings home), that there is a better world where all earthly thoughts and deeds, how secretly-concealed soever here, shall unfailingly bear their appropriate fruit: ill-feeling, ill-doing infallibly entailing sorrow and suffering; well-feeling and well-doing as inevitably bringing about an after-life of satisfying happiness, such as it is not given to us here to conceive.

* I have not any doubt that some of the apparitions seen by Mr. Livermore—casting, as they did, a shadow on the wall and a reflection in a mirror—might, by proper appliances, have been photographed; and I regret much that it did not occur to Mr. L. to attempt this.

How satisfactory would it have been, in giving his narrative, to reproduce an actual photograph of Estelle, in all her spiritual beauty!

BOOK VI.

SPIRITUAL GIFTS OF THE FIRST CENTURY APPEARING IN OUR OWN TIMES.

"Now there are diversities of gifts, but the same spirit."—1 CORINTHIANS xii. 4.

CHAPTER I.

CURES BY SPIRITUAL AGENCY.

—"to another faith by the same spirit; to another the gift of healing by the same spirit."—1 CORINTHIANS xii. 9.

THE facts which go to attest the substantial coincidence between the signs and wonders related in the Gospels, and the spiritual epiphanies of the present day, merit a volume: but I can make room here in favor of that branch of the subject, for two brief chapters only.

Whenever this topic is fully treated, the results, to Christianity, will be beyond calculation. Now, after eighteen hundred years, we cannot conceive any evidence in proof of the Gospel narrative so strong as the fact (if fact it be), that wonderful works and spiritual gifts of similar character to those mentioned in the New Testament come to light among us now. If they do occur now, it is not conceivable that they were imagined, or invented, by the Evangelists and by Paul. If they do appear to-day and if we still set down the Gospel narrative as fable, I know not what fact, two thousand years old, can be established by any historical evidence whatever. Cæsar may not have lived in Rome, nor died in the senate chamber. Soc·

rates may never have spent his life in teaching philosophy, nor lost it in defence of the truths he uttered.

Of the various spiritual powers exercised by Christ, that of healing was the chief. His mission, according to his own view of it, was to bring health to the sick and glad tidings to the poor. When John the Baptist sent, asking: "Art thou he that should come, or look we for another?" Jesus, for answer, sent him word: "The blind receive their sight, and the lame walk, the lepers are cleansed, and the deaf hear, the dead are raised up, and the poor have the Gospel preached to them." * So also of his disciples.

This power has been claimed by the Church of Rome, as exercised by her holy men and women, and, after their death, by their relics. Among what may be called a dissenting sect of that Church—the Jansenists—it appeared, at one time, in wonderful phase. †

We have overwhelming proof at the present day that it is not confined to the Roman Church. The curative powers of what has been called vital magnetism are admitted by all, except the hopelessly prejudiced. This phase of the healing power has shown itself chiefly in France; sometimes on a great scale. The Marquis de Guibert, a benevolent French noble, established, on his estate of Fontchâteau, in the Commune of Tarascon, an hospital in which, during the six years from 1834 to 1840, upward of three thousand three hundred patients were treated by magnetic agency, gratuitously. The Marquis, a powerful magnetizer, operated personally; and has given the

* Matthew xi. 5.

† In 1656, at Port Royal. See *Footfalls*, p. 83. And again, in far more marvellous guise, in 1731 and for years thereafter, at the tomb of the Abbé Pâris. Those who are curious in such matters, will find details in a paper contributed by me to the *Atlantic Monthly*, entitled: *Convulsionists of St. Médard*, and published in the numbers for February and March, 1864. See also *Footfalls*, pp. 85–87.

detailed results in an elaborate report, in which each case, with its separate malady, is set forth.

Of the patients treated by him more than one half were thrown into somnambulic sleep, while upward of five hundred were wholly impassive to magnetic influence. *Nearly three-fifths* (1,948) *left the hospital cured;* and three hundred and seventy-five more were partially relieved.*

I do not allege that these are cures by spiritual agency; but they were wrought by an influence with which we are little acquainted; and which, in past ages, has been again and again mistaken for miraculous. It is an open question, also, whether a magnetizer, employing an occult and imponderable agent, and

* I have not been able to obtain the report itself. But its results are summed up in a French work, *Physiologie, Médecine et Métaphysique du Magnétisme,*" by Dr. CHARPIGNON, member of the Medical Faculty of Paris, and of several learned societies. He gives (at p. 274) the following table:

	Total Patients.	*Impassive.*	*Somnambules.*	*Cured.*
Men..........	1,194	180	424	663
Women.......	2,121	324	1,259	1,285
Totals........	3,315	504	1,683	1,948

Here are some interesting results. We find—

That of the women more than two-thirds were cured, and of the men more than one-half (0.55).

That of the women nearly three-fifths were affected by somnambulic influence, and of the men little more than a third.

That nearly an equal proportion of both sexes—a little more than one-sixth—were wholly impassive; nearly five-sixths being more or less susceptible.

Charpignon does not give a detailed list of the maladies; but he mentions that there were fourteen cases of contraction of the limbs, of which seven were cured.

He states, on the authority of a medical friend of his (Dr. Despine, who visited the hospital at Fontchâteau), that so great were the Marquis's powers of magnetization, that he could produce, in a few seconds, effects which he (Dr. Despine) and others required half an hour, or more, to obtain.

devoting himself, like the Marquis de Guibert, to the relief of human suffering, does not receive spiritual aid. I think the weight of evidence is in favor of the theory that he often does.

I am fortunate, however, in being able to furnish two narratives, attested by name, place, and date, in which I think it cannot rationally be denied that the curative agency was unmistakably spiritual. The first I obtained in this country, the second in Europe.

Paralysis of the Motor Nerve.

In the month of February, 1858, a lady, the wife of Mr. Davis, of Providence, Rhode Island, was residing at her home in the immediate vicinity of that city.

It happened, one morning, when a large and powerful horse was standing harnessed in front of the house, that a servant, passing carelessly close to the animal with a child's carriage in which was an infant daughter of Mrs. Davis, accidentally dropped the tongue of the carriage close to the horse's heels. Mrs. Davis, seeing the danger of her child, rushed to the horse's head and, seizing him suddenly by the bridle with her right hand, the animal reared violently so as almost to lift her from her feet. She succeeded, however, in leading him off from her child, which thus escaped unhurt.

At the moment she experienced no pain: afterward she went about her usual occupations, but felt faint and languid throughout the day. About ten o'clock P.M., sitting down to supper, she first noticed a pain in her elbow, and then, when she attempted to use her right hand, was unable to do so: she found it impossible to close three of the fingers of that hand; the index finger alone obeying the impulse of her will. After a time the pain increased and extended above the elbow.

In the course of the night the right leg also became affected, the pain extending to the hip. In the morning she discovered that she could not, by any effort of the will, move either the right arm or the right leg.

The physicians declared it to be a case of paralysis of the

motor nerve, caused chiefly by sudden excitement. For a long time it resisted all remedies. During seven weeks the paralysis continued unabated. In all that time she never used hand or arm: when she walked she had to drag the right leg after her The leg, too, became cold even to the hip, and all efforts to warm it were ineffectual.

In the month of April she experienced slight relief by the frequent use of electricity; but only so far that, by a special effort of the will she could partially move her hand and arm. Habitually she rested the elbow on her hip, or, when sitting in an arm-chair, raised it with the other hand so as to rest it on the chair-arm. Nor did she ever, until the incident about to be related, regain the power of straightening either leg or arm. Nor was the warmth of the leg at all restored: and when she walked she still had to drag it after her along the ground.

This continued, without alteration or improvement, until the month of July, 1858: and by this time she had become completely disheartened. Life seemed to her no longer worth having; a cripple for life; a burden to her friends; useless to her family. She gave way to tears and despondency.

In the early part of July a friend, Mrs. J——, wife of a gentleman well-known in New York literary circles, and who had been staying with Mrs. Davis, proposed to close her visit and return to that city. Suddenly Mrs. Davis experienced an impulse for which she could not at all account. It was an urgent desire to go to New York and visit Mrs. Underhill* (Leah Fox), with whom she was not acquainted, having merely heard of her through Mrs. J——. She said to that lady that if she would remain with her a day longer, she (Mrs. Davis) would accompany her to New York and visit Mrs. Underhill in hope of relief. Mrs. J—— consenting, they left Providence on the evening of July 3, notwithstanding the doubts expressed by Mr. Davis whether his wife would be able to endure the journey;

* Then Mrs. Brown. Mr. Brown died not long after; and, eventually, Mr. Underhill married his widow.

reached New York next morning, and proceeded at once to Mrs. Underhill's.

Mrs. Davis was so much exhausted on her arrival, that she kept her bed until the afternoon; when she, Mrs. J——, and Mrs. Underhill met in the parlor.

Loud raps being heard, it was proposed to sit down at the centre-table. Before doing so, however, Mrs. Underhill requested Mrs. Davis, for her own satisfaction, to examine the room and its furniture. Mrs. Davis, from motives of delicacy, at first declined; but as Mrs. Underhill urged her request, Mrs. D. finally made the examination in a thorough manner, discovered nothing under the tables or elsewhere to excite suspicion, and convinced herself that there was no one in the room. It being but three o'clock in the afternoon, there was bright day-light.

Soon after the ladies sat down, all their hands being on the table, Mrs. Davis felt the ankle of her right leg seized as by the firm grasp of a human hand, the foot raised and the heel placed in what seemed another hand.* The touch of the fingers and thumb was unmistakably distinct, and indicated that it was a right hand which grasped the ankle, while a left hand received the heel. After a time the hand which had seized the ankle released its grasp, and Mrs. Davis felt it make passes down the leg. These passes were continued about ten minutes. Mrs. Davis felt a sensation as of the circulation pervading the paralyzed limb; and the natural warmth, of which it had been for months deprived, gradually returned. At the expiration of the ten minutes, there was spelled out by raps: "Rise and walk."

Mrs. Davis arose and found, with an amazement which she said no words could describe, that she could walk as well as she ever did in her life. She paced up and down the room, to assure herself that it was a reality: the pain, the paralysis was

* The allegation, by rapping, was, that the agency was that of a deceased brother of Mrs. Davis.

gone; she could use the hitherto disabled leg as freely as the other. After more than four months of suffering and of decrepitude, she found the natural warmth and vigor of the limb suddenly and (as it would be commonly phrased) miraculously restored.

This terminated the sitting for the time: the arm still remaining paralyzed as before. But late in the evening, after the departure of several visitors, the ladies sat down again. This time, by rapping, a request was made to darken the room. After a brief delay the arm was manipulated as the leg had been, but with more force, as if rubbed downward from the shoulder by a smooth and somewhat elastic piece of metal, like the steel busk sometimes used in ladies' stays. After this had been continued for some time, what seemed to the touch a steel busk was laid in Mrs. Davis' right hand; and, by raps, a request was spelled out to close the fingers upon it. This she found herself able to do with a firm grasp. Then the busk was drawn forcibly from her hand.

From that time forth she recovered the use of her arm as completely as she had that of her leg. Nor has she had pain or any return of paralysis, or weakness, or loss of temperature, in either limb, from that day to the present time;* that is, during four years.

In communicating the above to me, as Mrs. Davis did, in presence of the same friend who had accompanied her to Mrs. Underhill's, Mrs. Davis kindly gave me permission to use her name.†

The next case is of a still more remarkable character.

* Written July, 1862, when this narrative was communicated to me.

† The above was related to me July 20, 1862, by Mrs. Davis herself. I wrote it out next day; and submitted the manuscript on the 24th of July to Mrs. Davis, in presence of Mrs. J——, for authentication. It was assented to by both ladies as correct.

The Instantaneous Cure.

It occurred on the thirteenth of April, 1858, at Passy, near Paris, in the parlor of Monsieur B——, a gentleman who formerly occupied a position of rank in the household of Louis Philippe.

The lady who was the subject of it, Mrs. Emma Kyd, is the wife of Mr. A. Kyd, a gentleman of independent fortune, son of the late General Kyd, of the British Army; and is the mother of several grown-up children. The family were then residing in Paris.

Mrs. Kyd had been, for more than half her life, a grievous sufferer. For twenty-five years she had had a disease of the heart, gradually increasing in violence. At the time of this narrative it had reached such a point as to cause, every day of her life, severe pain, and entirely to deprive her of anything like a quiet night's sleep. She could never rest except on the right side; the bedclothes were sensibly moved by the powerful beating of the heart; and if she sought relief by sitting up in an arm-chair, she was frequently unable to rest against the back of it, so violent were the palpitations. She walked with great difficulty, and only slowly and for a short distance; and had frequently to be carried upstairs. Though fond of singing, she had been compelled wholly to abandon it.

This, however, was only one of several diseases under which Mrs. Kyd was suffering. She had chronic diarrhœa, of six years' standing; and this had proceeded so far, that small portions of stale bread, and of roast meat and rice, with occasionally a little tea, constituted the entire range of her diet. Even with such restriction, she was compelled daily to resort to powerful medicine; nor could she safely travel for an hour, or make a visit to a friend, without first taking a preparatory dose. The disease frequently produced violent cramps and spasms. In addition she was afflicted with a falling of the womb of an aggravated character; together with a disease of the bladder, accom panied by obstruction enduring for many years, and producing severe pain. For this latter complaint she had consulted Dr. Phillips, of Paris.

Her life, as she herself expressed it to me, passed with constant reminders of her infirmities; and when she rose from a restless bed, to the sufferings of a new day, tears would gush from her eyes, at the hopeless prospect before her. Her husband had spent a little fortune in taking the advice of eminent medical men. Dr. Locock, Dr. Chambers, Sir Charles Clark, Dr. Chelius, of Heidelberg, and many others had been consulted; but in vain: nor did they hold out any hope, except of temporary alleviation.

It was under these circumstances that, a few days previous to the date above given, she had visited Monsieur B——, attracted by astounding reports touching the wonders of his psychograph, * and the extraordinary phenomena attendant on its writing.

Its first movements, so like those of a living being, aston-

* Now known among us under the name of *planchette.* So far as I am informed, Monsieur B—— was one of the first persons who ever made or used one. It need hardly be said that this little instrument has nothing mysterious about it. It is a mere physical contrivance to gather vital-magnetic power and facilitate involuntary writing It is easier, by outside agency, to put a castor-working planchette in motion than it is to influence the human arm or guide the human hand: that is all. The same power which causes the instrument to write would, if in stronger measure, cause the hand to write without its intervention.

I have seen Monsieur B——'s planchette write, as fast as an ordinary scribe: I have seen it write forward and backward, then write inverted, so that one had to place the writing in front of a mirror in order to read it. I have held a long and spirited debate with it on abstruse subjects; two daughters of Monsieur B—— having placed the tips of their fingers on its surface. I have had the pleasure of frequent conversation with these young ladies, who were sprightly and accomplished; they could talk charmingly on the commonplaces of the day or the last opera; but I am as sure that neither of them could have maintained such a debate for five minutes as I am that they could not converse with any one in Chinese or Arabic.

ished her beyond measure. After a little while it raised itself up, moved toward her and remained, for a considerable time, the pencil suspended in the air.

"What is it doing?" she exclaimed.

"I am only taking a look at you," was the reply instantly written out by the psychograph. After a time it added: "I see you have not come from mere idle curiosity, but from a better motive." Then it proceeded to set forth some of its peculiar doctrines, and concluded by requesting her to return in a day or two and to bring her husband with her.

The night between the twelfth and thirteenth of April was, to Mrs. Kyd, one of even more than usual suffering, and she awoke feeling utterly unable to make the promised visit. But she summoned courage; and, fortified as usual with a dose of medicine and having prepared another to be taken on her return, she drove, accompanied by her husband, to the house of Monsieur B——.

There she found seven or eight friends of Monsieur B—— assembled, and seated herself in a corner of the room to watch the proceedings. They were experimenting with the psychograph; two of Monsieur B——'s daughters lightly touching it, as usual.* The results obtained seemed even more astonishing than on the previous occasion; and, almost out of herself, she involuntarily exclaimed: "It seems so like something divine, that I think if it were to bid me do anything in the world, I would obey."

"Why, your faith is enormous, Mrs. Kyd," said some one present.

Shortly afterward the psychograph suddenly wrote: "Emma, come here!" She advanced to the table and it continued: "Get a chair and sit down." She did so: then it added: "More to the left and closer to me." She brought her chair close to that part of the table where the psychograph was.

* It ought here to be stated that both these young ladies are highly susceptible and lucid somnambules.

"You shall be cured," it wrote: "it shall be to you according to your faith."

Then, suddenly and to the utter astonishment of all present, it sprung (with the hands of the two assistants still upon it) from the table against her heart, remaining there for three or four seconds, pressing gently against her, with a sort of fluttering or tremulous motion; then, as suddenly, it sprang back to the table and instantly wrote:

"You are cured. Go home and do not take that nauseous draught which you had mixed up, against your return. Eat whatever you please, as you used to do before you were ill. Do all this nothing doubting, and be assured all will be well."

Mrs. Kyd informed me that no words could express the sudden revulsion of feeling—the emotion utterly unlike anything she had ever experienced in her life—which shot over her, causing her to believe that the cure was real. She seemed actually to *feel* (as she expressed it to me) the revolution throughout her entire frame, and the return of the several organs to their normal state. She breathed long and deeply, without effort or pain. She rose and walked; already, so it appeared to her, with renovated strength.

When she returned home she ascended the stairs lightly and without effort; in a word, as she had not been able to do for fifteen or twenty years past. This she repeated several times; scarcely believing, even then, in its possibility. The medicine was thrown out; and from that day to this,* she has not consulted a physician nor swallowed a single dose.

That day, at dinner, she looked at the various interdicted dishes which the day before she could not have touched without the severest penalty; hesitating still, with natural reluctance, to taste them. But then the injunction to eat, nothing doubting, recurred to her mind. She did so; felt no evil effects whatever, and spent a night of almost undisturbed repose such as for long years she had never been permitted to enjoy.

* Related to me in Paris, on the 18th of April, 1859.

More than a year has passed since then: and, during that period, she has not had the least return of any one of the maladies which had made of half her life one long martyrdom. To describe how gratefully and wonderingly she enjoyed her relief; or with what zest she entered upon her new life, which even day after day seemed to her more like some beautiful dream than any earthly reality—was, she declared to me, impossible.

The allegation, as written by the psychograph, was, that the cure was the result of Mrs. Kyd's strong faith.

The particulars of this marvellous case I had, first in somewhat general terms from Monsieur B——, the gentleman at whose house the circumstance occurred, and whom I met in London in January, 1859; and afterward, during a visit to Paris, in minute detail, from Mrs. Kyd herself, in the presence of her husband: he confirming the narrative in every point. From earnest desire to serve the cause of truth and in token of gratitude to God for benefit so unexpectedly received, Mrs. Kyd granted me permission, in publishing the case, to give her name; and to this her husband also assented. In view of the peculiarity of the circumstances, I at first felt reluctant to avail myself of so generous an offer; as, indeed I did also in Mrs. Davis's case. But on further reflection I decided that, in the interests of truth and spiritual science, I had no right to refuse such an opportunity of authentication.

I am authorized also to furnish Mr. Kyd's address to any medical man, or other earnest inquirer, who may desire direct testimony for what will usually be deemed incredible.

The public cannot have a better voucher for the sincerity of the narrators. I myself have stronger proof; for I became well acquainted with Mr. and Mrs. Kyd, and I have the additional testimony touching their intelligence and uprightness which any one acquainted with the world instinctively derives from daily intercourse with the earnest and the cultivated.

I may add, what has been stated to me by Monsieur B—— and confirmed by Mrs. Kyd herself, that he had given her no reason to believe that a cure could be effected through the intervention of the psychograph; nor, though he knew Mrs. Kyd was in bad health, was he apprised of any of the details of the case. Monsieur B—— also stated to me that Mrs. Kyd had paid his family many subsequent visits; and that it was long before she could see the psychograph, inanimate medium though it was, without shedding tears.

It should be stated that a previous cure, though by no means so striking a one, had been, as Monsieur B—— informed me, effected in a similar manner.

Mrs. Kyd also told me that she had since procured a psychograph; that, with her hands and those of one of her daughters upon it, they had, after several weeks' patience, succeeded in getting it to write as fluently as that of Monsieur B——; and that, even up to the present time, if Mrs. Kyd has a headache or other slight indisposition, by placing her hands upon it and retaining them there some time, the effect is to cast her into magnetic sleep and, in every case, to afford relief. Indeed she and her husband seemed to regard the little instrument as a familiar friend and adviser, to whom, when they felt need of information or counsel, they might resort.*

I might go on, filling a hundred pages with the details of cures wrought among us by magnetic or spiritual agency. What are called "healing mediums" are to be found, in city and country, by the hundreds; and though, doubtless, many are pretenders and many more often fail to relieve, that is only

* The above narrative, as here written out, was submitted by me, at Paris, on the twenty-third of April, 1859, to Mr. and Mrs. Kyd; and its accuracy in every particular assented to by them.

It may not be out of place here to repeat a caution already given. There is great temptation, when an inestimable blessing has thus been received through spiritual agency, to accept, without scruple or scrutiny, all opinions which may be obtained from the same wonder-working source. But this is dangerous as well as illogical. The power to cure is one thing; the capacity to utter truth unmixed with error quite another. We have proof of the former: we have no proof—indeed fallible creatures *can* have none—of the latter.

what happens in the case of thousands who have a legal right to add M. D. to their names.

But further detail is needless. The proof that the gift of healing inheres in certain favored natures is as complete, and as readily attainable, as that some men and women are born poets and others musicians.*

And space fails me to touch except on a single additional point. It has been sometimes alleged that Spiritualism tends to produce insanity. I have never known, or found proof, of such a case: yet doubtless such have occurred. We have hundreds of examples of mania caused by religious excitement; as at revivals or camp-meetings: and it would be strange if Spiritualism, when unwisely or extravagantly pursued, should prove an exception to the rule. There have, however, come to my knowledge two cases in which insanity has been cured, or averted, by spiritual influence; the subject, in both instances, being a widow.

For several years previous to 1860, a Mrs. Kendall had been an inmate of the Somerville Lunatic Asylum, near Boston; and she was considered by the resident physician of that institution one of his most dangerous patients. Her lunacy had been caused by the death of her husband, six years before; and she remained insane until January, 1860. At that time she was taken from the asylum, to be received into a family where there were several mediums. With them she remained many months; obtaining, from time to time, communications alleged to come from her deceased husband.

On the tenth of January, 1861, the above circumstances

* I have the full particulars from the patient himself—but no room here to relate them—of a cure effected by the well-known Dr. Newton. The subject was a New York merchant of high standing, and he told me that his case was regarded by friends and physicians as absolutely hopeless; and that he sought Dr. N. in sheer despair. Several manipulations, throughout two weeks, effected a marvellous and radical cure; and for years and until the day I saw him, there had been no relapse.

were stated to me by her son, Mr. F. A. Kendall. His mother was then at home, completely cured. He told me that he was not a Spiritualist; not having had what he deemed sufficient evidence: but he freely admitted that his mother's cure was due solely to her residence among Spiritualists, and to the consoling assurance which she there found that the husband to whom in life she had been devotedly attached still lived and still thought and cared for her.

The other lady is personally known to me, though I am not at liberty to give her name. I knew her when her husband was alive; and her devotion to him was such that I shared the fears which I sometimes heard expressed by other friends of hers, that if she lost him, the consequences might be fatal. To her despair, he enlisted when the war was at its height, reached the rank of Major and died in a New Orleans hospital.

When the news, no longer to be withheld, was finally broken to her, it produced a fit of frenzy; and for weeks she was drifting into hopeless insanity. She had never been a Spiritualist; indeed she usually, as I well remember, had treated the subject with ridicule: but a sister, visiting a medium in hopes of getting something for herself, received, instead, a message to the disconsolate widow. It was repeated to her; and it was the first thing that roused her out of brooding despair. She went herself to the medium, received numerous messages embodying incontrovertible tests of identity; brightened day by day: and when I met her, many months afterward, she had regained all her cheerfulness; and told me that she felt as if K—— (his pet name) were living and conversing with her still.

Thus, in our day, as in Christ's time, lunatics may, by spiritual influence, be restored to "their right mind." The time will come when this truth will be acted on by the managers of insane asylums.

CHAPTER II.

OTHER SPIRITUAL GIFTS.

DEEMING it highly important to run out the parallel between the spiritual gifts enumerated by Paul and by the Evangelists, and those which manifest themselves in our times, I had prepared five chapters, with narratives illustrating the general similarity between ancient and modern "signs and wonders;" to be here inserted.* But my manuscript has spread over an unexpected number of printed pages; so that lack of space and a desire that this book should be sold at a moderate price cause their exclusion. If I should live to write another work this omission may be supplied.

Meanwhile a few references, in this connection, may be acceptable.

Of the gift of prophecy, considered by Paul one of the chief (—"desire spiritual gifts, but rather that ye may prophesy" †), some very remarkable examples, exhibited during somnambulism, are given by French writers on physiology and vital magnetism ‡ of acknowledged reputation. In this volume an

* As will be seen by those who may have looked over a condensed table of contents included in advance specimen-sheets of this volume, already issued by the publishers.

† 1 Corinthians xiv. 1.

‡ See, for example, *Manuel Pratique du Magnétisme Animal*, par ALPHONSE TESTE, D.M. de la Faculté de Paris; membre de plusieurs societés savantes: 4th Ed. Paris, 1853; pp. 120–128. This book has been translated into several languages.

See also *Physiologie du Système Nerveux*, by Dr. GEORGET, of Paris, vol. ii. pp. 404, 405. As to Georget's character and standing, see *Footfalls*, pp. 53, 54.

example is supplied;* and in a former work of mine there are several. † Bunsen believed in this faculty. ‡

As illustrating St. Paul's text—"to another the word of knowledge by the same spirit,"—I had intended here to give a collection of what I have good reason to regard as spiritual communications to myself; but I now limit myself to one—an average specimen—relating to this very power of prevision. It purported to be from Violet, and I obtained it § through a non-professional medium. I entitle it

The proleptic Gift.

"There is a faculty which is the complement of memory. Memory causes that which does not now exist, but which did once exist, to become, as it were, present. So this other faculty—let us call it prevision—causes that which does not now exist but will hereafter exist, to appear—like the past when we remember it,—to be present. But the faculty of memory is one possessed, in a greater or less degree, by almost every one; while the faculty of prevision is the privilege of comparatively few: and it is enjoyed by these few in different degrees; sometimes only as a dim presentiment or premonition, sometimes as a clear prevision.

"Prevision, though it be not as common, is as natural a faculty, as memory: and it may present to us, quite as clearly and even more clearly than memory, that which (as regards time) is remote from us. Our minds may, under certain conditions, anticipate more distinctly than they can recall: for our own feelings in the present often mix less with our previsions than with our recallings.

* See narrative entitled *A Trifle Predicted*, in Book ii. chap. 4.

† In *Footfalls* will be found the following examples of presentiment, or prophetic faculty, in its various phases: *The Negro Servant*, p. 204; *The Fishing Party*, p. 151; *How Senator Linn's Life was Saved*, p. 453; and others.

‡ See preceding page 178. § November 15, 1861.

"As there is, in reality, no up or down—these terms being relative only—so, as to time, there is, in one sense, no past or future. All IS.

"If this faculty of prevision had not shown itself, at times, throughout all the recorded past history of the world, prophets and prophecy would not be the common words they are."

This communication furnishes, at all events, material for thought. In connection with a subject which we cannot expect, in this world, fully to comprehend, I commend to the reader a remarkable and suggestive little pamphlet-volume entitled, "The Stars and the Earth;" published some twelve or fifteen years since, by Baillière, London; and since republished in this country.*

As regards the gift designated in the text—"to another discerning of spirits"—it is the less important that I should here advert; seeing that I have furnished examples both in this volume † and in a former work.‡

As regards the Pentecostal epiphany—"to another divers kinds of tongues,"—the most remarkable modern example has been already alluded to; namely the phenomena that came to light in London, among the Rev. Mr. Irving's congregation,

* Mr. Baillière informed me that the manuscript of this little treatise came to him anonymously, accompanied by a sum of money to defray part of the expense of publication; and that all his exertions to discover the author had been unavailing. A rare example of literary bashfulness!

† As *Sister Elizabeth*, preceding page 401; the vision of *Violet* by Mrs. B—— of Cleveland, Book iv. chapter 3; the vision to *Mr. Bach* in dream, Book iv. chapter 2; and others.

‡ See *Footfalls:* the continuous visions of *Oberlin*, p. 364; *The Dead Body and the Boat-cloak*, pp. 367, 368; *Apparition in India*, p. 369; *The Brother's appearance to the Sister*, p. 372; visions of *Madame Hauffe*, pp. 396–400; *The Old Kent Manor-house*, pp. 415–417; and others.

and which, as we have seen,* were deemed genuine by so sound a thinker as Baden Powell.

Mr. Livermore also testifies to the fact that he received, through Miss Fox, messages in languages unknown alike to her and to himself.† I examined one of these (in good German) the day after it was received.

Then there was the power which Jesus exercised by Jacob's well—the perception of the hidden Past—causing the Samaritan woman's exclamation to her neighbors: "Come! see a man who told me all things that ever I did." The same faculty was possessed, as in his autobiography he informs us,‡ by a well-known and much-esteemed German author.

Finally we have Paul's words:—"to another the working of miracles" (dunameon): referring to other spiritual powers or phenomena, not specified. We can but conjecture what these were.

I have myself either personally witnessed, or had trustworthy evidence for various phenomena, *seemingly* more miraculous than any related in this book; as the powers of levitation,§ of elongation, of handling glowing coals without injury, and the like.

* Prefatory Address, sec. 14; preceding page 178.

† See Mr. Livermore's letter to the author, at the close of chapter 4, Book v.

‡ *Eine Selbstschau*, von HEINRICH ZSCHOKKE, 4th Ed. New York reprint, 1851; pp. 283–287. Zschokke's works are collected in forty volumes.

§ Lord Lindsay, in a recent letter to the (London) *Spiritualist*, narrates the following incident:

"I was sitting with Mr. Home and Lord Adare, and a cousin of his. During the sitting Mr. Home went into a trance, and in that state was carried out of the window in the room next to where we were, and was brought in at our window. The distance between the windows was about seven feet six inches, and there was not the slightest foothold between them, nor was there more than a twelve-inch projection to each window, which served as a ledge to put flowers on. We heard the window in the next room lifted up, and almost immediately after

As to some of these manifestations I am not, for the present, at liberty, even did space permit, to give to the public the evidence which is in my hands.

I do not doubt that, as the years pass by, additional proof will accumulate that Christ's promise to his followers—that they should do the works that he did and greater works still *—is in progress of fulfilment among us.

we saw Home floating in the air outside our window. The moon was shining into the room; my back was to the light, and I saw the shadow on the wall of the window-sill, and Home's feet about six inches above it. He remained in this position for a few seconds, then raised the window and glided into the room feet foremost and sat down. Lord Adare then went into the next room to look at the window from which he had been carried. It was raised about eighteen inches, and he expressed his wonder how Mr. Home had been taken through so narrow an aperture. Home said (still in trance): 'I will show you;' and then, with his back to the window, he leaned back, and was shot out of the aperture head first, with body rigid, and then returned quite quietly. The window was about seventy feet from the ground."

* John xiv. 12.

BOOK VII.

ADDRESSED TO CHRISTIAN BELIEVERS IN IMMUTABLE LAW AND IN RELIGIOUS PROGRESS.

THE CONCLUSION OF THE WHOLE MATTER.

CHAPTER I.

SUMMARY.

AN author who assumes to write with a view to the improvement of his race owes it to his readers, ere he takes leave of them, to sum up clearly what he seeks to do, and how he seeks to do it.

I address this summary to those who have convinced themselves of the universal and persistent reign of Law, and who have faith in constant spiritual progress and in the ultimate triumph of Christ's teachings as the religion of Civilization. I specially address such believers, because they will best appreciate the general tenor of argument throughout this book.

Consider, I pray you, the following brief propositions, in connection with each other.

The teachings of Christ, as set forth in the Gospel narratives, so intimately connect themselves with the wonderful powers (dunameis) there ascribed to him, and with his claim to be the Anointed Messenger of God, and with his alleged appearance to his disciples after death, that if the claim be rejected and the phenomena denied, faith in the teachings will be rudely shaken; the most rudely in the most candid and upright minds. Neither Strauss nor Rénan speak of Christ, in terms, as an impostor; yet the virtual effect of their theories touching the signs and wonders of the first century, is to represent him as one who lent himself to deceit. But a spiritual system which had its origin in deceit presents slender claim to become the supreme religion of a civilized world.

The Church of Rome recognizes this truth. But because she does not believe in invariable law as the rule of God's government, nor in spiritual phenomena occurring under natural law, she regards the wonderful works and gifts of which we read in the Gospels, as miracles, wrought by one of the Persons of the Godhead eighteen hundred years ago, and still wrought by Him within the jurisdiction of a single Church. She sets down all persons who deny miracles as denying that these works and gifts ever had existence; and she declares all such persons to be anathema; that is, accursed of God.

You, believing in invariable law and believing also in Christ, as Civilization's great Spiritual Teacher, can say to the Church of Rome: "We admit that the works were done and that the spiritual gifts were exercised: we deny, however, that they were miraculous."

But the Church of Rome has a right to reply: "Your theory is illogical. You say the works and gifts in question occurred under natural law, and you assert that all natural laws are universal and perpetual. If so, the law under which these works and gifts appeared must have remained unchanged, and must be still operative at the present day; and, under that law, similar signs and wonders must be occurring now throughout the world. But this does not happen. They occur within our Holy Church—the only Church of Christ—and nowhere else. They are still wrought by Christ; and they are wrought by him, not under a general law, but among us exclusively and miraculously, in proof that the Catholic Church is his Church, and that he recognizes no other."

It is a very strong argument. It has convinced millions. To its power is mainly attributable the success of the Tractarian movement at the English University of Oxford, in 1832, carrying over such vigorous thinkers as John Henry Newman and others of his school. To its power is to be ascribed much of that enthusiasm and earnest conviction and self-sacrificing faith which has ever marked the Church of Rome. The phenomena do occur. In favor of her claims that Church has the evidence of her senses; the same evidence which Christ's disciples had. Thousands witness the wonders. On them she bases her right to canonize. Through them her greatest triumphs have been achieved.

Now, what are you to reply? That the phenomena do not occur within the precincts of Roman Catholicism? That allegation has been tried and has failed: men continue to believe that they do occur. You will be beaten on that issue, as we have seen that for the last three hundred years you have been. If I have proved to you, in the preceding pages, that similar phenomena may be observed outside the precincts of the Roman Church, why not within these precincts? But if I have not proved this, then where do you stand? What can you reply to the Catholicism of Rome?

You cannot deny that a universal, invariable law which was in operation in the first century must be in operation still. And if you fail to show, by modern results, that it *is* in operation to-day, then the Church of Rome reasons fairly when she tells you that it never had existence; therefore that Christ's wonderful works were *not* done under law; therefore that, if they be not miracles, they are fables. She places before you the naked alternative—Rénan or St. Peter.

If you have any mode of escape from such a dilemma, other than by the path which this volume indicates, I pray you to come forward and set it forth.

And if you cannot suggest any other, think where you stand!

On one side a Church which claims exclusive infallibility, and with it a right which properly inheres in the Infallible—the right to persecute even unto death; a Church which claims the right to circumscribe scientific inquiry; a Church which pronounces her doctrines to be irreformable and her creed to be a finality; a Church which denies to humankind religious progress.

On the other hand a Christianity which had birth in fabulous legends; a Spiritual System of which the historians—impostors or self-deceivers—narrate lies; a system pretending to bring immortality to light, yet assuming, as crucial test whereby to establish that great truth, a childish superstition. For such—with all due respect to the talents and the sincerity of the man—is Rénan's Christianity.

With the issue thus made up, I think the Pope will have the best of it. I see no reasonable ground for the assurance that the brilliant Frenchman's rationalism will not go down before the Church of Rome.

As little do I believe that Secularism will prevail against her. It has nothing to offer but this world, and that is insufficient for man.

But this is dealing in negatives only. "Leave these," you will say to me, "and let your summary inform us, plainly and briefly, what system, in your opinion, will prevail."

Willingly. A system that can reply thus to Papal argument: "We admit that the natural law under which the signs and wonders of the Gospels occurred is in operation still. We admit that similar signs and wonders have occurred, and still occur, within your Church. We add that they occur, as we can testify, outside of your Church also. They are œcumenical. Whether within your Church or without it, they occur in accordance with universal and enduring law. They afford proof, as strong as that which was vouchsafed to the apostles, of immortality: but they afford no proof whatever that Roman Catholics are God's children of preference, or that, outside of St. Peter's fold, there is no true religious life."

It suffices not, however, to have a system that can reply to an opponent's argument. If we would succeed against that opponent, we must discard the errors upon which our opposition to the Roman Church is, or should be, based. We must discard—

Belief in every phase of the INFALLIBLE, in connection with any religious matter whatever.

Belief in the MIRACULOUS, past or present.

Belief in the right of PERSECUTION; whether by ecclesiastical excommunication or social outlawry; whether by employment of rack and fagot, or by suborning of public opinion.

Belief in the EXCLUSIVE, as applied to any Church or sect, supposed to be God's favorite.

Belief in a FINALITY, as found in any branch of knowledge, including religion.

Belief in Vicarious Atonement, in Imputed Righteousness, in a personal Devil, in an Eternal Hell and in Original Depravity.

It may be added—though this is a Protestant rather than a Roman Catholic error—belief in the saving efficacy of faith without works.

There remains another duty, as imperative. If, misled by a wholesale spirit of condemnation, we have rejected certain valuable tenets of the Old Faith, because the form in which they appeared pleased us not, we ought to reconsider our rejection. Great truths are often covered up in unseemly garb. Let us reflect whether we may not properly admit our belief—

Not in a Purgatory of flames, whence sinners are rescued by virtue of the Church's intercession; but in a state of progression, intermediate between the life which now is and the higher phases of another.

Not in the Intercession of Saints, for we need not holy men to remonstrate in our favor with God, as some of the Jewish prophets of old assumed to do; but in grateful recipiency of such guardian aid and wise counsel as may come to us from the denizens of a better world.

Not in the efficacy of paid masses that find favor in God's sight and induce him to release from suffering in penal fires those to whose benefit these ecclesiastical ceremonies inure;

but in the influence of fervent prayer, offered here below, to aid a soul struggling upward to the light, whether the struggle be on our earth, or in that other life, a supplement to this, where a spirit laden with sin equally needs, ere it rises to better things, effort and repentance. *

For the rest, I think that he is the most likely to distinguish Christianity in its purity, who, with ears happily closed to the harsh murmurs of the scholiasts † reads, in the spirit of a cultivated child, the teachings ascribed by the Synoptical Gospels to Jesus; interpreting these by that inward light—God's holy spark within us—to which Christ himself so often refers.

I hope that in preceding chapters I may have succeeded in giving you, in a general way, my idea of the aspect of Christianity when divested of canonical cerements. Here, ere I close, I may briefly epitomize. It seems proper in discarding so much that is called orthodox, to advert to the grand truths that remain.

* See, for an example, how repentance may, by its regenerating influence, change the character and condition of a criminal in the next world; and how prayers and counsel from this sphere may bear fruit in another, *Footfalls*, pp. 396, 397, 399. The incident there given is very suggestive.

† "Wen, als Knaben, ihr einst Smintheus Anacreons
Fabelhafte Gespielinnen,
Dichterische Tauben umflogt, und sein mäonish Ohr
Vor dem Lerme der Scholien
Sanft zugirrtet—" KLOPSTOCK.

CHAPTER II.

WHAT UNDERLIES CHRIST'S TEACHINGS, AS FOUNDATION-MOTIVE.

"And now abideth Faith, Hope, and Love, these three, but the greatest of these is Love."—1 CORINTHIANS xiii. 13.

"Thy kingdom come!"—MATTHEW vi. 10.

"REPENT! for the kingdom of Heaven is at hand:" these, as we have seen, are the earliest recorded words of Christ's public discourse.

The Pharisees asked him: "When shall the kingdom of God come?"

And he replied: "The kingdom of God cometh not with observation: neither shall they say 'Lo here!' or 'Lo there!' For behold! the kingdom of God is within you."

—Is within us. The light within. The divine, indwelling spirit of truth. How far—passing by Christ's words—do we wander, seeking that which is in our own hearts!

We think by vast searchings to find out God and his kingdom and his Spirit. But the Spirit of God is not in the fierce wind of Dogmatism, desolating in its sweep; it is not in the earthquake of warring creeds, rending and convulsing the religious world; it is not in that fire of zeal which persecutes and consumes; it is in the still, small voice which, so it be not quenched, speaks from the soul of every one of us.

—Often obscured; stifled sometimes by adverse influence and vile surroundings: not unheeded only, alas! unheard: yet as surely existing, down under the crust, in the Bushman, or in the Caffre, or in the nomadic outcast of Civilization, as shining in the Christian who lives the nearest to the bidding of his Lord.

"Thy kingdom come!"

We repeat a thousand times these words of Christ's prayer, for once that we fully appreciate their deep meaning: forgetting that the kingdom whose advent we implore is (if we accept Christ's interpretation) a sovereignty of which we cannot witness the coming; to which we cannot assign this place or that; seeing that we bear it ever about us. We pray, even if we know it not, that the spirit of God within us may assert itself and rule. We pray for the sovereignty of enlightened conscience. We pray for the coming of ethical, of spiritual development; and we pray that, when it comes, it may be the governing power of our race.

Conscience is God's vicegerent, rightfully ruling the heart of man. Under her rule alone is human life satisfactory. That is Christ's doctrine. How simply and how strongly has he expressed this!

"Blessed are they which do hunger and thirst after righteousness: for they shall be filled."

—Hunger and thirst, not after this dogma or that sect; not after ritual or ceremonial or long prayers in the synagogues or much speaking; nor yet after silver and gold: hunger and thirst after THE RIGHT—that Kingdom of Heaven within.

Christ's plan is—right-doing because it *is* the right. Right-doing, come what will of it, for that is God's affair. Accept the consequences. Do we not pray: "Thy will be done!"

Things may seem to go ill. Men may revile and persecute and speak evil. No matter. Even then, Jesus declares, is the right-doer blessed. He may seem forsaken; bread itself may be scant: yet, in the end, it is he alone who shall be filled. If we seek first God's Right, all else—that is Christ's assertion—shall be added unto us.

Yet he states this as a fact, not puts it forward as a motive. The motive on which he relies is not the prospect of gain; it is the hunger and thirst. We may conform to man's law through forced obedience, fear of penalty, hope of reward. God's law can be fulfilled through love alone.

Christ has nowhere said that they are blessed who act righteously in order to win Heaven or escape Hell. Fear, a base motive, enters not at all into his scheme. He does not, like the Psalmist, inculcate the fear of God: * *his* wisdom has a far nobler beginning. It is based on perfect love—that love which casteth out fear.

The poet expressed a thoroughly Christian sentiment when he prayed:

> "What Conscience dictates to be done
> Or warns me not to do;
> This teach me, more than Hell, to shun
> That, more than Heaven, pursue."

This matter of basic motive underlying a religion is of vast practical importance. We poorly appreciate Christ's spiritual polity if we fail to perceive that it trusts, for a world's reform, to awakening in man the slumbering love of the Right, for its own sake; not to arousing his cupidity or playing on his fears. If a child, passing from under his teacher's hand, grow to manhood honest merely because he thinks that honesty is the best policy, he may be a fair dealer, and so far commendable; but

* If this startle any one, I beg him to examine, for himself, whether, in the entire Gospel record, there occur, even once, the direct injunction by Christ, "Fear God:" an injunction repeated, a hundred times, under the Old Dispensation. He will find, in Matthew (x. 28), this: "Fear not them which kill the body, but are not able to kill the soul: but rather fear him which is able to destroy both body and soul in Hell."

Yet the very words next following are these:

"Are not two sparrows sold for a farthing? and one of them shall not fall to the ground without your Father. But the very hairs of your head are all numbered. *Fear ye not*, therefore; ye are of more value than many sparrows."

The fair interpretation evidently is this: "It is more reasonable to fear one who has power over both body and soul than one who has power over the body only. But fear not your Heavenly Father; for ye are under his constant care."

With this accords the spirit of the whole record. "Fear not, little flock," said Christ. And he declared that his disciples should be known by their love, not by their fears.

he is not a disciple of Christ. If a professor of religion exhibit the liveliest zeal for his Church, actuated by no higher principle than that which caused Louis XIV. to repeal the Edict of Nantes—namely, to save a worthless soul from Hell—he may be a useful Church member, but he is not a Christian. There *is* no Christianity except that which has for foundation the indwelling love of the Right.

Let us not despair that, some day, such may become the basis of civilization's morality, public and private. A little introvision may encourage. When we have been looking back upon our early youth, has the thought never come over us that we are not what we might have been—that our nature was better than our education? Do we not sometimes feel—the dullest among us—that there are springs of virtue within us that have rarely been touched; generous impulses that have seldom been awakened; noble aspirations that have never found field of action? And do such convictions come to us alone? Shall we stand up in the temple and thank God that we are not as other men? Is it not written that man was created in the image of God?

Let it not discourage us that such a change of motive from the ruling selfishness of the day involves a reform radical even to regeneration. Christ admitted that. He saw how blind to the heaven within was the world around him. "Except a man be born again he cannot see the kingdom of God."

A consideration which will suggest itself to every one here intervenes.

Conscience alone, if it be uninstructed and undeveloped, suffices not, how earnest soever, to reform the world. The most sincere love of the Right can work only according to light and knowledge: but the light may be feeble and the knowledge scant.

Beyond the result to be hoped from the general progress of Civilization, does Christ's system open up to us no special source whence to supply this need?

The reply connects itself with a subject treated of in one of the most important chapters of this volume.* Jesus, as I have already reminded you, said to his followers, at the close of his earthly life:

"I have yet many things to say to you, but ye cannot bear them now. Howbeit when he, the spirit of truth, shall come, he will guide you into all truth: for he shall not speak of himself, but whatsoever he shall hear, that shall he speak."

Whether Christ, in virtue of his proleptic power, foresaw that it entered into the economy of God, at a certain stage of human progress, to vouchsafe unto man mediate spiritual revealings, coming to him perennially from a wiser world than this; whether the Author of Christianity here indicates the source whence he believes that the human conscience (so soon as the world can bear it) shall derive light and knowledge: that I leave for you to decide. In the preceding pages I have furnished you what aid I could, in making up your decision.

This, however, I pray you to observe: that you have to decide not at all whether the mass of alleged spiritual communications of the day can fitly educate conscience; † but whether, when prudence and reverence preside, a Spirit of truth, from an ultramundane sphere, speaking not of itself but from the knowledge which a heavenly residence imparts, may not be the medium, promised by Christ, for the regeneration of mankind.

* Book i. chapter 2.

† What impartial historian would judge the Protestantism of Luther's day by the extravagances of the Anabaptists, or the atrocities of the Peasants' War?

Some of the best and most intelligent friends I have are endowed with one or more of those spiritual gifts of mediumship, as to which Paul declares that we should all desire them: and many more share my own convictions touching the great truths of Spiritualism. Shall I discard these excellent friends, or hear them arraigned for their belief without solemn protest, merely because the new faith has, like early Lutheranism, attracted its waifs and strays; or because it has been often interpreted, like Lutheranism, by those whose zeal outruns their knowledge?

—Promised conditionally. The basis of all—the indispensable condition-precedent—is loyalty to conscience. The promise is to those who hunger and thirst after the Right. It is *their* hunger, *their* thirst, which, from a spiritual source, shall be stilled.

I check the temptation to enlarge on this. A recapitulation must not stretch out into a second work. Yet permit me to add a disclaimer, not needed for thoughtful minds, but which may avert misconstruction.

I have not been asserting—far be it from me—that, in our day and generation, severity is always misplaced, or that legal penalties are useless; still less, that we should not carefully explain to children the suffering they incur by doing evil, the pleasure which results from doing well: that is an educator's bounden duty. I but say that Christ discards—as the world will some day discard—force and fear and selfish gain as motives. I but remind you that Christ trusts, for a world's reformation, to influences higher, nobler than these—to an impulse strong as hunger, strong as thirst,—to a love seeking not her own, rejoicing in the truth, that shall draw men, as by chain of steel, to do that which is right.

Other characteristics of Christ's teachings will readily suggest themselves. The element of forgiveness, in a degree unknown among us yet. An erring brother pardoned even to seventy times seven. The merciful blessed; they shall obtain mercy. A frail offender, excommunicated by society, set free, uncondemned, and bidden to sin no more.

Beneficence, especially to the weary and heavy-laden, is another marked feature. Helping the poor. Ministering to the stranger, the hungry, the naked, the sick and those in bonds. That which we do unto them we do unto God.

We are warned against the danger of riches; against overmuch thought for the morrow; against eager seeking of place or power. The treasures which moth and rust corrupt, the uppermost rooms at feasts and the chief seats in synagogues are declared to be objects unworthy to engross the heart of man.

There are enjoined meekness, peace even to non-resistance of evil, purity as much in thought as in action, resignation under whatever God sends.

We are encouraged to have faith and hope, based on the assurance that the Father knows our needs and will provide, before we ask Him; but, above all and beyond all, as stamp and witness of our discipleship, as the very fulfilment of God's behests, we are incited to something greater than faith, greater than hope—uplifting as their influence is—even to the supreme law of all—LOVE.

A mere skeleton sketch is this; yet it is all that space permits. Is not such a Spiritual System worthy to be called inspired? Is it not profitable for doctrine, for reproof, for correction and for instruction in righteousness?

May this generation prosecute more and more careful researches into that Debatable Land on the confines of which we have been straying! Aided by spirits that have passed on, in advance of our spirits, under the triumphal death-change and into the beautiful Beyond—the still, small voice our monitor, Christ our chief guide—safely shall we question the Unexplored: safely and profitably. . We need the lessons that are taught by its laws. We need the evidence that is supplied by its phenomena. In the Border-land between two worlds we come upon much-needed influences, far more powerful than any of earth: gracious influences fitted to fortify degenerate morality and foster spiritual growth.

THE END.

BY THE AUTHOR OF THIS VOLUME.

Footfalls on the Boundary of Another World.

WITH NARRATIVE ILLUSTRATIONS.

Of this work there have been sold, in this country and in England, about twenty thousand copies, and in both countries it won notices from almost all the leading periodicals. A fair example of its reception is that it met in *All the Year Round* (September, 1860), from Charles Dickens; who, after dissenting from many of its conclusions, said: "I rise from the perusal of this book with a high regard for Mr. Owen personally. He is a gentleman of a sweet temper, and expresses himself as a gentleman should. He is a good writer, and has an admirable power of telling a story. That one of his stories which is called *The Rescue*, is by far the best of its kind to be found. Excellent throughout, it is told with a singular propriety, modesty, clearness, and force."

Beyond the Breakers.

A NOVEL FOUNDED ON VILLAGE LIFE IN THE WEST.

"All readers of taste, culture, and thought will feel attracted and impressed by it. We have, for ourselves, read it with deep interest and genuine pleasure, and can say for it what we can say for few novels of the day—that we hope sometime to read it over again."—*New York Independent.*

"The chief characteristic of this book is the knowledge of the human heart which its author displays, and the quickness with which he brings before us its most hidden secrets. Mr. OWEN shows his skill in treating that kind of preternatural influence which may be connected with common life, and we commend the work for its pure morality, its sober pleasantry, and unassuming simplicity. The narrative, though sometimes curiously elaborated, is so well managed that, at its close, the impression is most satisfactory."—*Hearth and Home.*

"It is a love-story full of interesting incident, which we can safely recommend to novel-readers in search of a thoroughly entertaining sketch of American life."—*Portland Transcript.*

"Mr. OWEN'S narrative style is exceedingly good, simple, clear, and direct."—*N. Y. Evening Post.*

"Mr. OWEN'S novel is particularly good."—*N. Y. Commercial Advertiser.*

"Characteristic and clever; improves as it advances."—*Philadelphia Press.*

"The author finds, in a western village, the elements of romance in an unusual degree."—*Springfield Republican.*

"Full of the results of a life of deep thought."—*Newark Daily Advertiser.*

"Full of exciting interest."—*Detroit Post.*

"Of commanding interest, which deepens as it proceeds, and far higher in tone than the sensation novels of the day." — *Watson's Art Journal.*

"Whoever commences its perusal will be constrained to follow the writer to the last page."—*Detroit Tribune.*

"A straightforward, vigorous, American story."—*Chicago Journal.*

"An honest book, with a valuable moral lesson."—*St. Louis Times.*

A Catalogue of

BOOKS

PUBLISHED BY

CARLETON & CO.,

NEW YORK

Madison Square,

corner of

5th Avenue and Broadway.

1872.

G. W. Carleton. *G. W. Dillingham.*

"There is a kind of physiognomy in the titles of books no less than in the faces of men, by which a skilful observer will know as well what to expect from the one as the other."—BUTLER.

NEW BOOKS

Recently Published by

G. W. CARLETON & CO., New York,

Madison Square, Fifth Avenue and Broadway.

N.B.—THE PUBLISHERS, upon receipt of the price in advance, will send any of the following Books by mail, POSTAGE FREE, to any part of the United States. This convenient and very safe mode may be adopted when the neighboring Booksellers are not supplied with the desired work.

Marion Harland.

ALONE.—	A novel.		12mo. cloth,	$1.50
HIDDEN PATH.—	do.		do.	$1.50
MOSS SIDE.—	do.		do.	$1.50
NEMESIS.—	do.		do.	$1.50
MIRIAM.—	do.		do.	$1.50
AT LAST.—	do.	*Just Published.*	do.	$1.50
HELEN GARDNER.—	do.		do.	$1.50
SUNNYBANK.—	do.		do.	$1.50
HUSBANDS AND HOMES.—	do.		do.	$1.50
RUBY'S HUSBAND.—	do.		do.	$1.50
PHEMIE'S TEMPTATION.—	do.		do.	$1.50
THE EMPTY HEART.—	do.		do.	$1.50

Miss Muloch.

JOHN HALIFAX.—A novel.	With illustration.	12mo. cloth,	$1.75
A LIFE FOR A LIFE.—	do.	do.	$1.75

Charlotte Bronte (Currer Bell).

JANE EYRE.—	A novel.	With illustration.	12mo. cloth,	$1.75
THE PROFESSOR.—	do.	do.	do.	$1.75
SHIRLEY.—	do.	do.	do.	$1.75
VILLETTE.—	do.	do.	do.	$1.75

Hand-Books of Society.

THE HABITS OF GOOD SOCIETY; nice points of taste, good manners, and the art of making oneself agreeable. 12mo. $1.75

THE ART OF CONVERSATION.—A sensible work, for every one who wishes to be an agreeable talker or listener. 12mo. $1.50

ARTS OF WRITING, READING, AND SPEAKING.—An excellent book for self-instruction and improvement. 12mo. clo., $1.50

A NEW DIAMOND EDITION of the above three popular books.—Small size, elegantly bound, and put in a box. - $3.00

Mrs. A. P. Hill.

MRS. HILL'S NEW COOKERY BOOK, and receipts. 12mo. cloth, $2.00

Mary J. Holmes.

'LENA RIVERS.—	A novel.	12mo.	cloth,	$1.50
DARKNESS AND DAYLIGHT.—	do.		do.	$1.50
TEMPEST AND SUNSHINE.—	do.		do.	$1.50
MARIAN GREY.—	do.		do.	$1.50
MEADOW BROOK.—	do.		do.	$1.50
ENGLISH ORPHANS.—	do.		do.	$1.50
DORA DEANE.—	do.		do.	$1.50
COUSIN MAUDE.—	do.		do.	$1.50
HOMESTEAD ON THE HILLSIDE.—	do.		do.	$1.50
HUGH WORTHINGTON.—	do.		do.	$1.50
THE CAMERON PRIDE.—	do.		do.	$1.50
ROSE MATHER.—	do.		do.	$1.50
ETHELYN'S MISTAKE.—	do.		do.	$1.50
MILLBANK.—	*Just published.*		do.	$1.50

Augusta J. Evans.

BEULAH.—	A novel.	12mo.	cloth,	$1.75
MACARIA.—	do.		do.	$1.75
ST. ELMO.—	do.		do.	$2.00
VASHTI.—	do.		do.	$2.00
INEZ.—	do.		do.	$1.75

Robert Dale Owen.

THE DEBATABLE LAND. 12mo. cloth. $2.00

The Crusoe Library.

ROBINSON CRUSOE.—	A handsome illus. edition.	12mo.	$1.50
SWISS FAMILY ROBINSON.—	do.	do.	$1.50
THE ARABIAN NIGHTS.—	do.	do.	$1.50

Captain Mayne Reid.—Illustrated.

THE SCALP HUNTERS.—	Far West Series	12mo. clo.,	$1.50
THE WAR TRAIL.—		do.	$1.50
THE HUNTER'S FEAST.—		do.	$1.50
THE TIGER HUNTER.—		do.	$1.50
OSCEOLA, THE SEMINOLE.—	Prairie Series	do.	$1.50
THE QUADROON.—		do.	$1.50
RANGERS AND REGULATORS.—		do.	$1.50
THE WHITE GAUNTLET.—		do.	$1.50
WILD LIFE.—	Pioneer Series	do.	$1.50
THE HEADLESS HORSEMAN.—		do.	$1.50
LOST LENORE.—		do.	$1.50
THE WOOD RANGERS.—		do.	$1.50
THE WHITE CHIEF.—	Wild Forest Series	do.	$1.50
THE WILD HUNTRESS.—		do.	$1.50
THE MAROON.—		do.	$1.50
THE RIFLE RANGERS.—		do.	$1.50

Comic Books—Illustrated.

ARTEMUS WARD, His Book.—Letters, etc. 12mo. cl., $1.50
DO. His Travels—Mormons, etc. do. $1.50
DO. In London.—Punch Letters. do. $1.50
DO. His Panorama and Lecture. do. $1.50
DO. Sandwiches for Railroad. . . .25
JOSH BILLINGS ON ICE, and other things.— do. $1.50
DO. His Book of Proverbs, etc. do. $1.50
DO. Farmer's Allmanax. . . .25
FANNY FERN.—Folly as it Flies. . . do. $1.50
DO. Gingersnaps . . . . do. $1.50
VERDANT GREEN.—A racy English college story. do. $1.50
MILES O'REILLY.—His Book of Adventures. do. $1.50
ORPHEUS C. KERR.—Kerr Papers, 4 vols. in one. do. $2.00
DO. Avery Glibun. A novel. . . . $2.00
DO. The Cloven Foot. do. do. $1.50
BALLAD OF LORD BATEMAN.—Illustrated by Cruikshank. .25

A. S. Roe's Works.

A LONG LOOK AHEAD.— A novel. . 12mo. cloth, $1.50
TO LOVE AND TO BE LOVED.— do. . . do. $1.50
TIME AND TIDE.— do. . . do. $1.50
I'VE BEEN THINKING.— do. . . do. $1.50
THE STAR AND THE CLOUD.— do. . . do. $1.50
TRUE TO THE LAST.— do. . . do. $1.50
HOW COULD HE HELP IT?— do. . . do. $1.50
LIKE AND UNLIKE.— do. . . do. $1.50
LOOKING AROUND.— do. . . do. $1.50
WOMAN OUR ANGEL.— do. . . do. $1.50
THE CLOUD ON THE HEART.— do. . . do. $1.50
RESOLUTION.— do. . . do. $1.50

Joseph Rodman Drake.

THE CULPRIT FAY.—A faery poem, with 100 illustrations. $2.00
DO. Superbly bound in turkey morocco. $5.00

"Brick" Pomeroy.

SENSE.—An illustrated vol. of fireside musings. 12mo. cl., $1.50
NONSENSE.— do. do. comic sketches. do. $1.50
OUR SATURDAY NIGHTS. do. pathos and sentiment. $1.50
BRICK DUST.—Comic sketches $1.50
GOLD DUST.—Fireside musings. $1.50

John Esten Cooke.

FAIRFAX.— A brilliant new novel. . 12mo. cloth, $1.50
HILT TO HILT.— do. . . . . do. $1.50
HAMMER AND RAPIER.— do. . . . . do. $1.50
OUT OF THE FOAM.— do. *Just published.* do. $1.50

Victor Hugo.

LES MISERABLES.—The celebrated novel, 8vo. cloth. $2.50
" Two vol. edition, fine paper, do. - 5.00
" In the Spanish language, do. - 5.00

Algernon Charles Swinburne.

LAUS VENERIS, AND OTHER POEMS.—Elegant new ed. - $1.50
FRENCH LOVE-SONGS.—By the best French Authors. - 1.50

Author "New Gospel of Peace."

THE CHRONICLES OF GOTHAM.—A rich modern satire. - $ .25
THE FALL OF MAN.—A satire on the Darwin Theory. - 50

Julie P. Smith.

WIDOW GOLDSMITH'S DAUGHTER.—A novel. 12mo. cloth. $1.75
CHRIS AND OTHO.— do. do. - 1.75
THE WIDOWER.— do. do. - 1.75
THE MARRIED BELLE.— do. (in press). - 1.75

Mansfield T. Walworth.

WARWICK.—A new novel. - - - 12mo. cloth. $1.75
LULU.— do. - - - do. - 1.75
HOTSPUR.— do. - - - do. - 1.75
STORMCLIFF.— do. - - - do. - 1.75
DELAPLAINE.— do. Just Published. do. - 1.75

Richard B. Kimball.

WAS HE SUCCESSFUL?— A novel. - 12mo. cloth. $1.75
UNDERCURRENTS.— do. - do. - 1.75
SAINT LEGER.— do. - do. - 1.75
ROMANCE OF STUDENT LIFE. do. - do. - 1.75
IN THE TROPICS.— do. - do. - 1.75
HENRY POWERS, Banker.— do. - do. - 1 75
TO-DAY.— do. - do. - 1.75

M. Michelet's Remarkable Works.

LOVE (L'AMOUR).—Translated from the French. 12mo. cl. $1.50
WOMAN (LA FEMME).— do. - do. - 1.50

Ernest Renan.

THE LIFE OF JESUS.—Trans'ted from the French. 12mo. cl. $1.75
LIVES OF THE APOSTLES.— do. do. - 1.75
THE LIFE OF SAINT PAUL— do. do. - 1.75
THE BIBLE IN INDIA— do. of Joccoliot. 2.00

Popular Italian Novels.

DOCTOR ANTONIO.—A love story. By Ruffini. 12mo. cl. $1.75
BEATRICE CENCI.—By Guerrazzi, with Portrait. do. - 1.75

Geo. W. Carleton.

OUR ARTIST IN CUBA.—With 50 comic illustrations. - $1.50
OUR ARTIST IN PERU.— do. do. - 1.50
OUR ARTIST IN AFRICA.—(In press). do. - 1.50

Miscellaneous Works.

RUTLEDGE.—A novel of remarkable interest and power.	
THE SUTHERLANDS.— do. Author of Rutledge.	
FRANK WARRINGTON.— do. do.	
SAINT PHILIP'S.— do. do.	
LOUIE.— do. do.	
ROUND HEARTS.— do. do.	
A ROSARY FOR LENT.—Devotional Readings. do.	
MAURICE.—A novel from the French of F. Bechard. -	1.50
MOTHER GOOSE.—Set to music, and with illustrations. -	
BRAZEN GATES.—A new child's book, illustrated. -	1.50
THE ART OF AMUSING.—Book of home amusements. -	1.50
STOLEN WATERS.—A fascinating novel. Celia Gardner.	1.50
HEART HUNGRY.—A novel. By Maria J. Westmoreland.	1.50
THE SEVENTH VIAL.—A new work. Dr. John Cumming.	2.00
THE GREAT TRIBULATION.—new ed. do.	2.00
THE GREAT PREPARATION.— do. do.	2.00
THE GREAT CONSUMMATION.—do. do.	2.00
THE LAST WARNING CRY.— do. do.	1.50
ANTIDOTE TO "THE GATES AJAR."— - - -	25
HOUSES NOT MADE WITH HANDS.—Hoppin's Illus. -	1.00
BEAUTY IS POWER.—An admirable book for ladies. -	1.50
ITALIAN LIFE AND LEGENDS.—By Anna Cora Ritchie. -	1.50
LIFE AND DEATH.—A new American novel. - -	1.50
HOW TO MAKE MONEY; AND HOW TO KEEP IT.—Davies.	1.50
THE CLOISTER AND THE HEARTH.—By Charles Reade.	1.50
TALES FROM THE OPERAS.—The Plots of all the Operas.	1.50
ADVENTURES OF A HONEYMOON.—A love-story. .	1.50
AMONG THE PINES.—Down South. By Edmund Kirke.	1.50
MY SOUTHERN FRIENDS.— do. do. -	1.50
DOWN IN TENNESSEE.— do. do. -	1.50
ADRIFT IN DIXIE.— do. do. -	1.50
AMONG THE GUERILLAS.— do. do. -	1.50
A BOOK ABOUT LAWYERS.—Bright and interesting. -	2.00
A BOOK ABOUT DOCTORS.— do. do. - -	2.00
WOMAN, LOVE, AND MARRIAGE.—By Fred. Saunders. -	1.50
PRISON LIFE OF JEFFERSON DAVIS.—By J. J. Craven.	1.50
POEMS, BY L. G. THOMAS.— - - - -	1.50
PASTIMES WITH MY LITTLE FRIENDS.—Mrs. Bennett. -	1.50
THE SQUIBOB PAPERS.—A comic book. John Phœnix. -	1.50
COUSIN PAUL.—A new American novel. - - -	1.75
JARGAL.—A novel from the French of Victor Hugo. -	1.75
CLAUDE GUEUX.— do. do. do. -	1.50
LIFE OF VICTOR HUGO.— do do. -	2.00
CHRISTMAS HOLLY.—By Marion Harland, Illustrated. -	1.50
THE RUSSIAN BALL.—An illustrated satirical Poem. -	.25
THE SNOBLACE BALL.— do. do. -	25
THE PRINCE OF KASHNA.—Edited by R. B. Kimball. -	1.75

Miscellaneous Works.

A LOST LIFE.—A novel by Emily H. Moore $1.50
CROWN JEWELS.— do. Mrs. Emma L. Moffett. $1.75
ADRIFT WITH A VENGEANCE.— Kinahan Cornwallis. . $1.50
THE FRANCO-PRUSSIAN WAR IN 1870.—By M. D. Landon. $2.00
DREAM MUSIC.—Poems by Frederic Rowland Marvin. . $1.50
RAMBLES IN CUBA.—By an American Lady. . . $1.50
BEHIND THE SCENES, in the White House.—Keckley. . $2.00
YACHTMAN'S PRIMER.—For Amateur Sailors.—Warren. 50
RURAL ARCHITECTURE.—By M. Field. With illustrations. $2.00
TREATISE ON DEAFNESS.—By Dr. E. B. Lighthill. . . $1.50
WOMEN AND THEATRES.—A new book, by Olive Logan. $1.50
WARWICK.—A new novel by Mansfield Tracy Walworth. $1.75
SIBYL HUNTINGTON.—A novel by Mrs. J. C. R. Dorr. . $1.75
LIVING WRITERS OF THE SOUTH.—By Prof. Davidson. . $2.00
STRANGE VISITORS.—A book from the Spirit World. . $1.50
UP BROADWAY, and its Sequel.—A story by Eleanor Kirk. $1.50
MILITARY RECORD, of Appointments in the U.S. Army. $5.00
HONOR BRIGHT.—A new American novel. . . . $1.50
MALBROOK.— do. do. do. . . . $1.50
GUILTY OR NOT GUILTY.— do. do. . . . $1.75
ROBERT GREATHOUSE.—A new novel by John F. Swift . $2.00
THE GOLDEN CROSS, and poems by Irving Van Wart, jr. $1.50
ATHALIAH.—A new novel by Joseph H. Greene, jr. . $1.75
REGINA, and other poems.—By Eliza Cruger. . . $1.50
THE WICKEDEST WOMAN IN NEW YORK.—By C. H. Webb. 50
MONTALBAN.—A new American novel. . . . $1.75
MADEMOISELLE MERQUEM.—A novel by George Sand. . $1.75
THE IMPENDING CRISIS OF THE SOUTH.—By H. R. Helper. $2.00
NOJOQUE—A Question for a Continent.— do. . $2.00
PARIS IN 1867.—By Henry Morford. $1.75
THE BISHOP'S SON.—A novel by Alice Cary. . . $1.75
CRUISE OF THE ALABAMA AND SUMTER.—By Capt. Semmes. $1.50
HELEN COURTENAY.—A novel, author "Vernon Grove." $1.75
SOUVENIRS OF TRAVEL.—By Madame Octavia W. LeVert. $2.00
VANQUISHED.—A novel by Agnes Leonard. . . $1.75
WILL-O'-THE-WISP.—A child's book, from the German . $1.50
FOUR OAKS.—A novel by Kamba Thorpe. . . . $1.75
THE CHRISTMAS FONT.—A child's book, by M. J. Holmes. $1 00
POEMS, BY SARAH T. BOLTON. $1.50
MARY BRANDEGEE—A novel by Cuyler Pine. . . $1.75
RENSHAWE.— do. do. . . . $1.75
MOUNT CALVARY.—By Matthew Hale Smith. . . $2.00
PROMETHEUS IN ATLANTIS.—A prophecy. . . $2.00
TITAN AGONISTES.—An American novel. . . $2.00